KU-647-625

Contents

Preface   vii

Prologue   xii

Chapter 1 The Cultural Basis of the Pluralist Dilemma   1

Chapter 2 Britain   15

Chapter 3 Canada   43

Chapter 4 Fiji   77

Chapter 5 The UnitedStates   104

Chapter 6 Hawaii   141

Chapter 7 Australia   166

Chapter 8 The Ideology of Pluralism in Comparative   218
           Perspective

Bibliography   245

Index   265

Preface

In 1944 Gunnar Myrdal's *The American Dilemma: The Negro Problem and Modern Democracy* was published. It pointed to the contradiction and conflict between the American ideals of democracy, fair play, and justice on the one hand, and American practices that discriminated against Negroes on the other. The book became a classic, and a milestone in the long journey of those writers who have attempted through their books to explain the nature of the contradiction between those who hold power and those who do not, between the rhetoric that preaches compassion, charity, and tolerance, and the practice that denies these and other features of a just society to those people who are discriminated against. This book, *The Pluralist Dilemma in Education: Six Case Studies*, is another step in the journey.

The ideas and beliefs people and groups hold — their ideologies — exert a powerful influence over the way they go about their activities. This applies as much to politicians, bureaucrats, trade unionists and other holders of power as to the man in the street. Probably nowhere is the influence of ideologies more obvious and pervasive than in education. *The Pluralist Dilemma in Education* looks at the effects of ideologies on the educational provisions in six case studies: Britain, Canada, the United States, Hawaii, Fiji, and Australia. In each, the central concern is to show what educational ideologies and models of society are held, and how these affect what is being done through the curriculum to overcome the problems posed by pluralism.

The background information for the book comes from a survey of teacher education in the six countries studied. This was carried out during 1978 and 1979 as a research project commissioned by the Education Research and Development Committee, Canberra, Australia. The project adopted a policy-research style, as this was seen to match the expressed desire of the Committee's Priority Area Advisory Group for Multicultural Education to obtain facts about overseas developments and research in pluralist education. The group accepted that the findings of the research could be 'decision-oriented' (Coleman, 1972) and suitable for wider dissemination to policy makers in Australian education, rather than 'conclusion-oriented' and destined for theoretical academic publication.

Many of the findings in the following chapters have clear policy implications and do not deserve the latter fate. They describe and analyse a great variety of problems other countries are meeting in providing pluralist education at the time the study was carried out, while hinting at an inescapable conclusion — that the task may well be impossible. This seeming paradox emerges from one factor which is common to all the case studies — the clear dominance exerted by the multicultural ideology in official thinking. In Canada and Australia it is official government policy, and enshrined in parliamentary legislation. In Britain and Fiji, it is becoming official orthodoxy in education, to replace the previous multiracial ideology. In the United States, the multicultural approach persists in many guises, despite the recent official support for a multiethnic approach which promises at least on paper, a more incisive attack on the dilemmas in pluralist education. Hawaii, following American experience and approaches of the late 1960s, has also opted for multiculturalism.

One might think that such unanimity in adopting the multicultural ideology at the official level means that there is broad agreement on what it means both in theory and practice. This is not so. In all the case studies immense confusion exists about what multiculturalism and multicultural education mean, definitions and conceptual models compete with one another, multiethnic education and other philosophies are proposed as alternatives, and in general, a great deal of the curriculum is in a 'mess', 'muddle', 'buzzing confusion'. Some counter-ideologists claim that multiculturalism is nothing more than a 'massive con job', 'everything to all men', 'a political sham'. The journey towards the just society seems to be as rocky as ever.

Why is this latest attempt to solve the 'American dilemma' so obviously failing to get beyond the trite, naïve, 'sticking plaster' approaches to explaining and educating about the complexities of ethnoculturally pluralist societies such as those forming the six case studies in this book? To answer that question we can look to ignorance and lack of technical expertise on the part of educational planners; cynical manipulation of the label 'multicultural' on the part of those who use it only to support applications for research and development grants; confusion and even competition between ethnic groups themselves to have one approach to multicultural education adopted over another because it suits their particular needs; and resistance by academic 'knowledge managers' to an approach that threatens their conservative theories and models of society. All these and other reasons can be put forward.

But the conclusion of this book points towards another, more intractable problem. Each pluralist society has its dominant ethnocultural group, which controls power over the access other ethnocultural groups have to social rewards and economic resources. Part of this control is exercised through education, and in particular through the curriculum.

Multiculturalism, in all its confusion, may be a subtle way of appearing to give members of ethnocultural groups what they want in education while in reality giving them little that will enhance their life chances, because a great deal of multicultural education emphasizes only life styles, in a safe, bland and politically neutral panacea.

I come to this conclusion through a logical argument developed in the following chapters. Chapter 1 outlines a theoretical model for considering education, as we understand it in Western societies, to be an institutionalized way of formally transmitting the culture of a society. Schools and other enculturation agencies employ a curriculum as their main strategy for ordering the selection of knowledge for which they are responsible. Among the many aspects of the curriculum which are considered, that of the selection process itself is crucial. It entails 'knowledge managers' of various kinds coming to value-based decisions about the type of society which the education system serves. Some of these decisions take account of the empirical realities of the society, others are more ideological. All decisions inevitably involve control over the type of knowledge to be transmitted, to whom, under what conditions and so on. In short, knowledge managers can control power through the way they make knowledge accessible to children. Those social and ethnic groups whose children are deemed more 'worthy' of receiving more knowledge than other children, or of receiving it under more favourable circumstances, will be related to the way knowledge managers interpret the place and status of these groups in their society. In a culturally pluralist society, the way is thus open for knowledge managers to control the life chances of children from 'unworthy' ethnic groups through the education system — a form of ethnic hegemony.

This perspective provides the underlying rationale for the analysis of each of the case studies in this book. To maintain cross-national comparability, each is considered in exactly the same way. A brief demographic description is accompanied by a summary of the main historical developments in thinking about the nature of the society's pluralist characteristics and their influence on education. This provides an overview of the socio-historical context, within which the current 'ideologies' and 'counter-ideologies' relating to pluralist education are examined.

The final chapter draws together the implications of the findings from the case studies, within the same theoretical perspective. It shows that multicultural education appears to have become the favoured approach in all the case studies, but involves so much confusion over terminology, aims and objectives, that its effectiveness in assisting children from ethnic backgrounds to improve their life chances must be seriously questioned. If the logic of the first chapter holds, this is what we might have expected. Multicultural education, despite its apparent egalitarian appeal, is merely another but more subtle way of exercising ethnic hegemony by the dominant group.

The apparent inevitability of this raises a further issue, namely, the *dilemma of pluralism* that has long been recognized in political thought. This is the problem of reconciling the diverse political claims of constituent groups and individuals in a pluralist society with the claims of the nation-state as a whole. In education, this is the problem of deciding how much diversity to allow in curriculum planning as against the degree of centralized control necessary to have at least a minimal, common core selection of the culture transmitted to each generation of children, who will ultimately grow up to be citizens. If the society is to survive, the latter is essential, and this key fact may well be the underlying reason why all approaches to catering for pluralist elements in society could be doomed to fail.

Seen in this light, multicultural education may be a way of obeying the *survival imperative*, while at least appearing to give ethnic minorities what they want. In the final analysis, it may just be the latest in the long line of attempts in the search for what could be a chimera — *the* solution to the pluralist dilemma.

I wish to acknowledge the financial and other support of the Education Research and Development Committee, and its Priority Area Advisory Group on Multicultural Education, which enabled me to carry out the research on which this book is based. In particular, I am most grateful for the advice of its chairman, Barbara Falk, and also of Larry Saha, which helped me to transform a lengthy academic document into something more readable. My thanks are also due to Marion Amies for research assistance and meticulous editing to prepare the final draft manuscript, and to Jenny Matthews and Peter Musgrave for advice on the theoretical model.

The case studies in this book are based on material from the Survey of Teacher Education for Pluralist Societies (the STEPS project) carried out during the second half of 1978. As some 130 organizations or individuals were consulted during this period, it is not possible here to acknowledge all the help, the many kindnesses and warm hospitality I received during my often hectic travels around the countries concerned. They are acknowledged in full in part 2 of the STEPS report, *Pluralism, Teacher Education, and Ideology* (Bullivant, 1979a). Many of the people with whom I held discussions are cited throughout this book.

However, there are several to whom I owe a special debt of gratitude for help 'beyond the call of duty'. At the risk of making an invidious selection I wish to thank the following: Ian and Jenny Allen, Simon Fraser University, Vancouver; Tupeni Baba, University of the South Pacific, Suva; Michael Banton, then at the S.S.R.C. Research Unit on Ethnic Relations at the University of Bristol; Madeleine Blakeley, General Secretary of the National Association for Multiracial Education (U.K.); Ted Booth, University of the South Pacific, Suva; Carl P. Epstein, Ethnic Heritage Studies Branch, Department of Health Education and Welfare, Washington, D.C.; Lawrence and Betty Fish,

Northwest Regional Educational Laboratory, Portland, Oregon; Leo Hamnett, at the Culture Learning Institute, East-West Center, Honolulu; Arthur J. King (Jnr.) Curriculum Research and Development Group, University of Hawaii Laboratory School, Honolulu; Horace Lashley, Commission for Racial Equality, London; Denis Lawton, Institute of Education, University of London; John R. Mallea, Ontario Institute for Studies in Education, Toronto; Geoffrey Mason, University of Victoria, B.C.; Hari Ram, Ministry of Education, Youth and Sport, Suva; Joe and Sandy Rubin, Allyn Spence, of the College of Education, University of Arizona, Tucson; Lawrence Stenhouse, Centre for Applied Research in Education, University of East Anglia, Norwich; Greg Trifonovitch, Culture Learning Institute, East-West Center, Honolulu.

Finally, the conclusions I come to and the opinions I express are my own, generated by the theoretical model which I have adopted to interpret the voluminous data from STEPS, only part of which could be used for this book. Many will quarrel with both model and opinion, and that is their privilege. However, they might ponder two aspects of education in Western democracies. One is a paradox, the other essential, especially in the age of the cybernetic revolution and the emergence of the 'knowledge society'. Firstly, for all its imperfections, multicultural education by perpetuating ethnic hegemony may be functional in assisting democratic societies to survive. Secondly, those weaknesses which do exist may be allowing a more traditional, knowledge-based form of education and curriculum to become established, which in the long term may prove to be the saving of our kind of society. The underlying reason for this has been admirably expressed by A.N. Whitehead: 'The rule is absolute — the nation that does not value trained intelligence is doomed.'

Brian M. Bullivant
Monash University
Melbourne, 1980

Prologue

A society is a group of unequal
beings organized to meet common
needs. . . . The just society . . .
is one in which sufficient order
protects members, whatever their
diverse endowments, and sufficient
disorder provides every individual
with full opportunity to develop
his genetic endowment, whatever
that may be.
ROBERT ARDREY

Any action which encourages only
the identity of groups and thus
their continued existence may lead
to a situation where separate groups
compete with each other for economic,
social and political power.
AUSTRALIAN SCHOOLS COMMISSION

The conceptual trick is to acknowledge
diversity of cultures within the society
but assume that culture deals mainly with
styles and cooking recipes and has
relatively little impact on ambitions,
moral judgements and public goals.
C.H. ENLOE

CHAPTER 1

The Cultural Basis of the Pluralist Dilemma

Thinking about the nature of society and the most effective education system for it can be traced back to Plato's *Republic*. The same concern has surfaced more recently in the various debates about the pluralist composition of many Western societies, which have resulted from the demographic, social and cultural changes brought about by the waves of settlers each has experienced at different times in the last two centuries. The first country to undergo these changes was the United States, followed, in the post-war period, by Canada, Australia, New Zealand, and Great Britain. 'All passed through phases when established social arrangements were stretched, strained, changed, overturned or replaced in the face of new situations created by high rates of immigration of people of diverse cultural origins' (Martin, 1978:15). In each country there have been, and continue to be, discussions and arguments about the nature of the society and how best to reconcile the legitimate claims of the nation-state with those of citizens who are from different social, economic and cultural backgrounds. This, in essence, is the pluralist dilemma.

A major part of the debate has focused on education, as this key social institution is responsible for producing citizens on the one hand and individuals on the other. As future citizens, children must be equipped with some common sentiments, knowledge and skills to play their part in furthering the welfare and aims of the nation-state. As individuals they should be equipped with whatever it takes to enable them to lead lives that are personally satisfying, provided they are not inimical to those of other individuals or the welfare of the state. Education to achieve these twin aims is relatively straightforward when children come from backgrounds that are broadly similar in cultural and socio-economic composition. When these are dissimilar, as can occur in societies that are multiethnic, i.e., composed of a number of distinguishable ethnic groups, the pluralist dilemma affects education. The remainder of this chapter outlines a theoretical model to bring these kinds of issues into sharper focus, and to provide a framework which can be used to analyse the pluralist dilemma in the six case studies presented in subsequent chapters.

The cultural foundations of education

The institution of education is closely related to the culture of a society, and this relationship is now fully recognized and accepted by most cultural anthropologists. There is less agreement about what culture is, but for the purposes of developing a useful model there is no need to get into this debate. As will become apparent, culture is taken to exist as part of a socio-cultural system, and can be identified and analysed. A social group or a whole society should be thought of separately from its culture, to avoid the common mistake of thinking that people live in or belong to a culture. Strictly they do not; people belong to or live in groups, as Schneider and Bonjean (1973:118) emphasize. People are born into a social group, and inherit its culture. They also play their part in modifying and adapting the culture, so that it is not a static feature of a society, but is constantly changing in response to the circumstances in which the society finds itself.

The importance of culture rests on what it is for. Here I draw upon the ideas of Laura Thompson (1969), Yehudi Cohen (1971), Peter Bock (1969), and Schneider and Bonjean (1973), each of whom and in various ways see culture as a form of problem-solving device or survival 'programme' which enables a social group to cope with the problems of living within its environment. More properly, we should say that culture enables a social group to cope with what its members define its environment to be. Strictly, we cope with 'reality-out-there' through a perceptual filter or screen provided by the way we look at the world around us. More usefully, that environment can be thought of as consisting of three conceptually separate, interdependent 'sub-environments' or definitions of the situation. The first is the natural or geographical environment and habitat, with its biotic and natural resources. The second is the social environment, consisting of the other social groups with which a society comes into contact, and the social relationships of the society itself in the sense of a demographic aggregate. The third is more speculative, but is needed to explain the often elaborate nature of a culture which enshrines a religious world view. This is the 'metaphysical environment', which embodies the social group's definitions of what is 'out there' in terms of supernatural beings, inexplicable natural phenomena, forces, and crucial dilemmas of life.

A related perspective, emerging among some anthropologists of education, is to see culture in terms of 'knowledge', 'meanings', and 'conceptions'. For instance, Ward Goodenough (1964:36) maintains that

> A society's culture consists of whatever it is one has to know or believe in order to operate in a manner acceptable to its members . . . . Culture, being what people have to learn as distinct from their biological heritage, must consist of the end product of learning: knowledge, in the most general, if relative, sense of the term.

Marion Dobbert (1976:207) takes an almost cybernetic, systems theory view:

> Culture is a system for mapping information from an environment. This information is stored in shared conceptual patterns, in patterns for social interaction and in patterns for getting a living.

The idea that culture involves knowledge, needs to be learned, relates to the environment in which a group finds itself, and is also a form of perceptual 'template' through which stimuli from the environment can be 'mapped' makes a definition that endeavours to incorporate all of these ideas useful in the context of an analysis of education. However, it is also important to draw attention to the mechanism or mode through which culture is transmitted, and also to take into account the mutability of culture in response to a social group's changing definitions of its environment and survival problems. The following definition is offered with these ideas in mind. Culture is a patterned system of knowledge and conceptions, embodied in symbolic and non-symbolic communication modes, which a society has evolved from the past, and progressively modifies and augments to give meaning to and cope with the present and anticipated future problems of its existence.

The most important of the communication modes is language, but, in passing, it is worth noting that in the view of some structural anthropologists and semiologists other modes, such as signs and signals, are involved. For example Leach (1976:10) maintains that '*all* the various non-verbal dimensions of culture . . . are organised in patterned sets so as to incorporate coded information in a manner analogous to the sounds and words and sentences of a natural language'.

Language occupies pride of place among the communication modes, and this fact assumes considerable importance for a system of education that tries to cope with pluralist conditions in society. The kind of programme that typically arrives first on the scene relates to language learning, e.g., bilingual education, Teaching English as a Second Language (TESL), and so on. Essentially, what is happening through such programmes is an attempt to partially reconstruct the 'reality' of a child from another socio-cultural group, i.e., a form of knowledge or reality control. This interpretation is an inevitable conclusion when one takes into account the several functions of language (Berger & Luckmann, 1971: 85 – 86):

> Language objectivates the shared experiences and makes them available to all within the linguistic community, thus becoming both the basis and the instrument of the collective stock of knowledge [i.e., culture]. Furthermore,

language provides the means for objectifying new experiences, allowing their incorporation into the already existing stock of knowledge, and it is the most important means by which the objectivated and objectified sedimentations are transmitted in the tradition of the collectivity in question.

Several other points about our use of culture need to be made at this juncture. First, it should not need to be stressed that culture is being used in the technical, anthropological sense — the discipline with which it is most closely associated — rather than in the way the man in the street would use the word. Second, culture represents both an accumulation of knowledge and conceptions from the past (cf. Berger & Luckmann's 'sedimentations', 1971:85), and the knowledge evolved to meet current and future problems of existence. As Bourdieu aptly comments (1971:192):

> Culture is not merely a common code or even a common catalogue of answers to recurring problems; it is a common set of previously assimilated master patterns from which, by an 'art of invention' similar to that involved in the writing of music, an infinite number of individual patterns directly applicable to specific situations are generated.

One of the most intractable problems in education and the curriculum relates to these twin aspects of culture — the historical and the current situational — namely how to balance knowledge preserved from the past with the rapidly expanding knowledge generated in the present. For instance this problem assumes importance when deciding what ethnic traditions should be encouraged and retained in a pluralist society. Third, although knowledge and conceptions have been emphasized, it should be pointed out that the latter embody such affective aspects as attitudes, beliefs, and values. Together these provide a sociocultural group or society with a 'world view', which incorporates both its own place and purpose in the universal scheme of things and its relationships with other groups and societies.

Curriculum: the strategy of culture transmission

The function of the school curriculum and the education system in transmitting the culture of a society is now becoming recognized by theorists other than anthropologists, among whom the concept of enculturation has long been accepted. Lawton, for instance, suggests (1975:6−7):

> It seems to me that the school curriculum (in the wider sense) is essentially *a selection from the culture of a society*. Certain aspects of our way of life, certain kinds of knowledge, certain attitudes and values are regarded as so important that their transmission to the next generation is not left to chance in our society but is entrusted to specially-trained professionals (teachers) in elaborate and expensive institutions (schools).

Phenix (1964:3) takes the enculturation concept for granted, and stresses the inherent ethnocentricity of the education process: 'Since education is the means of perpetuating culture from generation to generation, it is natural that the partiality of outlook endemic in the culture generally would be found also in education.'

The importance of Lawton's definition is the explicit recognition given to the transmission of knowledge, attitudes and values, which have long been recognized as key aspects of culture. Another important aspect is his recognition of the need for a selection to be made from the total culture. This is inevitable, because the amount of knowledge is so vast in modern societies, due to the knowledge explosion in recent decades, that transmitting everything in the cultural stock is impossible. For a number of years, since my early attempts to grapple with this concept in 1970, I have adopted the same perspective, and put forward a definition of curriculum which incorporates a number of ideas that are central to the development of the argument in the rest of this chapter. The curriculum is a selection from a socio-cultural group's stock of valued traditional and current public knowledge, conceptions, and experiences, usually purposefully organized in programmatic sequence by such institutionalized agencies of culture transmission (enculturation) as schools. In such agencies, the programme typically takes the form of syllabuses and their constituent parts or units.

The definition incorporates a number of features of the curriculum as it might be adopted in a school. It is conceptualized as involving three levels or stages of operation which add a process dimension to an essentially structural-functional model. These levels are *selection, organization*, and *implementation*. The first level necessitates making decisions about the kinds and quantities of knowledge, conceptions and other experiences that should be selected from the stock of public cultural knowledge.

The second level involves making decisions about such factors as allocation of teaching staff, rooms, timetabling, materials, and equipment. These are basically 'economic' decisions. There are also other decisions at this level that relate to the programming of the learning sequences on a school basis. Many of these decisions are best made in the light of recognized learning theories such as those of Piaget (1958) and Bloom (1971), rather than on an *ad hoc* basis.

Similar types of decisions extend into the implementation level of the classroom, where the actual teacher – pupil interactions take place. The classroom is a 'learning – stimulus mix' where all kinds of human, material, and temporal resources have to be juggled and deployed (see discussion in Bullivant, (1973b, Ch.7; 1981). In addition, the social, economic and cultural backgrounds of the pupils have to be taken into account, especially in classrooms which include children from different ethnic groups.

Although control over the dissemination of public knowledge can be exercised at all three levels of the curriculum, the level of selection is of central importance for our argument, and will be considered on its own. Like the other levels, it involves making a number of value judgements based on various criteria. Those at the selection stage are philosophical and sociological. The former consider such matters as the type of knowledge that might be selected: for example, whether discipline-based (Hirst, 1974) or based on 'essential meanings' (Phenix, 1964); what types and amount of knowledge should be compulsory for children to learn and what elective or optional (White, 1973; Lawton, 1975; Barrow, 1976); in a polyethnic society, what 'cultural universals' should be preserved in the selection and what 'cultural alternatives' (Lawton, 1975:85 ff.; Bullivant, 1978b, 1981).

The last type of philosophical value judgements is closely related to the decisions about selection which have to be made on sociological grounds. Here there are two main issues. The first concerns selecting the kinds of knowledge and experiences that will equip a child to take his or her place in society. In this case it is necessary to base judgements on socio-economic, demographic, and other empirical data that describe society as it is, or provide a basis for forecasting, with some confidence, how it might be some years hence. Such judgements are substantive, and enable one to make truth-claims about the society.

The second kind of issue is more philosophical, but still concerns the nature of society. In this case, it is the type of society which people think ought to be, and can be, achieved some time in the future. Statements based on this kind of viewpoint are essentially normative theories. They 'prescribe the means of attaining certain goals . . . [which] are determined by the values (axioms) upon which the theory is based' (Theodorson & Theodorson, 1970: 438). Whereas a substantive statement (theory) is descriptive, a normative theory is prescriptive and programmatic, i.e., it implies or makes explicit 'a systematic course of action for the solution of a social problem' (1970:438).

Both substantive and normative theories involve an element of conceptual mapping and delineating models of society. This task is not easy, even in a society that is broadly homogeneous demographically and culturally. It is far more complex when other dimensions of pluralism have to be taken into account, such as race, religion, culture and ethnicity. It is at this point that the kinds of people who have the responsibility for the actual selection of knowledge, or who are in a position to influence their choice, become crucial.

Knowledge managers: agents of culture transmission

Schools are normally staffed by formally appointed teachers, who can be regarded as the agents of a society responsible for the formal transmission of its culture. They are assisted by a wide range of others concerned with education — bureaucrats, educational administrators, curriculum development organizations, teachers' subject associations. As I have shown elsewhere (Bullivant, 1972; 1973a), together with teachers, such groups can exercise considerable influence not only over what knowledge is selected for the curriculum and how it should be organized and implemented, but even over what should be taken as knowledge, and, in the final analysis, what 'reality' should be. I use *knowledge managers* as a collective term for those who have this type of control.

All agents share at least two things in common. Their work involves learning and mastering a considerable part of the knowledge and conceptions that form the culture. Second, acquisition of this knowledge, if not the skills to impart it, necessitates a period of formal training. Both aspects will be programmed in a manner that matches the culture of the society from which the agents are drawn. This is to say, so essential is the task of culture transmission, that the training of agents responsible for it can be conceptualized just like any other institution of the society. In this case it is the institution of teacher (formal enculturation agent) education or training. Like the institution of schooling and education, it entails organizations such as colleges and university departments of education, statuses and roles, which are held and performed by those in the organizations, more-or-less agreed norms and activities, together with supporting materials, apparatus and equipment.

There may be grounds now for thinking that the professional responsibilities teachers have as agents of society have been underemphasized in much teacher training in the Western democracies since the Second World War. In an attempt to counter what were seen as authoritarian methods and regimentation in much schooling, stress has been laid on a more individualistic approach to the 'art' of teaching, in which the teacher's task is more to respond to the logic of each different classroom situation, rather than apply a previously learned sequence of teaching 'methods' or 'general principles'. A similar trend has been quite apparent in schools with the swing away from 'traditional' instruction towards more 'progressive', self-directed learning for children.

Both trends have been necessary to reduce the formalism that characterized much of pre-war education. It may well be that both have been taken to extremes of individualism in which the legitimate claim of the society to have the culture transmitted by responsible agents has been ignored. Worthwhile as self-determination is for the individual, whether teacher or pupil, it can lead to a 'pluralism' in education that works against the 'civism' necessary for the good of the common political community and nation state (Butts, 1977).

Accompanying this trend in the post-war period (and even apparent in some earlier writing, e.g., Conant, 1952) has been an ideological assumption that the evils of industrial society can be altered for the better through schooling. Implicitly, if not explicitly, this has encouraged teachers to see their role partly as that of agents of social change and reformers of society. In such thinking the claims of the enculturation imperative have been either ignored or relegated in importance. Again, the tendency has been for individualism and educational pluralism to be stressed in the hope that the products of the schools and the schooling process itself will somehow bring about the desired social reformation. It is now clear from the writings of such theorists as Bernstein (1970), Jencks (1973), and others, that such thinking is fallacious. However, it has left a pernicious legacy in the education systems of Western democracies which has yet to be eradicated.

In a recent publication (the 'Green Paper') in Britain (Cmnd. 6869, 1977:2), Shirley Williams (Secretary of State for Education and Science) and John Morris (Secretary of State for Wales) give explicit recognition to the need to redress the balance against individualism and towards the prior claims of society as a whole. Discussing the mounting criticisms of the education system and the quality of its products, they comment:

> Underlying all this [criticism] was the feeling that the educational system was out of touch with the fundamental need for Britain to survive economically in a highly competitive world through the efficiency of its industry and commerce. . . .

> Education, like any other public service, is answerable to the society which it serves and which pays for it, so these criticisms must be given a fair hearing.

The Secretaries' comments are also relevant for other democracies that have experienced extremes of individualism in education. They have been based on the naïve assumption that democracy is best served by developing the uniqueness of individuals without the corollary that, once developed, it should be put to constructive use in the service of the political community. The distortion we are now experiencing in education has occurred because of the extension of the 'doctrine' of uniqueness to the 'right' for every individual to 'do his own thing' regardless of the common good. The fallacy of this extension is self-obvious. From the anthropological perspective adopted here, for any society to survive, its culture — a socio-biological survival device — must be passed on to each successive generation in such a way that the claims of society are given priority over the wants of individuals. Any education system neglects these twin imperatives of survival and enculturation at its peril, and that of the society it claims to serve.

The distribution of knowledge and power

Thanks to recent literature on the sociology of knowledge (e.g., Young, 1971) and phenomenological perspectives on the curriculum, it is now accepted that the distribution of and access to public knowledge, i.e., the selection from the cultural stock, is not uniform throughout any one society. Instead, it varies from sub-group to sub-group so that some have more access to knowledge than others and can gain an advantage in obtaining better life chances and social rewards in those jobs and professions which depend on the possession of knowledge, obtained largely through education and schooling. To stress this close relationship, which is inherent in the way we have defined culture, Foucault (1977) has coined the term 'knowledge/power'.

The uneven distribution of knowledge is also seen as one of the ways by which some individuals and sub-groups within a society maintain their power and control over others. Most of this kind of analysis has typically focused on class and social stratification differences in the distribution of knowledge, in an attempt to show that one class (usually the upper) holds a disproportionate share of power in comparison with the lower classes. In what has become a much-quoted passage, Bernstein (1971:47) has put the essence of this point of view:

> How a society selects, classifies, distributes, transmits and evaluates the educational knowledge it considers to be public, reflects both the distribution of power and the principles of social control.

We do not need to confine our analysis to one that is based solely on class lines, as there are other groups in a society that try to control power through education in ways that are unrelated to the class system. Some are interest or pressure groups who want to push one view of education. An example in Australia is the League of Light, a moralistic, fundamentalist group with extreme views on personal and family purity. It has played a major part in certain Australian states in trying the have the MACOS Social Studies course removed from the curriculum on the grounds that certain sections of the kit are alleged to encourage a more divergent, culturally relativistic mode of thinking towards sexual mores.

Other individuals and groups are more closely concerned with educational decision making as Harman (1978:22) suggests:

> Policy processes in education today are not the sole preserve of any one group or set of individuals. Instead a range of different groups and individuals participate. These include high elected officials (Ministers, Prime Ministers, Presidents, Governors), legislatures, cabinets, official boards and committees, interest groups, lay members of school boards or university councils, teachers, students, parents and administrators. Of course, different participants are involved in different ways. . . . Who participates and how also vary over time, from place to place, from context to context, and from issue to issue.

In every culturally pluralist society there are groups that can be distinguished on cultural or ethnic grounds. These also try to obtain access to a form of education that best suits their needs. For instance, in the 1960s, the Black Power movement in the United States had as one of its aims the improvement of education for black children. Other ethnic groups such as Chicanos (Mexican-Americans) and Puerto Ricans have also pushed their claims for preferential treatment in education. In Canada, in addition to the French-speaking Canadians (francophones), the 'other ethnic groups' have been a major force. They have urged that multilingualism should be catered for in the curriculum rather than bilingualism (English and French), which is the present, official government policy. In each of these cases, it is reasonable to interpret such claims for preferential treatment as a way of overcoming the control over 'knowledge/power', or ethnic hegemony, exercised by the dominant ethnic group or *Staatsvolk* (Connor, 1973:2).

Each of the groups used as examples above may attempt to influence the way knowledge managers select, organize, and implement the curriculum. They may also try to influence what knowledge actually is, or what are 'relevant, desirable or necessary objects of knowledge' (Martin, 1978:20). This may be attempted in two main ways. The first is by commission, i.e., definitions of knowledge may be proposed, or limits to what is to be taken as knowledge laid down. The second is by omission, and is achieved by obfuscating central issues, or by ducking important problems of definition by implying that they are non-issues. When such tactics are used by highly placed and powerful 'accredited reality definers' (Esland, 1971:82), such as an eminent professor in the knowledge-management hierarchy, or the Australian Schools Commission, 'the parameters of any particular body of knowledge are thus embedded within larger constructs, which automatically negate or neutralize alternative definitions of what legitimately belongs to that body of knowledge' (Martin, 1978:21).

Martin has also extended this analysis to the way already existing knowledge is 'managed':

> The content of social knowledge also consists largely of taken-for-granted elements which, most of the time, no one is aware of constructing: they are simply there. But for its survival such taken-for-granted knowledge must be continually confirmed, and this process of confirmation shades over into the business of constructing new knowledge or moving knowledge from one domain where it is established to another where it is new. In societies like our own with a complex structure and technology (including a complex communication system), the affirming-constructing process goes on as a self-conscious part of managing the society's affairs and is often highly institutionalised.

The ideological foundation of 'knowledge/power'

The term ideology can be used in relation to a cultural institution as the cluster of values, ideas and beliefs that justify and validate its form and operation. A comparable, but broader, view is also taken of those over-arching systems of opinion which, in this case, influence the activities of knowledge managers and those associated with them. Such systems of opinion may also be termed ideologies. Where they concern the nature of a society, the function education should serve in relation to it, and the distribution and control over knowledge/power, they have an obvious bearing on the curriculum.

The concept of an ideology has been subjected to a great deal of discussion, much of it polemical as the term can be used in a pejorative sense. We do not need to repeat the debate here; instead, the definition of Julius Gould is adopted as being quite suitable for the arguments developed in this book. An ideology is 'a pattern of beliefs and concepts both factual and normative which purport to explain complex social phenomena with a view to directing and simplifying socio-political choices, facing individuals and groups' (Gould, 1964: 315 – 16). The distinction between normative and factual is an important one, and will recur in the case studies that follow. Ideologies can take the form of substantive statements or truth-claims about the nature of society and its education system. These are essentially descriptive, and can be tested to see if they are accurate by examining the facts. But, because normative statements are ideal-future claims about what society and its education *should* be, they are clearly prescriptive, and consequently cannot be tested by examining the facts. All we can do is to see how consistent they are in relation to known theories about education, and whether their ideas are logically sound and are based on commonly understood or properly defined concepts. In short, ideologies that are factual can be given a number of reality tests; ideologies that are normative can be given consistency tests, to see whether they have some substance or are merely empty rhetoric, and used to push one political point of view against others. Often the rhetorical nature of an ideology will become apparent when its generalizations do not lead to educational outcomes and detailed policies.

An ideology is used by its holders, i.e., ideologists, to maintain the *status quo* in society, and to maintain the existing power relationships between its constituent parts. Opposing it can be one or more counter-ideologies that endeavour to promote activities which seek a change in the prevailing state of affairs. Mannheim (1968: 86ff.) has described the tensions that can be generated between ideologies and counter-ideologies, especially when those who profess the former distort knowledge by deliberately failing to take account of the new realities of the situation.

The purposes of the confrontation between those who hold ideologies and counter-ideologies are discussed by Vaughan and Archer (1971).

Ideology is not only a component of successful domination and assertion but also defines the means by which educational goals can be implemented.

Therefore it not only functions as a source of legitimation for domination and assertion, but also a wider educational philosophy for the dominant and assertive groups. Bearing these points in mind, the ideology adopted by either type of group can be said to serve three distinct purposes — those of legitimation, negation and specification. While each of these may not be stressed to the same degree, they must be considered related to one another within a given educational ideology.

The negation of the sources of legitimation proposed by dominant groups is the main tactic of assertive ideologists, i.e., those persons who are trying to establish a counter-ideology. This is particularly likely to be the case in the early stages of an ideological confrontation. In turn, the challenged dominant group retaliates by reformulating its ideology to negate claims of the counter-ideology, so as to strengthen its source of legitimation. Going to further lengths, each of the opposing groups can specify the 'blue-print' to be implemented within educational establishments in such areas as goals and curricula. By these means, ideologies and counter-ideologies gain credibility by showing the world that they are not just words but are possible of realization in terms of concrete programmes.

Ideological dominance can occur in another way which relates the argument back to the central concern of control over knowledge/power. As Martin suggests (1978: 22):

> . . . the dominance of some parties implies their capacity to define interests and identities, to monopolise access to knowledge and its construction and to assert that certain knowledge is valid, irrespective of whether it has been validated in the way claimed, or not. To the extent that certain parties dominate the construction of knowledge to the exclusion of others, the knowledge so produced is ideological.

An even more covert way of maintaining ideological dominance is through ruling out certain objects as objects of public knowledge by what Bachrach and Baratz (1970: 43 – 44) call 'non-decision making' (see also Martin, 1978:23). 'A non-decision . . . is a decision that results in suppression or thwarting of a latent or manifest challenge to the values or interests of the decision-maker.' This is very similar to one of the 'maze games' I have described in relation to the lack of progress that has occurred in migrant education (Bullivant, 1976).

A further way of maintaining ideological dominance is by refusing to spell out the ideology in detail. Instead, to put across the ideas and beliefs he holds, the ideologist relies on a label or a phrase. These can easily become mere rhetoric. For example, the educational ideology referred to by the shorthand slogan 'equality of opportunity' consists of a whole cluster of beliefs and values. They concern ideas of justice, the basic notion of 'equality', the chance to make the most of one's endowed potential, differential treatment of disadvantaged or deprived children to make up their assumed deficits, a broad concept of compensation, which almost stands as an ideology in itself, and similar ideas. Very often these are not fully examined, but are accepted almost as an article of faith.

Shorthand ideologies of this type admit of almost infinite opportunities for obfuscating the issue, and taking refuge in further permutations and combinations of jargon to avoid being pinned down to what the ideological content of a slogan really means. The main tactic of the counter-ideologist is to insist that such ideologists define their terms and adopt theoretically respectable concepts if they want to be taken seriously and have their views accepted. Not surprisingly, the counter-ideologist's plea often falls on deaf ears.

Ideologies and counter-ideologies do not arise in a vacuum. They reflect the opinions of those who hold them, but they in turn are affected by forces from the society in which they live. Some of these have been influenced by the past history of the society; others are responses to its current situation. In short, ideologies and ideologists, counter-ideologies and counter-ideologists should all be seen in their socio-historical context, as Mannheim (1968: xxix – xxx) implies:

> The sociology of knowledge concerns itself not merely with the ideas and modes of thinking that happen to flourish, but with the whole social setting in which this occurs. This must necessarily take account of the factors that are responsible for the acceptance or the rejection of certain ideas by certain groups in society, and of the motives and interests that prompt certain groups consciously to promote those ideas and to disseminate them among wider sections.

Analysing the pluralist dilemma: the case study approach

It is now accepted that education in most Western societies since the Second World War has been influenced by a succession of ideologies and counter-ideologies. Those relating to the nature of pluralism are the most recent in a line of antecedent ideologies that have stressed other aspects of education. Each of the case studies in the following chapters attempts to identify the major ideologists and counter-ideologists, and traces their ideologies and counter-ideologies about the nature of the societies concerned, and how they influence educational provisions, and the work of knowledge managers.

The framework for the analysis is the logical model that has been developed from the concepts culture, enculturation, curriculum, and ideology. No claim is made that it is the only model which could have been developed. Whether it is right or wrong is beside the point as theoretical models cannot be attacked on such grounds. Rather it is the model's usefulness as an exploratory and explanatory construct that is the issue. From this point of view, it can be claimed with confidence that the model is both useful and powerful, to judge from the quality of the information it generated during the cross-national survey on which this book is based. The same confidence is held about the level of analysis the model has generated in each of the six case studies.

What emerges points to the pluralist dilemma. Western democracies can no longer ignore the very obvious fact that pluralism contains the seeds of competition and even conflict over the allocation of access to social rewards and economic resources through education. Ideologically, at least in theory, democracies are committed to policies that endeavour to protect and cater for individual and group rights. The dilemma is a very real one: allowing democracy full rein may cater for the educational wants of individuals and groups that are part of a society's pluralist composition, but doing so risks weakening the cohesion of the nation-state by interfering with the enculturation imperative — the need to have enough of a common culture passed on to each generation of children. How educationists in six societies view the pluralist dilemma is described in the case studies in the following chapters.

CHAPTER 2

Britain

This chapter describes some of the main features of the education system and policies relating to education in Britain, with particular reference to the problems posed by pluralism and the official and semi-official attempts to conceptualize it. The Scottish education system is not dealt with in any detail.

The socio-historical context

The current demographic pattern

The total British population in 1971 was 53 874 000. Of these people a total of 5.5 per cent were born overseas (Nissel & Lewis, 1974:83). As table 1 shows, of this proportion 1.8 per cent was born in foreign countries (including South Africa), 0.3 per cent in Canada, Australia and New Zealand (members of the Old Commonwealth), 2.1 per cent in the New Commonwealth (including Pakistan) and 1.3 per cent in the Irish Republic.[1]

TABLE 1   People born overseas, 1971 census

Birthplace	Number of people as percentage of total population
Foreign countries (including South Africa)	1.8
Canada, Australia, New Zealand	0.3
New Commonwealth (including Pakistan)	2.1
Irish Republic	1.3
Total born overseas	5.5
Total born in Britain	94.5

Immigration statistics indicate that in round figures 2.9 per cent of the total population in Britain in 1974 originated from the New Commonwealth ('coloured') countries (Smith, 1977:21). This low figure is surprising in view of the high visibility and seemingly ubiquitous presence of New Commonwealth people as one goes around the country. The opposite social and demographic reality indicated by the statistics is incontrovertible. 'It is most important . . . that the relatively small size of the minority population should be firmly established and constantly borne in mind' (1977:21).

Even the addition of figures for immigrants and their children from countries other than the New Commonwealth does not markedly inflate the total number of those born overseas. Nor does it suggest a markedly diverse ethnic 'mix' in the population. A table showing the origin of pupils published by the Department of Education and Science (DES) indicates how this is apparent in the school population. As they reflect the type of situation for which teachers are being trained, the figures indicated in table 2 are probably more helpful in showing the social and demographic characteristics of Britain. The figures give the numbers of pupils of overseas origin, as defined above, in maintained and special schools who might need special educational help and attention. Children of mixed immigrant and non-immigrant parentage, and children from the Republic of Ireland are excluded (Fuller, 1974:175).

TABLE 2   Immigrant pupils (aged 5 – 18) in Primary and Secondary schools by country of origin, 1972

Countries	Number	Percentage
West Indies*	101 898	36.4
India*	56 193	20.1
Pakistan*	30 629	10.9
Kenya (Asian origin)*	17 340	6.2
Africa*	15 829	5.7
Other Commonwealth countries in Asia*	8 008	2.9
Italy	12 009	4.3
Cyprus (Greek)*	9 504	3.4
Cyprus (Turkish)*	4 461	1.6
Spain	3 275	1.2
Poland	1 958	0.7
Other European	5 980	2.1
Australia/Canada/New Zealand	2 455	0.9
Gibraltar/Malta*	1 252	0.4
Rest of the world	9 081	3.2
Total	279 872	100.0

Source: Department of Education and Science, *Statistics of Education*, vol. 1 (London: H.M.S.O., 1972).
*New Commonwealth countries.

It is again quite clear that the major groups of children are from New Commonwealth countries, constituting 245 114 pupils (87.58 per cent) out of a total of 279 872 immigrant children. Like the figures for the British population as a whole, it is essential to appreciate that these immigrant children form only a tiny minority, 3.3 per cent in 1972, of the total school population (1974:175).

The impression of high ethnic visibility that the observer gets when touring the country is partly due to the regional concentrations of immigrants in certain areas. For instance, Fuller points out (1974:175 – 76) that Cypriots are largely settled in a few London boroughs, and thus constitute significant minorities in particular schools. Acquaintance with only these would lead one to exaggerate the numbers of Cypriot children in the school population.

West Indians are heavily concentrated in the south-east of Britain (66 per cent) and also in the West Midlands (17 per cent). The comparable figures for the general population in these two areas are 36 per cent and 10 per cent respectively. The rest of England and Wales (North, East Anglia, South-West and Wales) contain 3 per cent of the West Indians as compared with 23 per cent of the general population.

The main concentration of Pakistanis and Bangladeshis is in the West Midlands (33 per cent) compared with 10 per cent of the general population. A secondary concentration (30 per cent) is in Yorkshire and Humberside. All Asians (Pakistanis, Bangladeshis, Indians and African Asians) constitute 27 per cent of the total minority groups in the West Midlands compared with 10 per cent of the general population. However, it is important to note that this broad figure conceals important variations in the distribution of the various groups that comprise 'Asians'. Indians are concentrated in London and the South-East (43 per cent) and in the West Midlands (31 per cent). African Asians also favour these two regions (61 per cent and 14 per cent), but Pakistanis and Bangladeshis do not favour London and the South-East. The category 'Asians' thus needs to be interpreted with care. 'There is no single Asian community, but a number of distinct communities which are geographically grouped in different ways' (Smith, 1977:37).

In sum, it is clear that most of the Asian and West Indian immigrants from the New Commonwealth are living in London and the South-East and the West Midlands (74 per cent) in comparison with 46 per cent of the general population of adults. The remaining adults from these groups are spread very thinly over the rest of the country. As Smith comments (1977:35): 'It is this basic fact that leads to much of the widespread exaggeration of the numbers of Asians and West Indians in Britain. People notice the concentrations, but forget about the large areas where the minority groups are very uncommon indeed.'

Asian and other religions

As it has a bearing on the education provided in schools and consequently an effect on teacher education, mention should be made of the religious complexity of the Asian group, especially as it cuts across national origins. As Smith notes (1977:31 ff.) the great majority of Pakistanis are Moslems. Indians and African Asians belong to three main religious groups — Islam, Hinduism and Sikhism. There is also a small minority of Christians. Hinduism is by far the most common religion among African Asians.[2] Sikhism is the most common among Indians, even though it is a minority religion on the Indian subcontinent. Indians professing Islam constitute a larger proportion of the Indian population in Britain than they do in India.

Mention should also be made of the growing popularity of Rastafarianism among some West Indians, especially the younger generation. This appears to be a semi-religious, quasi-millenarian movement based among other aspects on the belief in the divinity of Haile Selassie, former emperor of Ethiopia. Symbols of group identification among members of the Rastafarian movement are special hairstyles among men ('locks'), coloured badges or buttons pinned to clothing, Reggae music, and, more dubiously, smoking 'ganja' (Indian hemp or marijuana). All these are functional in providing the bases for a collective ethnic identity for West Indians, even though 'ganja' is technically a deviant activity. The movement also has overtones of political ('Black Power') activism (Barrett, 1978:149 – 65).

Two further demographic factors bearing on the education system need to be mentioned. People born in New Commonwealth countries tend to be younger than the population as a whole (Kohler, 1974:9; Smith, 1977:35). The adult population is concentrated within the age range 25 – 54, and there is an unusually high proportion of children. Secondly, due to immigration restrictions, the number of New Commonwealth people entering Britain is reducing. More and more the demographic pattern will be influenced by the children born of parents from the New Commonwealth. These children will also be 'coloured', but more importantly they will have full, British citizenship.

Socio-economic 'class' structure

The detailed analysis in the PEP Report (Smith, 1977) shows clearly that immigrants from the New Commonwealth are severely disadvantaged compared with whites. The former have higher levels of unemployment; lower levels of earnings despite, in some cases, the possession of higher professional qualifications; lower job levels; and larger proportions doing shiftwork. There are important differences between the various groups that make up the New Commonwealth minorities, but, in general, the overall picture of their lower class status still holds as table 3 indicates.

Historical context

Immigration

Although small groups of racial and ethnic minority peoples have been part of the British social structure for centuries, the current situation is

TABLE 3 Job level analysed by country of origin: men

Men in job market who have worked	White	West Indian	Pakistani/ Bangladeshis	Indian	African Asians
unweighted	996	634	495	508	226
weighted	1594	2896	1391	1867	1050
Job level (socio-economic group)	%	%	%	%	%
Professional/ management	23 ⎫	2 ⎫	4 ⎫	8 ⎫	10 ⎫
	⎬ 40	⎬ 8	⎬ 8	⎬ 20	⎬ 30
White-collar	17 ⎭	6 ⎭	4 ⎭	12 ⎭	20 ⎭
Skilled manual	42	59	33	44	44
Semi-skilled manual	12 ⎫	23 ⎫	38 ⎫	27 ⎫	24 ⎫
	⎬ 18	⎬ 32	⎬ 58	⎬ 36	⎬ 26
Unskilled manual	6 ⎭	9 ⎭	20 ⎭	9 ⎭	2 ⎭
Not classified	1	1	1	*	*

Note: Among West Indian, Indian and African Asian women, job levels are distinctly lower than for white women, though the differences are less striking than they were in the case of men. Among working women generally, 29 per cent are doing semi-skilled and unskilled jobs; this compares with 47 per cent of West Indian women, 58 per cent of Indians and 48 per cent of African Asians. (This proportion is probably higher still for Pakistani women, but the sample size is too small for separate analysis.)
Source: *The* PEP *Report* (Smith, 1977:73).
*Less than 0.05 per cent.

largely the result of post-Second World War population changes due to immigration from Britain's former colonies. All main references comment on the recentness of this phenomenon. 'Twenty years ago black and brown people were an insignificant fraction of the population of Britain. . . . Racial minority groups, and the issues of race relations, have come to Britain recently, but there is general agreement that they have come to stay' (Smith, 1977:14). The history of this wave of migration does not need to be treated in detail, as the main object of this section is to establish the development of those currents of social thought that form the climate of public opinion about immigrants. This is now part of the context in which statements and decisions about the education of immigrant children are being made.

Immigrants from Britain's ex-colonies were entitled to come to Britain as they had had British nationality conferred upon them as part of the country's colonial policy. This created a situation in which migration to Britain was always possible. Those who migrated were motivated by the better work prospects, higher standard of living, and better education and social security there compared with the former colonies in which they lived. Historical events in these provided the impetus which motivated people to migrate. The first was the partition of India, in 1947, into India and Pakistan, which created numbers of rootless refugees living in uncertain circumstances. They were attracted by the better conditions in Britain and generated the late 1950s wave of immigration. The second event during the post-1968 period was the political persecution of Asians in Africa by the newly emergent black, nationalist states. This persecution 'created an entirely new class of migrants, for whom emigration was primarily a means of escape' (Smith, 1977:24). Their numbers added to those of the earlier wave.

The economic conditions in Britain during those periods also favoured immigration. In the 1950s, when the immigration boom was gathering force, Britain was enjoying a temporary economic boom period in which labour was short. Immigration was not initially discouraged; some enterprises even recruited overseas labour, and thus created a powerful incentive which compounded the effects of refugee status and political persecution. Two dominant preoccupations arose in the receiving society as a result of the inflow of immigrants caused by these various factors. The first concerned the immigrants' citizenship rights and rate of inflow, the second concerned their participation in the labour force and wider society.

In the early years, between 1950 and 1960, there was a general ignorance of the situation because the inflow had been proceeding quietly, with little publicity or fuss. The racial disturbances in Nottingham and Notting Hill in late 1958, however, jolted the complacency of many people (Griffith et al., 1960: 3). Initial reactions on the part of the government during the early stages have 'been described as *laissez-faire*; that is, there was no policy' (Smith, 1977:25). Certainly, there were no immediate moves to introduce laws through Parliament that would curb racial disturbances and the growing 'colour' problem. The Home Secretary of the time, Mr Butler, told the Annual Conference of the Association of Chief Police Officers, on 10 June 1959, that 'Racial discrimination is not and must not be part of our law' (Griffith et al., 1960:127). With the increasing numbers of highly visible immigrants in the community a concern gradually developed to restrict their entry, seen by many as an uncontrollable flood. This was attempted by the passing of a series of increasingly restrictive immigration Acts in 1962, 1968, and 1971.[3] Smith notes (1977:26): 'Thus in three stages from 1962 onwards the right of entry to Britain has been withdrawn from most of the population of the New Commonwealth countries, and a strict control of immigration has been imposed.' The impression this gives of well-thought-through official policies may not accord with the reality. As Krausz comments (1971:62), 'The record of the major political parties and most of their supporters could be assessed as showing their attitudes to have been flexible; in a more critical appraisal one would, however, describe the policies and utterances as muddled.'

In the equally difficult area of participation in the labour force and in society as a whole, the policies and attitudes seem to have reflected the middle-class tendency to be evasive on important issues or to see the problem as one 'to be ignored or treated blandly' coupled with 'a desire among most upper and middle class institutions to keep Britain civilized in racial matters' (Hiro, 1971:316, 318). Statements by politicians were based on assimilationist and integrationist assumptions. On 4 June 1959, after the Notting Hill disturbances, the Home Secretary gave the House of Commons the assurance that 'every effort will continue to be made in areas where there is a large coloured population to encourage their effective integration into the community (Griffith et al., 1960:126). The General Council of the TUC (Trade Union Congress) in its 1958 report favoured social integration, an absence of discrimination, and racial harmony along accepted socialist lines, but recognized that these were very difficult to achieve. Top-level spokesmen of the organization have tended to voice similar sentiments but at the rank-and-file levels of the workshop floor, where members' personal livelihood and competition with immigrants for jobs become salient issues, a much greater ambivalence towards the problem exists. One of the most extreme examples of this occurred in the summer of 1968, when London dockers marched to Parliament House in a panic reaction against floods of immigrants. Krausz (1971:64–65) comments of this event that, 'Here was a march of left-wing Trade Unionists in support of the views of right-wing politicians indulging in scapegoating at a time of economic trouble; for many people this was reminiscent of the unsettled period in Germany between the wars.'

This event had its roots in economic difficulties, but it is quite apparent from all writers that a dominant concern has also been the discrimination and prejudice displayed towards New Commonwealth immigrants on the grounds of their colour.[4] According to Foot (1965:231): 'The tendency of anti-immigrant propaganda over the last three years indicates that colour is establishing itself as a crucial feature of British politics.' However, he also suggests — somewhat polemically — that economic factors are still the major concern (1965:236):

> What hampers them [Commonwealth coloured immigrants] more than any other single disability is their formation into a sub-proletariat, working in jobs at the bottom of the wage scale, without proper trade union organization, in appalling conditions for long hours of overtime. As a sub-proletariat, they incur the worst forms of snobbery from their neighbours.

The evidence presented by the PEP Report also indicates clearly that colour or race is only one of many factors causing the way immigrants are treated, despite strategy embodied in the 1976 Race Relations Act which Smith (1977:320) sees as having some chance of success. He also points to economic issues:

> The gap between whites and the minority groups in terms of jobs, earnings, housing and standard of living is partly the result of racial discrimination and partly of other factors which have combined with each other and with

discrimination over a period of twenty years or more to produce the present situation.

Two organizations that might have been expected to play a major part in overcoming prejudice and discrimination in both economic and social areas of life are the trade unions and the Church. Most commentators are critical of the efforts of these bodies, especially at the lower levels of workplace and worship respectively. Banton (1959), among several others, gives evidence pointing to the basic lack of concern shown towards immigrants.

In an analysis utilizing the theories of Bogardus, Foot (1965:229) has attempted to pinpoint the British experience in relation to a cycle of reactions to immigrants by the host community. Stages in the Bogardus cycle are: (1) curiosity; (2) economic welcome; (3) industrial and social antagonism; (4) legislative antagonism; (5) fair-play tendencies; (6) quiescence; and (7) second-generation difficulties. Whilst commenting that the Bogardus cycle is helpful to understanding the British experience without exactly fitting it, Foot concludes (1965:229):

> The first four stages (curiosity, economic welcome, social and legislative antagonism) fit the process of Commonwealth immigration exactly. Unhappily, however, there is less sign of 'quiescence after fifteen years of Commonwealth immigration than there was after fifteen years of Irish or Jewish immigration. All the signs point gloomily towards increased antagonism.

It is important to stress that the question of assimilation and integration should not be considered solely from the point of view of the receiving society. The immigrants themselves have important opinions and desires that must be taken into account, as they too contribute to the dynamics of the situation within which decisions, claims and counterclaims about education and teacher training have to be taken. Henderson (Griffith et al., 1960:82) distinguishes between accommodating and assimilating groups. The former are those who are content to live on the outside of the broader community, asking little more of it than work of a kind and a place to live. She mentions Hindu Indians and Pakistani Moslems in this context. The latter are those who want to belong to the wider community, even to the point of gradually losing their own distinct ways. Henderson cites West Indians and, to a lesser extent, West Africans in this category. For the accommodating groups an official policy of assimilation would be far more threatening than it would be for the assimilating groups. Although Henderson's comments were written at the time of the Notting Hill disturbances, it would appear that the 'liberal lobby' favoured integration at least until Enoch Powell's inflammatory entry into the field of race relations by his Walsall speech in 1968. The same current of opinion was also promoted quite energetically by the mass media, including the British Broadcasting Commission's television programmes of the 1960s (Hiro, 1971:321 – 22).

The education system began to pay attention to problems of pluralism in the second half of the 1960s. Prior to this it was assimilationist. In 1963 the Robbins Committee (1963:7) saw one of the aims of higher education as 'the transmission of a common culture and common standards of citizenship'. Fuller (1974:184 – 85) sums up this period:

> Certainly, during the early 1960s it was assumed that education had a major role to play in bringing about racial harmony through encouraging cultural assimilation. This thinking can best be summed up by the major teachers' union statement in 1963 '. . . it is not the duty of the school either to foster or discourage the expression of national characteristics in minority groups [National Union of Teachers, Evidence Submitted to Commonwealth Immigrants Advisory Council, N.U.T., London, 1963]'.

Fuller (1974:185) and Rose (1969) trace the developments in education that took place in the 1960s. There was concern over the numbers of immigrant children schools could 'absorb' before they became too numerous to benefit from contact with a majority of white, indigenous children. Little teaching about race relations was attempted. A general *laissez-faire* approach pervaded schools and the system. Until 1966 no statistics were collected on immigrant pupils. Although restrictions on teacher quotas in areas of immigrant education had been lifted, resources were not available to train teachers of English as a second language, the dominant concern at the time. As a way of reassuring white parents and responding to their fears that standards in schools were dropping, the central government adopted policy recommendations to disperse immigrants and thus avoid their concentration in particular schools. As Fuller comments about these developments (1974:185):

> In a nutshell, the problem of race and education was seen during these years as basically an immigrant problem, a problem of numbers, the aim of education being to encourage immigrants to assimilate and whites to be tolerant.

Changes in the organization of the education system

The British education system is still going through a period of major reorganization, and no picture of the historical influences on education would be complete without some brief review of the changes that have occurred in the last decade. The famous Green Paper (Cmnd. 6869, 1977:1) takes its direction from the results of these changes to date, and foreshadows the anticipated outcomes of others that will flow from the gradual evolution of Labour Government Policy, first set out in the Education Act of 1944.

The change in school structure has been towards comprehensive reorganization. In England and Wales this has largely been pursued to eliminate selection (1977:3). Until 1977 when it was at its peak, the school population had been increasing steadily. Forecasts now indicate that it will decline for the next decade or more. The two features of comprehensive reorganization and increasing school population have dominated educational debate and planning during the past decade. A further important change was the introduction of the Certificate of Secondary Education (CSE) in 1965 to complement the General Certificate of Education (GCE). General overseeing of examinations is the responsibility of the Schools Council which acts on behalf of the Secretary of State for Education and Science (Central Office of Information, 1978:23). Future changes in this system are also envisaged, to give a common system of examining at 16-plus which would replace the CSE and GCE 'O' Level examinations. Recommendations to this effect have been put to the government.

The 1960s and early 1970s also saw a great expansion in the numbers of teachers and teacher training facilities to meet the increase in the school population, coupled with 'strenuous efforts to persuade former teachers to return to service' (Cmnd. 6869, 1977:24). The peak year was 1973, with over 40 000 newly qualified teachers completing their training. Numbers do not necessarily mean quality, however, and the Secretaries of State for Education and Science for England and for Wales concede that there is 'some degree of "mismatch" between the needs of the schools and the capacity of the present teaching force to meet them. Shortages of teachers of particular subjects persist and school curricula have often had to be trimmed to square with the staff available' (1977:25).

In 1972 the James Report, *Teacher Education and Training*, was published and led to many important changes. Of these the most significant has been the introduction and development of three- and four-year Bachelor of Education (B.Ed.) courses for initial teacher training. Graduates are no longer automatically qualified to teach without obtaining additional teaching qualifications, as they were prior to 1970. In that year for primary teachers, and since 1974 for secondary teachers, a year's professional training became mandatory for newly qualified graduates wishing to teach (COI, 1978:33 – 34). The government plans to carry these changes even further to achieve its policy of having an all-graduate entry to the teaching profession. The non-graduate, three-year Certificate of Education courses still offered by some training bodies are to be phased out, and no entrants to them will be accepted after the academic year 1979 – 80.

Accompanying these policies have been quite sweeping changes to the organization of training colleges. Many are merging with the polytechnics or further education colleges, with the result that single institutions now provide a wide range of courses. Some colleges have remained separate, but have broadened their offerings to include more general courses of higher education. Others continue to be solely or mainly concerned with teacher education. A sizeable number of colleges are closing. The view of the government is that the reduction in the teaching force is necessary in response to declining pupil numbers — 1977 projections forecast a reduction of about 2 million pupils by 1989. The sweeping changes are also seen as a way of achieving 'flexibility' in the system (1978:34).

There seems little doubt that these changes are having a profound effect on the morale of the teaching service, which in turn is a further component of the socio-historical climate in Britain. The Director of the Derby Lonsdale College of Higher Education, Ken Millins, is one among many academics and teacher educators who deplore what has occurred. In his opinion, the overall provision for and standard of teacher education has regressed. 'The government has destroyed teacher education in the last two years' is a common comment. With the destruction have come anxiety about future career prospects, a period of stagnation with many teachers without jobs, poor job mobility and promotion prospects, and hostility to the government.

It seems little wonder, then, that in the area of teacher training and education for pluralist Britain the situation and thinking 'are on the whole complex . . . a sort of muddle, with muddled thinking at the top . . . and muddle at the bottom' according to Madeleine Blakeley, the General Secretary of the National Association for Multiracial Education. Her opinion reinforces those of Millins and others that the time has come for educationists to hold on to what has been accomplished in pluralist education, limited though it may have been.

A final component of the historical and social context in Britain is the wider political framework within which the country now operates as a signatory to, and member of, the European Economic Community. The Council Directive of 25 July 1977 sets out its requirements on the education of the children of migrant workers. The purpose of the requirements is to 'improve the conditions of freedom of movement for workers relating in particular to reception and to the education of their children'. To these ends 'they should be able to receive suitable tuition including teaching of the language of the host State. Member States should also take, in conjunction with the Member States of origin, appropriate measures to promote the teaching of the mother tongue and the culture of the country of origin of the abovementioned children, with a view principally to facilitating their possible reintegration into the Member State of origin.' A further requirement is that 'Member States shall take the measures necessary for the training and further training of the teachers who are to provide this tuition'.

Ideologies and ideologists

The forces and tensions within the socio-historical context are reflected in the diversity of interpretations of the kind of pluralism that the British situation displays. Thinking about the problem is at an embryonic stage, which seems to suggest that, until relatively recently, British educationists have been content to accept the received tradition concerning pluralism in Britain. In the opinion of Tuku Mukherjee, a senior lecturer in multicultural education at Southlands College of Education in Wimbledon, London:

> The issue is that the education system here is so ethnocentric. For the first time it has got to look at itself, and that's a difficult thing to do. To admit to oneself that one has been wrong is very difficult, but as soon as you are able to do it, you are half way to recovery. The system hasn't been able to do that yet, but it is just beginning to think about it.

Distinguishing ideologies from counter-ideologies is difficult, but one useful measure is the degree to which the evolving ideas depart from the essentially conservative socio-historical context described above.

Received traditions in knowledge management

The Schools Council and the National Foundation for Educational Research (NFER) are independent bodies which control both the creation and dissemination of a considerable amount of 'educational knowledge'. Neither body holds official views about British society and the direction its education system should take, but by the kind of educational projects each takes on under its aegis it inevitably encourages certain views about both issues and discourages others. For instance, Mike Feeley, ex-President of the National Association for Multiracial Education (NAME), commented in 1976 that the Schools Council spends twice as much on single (English) language development as on multilanguage programmes and that this proportion is some indication of official priorities.[5]

The projects carried out by both organizations to date, in title at least, have tended to stress the multiracial aspects of education in Britain. In 1972, NFER published the study of multiracial schools carried out by Townsend and Brittan, (1972). This was followed in 1973 by the Schools Council Working Paper no. 50 on multiracial education, also by Townsend and Brittan. The latter was a report of a survey conducted by the NFER among schools throughout England. In broad terms, it was found that many of the schools who responded supported a cultural assimilationist and integrationist position for racial minorities. Many of the headteachers interviewed seemed willing to educate children of overseas origin, but in the English tradition. Even the headteachers of some schools with culturally different children were against multiracial education or other kinds of instruction which emphasized cultural or racial differences in children.

In 1974 the NFER published the results of a commissioned research project undertaken by Dr. F. Taylor of Goldsmiths College, (Taylor, 1974). Giles notes (1977:2) that Dr Taylor makes it clear that there are many people concerned with, and looking at, multiracial education in

Britain. However, there is also a large groundswell of teachers and headmasters who do not want to have anything to do with race relations. Giles reached a similar conclusion, based on his own research into West Indian children's education (1977:7):

> Most of the heads and teachers I interviewed did not feel they could justify or support a policy or programme designed to address the special needs of disadvantaged West Indian students which ignored similar needs among the indigenous white population and other culturally different, socially disadvantaged pupils.

A major project carried out by an NFER/Schools Council team is Education for a Multiracial Society. This was sponsored by the National Union of Teachers and the National Association for Multiracial Education. Relations between these two bodies became strained during the last six months of the project's life, however, and when the project report was presented to the Schools Council late in 1977, it had to pass through a number of its vetting committees. The final committee, which was dominated by representatives from the National Union of Teachers (as are all other Schools Council committees), quashed the report and banned its publication on the grounds that it was unfair to teachers. It was alleged that the report attacks bad teaching and teachers' racist attitudes.

Rather ironically, however, and in a distinct sense of anti-climax, chapter 1 of the report was 'leaked' and published in *New Society* in February 1978. All it said was that teachers of infants and juniors did not realize how much children are conscious of races and, in fact, how grossly prejudiced they can be, largely as a result of acquiring racist attitudes from their parents. In discussion, Penny Manners of Garnett College commented on this reaction: 'It was quite extraordinary how threatened teachers felt . . . but to anybody who knows about these things at all the fact that the chapters were suppressed is totally unremarkable.'

Certainly the Schools Council has some reputation for blocking unfavourable reports or not supporting sensitive projects. The most notorious case was the withdrawal of support from Lawrence Stenhouse and the Nuffield/Schools Council Humanities Curriculum Project when the race relations kit was being developed and tested. In the case of the Schools Council Social Education Project, Madeleine Blakeley believes it never got published because it was trying to give children the skills to 'beat' society. Finally, there was the Schools Council Project on Social and Cultural Change and the Implications for Secondary Education in Wales, which showed up deficiencies within the system as a whole and expressed critical views obtained from many sources of various happenings within education. These views were received with 'guarded enthusiasm' but this did not extend to supporting general publication of the report.[6]

The National Union of Teachers (NUT) has recently come out in favour of race relations and multicultural studies, according to John Callander of the Commonwealth Institute. In mid-1978 at a meeting of its Council Executive a joint NUT/Schools Council project was approved to produce suitable materials for multicultural education. These materials would be used nationally and not only in those areas with few coloured immigrants. It remains to be seen what impact if any this will have in school systems. As Eggleston points out about the work of the Schools Council (1977:124): 'Even when decisions have been made, projects completed and final reprints published, the Council has no mandatory power to put them into practice: the final decision remains with the school and the teacher.' Moreover, all the Council's decision-making committees have a majority of teachers' unions' representatives in their membership (1977:123).

Eggleston also maintains that the Schools Council puts an emphasis on 'good practice' that is derived from a 'received perspective' (1977:132). This entails the Council in

> . . . making curricular recommendations within the traditionally accepted definitions of knowledge and ability and enforcing them by its indirect but effective control of 'new resources' and the authority that derives from the nature of its sponsorship and the size of its budget. A number of commentators see the Schools Council and curriculum development as a whole as authoritarian (1977:129–30).

We can assume with some confidence that the role of the Schools Council and the official teachers' organizations is largely to preserve the *status quo* — the received tradition. Thus their models of society are likely to reflect an ideology that favours a fairly passive stance. Organizations such as these are not going to 'rock the boat' or embark on courses of action that necessitate redefinitions of the situation and alternative ideologies. As an example, we might cite the NUT statement of 1973 which encourages 'respect' rather than 'tolerance' towards ethnic minorities (Fuller, 1974:186):

> The extent to which schools can and should transmit the cultural and religious values of the nation or race is perhaps arguable, but it is difficult to deny to children of one race or nation what is automatically done for others . . . the emphasis for the future must lie in the concept of an education directed towards the needs of a multiracial society, and not to the specific and isolated question of educating children from immigrant families, with often the unacknowledged aims of converting them into good Europeans!

Coming from an organization which played a major role in suppressing the findings of the Schools Council/NFER report, *Education for a Multiracial Society*, despite its involvement as a sponsor of this project, one can only take it that this ideological statement was never really intended to be put into practice, and remains largely rhetoric.

The Department of Education and Science (DES) is concerned with official government policy towards the education of all children in Britain, and its decisions and recommendations are some guide to its thinking about the nature of pluralism. They are formulated by the bureaucracy and put into effect by a Her Majesty's Inspectors (HMIs) who are bound by the Government's official publication. This formidable body forms one of the important 'specialist agencies and *cadres* within the education service itself', which began with 'a powerful executive and supervisory power' and 'has, through greatly increasing emphasis on advisory roles and the monitoring of innovation, played an unobtrusive but central part in curriculum affairs' (Eggleston, 1977:47).

Three HMIs in particular are involved with pluralist education. Eric Bolton has national responsibility for multiracial education.[8] Colin Roberts was the former director of the Centre for Information and Advice on Educational Disadvantage in Manchester. John Woodend is attached to the Education Disadvantage Unit operating in the Inner London area. As ideologists their views are important, because each has been active in taking part in courses run for teachers by DES, and in its annual course on multiracial education and race relations.

Government policy, according to the HMIs, blends recognition of the pluralist nature of British society with conventional deprivation or compensatory ideology. This enables the government to accept that 'ours is now a multiracial and multicultural society' on the one hand (Cmnd. 6869, 1977:4) but propose solutions for the problems such pluralism generates as part of a wider 'package' of social welfare and equality of educational and employment opportunity (Cmnd. 7186, 1978:3). Although this would seem to be a new approach to the problems of ethnic minorities, it has roots in earlier government thinking about their position in British society, and is basically assimilationist, as it still sees a *racial* problem as one part of a wider context of social and economic deprivation that affects all disadvantaged groups.

The latest DES thinking seems to represent a policy shift to accepting the reality of urban deprivation. This is now seen as closely connected with lack of fluency in English and the general educational disadvantage among ethnic minorities. The logic of their solution then becomes clearer, if not totally acceptable, to those who press for separate solutions to minority problems. DES adopts a social alleviation policy model to alleviate racial discrimination. The racial problems associated with 'ghetto' areas are tackled by proposing *social* solutions. If successful, it is hoped that these will also lead to getting rid of ethnic minority problems. Both the government and DES have a growing awareness of multiracial problems, but are less willing to get programmes off the ground solely for ethnic minority groups. This, too, has historical roots in the government's general hope that a society with positive multiethnic aspects might be achieved, coupled with the fear that this could be socially divisive. In consequence the government is not proceeding too quickly and keeps a brake on going multiethnic and multicultural in its thinking.

A further complicating factor is the problem of second and third generation ethnic minority children, who see themselves as British, but are not seen in the same way by the majority of the population. Ethnic groups want cohesion, with very strong sentimental links with their countries of origin, but with no very strong, real desire to go back to them. Young people from ethnic groups are tending to establish themselves as 'hyphenated ethnics'. Many are urban, British-born, more liberated than their parents but still not totally Westernized, and are driven in on themselves by poor race relations and a white backlash. Hyphenated ethnicity is seen as a way of establishing some self-identity in such conditions.

Government thinking also includes a concern for bringing a greater international perspective into the curriculum, as seems clear from the Green Paper (Cmnd. 6869, 1977:41):

> Our society is a multicultural, multiracial one, and the curriculum should reflect a sympathetic understanding of the different cultures and races that now make up our society. We also live in a complex, interdependent world, and many of our problems in Britain require international solutions. The curriculum should therefore reflect our need to know about and understand other countries.

An international perspective is also the concern of the Commonwealth Institute in London, but despite its recent adoption of more innovative programmes, it is basically conservative, although it does show willingness to move with the times. According to its Chief Education Officer in 1978, John Callander, there is no common ground in tackling the problems of pluralism, and it is difficult to identify a dominant ideology. The Institute's programmes reflect this uncertainty, especially in the tendency to use technical terms like multiracial, multicultural, and multiethnic interchangeably and apparently synonymously.

In general, the Institute's present policy is to move away from a multiracial approach and from programmes that stress Black studies, because these are too sensitive in the present British context. Instead, programmes try to adopt a 'well-rounded attitude' towards pluralist education, with the aim of helping teachers to 'open windows on the world' for children. From its publications and lavish display materials in a striking exhibition hall, it is obvious that the Institute stresses the importance of the heritages, traditions, festivals and customs of the Commonwealth countries as a basis for understanding the characteristics of British pluralism. This is made clear in a brochure produced for Commonwealth Day 1977 (Commonwealth Institute, 1977:3):

> We must also learn to live fully and harmoniously at a national and local level. Britain now has a multi-racial and multi-cultural society with most of

the ethnic minorities having their roots in overseas Commonwealth countries. The link between preparation for living in this kind of society and studies of the Commonwealth countries is obvious.

An exhibition entitled 'The Richer Heritage' was held at the Institute in June 1978 and followed the same approach. Although the term multi-ethnic appears in the publicity literature, reflecting the new thinking of the Inner London Education Authority (ILEA), most of the exhibition stressed the variety of cultural traditions represented in Inner London schools. The conservative emphasis is quite clear in the introduction to a supplement to *Contact*, published for the exhibition by ILEA. The Authority's Education Officer, Peter Newsam, notes (1978:2): 'Heritage is something which comes to us from the past and, rich or poor, there it is.'

The terminological uncertainty typical of the early stage in the evolution of an ideology of pluralism is neatly illustrated by a Commonwealth Institute brochure *A Teacher's Guide to Study Resources* (p.6):

> Schools also accept responsibility for preparing young people to live fully and harmoniously in the local and national context. In Britain, we now have a multi-racial and multi-ethnic society with most of the ethnic minorities having their roots in overseas Commonwealth countries . . . Studies related to the Commonwealth and its member countries provide an excellent vehicle for this aspect of education at all levels in the school system.

Early revisionist ideas

In June 1977, the legislated date when the 1976 Race Relations Act became effective, the London-based Community Relations Commission (CRC) amalgamated with the Commission for Racial Equality. The CRC had always been very active in the field of educational policies for pluralism, and its monthly bulletin, *Education and Community Relations*, had provided a useful and informative forum for exchange of views on the topic, as well as information about curricula, conferences, seminars, and training courses for teachers.

The most relevant document published by the CRC in its time was *Teacher Education for a Multi-cultural Society* (Joint Working Party: 1974) which might be seen as a specification exercise. This is the report of a Joint Working Party of the Community Relations Commission and the Association of Teachers in Colleges and Departments of Education. As the title indicates, and the opening sentence of the report reiterates, 'Britain is a multi-cultural society'. Like the Commonwealth Institute, the Community Relations Commission functioned during the early stage in the evolution of pluralist thinking, and the report tends to suggest this (Joint Working Party, 1974:5):

> Our awareness of the many strands in our *culture* has been sharpened by recent changes in the *racial* composition of this society . . . What happens to them [black and brown people] in our schools is crucial to the development

of a *racially* just society. The training of teachers and other professionals should equip them to work towards such a society [italics added].

The Joint Working Party also tackled the problem of terminology. It is apparent that they had mixed success, however, judging from the anomalies indicated by the italics in the following passage (1974:5n):

> In this Report we have decided to use 'black' and 'brown' to describe members of the main minority *ethnic groups* in Britain today. We have used 'multi-racial' when referring to the composition of the population and 'multi-cultural' to indicate the diversity of historical background, linguistic patterns, religious beliefs and cultural and family customs which make up our *society*. [italics added]

A key problem noted by the Joint Working Party focuses on race relations. Increasingly, the teachers being trained in the colleges will be dealing with fewer and fewer immigrants, but more and more young black and brown Britons who have been born in the country and thus have, and are entitled to, the same rights to educational and occupational opportunities as their white classmates. This 'colour' problem has probably become the major preoccupation among educationists and policy makers in Britain. Attempts to conceptualize it differ, however, and in the case of the Joint Working Party's recommendations it would appear that the problem is subsumed under the rubric of multi-*cultural* education. This seems to contradict the Working Party's own definition of terms given above, from which one might have expected them to see the problem as being part of a multi*ethnic* society, i.e., one composed of several minority ethnic groups. Instead, culture rather than race seems to be singled out as the strategic issue. As the following passage indicates (1974:10), it is also extended to take into account socio-economic or class sub-cultures:

> . . . the teacher in particular must extend the ability he already has to deal constructively with pupils from different socio-economic backgrounds and encompass a still wider range of ethnic differences. In order to communicate effectively with a different outlook, class or culture from his, the teacher needs an understanding and appreciation of these sub-cultures, be they of a particular class, of black Londoners or of Bradford Pakistanis.

This confusion seems to dodge the central problem — that children from coloured groups are being discriminated against on the grounds of race alone. The Joint Working Party (1974:11) cites an ILEA study which showed

> . . . that even pupils from minority groups who have been fully educated in this country are still functioning across the primary curriculum at a level well below that of the indigenous population and comparisons within the schools suggested that minority pupils are not performing at the same level as underprivileged white pupils.

The National Foundation for Educational Research also surveyed the organization in multiracial schools (Townsend & Brittan, 1972). It found that West Indian, Indian and Pakistani children were often in the lower streams; and of the 230 multiracial schools surveyed, only one reported that black and brown pupils were frequently placed in the higher streams — and this was true only of Indian children.

The West Indian pupils are disadvantaged in schools to such an extent that a disproportionate number are found to have been placed in ESN (Educationally Subnormal) schools at both primary and secondary levels. This is despite the fact that, in its report on such schools, the ILEA concluded that 'some immigrant children, especially West Indians, may well have intellectual potential above the assessed I.Q., their level of achievement having been depressed by inadequate or narrow previous education' (Fuller, 1974:177).

The Joint Working Party's recommendations for the kind of teacher education needed to cope with this problem illustrate just how difficult it is to grasp the idea that the basic cause of the obvious discrimination has to do with race and not culture (Joint Working Party 1974:10). An alternative explanation is that such an interpretation is so politically sensitive that it has to be re-defined in cultural terms — a kinder euphemism.

> . . . those training to be teachers . . . will need specific preparation for working in a multi-cultural society. Such professionals will inevitably have a key role in building satisfactory race relations in Britain. The opportunities that they give to the first generation of black and brown Britons born here and passing through our educational system will be among the important determining factors of these relations.

As its name implies, the Commission for Racial Equality (CRE) is far less ambivalent about the function of education in Britain. Horace Lashley, the Commission's Senior Education Officer, made this quite clear. However, whether his views fully resolve the confusion about the nature of British society is debatable.

In his opinion, although it could be argued that Britain is nto a multiracial society, since only some three percent of the people are non-white, for a great many people the problems in education are being seen in terms of race. For them, race is the major issue. 'For the vast majority of blacks who are here, for government and governmental policy, as also happens for education and educational policy, Britain today is a multiracial society.' This description stresses the physical composition of the society but carries no curricular implications. All it suggests is that there are groups of people in Britain who are non-Anglo-Saxon, and that they are spread thinly over the country as a whole, with concentrations in major metropolitan regions. By extension, all 'multiracial' says is that there are racially different children in the classroom to be educated.

Multicultural education, according to Horace Lashley, does have curricular implications on the other hand. In this conceptualization we are looking at the composition of society and are seeing different groups of people with different values and different interests. This view has no racial connotations — Britain has working class, middle class and the rest as sub-groups within it. Multicultural education is education using the various cultural sub-groups within the society.

Multiethnic education involves talking about the ethno-cultural implications of the society. This means considering the Chinese, the West Indians, the Afro-West Indians, the Asians, the Pakistanis or whatever, as ethnic groups with their own cultural differences which influence their view of society. As a sociological description of society multiethnic is a preferred term, but from the point of view of an educationist the preferred model is the multicultural one, because it enables socio-economic, or 'class', sub-cultures to be considered, something which the multiethnic perspective neglects, according to Lashley.

However, there is a wider international dimension to the problem. The serious implications for schools of increased numbers of blacks in Britain, a result of the waves of coloured immigrants coming into the country, must be seen in relation to the changing relationships between Britain and her former colonies, and between the 'haves' and the developing countries, the 'have nots'. In conjunction with the results of the Vietnamese war and the Arab oil embargo, there is a set of new economic relationships, where for the first time non-whites are having a catastrophic effect on the economies of Europe.

This new international dimension of the 'coloured' problem has implications for the curriculum. Schools need to readjust from the Eurocentric view, with its pro-white education, to a world view and an internationally-oriented education. There needs to be an emphasis on breaking up the present curriculum to take into it all the experiences of *all* the children who are now in the country. Secondly, a greater internationalism must replace the present nationalism. A pluralistic viewpoint must replace the present integrationist ideology, and include such aspects as respect for each other's positions, for each other's cultures, and even for each other's values. It should also tend to talk in terms of equality of opportunity. Despite these ideal aims, however, an examination of the types of courses used in schools shows a preponderance of those that deal with ethnic heritage, folk traditions, aspects of countries of origin, regional and areas studies. Treatment of 'race' follows the traditional approach of trying to improve children's attitudes. These types of approaches are summarized in the following diagram.

Lashley's views echo those of the CRE's publication, the first issue of which appeared in April–May 1978. 'Like its forerunner it will maintain a policy of being a useful aid to teachers interested in the area of multi-racial, multi-cultural education' (CRE, 1978a:1). However, the CRE also envisages an expansion of the journal's role in what might

FORMS OF PLURALIST EDUCATION

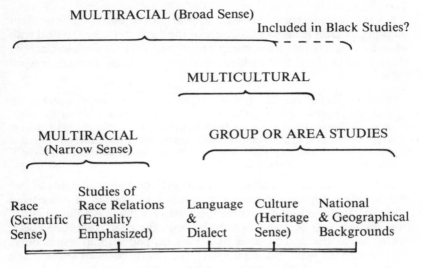

MULTIRACIAL (Broad Sense)

Included in Black Studies?

MULTICULTURAL

MULTIRACIAL
(Narrow Sense)

GROUP OR AREA STUDIES

| Race (Scientific Sense) | Studies of Race Relations (Equality Emphasized) | Language & Dialect | Culture (Heritage Sense) | National & Geographical Backgrounds |

TOPICS IN THE CURRICULUM

be seen as an exercise in legitimation, possibly in answer to the uncertainties and internal dissension that have occurred in the Commission since its establishment. 'In addition we intend to use the Journal as a vehicle for the exploration of the concept of multi-racial education, also to stimulate the creation of a *body of knowledge* concerned with this area.' Greater specification of the Commission's function appeared in the second, June – July, issue of (CRE, 1978b:1). It is clear that, in the field of education, the central concern is the promotion of equality of opportunity regardless of race or colour.

Working to overcome the problems of educational injustice on grounds of race is the prime concern of the National Association for Multiracial Education (NAME). This organization was formed in 1965 as ATEPO (Association for the Teaching of English to Pupils from Overseas), in response to what was seen at that time as the central issue. However, as its publicity brochure makes clear (NAME, n.d.:5), this organization considers itself to be more widely involved 'in making changes required in the education system which will further the development of a just multi-racial society'. This is defined (NAME, n.d.:6) as 'one in which all groups are tolerant and respectful of each other and have an equal opportunity to lead a decent life. . . . Minority groups are at a disadvantage in such areas of life as employment, housing and education.' Minority-group children suffer handicaps similar to those experienced by working-class children and arising from similar socio-economic causes. In addition, they 'are further handicapped by being on the receiving end of racial prejudice and discrimination' (NAME, n.d.:7).

NAME is concerned lest what appears to be current government thinking by DES leads to a lessening of the measures taken to deal with what are special minority group problems. This was made clear by Hugh Boulter (1978:5), President of NAME, at its conference in April 1978:

> We have become increasingly aware of the weakness of the argument which states that multi-racial education is only one aspect of educational disadvantage in general. The Centre for Information on Educational Disadvantage which was established in Manchester demonstrates all too clearly that in such a wide field as educational disadvantage the particular needs of multi-racial education are all too easily lost.

The extent of the muddled thinking and counter-arguments about this issue are apparent from the perceptive comments of Madeleine Blakeley. In her opinion, race has become very much a political issue, over the last year or eighteen months, with the result that it has been taken out of the narrow area of debate on educational issues only. Teachers do not want to align themselves on party political terms. They are scared and really do not want to know about race issues, and react by 'pushing them away' and concentrating on cultural differences.

Multicultural education is seen by the coloureds in this situation as being about black and white and discrimination. Their insistence on this can lead to tension with teachers who hold that the problem is really one of differences between cultures and the fears of people meeting new cultural situations. Tensions such as these can lead to 'a desperate situation' in places like Brixton (London Metropolitan suburb). Theorists in Britain have not come to a consensus about terms like multiracial, multicultural, and multiethnic; this would also be true of many teachers. As the conceptual muddle in Britain is typical of that which exists in other countries, Madeleine Blakeley's analysis is especially important:

> We started off by talking about immigrants, fairly obviously in the late sixties. We still haven't got rid of that. Immigrants are now seen as anybody who's a different colour. Coloureds are singled out; black minorities are in the greatest numbers. . . . Multi-racial is the term used in relation to inner city disadvantage, black problems, language deprivation, and so on. . . . The whole political implication of the term makes people shy away from multi-racial because they don't want to understand the relationship between black and white. So they'll say multicultural to get away from that.

Mainly as a result of the recommendations of the Green Paper, there are moves afoot to make a multiracial training component compulsory in all teacher training institutions. All teachers should be prepared for teaching in a multiracial society, but when that idea is put into practice what it usually comes down to is a term's course as part of professional studies training. Some colleges make this compulsory, but it is not common practice; more usually there is an optional elective system. Madeleine Blakeley believes the ideal situation would be one where every course in a teacher training programme included as its guiding philosophy a rationale that teachers are being prepared to teach in a multiracial society. 'Doing' multiracial education as a small topic is counter-productive. In line with this emphasis is the decision announced by the retiring editor that NAME's journal, *Multiracial School*, would be called *New Approaches to Multi Racial Education* as from July 1978.

Counter-ideologies and ideologists

There seems little doubt from the literature that there is a slowly growing climate of opinion which believes that a clarification and re-definition of the situation facing migrant and minority group children is necessary. At the time of the 'great debate' on education in Britain, instigated by the Secretary of State, a number of delegates from ethnic minority groups met on 12 March 1977 to hold their own discussions on the issues, and resolved to continue to argue for their priorities.[9] The delegates were provoked by the complete absence of multiethnic education from the debate's agenda. They made it clear that the four areas of the national debate were very limited and did not meet the overall concerns of ethnic minorities. These are that:

1 Education must be for a multiethnic, multicultural society and this must be reflected both in the initial and in-service training of teachers.
2 Ethnic minorities have the right to define their own needs and to be involved in the decision-making processes at all levels of the education service.
3 The education service tends to ignore the views and concerns of ethnic minorities on such matters as choice of school and curricula. It is regrettable that schools with a high percentage of ethnic minority pupils should have no ethnic minority governors or parent representatives. . . .

There is also clear evidence from the literature in the last two or three years that an 'ethnic perspective' is being used increasingly, and that it includes reference to the multiethnic society. Whether these views are merely a change of 'labels' or constitute significantly different conceptions of minority relations in Britain remains to be established in what follows.

During the discussion held at Garnett College, Penny Manners, who has responsibility for multicultural education, claimed that there are few educationists who can sort out the difference between multiracial, multiethnic and multicultural; generally they tend to use the terms synonymously.

> That battle has not got a great deal of significance here simply because we have not tried to define the differences and see what the implications are. . . . Multi-racial [is] beginning to be abandoned for multicultural . . . maybe we haven't bothered to define them because of all the other enormous things which do have to be bothered about. . . . The question of racism is very important.

It would seem that what counter-ideology there is, may be at an embryo stage — an interpretation that is borne out by the opinions of others, who may only tentatively be called counter-ideologists.

Tuku Mukherjee of Southlands College holds views very similar to those of Madeleine Blakeley. He believes that the emphasis should not be placed on seeing West Indians in Britain as a problem. Their situation is more of an educational *issue*. The danger with seeing their situation as a problem is that it becomes 'hived off' from education in general. Thinking about racial differences, multiculturalism and similar issues, on the other hand, should pervade the whole teacher education course. According to Mukherjee, at present this is not the case at Southlands College, but moves are under way to make it so in the future. In his opinion, attempts should be made to get the multicultural perspective to permeate through all the disciplines in courses. At present this does not happen, as those involved in multicultural studies lack authority and 'academic' prestige. Southlands College authorities have made the decision to increase both within their institution. Teaching staff for a multicultural studies programme will not be brought in from outside but will be seconded to the programme from other areas of specialization within the organization. This means that when they go back, they take the multicultural perspective with them to inform the work of the other disciplines and may even promote thinking about the need for their reorganization. People in the college are beginning to think about making multicultural studies a 'must'.

Both Southlands College and Garnett College are Associated Colleges of the University of London Institute of Education. They do not have full autonomy in setting their own curricula, but work through the Institute, which thus exercises considerable control over the type of knowledge, and the interpretations of the nature of British society, disseminated by teacher education courses. The Deputy Director of the Institute is Professor Denis Lawton, whose work has had considerable bearing on curriculum development theory. It is noteworthy that the Institute set up a Centre for Multicultural Education in 1979.

In commenting on the situation in Britian, Professor Lawton initially adopted a broader perspective than those cited earlier.

Curriculum in England is in such a mess, not for multi-cultural nor multi-ethnic reasons, but for historical reasons. We need to talk in terms of what could be a common curriculum everyone needs in society, regardless of where they come from. The idea has more or less been accepted, not universally or not officially by people like NUT, but latest pronouncements from DES seem to accept the idea of the need for a core curriculum based on the idea of a plurality of sub-cultures, but running through that what everyone needs to live and survive in, and enjoy, our type of society.

In this model, the lower working-class groups would be seen as sub-cultures, but with more in common with the rest of the community and society than there are differences. Professor Lawton stated that he would want to go on and look at geographical sub-cultures, social class sub-cultures, ethnic sub-cultures and the schools that serve them. Once the core curriculum has taken care of, say, between 50 and 75 per cent of the curriculum in these schools, one can then talk about the rest of the programme and the practical difficulties which sub-cultural variations pose.

It seems to me inevitable that the composition of the core elements in the curriculum must be related to the dominant society, even though this might be interpreted as a form of ethnic hegemony. Professor Lawton's reaction to this concept was remarkably frank:

> I fail to see how it could be otherwise, because if we are talking about white, Anglo-Saxon people, this is the culture we are in, a highly technological culture, a scientific culture and so on. . . . I'm not suggesting that it's not universalistic in some senses. . . . I think that science has to be. [To those ethnic minorities demanding that their traditions be catered for in the curriculum] I would want to say that by all means let's preserve your culture, but if you want to survive and prosper in our English society, you've got to come to terms with that as well as your own. . . . But the situation is that they learn to cope with our scientific, technological kind of culture, and still value very highly [their own] language, dancing and all the rest of it, which I would want to see as part of the periphery of the curriculum rather than the central core . . . as soon as you move away from the central core, which is based on what we've already got, a hundred years of tradition, I think you're in danger of not transmitting anything.

One major difficulty according to Lawton is that teachers and others concerned with education slide away from talking about either multi-cultural or multiethnic problems, but try to incorporate social class differences as well. Thus, when they talk about multicultural education, many people are really thinking about accommodating within the British educational system not only those from other ethnic communities but also those from the working classes, and people on the periphery of Britain, such as Welsh-speaking people in the far west and some Scottish Gaelic-speaking children.

Lawton's assessment of the dominant problem in Britain is very similar to that of Horace Lashley and of Madeleine Blakeley. In short, cultural and racial differences are operating to produce educational disadvantages for children from ethnic minority backgrounds. However, Lawton's solution links these problems with the issue of social class differences:

> I would want to see that in terms of, on the one hand, how can schools make our common core curriculum, or whatever we like to call it, relevant and appropriate to children from a variety of cultural backgrounds, race, or social class . . . that's part of the problem. The other part of the problem, which interlinks with it, is how do we at the same time demonstrate that the school values the cultures from which they come. It's a two-way process I think . . . welcoming their cultural differences, but at the same time making our core curriculum, our common culture, available and attractive to them. Both of these are enormously difficult problems.

Multiethnic education: counter-ideology or further revision?

To judge from its title, a new departure from the received tradition seems to have been established by the Inner London Education Authority's report *Multi-ethnic Education*, published on 8 November 1977. This constituted a 'radical reappraisal' of the service ILEA provides to London's multiethnic society, according to the recommendations made by its Chief Education Officer, Peter Newsam. As summarized in *ILEA News* (11 October 1977), immediate first steps would include:

(i)   a special 'whole school' project with primary and secondary schools in central Lambeth, and another plan to help teachers working with children and adults of Asian Origin;

(ii) new liaison arrangements for minority ethnic groups;

(iii) a major 'bank' of teaching materials and equipment for multi-ethnic schools;

(iv) a new 'inner-city team' spanning all the ILEA's work, from schools and colleges to youth and careers work;

(v)   accepting the need to collect statistics, where they have a specific education purpose, on the ethnic origins of staff and school and college students.

A sentence from the report sums up the overall logic behind its approach: 'It is for the Authority to provide an effective comprehensive education service capable of responding to the requirements of all groups and individuals and providing appropriate opportunities for all.'

There is an illuminating socio-historical background to this new thinking. According to Penny Manners, Peter Newsam and a group of prominent educationists visited New York, and were shocked by what they saw of the built-in disadvantages blacks were experiencing. They came back determined that the same thing should not happen in London. The report constitutes a new policy but, on Peter Newsam's own admission, it has not been fully thought through. Consequently, the Authority is having to evolve the policy gradually. It will become clear in time how great a counter-ideology its orientation will become.

Meanwhile, as is the case in the other countries discussed in this book, the multicultural ideology increases its influence. The establishment of the Centre for Multicultural Education at the University of London has its counterpart in the major research project now being undertaken at the University of Keele, under the direction of Professor John Eggleston. The purpose of this project is to develop strategies for educating teachers to cope with teaching in the multicultural society.

In an illuminating discussion, Professor Eggleston clarified the conceptual muddles that have been a theme in this chapter.[10] According to him, multi*racial* education is still of major concern with teachers, because they have children in their classrooms who are obviously different on racial grounds. Multi*cultural* education is the emerging concern, because culture is the central, all-embracing concept. In addition, it is more useful and recognizable for people who are not teachers. Multi*ethnic* education and the major issue of the rights ethnic minority groups have to equality of educational and employment opportunity constitute a very broad area, which people are shying away from and not really attempting to tackle. Although the term multi-ethnic may be most useful for teachers as a way of distinguishing those groups of children in the classroom who have problems, multicultural education is less sensitive. Teachers and other educationists favour multicultural education for an additional reason: it is politically supported.

Notes

1. New Commonwealth countries are: **Africa**: Ghana, Kenya, Malawi, Nigeria, Rhodesia, Sierra Leone, Tanzania, Uganda, Zambia, other countries; **America**: Barbados, Guyana, Jamaica, Trinidad and Tobago; **Asia and Oceania**: Ceylon, Cyprus, Hong Kong, India, Malaysia, Pakistan, Singapore; **Europe**: Gibraltar, Malta and Gozo.
2. African Asians are those who are racially Asians but have some connection with Africa. They form two main groups: (a) Asians who were born in Africa or children of Asians born there; (b) Asians who were born in the Indian subcontinent but who lived in Africa before emigrating to Britain, or the children of such people (Smith, 1977:30).
3. Commonwealth Immigrants Acts 1962 and 1968; the Immigration Act, 1971. Several amendments have been made to the last to further restrict immigration.
4. A major concern of the Race Relations Acts of 1968 and 1976 was to counter these tendencies.
5. Department of Education and Science course at Coventry College, 20–27 July 1976.

6. Personal communication from its former Director.
7. National Union of Teachers, *Evidence to Select Committee on Race Relations and Immigration* (NUT, London, 1973).
8. Eric Bolton has recently been promoted to other responsibilities.
9. Schools in England and Wales: Current Issues An Annotated Agenda for Discussion. The Agenda was issued by the Secretary of State in November 1976 for the discussions she held with 30 organizations, teachers' unions, local authorities, industry and universities. Comments on omissions in the agenda entitled 'Great Debate: whose agenda?' are published in the Community Relations Commission's *Education and Community Relations*, vol. 7, no. 1 (1977).
10. Personal communication, cited with permission, from a brief discussion at Monash University, March 1980.

CHAPTER 3

Canada

The debate over the nature of Canadian pluralism and educational provisions is now quite contentious. It has almost become institutionalized, with a considerable volume of official government literature propounding the current ideology and other theoretical analyses. As this chapter will show, the debate is much more clearly delineated in Canada, with the result that the sense of 'muddle' and 'mess', which seems to pervade educational thinking in Britain, is not nearly as acute. Here the ideological battle lines of the pluralist debate have been drawn fairly clearly and at times with a passion that is quite uncharacteristic of a predominantly English-speaking, 'British' country. This chapter is about the battle and its implications for education.

The socio-historical context

The current demographic pattern

At the time of the decennial census in 1971, the total Canadian population was 21 568 300 persons. Of these, 84.7 per cent was born in Canada, 4.3 per cent in the United Kingdom, 7.8 per cent in European countries, 0.8 per cent in Other Commonwealth countries, 1.4 per cent in the United States, and 0.6 per cent in Asiatic countries (Statistics Canada, 1977:193, Table 4.21).[1]

The ethnic composition of the Canadian population is best given in broad groups, in view of the large number of ethnic groups identified by the 1971 census and their very small size in relation to the whole population. In 1971, 44.6 per cent of the population was identified by ethnicity as being British (i.e., from the British Isles), 28.7 per cent French, 23.0 per cent Other European, and 1.3 per cent Asiatic. In the Other category, totalling 2.4 per cent, Eskimo made up 0.1 per cent, Native Indian 1.4 per cent, Negro 0.2 per cent, and West Indian 0.1 per cent. Table 3 summarizes the percentages of the main groups, and in the case of Other European lists those whose percentage is 0.5 or above. Asiatic ethnic groups are given in full.

TABLE 3   Selected population by ethnic group, percentages at 1971 census

Ethnic Group	1971 census %
British Isles	44.6
French	28.7
Other European (selected groups)	23.0
German	6.1
Greek	0.6
Hungarian	0.6
Italian	3.4
Jewish	1.4
Netherlands	2.0
Norwegian	0.8
Polish	1.5
Swedish	0.5
Ukranian	2.7
Yugoslavic	0.5
Asiatic	1.3
Chinese	0.6
Japanese	0.2
Other	0.6
Other	2.4
Eskimo	0.1
Native Indian	1.4
Negro	0.2
West Indian	0.1
Other and not stated	0.7

Source: Statistics Canada, 1977. *Canada Year Book 1976–77*, Special Edition. Ottawa: Minister of Supply and Services Canada.

The ethnic pattern has changed historically and it is anticipated that it will continue to change (Burnet, 1976:200). In the hundred years since 1871, the percentage of the population of British origin dropped from 60.5 per cent to 44.6 per cent, and the French from 31.1 to 28.7 per cent. In 1871, the 7.7 per cent of the population that was not British, French, Native Indian or Eskimo, was chiefly of German and Dutch origin. In 1971 the corresponding 23.4 per cent was drawn from virtually every people in the world. Of these West Indians, Chinese, and (Asian) Indians are among the newest and most rapidly expanding origin categories. Professor Burnet notes (1976:201) that there are increasing numbers of those of other than British, French, Native Indians or Inuit (Eskimo) origins who are Canadian by birth and breeding. Richmond and Lakshmana Rao (1976:186, 188–89) comment on the decline in the numbers of immigrants coming to Canada and also on the changing proportions coming from various regions, during the period 1968–75. Based on their figures: in 1968 Britain and Europe contributed 66 per cent of immigrants to Canada; by 1975 the proportion had declined to 39 per cent. As a proportion of total immigration to Canada in 1967, the Black and Asian group made up 14.6 per cent; by 1974 it was 36.6 per cent.

Figures for 1973–74 immigrants by country of last permanent residence give some indication of the composition of this trend. Of six major selected countries the United Kingdom provided 16 per cent of all immigrants, the United States 12.9 per cent, Portugal 7.4 per cent, Hong Kong 6.8 per cent, India 5.5 per cent, Jamaica 5.1 per cent, and all others 46.1 per cent.

Since part of the current debate over the nature of Canadian pluralism is about the stress to be given to languages, the figures for English, French, and other mother tongues are of some importance. In 1971 60.2 per cent of the population spoke English, 26.9 per cent spoke French, and 13.0 per cent spoke other mother tongues. The percentage of those speaking English represents an increase, in the decade from 1961, of 1.7 per cent. The percentage of French speakers is declining, on the other hand: by 1.2 per cent in the same period.

To get a clearer picture of the debate over bilingualism in Canada, it is helpful to see the figures for those speaking one or both of the official languages by province. Table 4 gives figures based on the 1971 census.

TABLE 4   Percentage distribution of the population speaking one or both of the official languages by province, 1971

Province	English only	French only	English and French	Neither English nor French
Newfoundland	98.0	0.1	1.8	0.1
Prince Edward Island	91.2	0.6	8.2	
Nova Scotia	92.6	0.5	6.7	0.1
New Brunswick	62.5	15.9	21.5	0.1
Quebec	10.5	60.9	27.6	1.1
Ontario	87.3	1.2	9.3	2.2
Manitoba	89.2	0.5	8.2	2.1
Saskatchewan	93.6	0.2	5.0	1.2
Alberta	93.7	0.2	5.0	1.1
British Columbia	94.1	0.1	4.6	1.2
Yukon Territory	93.2		6.6	0.2
Northwest Territories	73.3	0.3	6.1	20.4
Canada	67.1	18.0	13.4	1.5

Source: Statistics Canada, 1977. *Canada Year Book 1976–77*, Special Edition. Ottawa: Minister of Supply and Services Canada.

The heavy concentration of French speakers in Quebec is at once apparent, with a corresponding reduction in speakers of English. New Brunswick shows the next highest figures for French speakers and next lowest for English speakers.

An article (Valpay, 1978:A4), about the bilingual situation in Canada based on a 40-page report published by C.D. Howe Research Institute in Montreal, stresses the significance of the figures set out in table 4 and of more current statistics. Firstly, there is a deepening polarization and isolation of Canada's two official language groups. Secondly, there is a rapid assimilation of French-speaking persons outside Quebec into the anglophone community. This historical trend is gathering speed each year, and is due, in part, to a massive post-war immigration into the anglophone community and a rapid population shift from rural to urban Canada. The result is that the mainly rural francophone communities have been dissolved (1978:A4).

For purposes of analysis, the Howe Research Institute report refers to English Canada. This comprises four regions — British Columbia, the Prairies, Ontario less 11 counties in the north, and Atlantic Canada, less 7 counties in New Brunswick. In all of English Canada, according to the Howe Research Institute, not more than 3 per cent lays claim to being bilingual. In English Canada's seven provinces west of Ontario and east of New Brunswick, persons of French home language represent only 1.7 per cent of the population. They are outnumbered by anglophones 51 to 1. In southern Ontario the ratio is 90 to 1. As Valpay comments: 'For demographers, such overwhelming odds have historically meant one thing: linguistic genocide.' However, the overwhelming concentration of French people in Quebec, where about 80 per cent live, has profound symbolic and political implications for the future of Canada's pluralistic policies. As Porter points out (1975:270):

> French Canadians . . . have territory or a homeland which was conquered, a historical and immensely symbolic fact which makes some sense and gives an impetus to a separatist movement for an eventual French-speaking state of Quebec as the visionary solution to the deprived status that the French as an ethnic class have experienced.

Socio-economic structure

Lack of up-to-date data does not permit a full analysis of the socio-economic structure of Canada in relation to its ethnic groups. Data available at the time of the Royal Commission on Bilingualism and Biculturalism in 1963 were based on the 1961 census. They showed a marked differential pattern of occupational distribution, which indicated that male workers from British and Jewish ethnic groups predominate in upper status occupations, while male workers from French (francophone), Italian, German and Ukrainian groups predominate in middle and lower-middle status occupations. As Porter (1975:291) comments about more recent developments in Canada, which indicate the continuation of ethnic stratification,

> Immigrants from Britain and the United States continue to be heavily over-represented in the higher professional, managerial, and white-collar occupational levels, while those from Portugal and Greece are taking over from Italians at the lower levels of the immigrant labour force.

'Race' is an issue in Britain, Canada, and the United States. In the first two countries the problem has partly arisen because of the replacement of immigrants from European origin by those who are racially different from the receiving country. Porter's comments on developments in Canada contain, in principle, a salutary reminder that the same thing could occur in a country such as Australia (1975:292):

> Caribbean and Asian countries are now appearing as a new source of immigrants to Canada and will, because of early controls on immigration of Chinese and Japanese, and the previously small black population, make color a newly visible element in the structure of ethnic stratification.

In an attempt to explain the discrepancy between the level of occupations of the French ethnic group and the British ethnic group, the authors of the Report of the Royal Commission note the influence of education. Canadians of French origin have spent, on average, two years less at school than English-Canadians (RCBB, 1967, III:45). The Commissioners point out that if the labour force of French origin had had a level of education equivalent to that of the British, the observed differences in the occupational distribution of the two groups would be reduced by about 60 per cent (1967, 111:47).

In mitigation of this apparent unbalance, it should be pointed out that some French-Canadians have enjoyed high status and power in collaboration with English-speaking Canadians and foreign investors. As Porter has suggested (1975:269):

> This seeming contradiction between being a large deprived minority within Canada and having representatives in the structure of power can be explained in terms of the class structure of French Canada which until recently has been premodern, with a narrow band of classically educated élites and members of the learned professions at the top, and a mass of poorly educated at the bottom who increasingly left a rural way of life for the industrialized cities.

In view of the geographical size of Canada, it is also necessary to note the observation of Innis (1973:139) that region has a strong influence on income in Canada. Low average incomes are found in the Atlantic Provinces and Quebec (excluding metropolitan Montreal). Higher incomes are a feature in Montreal and the Prairies. The highest incomes are found in Ontario and British Columbia.

Historical context

Immigration

As in Great Britain, the history of recent immigration to Canada plays a significant role in influencing the socio-historical context. This has particularly been the case during the period after the Second World War. The much earlier formative period — of Canadian society and of the nation itself — also has some importance, however, as it gives a clue to much of the strong anglophone emphasis in language maintenance and the strength of British traditions. Troper (1977:6–7) has traced the roots of the Canadian political entity in the tension between being in North America — and yet not wanting to be part of it — on the one hand, and being very largely founded by Loyalists with a strong British Imperial legacy. These chose to be exiles in Canada after the American Revolution, and established the 'élite bedrock on which Canadian political culture and social organization would be constructed'.

Troper's analysis goes some way towards explaining two features which puzzle the visitor. Firstly, parts of Canada seem more British than Britain in place names, customs and other threads of the cultural weave. This is probably most apparent in parts of British Columbia, particularly on Vancouver Island and in Victoria, the capital of the province. Secondly, there seems to be a curious ambivalence towards Americans and things American. The excesses of American society and culture may be deplored, for example, but many of that nation's accomplishments in scientific and other fields are admired.

The anglophone emphasis, though coupled with the francophone legacy from the other 'founding' nation, the French, has had a strong influence on education in the English-Canadian school system. Citing the Canadian historian Arthur Lower (1958) and also Robert Stamp (1971:137), Troper (1977:8) points to the 'symbolic trappings of the Imperial tie within the system', which persisted, albeit in attenuated form, at least into the 1950s:

> In addition to the inclusion of British history and literature to the curriculum, not as separate from Canadian history and literature but as Canadian history and literature, English Canadian children were subject to a daily ritual of saluting the Union Jack, singing 'God Save the King' and pledges of allegiance to the crown. The Loyalists were reconstituted. In this new incarnation in the school history curriculum they appear not as Americans, which they were, but as noble British victims of American excess.

Australian educationists will undoubtedly remark on the same 'daily ritual' that is observed in some Australian schools to this day.

The massive post-war immigration has built on this foundation. Although immigration has been part of Canadian experience since the founding of the nation, it has escalated dramatically over the past 35 years. From 1945 to 1974 alone, over four million people entered the country as immigrants (Department of Manpower and Immigration Statistics cited in Ashworth, 1975:1). The successive waves of immigrants followed a pattern similar to that found in Australia; according to Burnet (1976:201) the trend has been for 'increasing numbers of the urbanized, educated, skilled, and politically sophisticated'. In the late 1940s people displaced from highly developed parts of Europe immigrated, to be followed in the 1950s by skilled and educated immigrants who were sought to fill positions in Canada's expanding economy to which the Canadian educational and training system was not geared. In the late 1960s immigrant selection procedures that were racially discriminatory were replaced by a policy of accepting those who were trained and educated (Porter, 1965:40–48; Burnet, 1976:201).

A further trend towards irregular settlement by immigrants has added to the complexity of language and cultural conditions in Canada (Greenfield, 1976:114).

> Responding to a policy which sees immigrants largely as an economic necessity, the new arrivals have clustered in the large cities where jobs were available and where services both formal and informal were available to help them with the problems of transition to an environment which was culturally and often linguistically alien.

Masemann (1978–79:30) notes that whereas the impact of immigration in the 1920s and 1930s was felt primarily in the Prairies and also in major urban centres such as Toronto and Montreal, the post-World War II focus shifted almost entirely away from the rural west. Major reception areas for immigrants have been Toronto and nearby Hamilton, and to a lesser extent Montreal and Vancouver. This trend did not apply to all immigrants. A study by O'Bryan, Reitz and Kuplowska (1976:26) shows that Greeks, Portuguese, Chinese and Italians are most highly urbanized, while Hungarians, Dutch, Germans, and Scandinavians are least urbanized, with less than 35 per cent of their numbers located in five major cities.

In conjunction with strong anglophone traditions, massive postwar immigration, and strong urban concentrations, the francophone element in Canadian society must be taken into account. Without some understanding of this, many of the tensions which exist between the Quebec separatists, the Québecois movement, and the rest of the nation can only appear bemusing.

Canada was first colonized by the French, beginning early in the seventeenth century, and only later by the British. On these grounds at least, then, the French should have equal status with the British, since they were one of the two founding nations or charter groups within the confederation. Despite the long passage of time since those very early days, and the conquest of the French in 1760, a strong sense of French nationalism and injustice continues to this day (McNaught, 1970:43). It is thus hardly surprising that, as Innis remarks (1973:9): 'For all practical purposes, the Canadian population at the time of Confederation [1867] was composed of two main groups. Since 1867, however, the continual increase of heterogeneity in the population has been most remarkable.' Despite this, the French-speaking Canadians remain firmly entrenched in Quebec and the Laurentide homeland, though not without some social and economic problems. These exacerbate the historical sense of injustice and separation from the rest of Canada, which has led to the fundamental duality in language, culture and community.

The francophone community is economically weaker than the anglophone and cannot easily attract immigrants. The economic imbalance leads to non-British, non-French groups gravitating inexorably towards the anglophone side. When it is recalled that the trend in recent years has been for immigrants to be more skilled than formerly, the implications are obvious: the francophone community is not receiving 'new blood' which will improve its income-earning power. As Innis notes (1973:132):

> The repercussions of this are felt in many fields, some of which lie within provincial jurisdiction, particularly in social and educational spheres. We caution readers against forming the impression . . . that the Francophone group is on an equal footing with the Anglophone; in fact its position is inferior in all sectors in Canada, and in a number of sectors in Quebec.

The strength of the tension between the anglophone and francophone sectors of Canadian society comes out in 'the long-standing hostility of so many of the English in Canada to learning French [which] is analogous to the hostility toward blackness that has marked black-white relations [in the United States] . . . the psychological elements are deep-layered, all the more so because Anglophones in Canada . . . are the dominant majority in both numbers and power' (Porter, 1975:268).

Attitudes and climate of opinion towards immigrants

With such a strong Imperial legacy and sense of anglophone dominance pervading its history, it would be surprising if official attitudes towards immigrants were other than assimilationist and Anglo-conformist. This is despite the occasional government rhetoric that might lead one to imagine otherwise. For example, as early as 1903, the then Prime Minister Sir Wilfred Laurier expressed his personal view: 'For here (in Canada), I want the marble to remain the marble; the granite to remain the granite; the oak to remain the oak; and out of all of these elements I would build a nation great among the nations of the world' (Minister of State Multiculturalism, 1978:1). However, for some considerable time after this, and indeed right up until the Second World War and on into its immediate aftermath, 'Rather than become citizens of Canada and the New World, immigrants were admonished to become good British subjects — citizens of the Empire'. Indeed, they had little option in the strict legal sense: prior to 1947 naturalization granted the status of British subject resident of Canada (Troper, 1977: 9 & n.).

During the same period in the United States, the melting-pot theory was the dominant ideology of assimilation. As Troper points out (1977:10ff):

The dramatic imagery of the melting-pot captured the imagination of some Canadians as well . . . [But] fearful lest the melting-pot portend miscegenation and a slow weakening of British blood lines and cultural superiority, other Canadians questioned the desirability of any melting-pot ideology in Canada. . . . The Anglo-conformist program, however, offered an ingenious alternative. Anglo-conformity did not seek to create 'a uniform race'. It was based upon behaviour modification. . . . In other words, Anglo-conformity did not require the foreigner to mix biologically with the Anglo-Saxon who was to act as his model. It only demanded that the foreigner behave as if he did.

Some educators' views of the process had an arrogance which contrasts markedly with those of our more enlightened present.

One advocate of Anglo-conformity observed [Anderson, 1918:55] that 'many of these people will be slow to understand and appreciate the higher ideals of our [British] civilization, but we have reason to hope that [with education] their offspring, born under the Union Jack, will grow up as valuable Canadian citizens'. (Troper, 1977:11)

In place of the melting-pot theory, a Canadian variant gradually developed, which was to become part of the official rhetoric in the post-Second World War period. As Professor Burnet has commented (1976:200):

During a relatively recent part of the period in which Canadians of British origin have defined the rules by which other groups had to act, the ideology concerning ethnic relations in Canada was summed up in the term mosaic, and its floral and gustatory analogues — bouquet, flower garden, salad, vegetable soup, stew. The mosaic was proudly contrasted with the American melting pot. However, less effort was expended by Canadian governments to maintain the mosaic than was spent by governments in the United States to keep the melting pot bubbling: in the public school systems and in broadcasting . . . no tangible aid was given to ethnic groups in preserving their old-world heritages, and, on the contrary, considerable pressure was exerted in the direction of 'integration' or 'assimilation'. The mosaic was lent support chiefly in speeches by governors general and by politicians.

Even after the Second World War assimilation ideology died hard. In 1947 Prime Minister Mackenzie King, outlining the federal government's immigration policy, stated that it should be restricted to those who could be absorbed. It was assimilationist and anti-non-white. 'He was no more interested in having a multicultural society than he was in having a multiracial society' (Palmer, 1976:98).

In contrast, the statement of Prime Minister John Diefenbaker in 1961 (Minister of State Multiculturalism, 1978:1) may be some indication of a change in official ideology, an expression of mosaic sentiment, or a recognition of the changing climate of the times. 'Canada is a garden . . . into which has been transplanted the hardiest and brightest flowers from many lands, each retaining in its new environment the best of the qualities for which it was loved and prized in its native land. . . .'

Certainly, in the opinion of Troper (1977:15), 'It was World War II and its aftermath which finally laid the British Imperial connection to rest, destroyed the myth on which Canadian political culture had developed and, therefore, made Anglo-conformity irrelevant.'

The post-war period also brought new types of immigrants. Not only were many better educated and more highly skilled, but the majority were refugees, political emigrés, or former soldiers from central and eastern Europe. They had strong nationalistic feelings about their motherland and did not readily assimilate into the Canadian mosaic. They acted in many instances to reinforce ethnic involvement within their respective communities. For the Hungarian, Chinese, Polish and Ukrainian communities in particular, such immigrants had the effect of strengthening and reaffirming a sense of ethnic identity (O'Bryan, Reitz & Kuplowska, 1976:11). Some, the intellectuals, also brought with them ideals about cultural pluralism and its values which they could readily articulate (Palmer, 1976:100).

The 1950s and 1960s were also a period of social upheaval in America and many parts of the Western world, with radical ideas, the Black Revolution in the United States, Black power movements and similar manifestations of an ethnic revitalization movement, the 'new pluralism' among many minority groups (Glazer & Moynihan, 1975:1 ff.). At the same time in Canada a similar wave of unrest and French-Canadian nationalism affected the two founding nations (Burnet, 1976:201).

The Quiet Revolution and the 'spectre of separatism' (Troper, 1977:17) provided the stimulus to make the Canadian government set up a Royal Commission on Bilingualism and Biculturalism in 1963. Under its terms of reference (RCBB, 1967:151) the Commission was authorized to:

> . . . inquire and report upon the existing state of bilingualism and bicultural-ism in Canada and to recommend what steps should be taken to develop the Canadian Confederation on the basis of an equal partnership between the two founding races, taking into account the contribution made by the other ethnic groups to the cultural enrichment of Canada and the measures to be taken to safeguard that contribution. . . .

The Commission held its preliminary meeting in September 1963, and on 6−7 November of the same year conducted its first public hearings in Ottawa. A 'multitude of briefs' were submitted for study, including 51 from various ethno-cultural organizations across the country. Twenty-three regional meetings were organized and conducted across Canada from Victoria to St Johns.

The mention of 'other ethnic groups' in the terms of reference was not allowed by them to remain purely an expression of tokenism, even though this was the initial intention of the government as Professor Jean Burnet, an influential B and B Commissioner at the time, makes clear (1976:202):

Although 'the other ethnic groups' received offhand recognition in the terms of reference of the Royal Commission on Bilingualism and Biculturalism, and somewhat greater recognition in the inclusion among the ten Commissioners of two Canadians (one of Polish background and the other of Ukrainian background) who had immigrated to Canada after World War II, it was not the original intention of the government to have the Commission probe deeply into their place in Canadian society. The extensive research programme of the Commission included little about them. . . .

The reaction of the 'other ethnic groups' — 'an economically resourceful, politically self-assured, increasingly articulate and socially restless third force' (Troper, 1977:17) — was to demand recognition by the Commission. Almost as an afterthought, it would appear, the Commission took up the issue of the place of 'other ethnic groups' in the Canadian mosaic, and in 1970 published its aspirations in Book IV, *The Cultural Contribution of the Other Ethnic Groups*. The federal government's response to its findings was presented to the House of Commons on 8 October 1971. The recommendations, ideology and policies that flowed from the Commission's report are taken up in a later part of this chapter. Suffice at this point to say that it virtually closed a whole era of historical influence. In Troper's words (1977:18): 'Twenty-five years after World War II ended the British Imperial connection was indeed dead. Its domestic missionary impulse, Anglo-conformity, was repudiated'.

Attitudes apparent in the education system

The education system itself is part of the context in which the pluralistic debate is occurring. Some mention has been made already in the preceding section of the Anglo-conformist philosophy behind the curriculum. Other criticisms have been voiced by Greenfield (1976:112). In his opinion the approach to second language and cultural programmes in Canadian schools demonstrates

> . . . a malaise which is common to Canadian education generally. We approach them technocratically, with little concern for what they are to do as long as we can convince ourselves that the programs are 'effective', acceptable to tax payers, and good for children. Whether the programs meet any of these criteria is seldom known, for they rarely receive searching analysis in terms of their relationship to the language and cultural questions which so obviously beset Canadian society.

Lest it be thought that such comments come only from disenchanted Canadian educationists, or 'knockers' — to use an Australian idiom — similar, but more general criticisms have been made by the examiners from the Organization for Economic Co-operation and Development (1975:para 24).

> In distinction from most other comparable industrialized countries, Canada has *neither* produced a politically motivated educational reform, rooted in a

conception of the country's future, nor has Canada blocked such reform, as has happened in a number of European countries. Instead, Canada has trodden out its own path, with an array of exceptionally active programmes for vast quantitative expansion and significant qualitative changes of the education system that are, however, derived from no explicitly stated, overall national conceptions of the country's interests.

Greenfield's (1976:112) evaluation of the OECD reactions is not without application to Australia: 'It seems unlikely in the face of increasing social, economic, and political problems, that Canada can much longer afford the luxury of mindless educational policies.'

In Canada, the organization and administration of public education is controlled by provincial and territorial governments through their own education departments and bureaucracy. As a result, organization, policies, and practice vary from province to province. The federal government plays no direct role in this responsibility, apart from its concern with schools for native Indian children. Schools are provided for Indians living on reserves. Approximately 60 per cent of reserve-based Indian children attend schools operated under provincial jurisdiction; the remainder attend federally operated schools. In all cases, the federal government assumes the total cost of these services. However, since the acceptance of the National Indian Brotherhood's paper 'Indian Control of Indian Education' in 1973, an increasing number of Indian bands are assuming control of their schools and other educational programmes. Since that date the involvement of the Department of Indian Affairs and Northern Development has been directed toward facilitating the transfer of educational programmes to Indian bands and working with Indian groups to develop appropriate curricula.

The federal government's involvement in other ways with the provinces is financial. In addition to financing retraining of adults, the federal government provides financial support to the provinces amounting to at least 50 per cent of operating costs of post-secondary education, and makes grants-in-aid for research personnel and equipment in universities.

The university system possesses distinctive differences from the Australian system. There are a number of French-language universities and colleges which were established by the French, based on the culture of Old France, and administered by Roman Catholic groups. These still retain their traditional characteristics but now conform almost entirely to the North American system of administration. The largest group of universities and colleges in Canada is administered by English-speaking staff, and offers instruction in English.

A further difference in Canada is the strength of the public (state) school system. Less than three per cent of children attend private, fee-paying schools. Originally, six-year-old children entered the eight-grade, publicly controlled elementary school each September. At about

14 years of age, a significant proportion of those who entered grade 1 moved on to a four- or five-year secondary school. This 8−4 model has been modified in many provinces, cities, or groups of schools. A number of variants are now found throughout Canada, including junior high schools, organization on a 6−3−3 or 6−3−4 plan, and even recently established community colleges. At the secondary level, three types of programmes are the general pattern — the academic university entrance course, the general course for those wishing to complete an academic type of programme before entering employment, and vocational courses for those wishing to enter skilled trades or pursue further training in technological fields.

As in Britain, and foreshadowed for Australia, the organization of teacher training in Canada is also undergoing modification, with the emphasis on making teaching an all-graduate profession. In part this is due to declining pupil enrolments in the public and elementary-secondary school system. In 1975−76 this decreased by 41 445 to a total of 5.59 million students from 5.63 million the previous year, continuing the downward trend that began in 1971−72 (Statistics Canada, 1977:303). It is of interest, in the light of the comments above about the maintenance of French in the education system, that Quebec continued to lead the trend in falling enrolments.

Whether these changes reflect a conscious official response to the massive changes taking place in Western industrial societies is debatable, in view of OECD comments noted above. At least the problem is given token recognition in the 1976 *Canada Handbook* (p. 156):

> The beginnings of the post-industrial society are upon us. As Daniel Bell and others have suggested, the creation of a service economy and the preeminence of professional and technical operations characterize the structure of a post-industrial society. Thus the problem of producing the required professional and technical manpower is one that education must face.

Ideologies and ideologists

The official, government ideology

By announcing the government's policy to the House of Commons on 8 October 1971, the Prime Minister, Pierre Trudeau, ensured maximum publicity and legitimation for its ideology (Minister of State Multiculturalism, 1978:45):

> A policy of multiculturalism within a bilingual framework commends itself to the Government as the most suitable means of assuring the cultural freedom of Canadians. Such a policy should help to break down discriminatory attitudes and cultural jealousies. National unity, if it is to mean anything in the deeply personal sense, must be founded on confidence in one's own individual identity; out of this can grow respect for that of others and a willingness to share ideas, attitudes and assumptions. A vigorous policy of

multiculturalism will help create this initial confidence. It can form the base of a society which is based on fair play for all.

The Government will support and encourage the various cultures and ethnic groups that give structure and vitality to our society. They will be encouraged to share their cultural expression and values with other Canadians and so contribute to a richer life for us all.

More specification of the ideology took the form of details of the four main types of support which the government would provide (1978: 45–56):

First, resources permitting, the government will seek to assist all Canadian cultural groups that have demonstrated a desire and effort to continue to develop a capacity to grow and contribute to Canada, and a clear need for assistance, the small and weak groups no less than the strong and highly organized.

Second, the government will assist members of all cultural groups to overcome cultural barriers to full participation in Canadian society.

Third, the government will promote creative encounters and interchange among all Canadian cultural groups in the interest of national unity.

Fourth, the government will continue to assist immigrants to acquire at least one of Canada's official languages in order to become full participants in Canadian society.

Since the first statement of the ideology and policies a number of enabling organizations and programmes have been established to put them into effect. A Minister of State responsible for Multiculturalism was appointed in November 1972 to administer the policy. Its implementation is carried out by the Multicultural Program of the Multiculturalism Directorate in the Department of the Secretary of State and by 'a number of federal cultural agencies which have developed special programs designed to promote better understanding of Canada's ethno-cultural groups and to provide these groups with specialized services' (Statistics Canada, 1976:61).

In May 1973 the Canadian Consultative Council on Multiculturalism (CCCM) was established as an advisory body to the Minister of State for Multiculturalism. Its members are appointed by the Minister from a cross-section of Canada's cultural communities. The Council is 'designed to assist members of Canada's diverse ethno-cultural groups, including those of English, French and native heritages, to be actively involved in a consultative process with the government' (Minister of State Multiculturalism, 1978:15). Since its establishment, a number of regional and national meetings under its auspices have been held. The First Canadian Conference on Multiculturalism was held in October 1973. Out of this came the first annual report of the CCCM, tabled in the House of Commons in June 1975. It discussed, among other matters, retention of language and culture, overcoming inequalities, community cultural and multiethnic centres, ethnic press and mass media, arts in a multicultural society and attitudes of youth towards multiculturalism. The Second Canadian Conference on Multiculturalism was held in February 1976, and was designed to hear viewpoints found in the two official language groups concerning the multicultural policy (Minister of State Multiculturalism, 1978:15). The outcomes of this, at times fiery, conference are discussed below.

The function of the Multiculturalism Directorate is to implement the variety of activities that support the multiculturalism policy. The Directorate's main objective is

> . . . to encourage and assist, within the framework of Canada's Official Languages Policy and in the spirit of existing human rights codes, the full realization of the multicultural nature of Canadian society through programs which promote the preservation and sharing of cultural heritages and which facilitate mutual appreciation and understanding among all Canadians. (1978:16)

The Directorate's programme has two broad approaches (1978:16):

> one is directed specifically towards Canadian cultural groups and organizations to help them to articulate their needs and achieve their individual aspirations and the other is directed at society at large to increase awareness and appreciation of the bilingual and multicultural nature of our country.

Activities for the former, many of which are initiated by cultural groups themselves, include conferences and seminars to discuss issues of concern; the collection and exhibition of art, craft works, and other cultural materials; the production of audio-visual and other resource material for use within one cultural group or shared between groups; the writing of creative literature and its publication in either of the official languages — French and English — or in the language of the cultural group itself. 'All in all the emphasis is on projects which can be seen to be meaningful in the development of a given group and which contribute to the objectives of the Multiculturalism policy.' (1978:16)

In order to promote the second aim of government policy — increased appreciation and awareness among the society at large of the bilingual and multicultural nature of Canada — the Directorate works in close connection with a range of subsidiary ideology-managing agencies such as the Canadian Radio-Television and Telecommunications Commission, the Canada Council, the National Library, the Public Archives, the National Museums, the Canadian Broadcasting Commission, the National Film Board, the Canadian Centre for Folk Culture Studies, folk arts councils and various national organizations of authors, artists, playwrights, publishers and educational resource developers. 'Multiculturalism is promoted also through a public relations program directed at the mass media, through information campaigns and through the encouragement of those projects which may have a particular impact on public opinion' (1978:16).

A feature of the Directorate's continuous monitoring activity is the Ethnic Press Analysis Service which analyses more than 200 ethnic newspapers and periodicals published in over 30 languages. This branch also carries on liaison activities with the Canadian Ethnic Press Foundation and its four affiliated press clubs of ethnic newspapers as well as the publication *Canadian Scene*.

Despite this impressive array of ideology-managing agencies, Canadian Consultative Council on Multiculturalism in its 1977 Report (1977:1) lamented: 'we were not involving the general public in a meaningful discussion on the various aspects of our policy on Multiculturalism. To this end in June 1977 we commenced a series of hearings and consultations in an attempt to reach both the enthnocultural communities and the youth of this country.' Dahlie (1976:89) reports that at the Second Biennial Conference of the CCCM, held in Ottawa on 13–15 February 1976 the chosen theme, 'Multiculturalism as State Policy', could have been interpreted as a pointed reaction to comments made by John Munro, Minister responsible for Multiculturalism at the end of 1975. These were taken by many members of the CCCM 'to indicate that the government had decided on a major shift in multicultural policy, away from an emphasis on support for ethno-cultural activities — colourful folkloric spectacles, drama, art and the like — toward a somewhat more vague concern for reducing intolerance and discrimination, with particular reference to the more recent "visible" minority groups'. The Conference was seen as an arena where the CCCM delegates could react to and counter specific threats posed by policy decisions, 'and exacerbated by the unenthusiastic response of the majority groups, Anglophone and Francophone alike, to the policy of multiculturalism itself'. It seems clear from Dahlie's analysis of the Conference, and its subsequent report, that much of it can be interpreted as ideological specification, to counter what seemed to be ideological negation, albeit from the government Minister with official responsibility for multiculturalism.

Multiculturalism within a bilingual framework and education policy

As was noted above, the federal government has no direct concern with the provision of education as this is within provincial jurisdiction. In the opinion of the CCCM (1977:7) this has resulted in its recommendations involving education being 'skirted' by the federal government. In its 1977 report, the CCCM reiterated the recommendations, and gave indication of a clear bias in favour of language learning.

The Council also felt strongly that the cultural contributions of ethnic groups should be reflected in curricula and course content, textbooks and the school system itself. In order that the Canadian education system should reflect the 'inescapable reality' of ethnic diversity and increasingly visible minority groups the Council recommended (1977:9):

That school curricula be developed and implemented in full consultation with qualified educators and representatives of the ethnocultural communities concerned, with a view to nurturing deeper insight into the various cultures in Canada;

That each province maintain a bank of approved curricular material, including audio-visual teaching aids, relevant to the linguistic and cultural pluralism of Canada.

The policies and recommendations of the CCCM also extend to Native Indians and Inuit (CCCM, 1977:10):

That the federal government assist in the development of the Indian identity so that local band councils, which are accepting increasing responsibility for the education of Indian children, can integrate the best aspects of modern Canadian society into their own unique cultural system;

That the federal government support the development of all culturally relevant curricula to reflect the rightful place of the native people in the life and history of Canada.

Multiculturalism in educational practice

If a counter-ideology can take the form of apathy, then much of Canadian post-secondary education and general programmes of teacher education have implicitly rejected multiculturalism. Symons (1975:123) has brought out how the post-secondary system has failed to respond to the dilemmas inherent in Canadian pluralism:

As things now stand, there are few other countries in the world with a developed post-secondary education system that pays so little attention to the study of their own culture, problems and circumstances in the University curriculum.

Programmes that have been developed often follow a sequence of educational ideas and innovations, with which some Australian educationists are all too familiar. Those which have been developed in Toronto provide an excellent example.

'Until 1970, all the programs [of the Toronto Board of Education] for immigrant children were directed toward the goal of initiating the child into the dominant Anglo-Canadian culture' (Masemann, 1978–79:32), with considerable emphasis being placed on the teaching of English — the technocratic approach to education cited from Greenfield above. There was little or no appreciation of the cultural and emotional cost to the immigrant child. In the 1970s, transitional language programmes for Italian children in kindergartens, bilingual/bicultural classes for Chinese students, and regular English as a Second Language classes for adults and children were provided. A further impetus, though not as great as orginally hoped, was provided by the recommendations of the Work Group on Multicultural Programs. This was set up by the Toronto Board of Education in May 1974. It submitted a watered down final report in 1976, after facing considerable criticism from the wider community and ethnic pressure groups. This stimulated increased counselling procedures and multicultural content in the curriculum (1978-79:42).

The Ontario Ministry of Education published its programme objectives in *The Formative Years*. This is a policy statement for Primary and Junior Divisions (grade 1 through to 6), in which the purposes of multicultural education are identified (Wells, 1978:3–5). A support document, (Ministry of Education, Ontario, 1977), also provides details on aims. Among other things, the programme is intended to give each child an opportunity to:

(i) develop and maintain confidence and a sense of self-worth;
(ii) develop and retain a personal identity by becoming acquainted with the historical roots of the community and culture of his or her origin, and by developing a sense of continuity with the past;
(iii) begin to understand and appreciate the points of view of ethnic and cultural groups other than his or her own;
(iv) develop an understanding of such concepts as *community, conflict, culture,* and interdependence;
(v) learn the social skills and attitudes upon which effective and responsible co-operation and participation depend;
(vi) provide the context in which the child can work out a personal system of values and begin to develop a way of analyzing value issues.

In his speech to Phi Delta Kappa, Toronto Chapter, in 1977, the Minister of Education also made it clear that further changes are imminent (1977:4):

> At the same time, we recognize that adding units on minority groups, or even a course on multicultural heritage, will not be sufficient to meet ongoing needs for curriculum change. We have introduced a review process to ensure that all our curriculum guidelines and support documents maintain a multicultural perspective. We are striving for a multicultural dimension in all curriculum . . . [but] a great deal needs to be done at the Intermediate and Senior levels, where there is a subject orientation.

An important opportunity for promoting and managing the official ideology is available through academic and general journals published by government departments or by university or other tertiary organizations. A journal's editorial policy (where stated), contents, and general style of articles give some indication of the ideological stance it adopts towards policies contained in the received perspective. One such journal in Canada is *Multiculturalism*, which by its title, policy and contents seems a classic vehicle for knowledge management and the official ideology. It is a quarterly magazine published by the Guidance Centre, Faculty of Education, University of Toronto, in collaboration with the Multicultural Development Branch of the Ministry of Culture and Recreation, Ontario. The first issue appeared in 1977. By and large, editorial policy (vol. 1, no. 1, 1977), articles and topics featured are consistent with the official government policy, and especially the emphasis followed by the Canadian Consultative Council on Multiculturalism. A feature of the journal is the number of photographs, both on the cover and in text, which show arts and crafts, dance, drama and other folk aspects of multiculturalism.

Have there been any shifts in the official federal government ideology since it was first formulated in 1971? What might be seen as an exercise in specification, or possibly a subtle reformulation of the ideology, was published in August 1978 as part of the Prime Minister's proposals for the renewal of the Canadian Federation (Trudeau, 1978), in a booklet distributed nationally and freely available at government agencies such as post offices. Among others, the following principles are listed, and give a curious sense of *déjà vu*:

Full Respect of Native Rights
The renewal of the Federation must fully respect the legitimate rights of the native peoples, recognize their rightful place in the Canadian mosaic as the first inhabitants of the country, and give them the means of enjoying full equality of opportunity.

The Full Development of the Two Linguistic Majorities
The renewal of the Federation must guarantee the linguistic equality of its two major communities, the English-speaking and the French-speaking, and assure that Canadian institutions exist to help each group to prosper.

The Enhancement of the Mosaic of Cultures
The renewal of the Federation must lead to respect for cultural diversity and for the right of every citizen, regardless of ethnic origin, to equal opportunity. Every cultural community should be able to rely on the support of governments in preserving its own cultural heritage and in discovering and appreciating those of other communities.

In the light of developments since 1971, reference to the 'Canadian mosaic' and 'linguistic equality' seem little more than pious rhetoric.

Counter-ideologies and ideologists

After meeting so much at the official level which appears to indicate that everything in the multicultural garden is flowering beautifully, it comes as some surprise to find a great deal of evidence to suggest that very strong counter-ideologies are being promoted by various social forces in Canada.

The groundswell of public opinion

Firstly there is a general, diffuse but articulate and influential array of opposing forces to the multiculturalism ideology. Their negative counter-ideologies come to the fore when major issues are open for public debate and allow the opposition to multiculturalism to be expressed and published, often quite polemically and stridently. In such a climate of conflicting viewpoints, it is not surprising to find that many teachers have been hesitant to react positively towards the official policy of multiculturalism within a bilingual framework. As Mallea and Young point out (1978, n.d.:9) innovations in education depend heavily on teachers' understanding and support. One might also add 'and on their respect for the quality of the ideology and the integrity of its advocates'. The Ontario Secondary School Teachers' Federation comments on the inevitable result when these are lacking:

> Over the last 30 years the goals of education have changed frequently. With each change, little has been done to acquaint teachers with the new concepts or ways to implement them. Classroom teachers have seldom been involved in formulating philosophical change; change was imposed from above without adequate preparation of teachers or teacher training institutions. The consequences have often been confusion over aims, contradictions between philosophy and practice and lowering of teacher morale.

Even the work of a high-powered official body can be negated and hampered by the groundswell of public opinion and the activities of conservative counter-ideologists, who wish to protect their own counter-ideologies and views of social reality, as the following cautionary tale illustrates. As mentioned, the Toronto Board of Education set up the Work Group on Multicultural Programs. It comprised a group of elected Board of Education Trustees, with the function and powers of an Advisory Committee to the Board as a whole.

Ostensibly, the Work Group was commissioned to 'investigate and explore the philosophy and programs related to the City's multicultural population . . . to examine current practices related to the operation of the Board's multicultural programs'. The Work Group was also asked to make recommendations on the above issues and to 'consider the financing and structural needs determined by the proposed policy' (Masemann, 1978–79:35). After a succession of public meetings and submission of briefs from interested parties, a draft report was published in 1975 and made available for further discussion. This led to a second round of submission of briefs, public meetings and individual comments, many of which opposed certain of the more innovatory and radical changes proposed by the draft report. The final report was published in 1976. It indicated quite clearly, after a three-year debate, 'to what extent Anglo-conformity still prevails as a mode of thought. It demonstrates that the shift in sentiment since World War II has not been such as to call into question the predominantly Anglo-cultural basis of the schools' (1978-79:39). The force of this counter-ideology led to a rejection of the demands of major ethnic groups in the community and negation of the official ideology, as Masemann goes on to state (1978-79:42):

> In essence, the immigrant community's requests for programs responsive to their language and culture, which clearly would have resulted in the diminution of the force of Anglo-Canadian culture in the school system, were rejected by vociferous community members, by some teaching personnel, and by the Ontario government. . . . In the end, the immigrants' cause lost to the realities of an official federal bilingual policy and benevolent Anglo-conformity.

One wonders what happened to the Prime Minister's hope, expressed in the 1971 speech to the House of Commons, that a policy of multi-culturalism in a bilingual framework 'should help to break down discriminatory attitudes and cultural jealousies'.

In such a climate, which would be more pronounced in the far more Anglo-atmosphere of British Columbia, it is thus not really surprising that the recent report of an official Committee on the Education and Training of Teachers (1978), gives no consideration whatsoever to wider societal issues and the type of society for which teachers are being trained. Instead, in a quite banal and authoritarian document, in which several of the official findings amount to no more than Chairman's personal opinions, most attention is devoted to 'bread-and-butter issues' such as selection of applicants for training; a five-year, degree-status, elementary 'generalist' programme for teachers; a five-year, degree-status, secondary 'specialist' programme; and other programmes for special and industrial education. Anglo-conformity *is* alive and well in British Columbia!

A further groundswell, rather than a formulated statement of a counter-ideology, concerns the slowly emerging problem of racism in Canada. The term multiracial is not used to describe the society, but the 'colour problem' exists in certain areas like Vancouver, Montreal, Toronto and its industrial satellite towns, where numbers of West Indians and Negroes are greater than in the remainder of Canada. Dr Kent Henderson, of the Ontario Institute for Studies in Education (O.I.S.E.), believes that the phenomenon of racial discrimination has not surfaced to the same extent as it has in Britain. As yet Canada is 'only two or three years into the question; Blacks have yet to emerge as a community'. However, there have been moves in Ontario, as in Britain, to link cultural disadvantage to lower-working-class and racial discrimination influences.

However, the matter is not being ignored entirely. For instance, the Ontario Ministry of Culture and Recreation published a special journal issue in 1976, 'Black Students in Urban Canada'. This came out of a multicultural conference sponsored by the Ontario Curriculum Studies Association. In the opinion of Wilson Head (1978:17):

> although there has been some activity at the local level, Canadian-born

Blacks have not until recently launched major attacks upon the prejudice and discrimination found in Canada . . . there have been numerous sporadic, more or less successful, attempts to organize Blacks against racism and bigotry. The formation of the National Black Coalition of Canada in 1969 was one of the most recent attempts.

Black Presence in Multi-Ethnic Canada edited by Professor Vince D'Oyley, is a source of detailed and often critical opposition to the policy of multiculturalism. In the introduction, Professor D'Oyley says of the book (1978:xix):

> *Black Presence in Multi-Ethnic Canada* can be said to reflect black life. Common experiences and perceptions emerge, new insights are offered into the nature of racism and the ramifications of the concept of multiculturalism for the black population are examined from many perspectives. The contradiction between the ideal model of inter-ethnic relations in a multi-cultural society and the reality of those relations, is deeply felt.

In British Columbia, the Teachers' Federation (1978–1979:section c) has published its 'BCTF Policies and Procedures Regarding Racism': 'the BCTF openly condemn all or any practice of discrimination on the basis of race in the communities and schools of this province'. In its submission (1978–79:11) to The Joint Board of Teacher Education Sub-committee, the BCTF briefly reviews causes of discrimination on socio-economic, racial, sex, poverty, and class grounds, and recommends (1978–79:11): 'That an integral part of any teacher education program deal with the varied cultural and socio-economic backgrounds of students and the implications of that for teaching and learning in schools'.

The academic debate

The main arguments and counter-ideologies against the multicultural ideology are found in the writings and public statements of academics, some journalists, and even a few politicians or public servants. In an analysis of the main themes (1976:103–5), Professor Howard Palmer of the Centre for Ethnic Studies at the University of Calgary, suggests that there are three debates going on in Canada at the present time:

> What we now have in English-speaking Canada is a debate between proponents of assimilation vs. proponents of multiculturalism, between proponents of biculturalism and multiculturalism, and between different proponents of multiculturalism.

From this one may establish that the counter-ideologists with which this section is concerned are assimilationists of various kinds, those polemicists who support biculturalism and bilingualism, and those issue-oriented social scientists who attack multiculturalism mainly on the theoretical and logical grounds that it is a defective model to describe and prescribe for Canadian society.

The assimilationists

In Dr Palmer's opinion, the late Professor John Porter was the most trenchant, obvious critic of multiculturalism and advocate of an assimilationist ideology. Porter can also be assigned to the third category of critics, to some extent, as his theory holds the multicultural model to be theoretically defective. The major theme of his attack (Porter, 1965, 1975) is that multiculturalism is detrimental to progress and to equality of opportunity.

To Porter, culture is a myth and is being made redundant in the face of the advance of Western science and technology. The policy of multiculturalism is performing a disservice by bolstering dying cultures, thus 'prevent[ing] those who cherished them from participating fully in the benefits of a universalistic post-industrial way of life' (Burnet, 1976:204). Ethnicity and the maintenance of cultural affiliation can produce a form of ethnic stratification or 'vertical mosaic' in which ethnicity combines with class to reduce social mobility and opportunity.

> It is my view that in Canada, in the emerging post-industrial phase, with its one culture of science and technology and its extensive transnational network, bilingualism can survive. But that phase can scarcely be bicultural, much less multicultural. (Porter, 1975:303)

Isajiw (1977) argues for partial and inevitable assimilation of ethnic groups in Canada. Adopting a theoretical framework similar to Porter's, he points to the force of technology and technological culture as integrating factors which bring ethnic groups together (1977:78). 'Technology has been doing this in the arena of industry and industry related occupations; technological culture does this by means of values and patterns into which ethnic groups assimilate.' However, the assimilation is not total; the 'new ethnicity' we are seeing in many pluralist countries is a search for identity rooted in the past, a way of countering the self-anonymization and impersonality of social relationships caused by technology and technological culture (1977:82):

> The turn to the past is symbolic. Some elements of the heritage come to be known, practised, or glorified. What is significant is that there is a process of selection of items from the cultural past; and, even relatively few items, such as pieces of ethnic folk art, folk dances, music, partial use of language, knowledge of some aspects of the group's history, etc., can become symbols of ethnic identity. . . . The 'new ethnicity' can be said to be a way in which ethnicity has adapted itself to the technological culture. As an identity phenomenon, it complements the technological culture by, as it were, filling in the gaps and the needs created by it.

The arguments of other assimilationists are less subtle and theoretical. For instance, Charles Lynch argued in an article in the *Montreal Gazette* (9 October 1971) that multiculturalism would perpetuate old world hatreds between various cultural groups (Palmer, 1976:103). He has not changed his opinion since that date. At the Second Biennial Conference of the Canadian Consultative Council on Multiculturalism, held in Ottawa during February 1976, Charles Lynch alleged that 'Multiculturalism is a "con game" played on the Canadian people' (Dahlie, 1976:90), and was in danger of degenerating into tokenism in the treatment of minorities (CCCM, 1976:15 ff.). At the same conference Douglas Fisher was cynical about multiculturalism; he favoured second generation assimilation and integration (1976:15). One of Fisher's concerns is that multiculturalism will foster the alleged authoritarian values of ethnic minorities (Palmer, 1976:102). The importance of the negative, counter-ideological views of both Lynch and Fisher should not be underestimated, as both are strategically placed as counter-ideologists. Lynch is Chief of Southam News Press; Fisher is a journalist for the *Toronto Sun*.

Two speakers at the CCCM Conference appear to have argued for a form of partial and inevitable assimilation, but on grounds different from those of Isajiw noted above. Arnold Edinborough argued that certain institutional aspects of Canadian society are not negotiable. These are the institutions of the Crown and a non-elected judiciary. Pluralism is only possible to a limited degree; some sharing and assimilation are inevitable (CCCM, 1976:14). Senator Eugene Forsey took a basically similar position in his presentation, 'Multiculturalism : An Anglo-Celtic View' (CCCM, 1976:61–64). There are certain non-negotiable common institutions such as the English language of commerce, the legal system, the parliamentary and government system, which are social facts that Quebec separatism would not alter.

The advocates of bilingualism and biculturalism

Without doubt, the most consistent and virulent opponents of the multicultural ideology are those who consider that the most appropriate model for Canada is the bilingual (anglophone/francophone) one. The majority of these counter-ideologists are francophone supporters, usually from Quebec or French-speaking backgrounds. Their views have deep and bitter political and historical origins.

As Dahlie comments (1976:90) of the 'Francophone View Points' presented at the 1976 CCCM Conference: 'While it was disheartening to find the extremely negative views of Rev. Father Leger Comeau expressed, there *is* an issue between the proponents of multiculturalism and those who see the policy as a threat to French culture in Canada.' However, it is apparent that the francophone position is far from being unanimous, at least outside Quebec. At the CCCM Conference, Professor Robert Painchaud, 'not speaking as an unqualified partisan of the French, stressed that there was no unanimity among the French in Western Canada with regard to the federal policy on pluralism. He noted also, in response to a question, that the "other ethnic groups" had been conspicuously silent whenever it came to supporting the aspirations of the French outside of Quebec' (Dahlie, 1976:90). Professor Painchaud's contention is that the sensitivity of the franco-phone communities across the Prairies and in British Columbia to continuing criticisms of bilingual Canada explains their reluctance to support and promote multiculturalism (CCCM, 1976:29).

A detailed criticism and series of counter-ideological proposals were presented to the same conference by Professor Leslie Laczko, speaking on behalf of a noted opponent of multiculturalism, Professor Guy Rocher (CCCM, 1976:47):

> At a time when 90 percent of the ethnic minorities in Quebec are opting for the English language and anglophone culture, thereby constituting one of the most serious threats both politically and culturally to the francophone community of Quebec, the federal government has undertaken to define Canada as a multicultural nation. It is a characteristic of our country that these paradoxes can exist, and that many Canadians are even unaware of them.

In this paper Professor Rocher has four reservations about multi-culturalism that constitute the main core of his counter-ideology. Firstly, as a new concept of Canadian society it seriously jeopardizes the future of bilingualism. This, it will be recalled, was the original con-cern of the government before the concern over the other ethnic groups brought about what was essentially a compromise ideology. Secondly, bilingualism is losing its cultural connotation. Thirdly, the notions of multiculturalism and unity seems incompatible; Professor Rocher does 'not believe that nationhood can be founded on multiculturalism.' Finally, the new multicultural policy represents a retrograde step as far as French Canadians are concerned. Burnet (1975:207) cites Rocher's views as exemplifying those of the chief critics of multiculturalism who 'are united in seeing its aim as buttressing the privileged position of English-Canadians of British origin and keeping all others — native Indians and Inuit, French-Canadians, and all of origins other than British — "in their place".' Rocher is primarily concerned about the fate of francophones. In his opinion multiculturalism 'offers too little chance for the survival and expansion of French-Canadian culture, and thus makes an independent French-speaking Quebec appear to be the last chance for a French-speaking nation in North America' (1975:207).

Another speaker, Suzanna Drouin, was equally emphatic (CCCM, 1976:56):

> We have to maintain French-speaking culture in Canada. . . . Canada must be a bilingual country with a French culture that will make it, if you like, different from other North American countries.

One outcome of this strong francophone point of view, noted by Green-field (1976:115) is the Quebec State Government's Bill 22, which makes the teaching of French and its use mandatory in schools and all business.

This is an attempt to balance the swing of newcomer immigrants into the English-speaking group. On a more ideological level the cry in French Canada is 'La survivance', coupled with a sense of history as 'a weapon in the contemporary struggle for survival' (Cook, 1971:135; Greenfield, 1976:120).

The bilingual/bicultural counter-ideology is also promoted by politicians in Quebec. Dr John Mallea, Assistant Director of the Ontario Institute for Studies in Education, has made it clear that the issue is still highly explosive, because it has taken on survival connotations. In a recent publication (Mallea, 1977:3 – 5) he points out that the White Paper on Language published by the Political Parti Québécois held that the French language is not just a means of expression, but is a medium for living. There must be respect for the minorities and their languages and their cultures in the new Quebec, but French must become the common language.

The same theme has been echoed by newspapers in Quebec, as might be expected, newspapers and journalists being powerful promoters of ideologies. For instance, an article entitled 'Multiculturalism seen as a threat by Quebecers' appearing in the Montreal *Gazette* in April 1976, analysed the French fears of substituting cultural pluralism for biculturalism. Quebecers were strongly resistant to multiculturalism as it had different connotations in English and French, and was seen by the latter as placing French Canadians on an equal footing with other ethnic groups, thus weakening French claims to be one of the two historical founding charter groups ('deux peuples fondateurs') in Canadian society.

> It is the equal footing with national bilingualism thus given to multiculturalism which is disquieting. Bilingualism and biculturalism help shore up the French of Quebec. Multiculturalism is seen to threaten and undermine it. (Mallea, 1977:3)

However, it is possible that the opposition to multiculturalism among some French-speakers does not match Premier René Lévesque's denunciation of it as 'artificial' and a 'vast verbal fraud', and it may not extend beyond Quebec. Lévesque himself is of the opinion that it was equally artificial to believe that bilingualism and biculturalism had any real existence outside Quebec (Mallea, 1977:4). According to Mallea, the Québécois intellectual community appears to be indifferent to the new policy. He cites Rocher's (1972) comment that the consequences of multiculturalism for Canada's cultural and political future had not been sufficiently recognized, particularly among francophones. The policy was 'ambigue, erronée et dangereuse'. It 'broke with the mandate given to the Royal Commission on Bilingualism and Biculturalism, rejected the concept of a bicultural Canada, and violated the image of a unitary Canada' (Mallea, 1977:4).

Proposals for alternatives to multiculturalism
Several counter-ideologists have reservations about the government's adherence to the official ideology, and are insisting that it be specified more clearly, to provide a tighter model of what multiculturalism really means. Other counter-ideologists suggest that the government should modify its ideology.

For instance, at the 1976 CCCM Conference Monique Bégin, Parliamentary Secretary to the Secretary of State for External Affairs, criticized the policy on the grounds of its profound ambiguities, which only came to light when the Canadian Consultative Council on Multiculturalism published its first report in 1975 (CCCM, 1976:4):

> In other words, I am saying that the objectives of multiculturalism in relation to national unity, and to the integration to active Canadian life of immigrants or older new Canadians, has [sic] never been clearly stated. Nor has the fine line between multiculturalism and multilingualism been drawn. I think the distinction between multiculturalism and immigration has never been made either. . . . Poor folklore dances, lousy handicrafts, local newspapers with nothing on Canada, or little clannish egocentric group meetings are not multiculturalism in my way of thinking.

Monique Bégin's critical comment on the 'folksy' element in multiculturalism is a very common theme. For instance, Associate Professor Mary Ashworth, of the Faculty of Education at the University of British Columbia (UBC), referred scathingly during discussions to the common fallacy that if one teaches sufficient folk elements in a syllabus, one is 'doing' multiculturalism. Such a 'basket-weaving spaghetti-eating' approach is all too common in schools but is a travesty of what multiculturalism could mean. She was equally critical of the 'bilingual framework' in the federal government policy. This was necessary appeasement on the part of Prime Minister Trudeau to avoid a political crisis triggered off by Quebec separatism, but it has no meaning in Vancouver and British Columbia. These provinces are a long way from Quebec, and have no opportunity to use French. For them the government's mandatory bilingualism is irritating. It would be no better to introduce multilingualism in Canada; this would be political suicide for the federal government. The concept of a multicultural society is not well received in Quebec; that of a multilingual society would be rejected entirely.

Despite the political dangers for the federal government if a multilingual component were linked with the multicultural, multilingualism is being advocated by some supporters of pluralism. As Palmer comments (1976:104):

> Another contentious issue . . . is the degree to which language maintenance is necessary to have a viable multicultural policy. Some supporters of multiculturalism accept the arguments of the B & B Commission that language and culture are inseparable but pursue the argument to conclude that if

Canada is to be a multicultural society it must also in some ways be a multi-lingual one.

One outspoken advocate of this position is Professor M.R. Lupul, who is an Albertan of Ukrainian origin, and whose viewpoint is probably shared by some other Westerners, especially those of Slavic origin (Burnet, 1975:206). In his (1973) paper, Lupul argues that multicultur-alism perpetuates the inequitable situation of the non-British-non-French groups because it is tied to official bilingualism.

The academic attack

Multiculturalism as an ideology comes under very strong attack by a number of educationists and social theorists in personal comments and academic writing. To Professor Vince D'Oyley, 'multiculturalism is a sop offered by the federal government'. He tends to use the term 'multi-ethnic' without definition in an attempt to emphasize that minority group rights are the key issue. Dr H. Troper of the Ontario Institute for Studies in Education considers multiculturalism to be a hydra. It changes its characteristics according to the people and the situation involved. It was largely a political gesture by the federal government to ethnic pressure groups, and in consequence a great deal of bombast and rhetoric has grown up around the ideology. Any sin of the past can be excused in the name of multiculturalism within a bilingual framework, and it also gives its blessing to good things in the present and future. It is a change of name rather than of content, and at present the federal government and provinces are playing one off against the other. It is, moreover, a game which has opened up opportunities for many outside the governments to take part in, without, however, having more than token commitment to the policy.

Dr. Jack Kehoe, Associate Professor in the Faculty of Education, UBC, is against multiculturalism on more technical grounds — i.e., because it implicitly recognizes a culturally relativistic position, which characterizes much writing on the subject, but is contrary to the United Nations Universal Declaration of Human Rights. This proscribes certain cultural practices (e.g., arranged marriages) as being unethical. In Dr Kehoe's opinion, a lot of the curricular material generated by multiculturalism is based on quite naïve misconceptions. For instance, research has shown that knowledge or 'understanding' of other cultures does not lead to tolerance, neither does material that is 'interesting'. A great deal more work needs to be done on attitude research in Canada, but no funding is forthcoming for this purpose.

A more detailed view of alternatives to multiculturalism comes from Professor Jorgen Dahlie, Chairman of the Division of Educational Foundations in the Faculty of Education, UBC. Multiculturalism in a bilingual framework was a politically motivated ideology, conse-quently it is a bankrupt model, as it tries to make everybody happy by *ad hoc* things like a grant for a folk dance here, the endowment of a university Chair in Hungarian there. What is needed is a deeper, profound and organic appreciation of what it means to live in a diverse society. The exotic approach to teaching about groups is wrong because it will not achieve this depth. The government is well-intentioned, but operates basically at a surface level. Materials on the multicultural society are prepared for schools, but are essentially only a token effort.

Professor Dahlie argues for a multiethnic model of society in which ethnicity is no longer used in a derogatory sense; and he rejects Porter's suggestion in *The Vertical Mosaic* that the concept of ethnicity should be thrown out as impeding the development of a homogeneous society. To Dahlie, ethnic identity and personal 'cultural baggage' *are* important in the life of members of ethnic groups, and should be retained and used as an inescapable part of a person's life and work. An important part of the cultural baggage is ethnic heritage. There is no mileage to be gained in adopting a racial model of society, particularly in British Columbia where people react negatively towards the sensitive issue of race. The quest for equality in society is better achieved through the type of analysis that can be done using the multiethnic model.

Dr Bill Cross, Associate Professor in the Faculty of Education, University of Victoria, was not happy about the multicultural model, and considered it a political gimmick rather than a genuinely thought-through policy. Its effect on the school curriculum in British Columbia at least had been minimal.

Referring specifically to Native Indian programmes, and the research in this area that he is conducting in the Faculty of Education, University of Victoria, Dr A.R. King criticized the monolithic nature of federal government thinking and the projects it fosters. Smaller-scale projects operating through local resource centres would have much greater potential. Operationally, the multicultural mosaic is an invention of immigrant ideology. Native Indians do not agree with it, and do not identify with pluralism, as their world view sets them apart ecologically from the mosaic. In any case, the official bilingual/bicultural policy is a 'mythology', and is not in accord with the reality of Canadian society. Ethnic minorities form 'a seething cauldron of competition for resources', and this is not catered for by adopting the multicultural perspective.

A group of academic theorists is taking a conflict, resource competition model as the focus of their analysis and criticism of the multicultural model. At the 1976 CCCM Conference, Rosemary Brown, a Member of the Legislative Assembly of British Columbia, argued from an ideological perspective of the left (Brown, 1976:8):

> The recognition that our society has been composed of many cultural groups, being a mosaic, must not blind us to the frequent cynical use of this fact for political purposes. . . .

Multiculturalism must not be a way of avoiding the basic social issues of an advanced class society. . . . If we view ethnic groups only from a cultural perspective and ignore class relationships, we fall into a posture of patronizing and condescending. Ethnic people are not separate from but are part of, and located in, a class society just like everyone else. The status of their culture, our culture, exists in direct relationship to their status, our status, in the economic and political structure.

Davis (1975) asks a basically similar question:

Is the federal multicultural policy serious about attempting to overcome social and economic inequalities between ethnic groups and make the Canadian mosaic less vertical or is multiculturalism simply a means of 'containing' the demands of ethnic minorities without envisaging basic changes in the power structure of Canadian society?

In a publication which adopts a similar, class-focused analysis, the contrast between much of what passes for multiculturalism and what should pass is bitterly brought out by Jackie Wilson (1978:185).

The Canadian multiculturalism policy seems to guarantee that we can each do our little dances and flash our pretty, lacy petticoats while we drink our ethnic drinks and admire each other's handicrafts, as long as we realize that in reality the mosaic is vertically organized. It says little about meeting the needs of those of us whose place is at the bottom of that vertical column, who can not find decent employment or housing, whose creative spirit is crushed by poverty and incessant insecurity, whose children are destined only to replace us in our bottom slots. It does not speak to the injustice that pervades our daily lives if our hair style or skin color is unlike that of the members at the top of the column. . . . Multiculturalism does not guarantee us the right to use the public thoroughfares free of harassment, or to conduct our lives in peace and dignity. These are the issues that a truly multicultural society must address. Only then will the ethnic displays be an expression of the joy that is the natural inheritance of the human heart.

Dr Kent Henderson of OISE points out that a conflict model makes sense in a pluralist society in a period when the demands of its constituent minority groups are emerging clearly. It is possible that Canadian society is just approaching this stage. Until very recently immigrant groups were so new that it was difficult for them to recognize and articulate their disadvantage and the discrepancy of standards compared with other more privileged groups. Ethnic consciousness does not really emerge until the immigrant has been settled in for four or five years, and begins to see that he is disadvantaged.

A class-based approach to the problems of Toronto was used to produce a curriculum unit on the working-class child and the city as part of a curriculum project, *Canada and the Third World*, directed by Fran Endicott of OISE in collaboration with Barbara Thomas and the Co-operative Schools Group on Third World Education based at the Development Education Centre in Toronto. A publication produced by the team, *The Problem Exists Because it Exists in the World*, takes racism and discrimination as a major theme in response to this growing problem in Toronto.

Dr Endicott stressed that neither a multicultural approach nor a third-world approach to examining these problems is effective, as they fragment the problems and suggest that more is being done than is actually the case. This can often produce a white backlash. In reality, ethnic groups in Toronto are split into socio-economic classes, but it is being put about by some ethnic groups that what is needed is cultural maintenance and ethnic teachers in schools. Ethnics are split on these issues, and even a multiethnic model is then dangerous as it is separatist and divisive. Such terms only cloud the issue. What is required is a class-based analysis to show that problems in Canadian society are due to the class structure and not the diversity of cultures. In education for Black people, programmes are needed to encourage inter-ethnic co-operation between Black and White, and should demand justice and social rights in such areas as schools, medical and social welfare, housing facilities and so on.

To some extent the cross-cultural education programmes at OISE try to tackle some of these issues, according to Professor George Bancroft and Dr Keith McLeod, who have major teaching responsibility in this area. Professor Bancroft disagrees with the multicultural society ideology of the federal government. He claims it is only 'sloganeering' and believes it has diverted attention away from Native Indians and Inuit (Eskimos) because the policy is dominated by government thinking about migrants. Indians and Eskimos are an afterthought, but they are becoming increasingly restive about their marginal position in society, and are beginning to press their demands. Professor Bancroft uses a community-centred theme in his courses.

Dr McLeod sees the current ideology of multiculturalism as being a 'loaded' one. It is necessary to realize that both ethnicity and cultural pluralism have a part to play in Canadian society. For too long ethnicity has been seen in terms of 'singing and dancing only', but now questions of power and conflict are becoming increasingly discussed, in addition to the cultural aspects of pluralism. Both as editor of *Multiculturalism* and in his courses in the cross-cultural and multicultural studies teaching programmes Dr McLeod tries to steer a middle course between the folk-culture/ethnicity approach on the one hand and the resource competition/power conflict perspective on the other.

Dr Aaron Wolfgang, also at OISE, takes these concerns even further, by stressing that the multiethnic perspective is here to stay but on a world scene. The world is 'becoming stratified in terms of ethnicity' and this phenomenon cannot be reversed. Many world conflicts are based on ethnicity. In a country like Canada, mainstream values are bankrupt, so people from ethnic groups look for ethnic identity for reassurance.

A reconciliation of viewpoints

The views of Jean Burnet, the highly respected Professor of Sociology at Glendon College, York University, seem to be an attempt to reconcile the conflicting opinions being expressed in Canada. Her experience as a former RCBB Commissioner gives her a unique perspective for arriving at an overall assessment of the current situation in Canada.

To some extent, the criticisms of the government's policy of multiculturalism within a bilingual framework voiced by Rocher, Lupul and Porter arise because the policy was misnamed by the Royal Commission (Burnet, 1975:208). The Commission did not intend that multiculturalism should be interpreted in the sense of being 'the full and vital maintenance of distinctive ways of life by all of Canada's peoples within a single society' (Burnet, 1976:204). In actuality this is impossible to attain. Evidence suggests that the aim was more to encourage and recognize ethnicity in the sense used by Glazer and Moynihan (1975) and most of their collaborators.[2] Professor Burnet agrees that multiculturalism is a misleading and inaccurate term since most ethnic minorities do not preserve complete cultures in the technical sense. Instead, they want to preserve a sense of identity. Folk dances and costumes, handicrafts, traditional customs, and even languages are symbols of group identity rather than elements of complete, self-contained cultures (Palmer, 1976:104; Burnet, 1976:204).

Programmes fostered by federal government agencies have tended to stress folk culture often more than ethnic language maintenance, thus incurring the dissatisfaction of ethnic minority spokesmen who want more attention to language. But 'both emphases can be related at least as logically to a policy of invigoration of ethnic groups as to policy of culture maintenance' (Burnet, 1976:204). However, there is an important difference between the Canadian situation and some other multiethnic societies. In the Canadian context neither of these symbolic elements of ethnicity is being retained as a form of heritage, or even revived. Rather each is being learned anew. In the case of language, 'the dissemination of the standard or the literary language in Canada, then, again seems intended to unify a highly differentiated group rather than to maintain or preserve a culture brought to Canada from elsewhere' (Burnet, 1976:205).

The key to federal government policy is the maintenance of ethnic groups in the sense of encouraging those that wish to do so 'to set up or to maintain their ethnic organizations and their cultural symbols, because preserving one's identity is considered to be consistent with acquiring a Canadian identity and taking part in Canadian society and culture' (Burnet, 1975:209). Indeed, were it not for the disrepute in academic circles of the term ethnic in the 1960s and the decision of the Royal Commission on Bilingualism and Biculturalism to avoid using the term in its report, it is likely that the government policy would have been to encourage polyethnicity in a bilingual framework (Burnet, 1976:205).

To Findlay (1975:216), 'the Canadian situation is of special interest because of the way in which it is both institutionally pluralist and multi-ethnic'. Findlay later qualifies his assertion by suggesting that poly-ethnic is a better term. '[Canada] some might even say [is] "polyethnic perverse".' However, at another level of abstraction, based on the ethnic complexity of Canadian society, 'Canada is undeniably multi-cultural . . . [but] acceptance of the fact that Canada is in one sense multicultural does not sufficiently take into account the complexities involved, nor is it very illuminating in considering the efficacy of multi-cultural policies' (1975:217).

The complexity of assessing the feasibility of multiculturalism is thus due to the various factors that have to be taken into any analysis. According to Findlay (1975:219) these are firstly the polyethnic nature of the country's population and the linguistic institutional duality, due regard being given to the 'historical and current differences in immigra-tion patterns for the various descent groups involved'. In addition, it is also necessary to have 'some recognition of the relationships between ethnicity and social status and power within the context of the continu-ing evolution of the technological and large-scale organizational features of contemporary society'. By over-emphasizing one variant of pluralism such as cultural pluralism (i.e., multiculturalism) major social problems can be obscured.

Lupul (1978:15) focuses on other aspects of the socio-historical context, which have produced a situation in education where, apart from the provision of some third (ethnic) languages, 'in terms of other aspects of the school curriculum, Canada's multi-ethnic or multicul-tural reality has as yet hardly made a dent'. A gross lack of teaching materials at all levels about multiculturalism as an ideology, and a basic ignorance of teachers about ethnicity have produced a

. . . whole dreadful situation [which] is but a reflection of the overall indif-ference of most Canadians to cultural diversity rooted in ethnicity. To most, ethnicity is synonymous with immigrants, exotic dishes, and folk festivals. Ethnicity as a creative basis to help give Canada a living multiculturalism as its national identity is understood by very few. To the French Canadians, multiculturalism is a threat to be shunned; to the Anglo-Celtic Canadians it is a slogan to be trotted out on ceremonial occasions. It is either too serious or not serious enough to be taken seriously. In the situation the French fear it, the Anglo-Celtics patronize it, and 'the others' grow to view it cynically.

What of the future of multiculturalism in a bilingual framework? Asked this question, Professor Burnet pointed out that parents faced a choice between maintaining their ethnic heritage and/or opting for the Western industrial culture. The choice at the personal level is difficult. At the political level a lot will depend on the way Quebec moves. If it separates from the federation the result could be two multiethnic societies. Both could be repressive and all developments to date would go by the board. Of the fate of multiculturalism Professor Burnet holds the following view (1975:211):

> Multiculturalism within a bilingual framework, if it is interpreted as intended — that is, as encouraging those members of ethnic groups who want to do so — to maintain a proud sense of the contribution of their group to Canadian society . . . becomes something very North American: voluntary marginal differentiation among peoples who are equal participants in the society. If it is interpreted in a second way — as enabling various peoples to transfer foreign cultures and languages as living wholes into a new place and time — multiculturalism is doomed.

Notes

1. A quinquennial Census in 1976 established the total population on June 1 to be 22 992 604. Up-dated figures on ethnicity are not available from this Census. (Statistics Canada, 1977:164).
2. Ethnicity entails the insistence by members of ethnic groups 'on the significance of their group distinctiveness and identity and on their rights that derive from this group character' (Glazer & Moynihan, 1975:2–3).

CHAPTER 4

Fiji

In contrast to Britain and Canada, Fiji is small geographically, and has only one-fiftieth the population of Canada. The general question asked in this chapter, therefore, is whether Fiji experiences fewer problems of pluralism than the larger countries examined in this book.

The socio-historical context

The current demographic and cultural pattern

On September 13, 1976 when the decennial census was taken the total population of Fiji was just over half a million people (588 068). This represented an increase of 111 341 (20.5 per cent approximately) in the decade since 1966 when the total population was 467 727. This increase is being maintained: estimates from the Bureau of Statistics for December 31, 1977 gave the total as 601, 485. Changes in the ethnic composition of the population since 1966 together with estimates for December 31, 1977 are given in table 5.

In both overall numbers and as percentages of the total population Chinese and Europeans show a decline. Compared with the Indian and Fijian totals they are a negligible part of the population numerically but, as will become apparent, they hold high-status occupations and power to a disproportionate degree. Although numbers show an increase, the percentages of Part-Europeans and Other Pacific Islanders have declined during the decade. The most significant increases in totals are those of Fijians and Indians, but the latter show a slight percentage decline, whereas the former have increased by almost 2 per cent compared with the figure for the previous census. Bakker (1977:9–10) has pointed out that since 1966 the mortality levels have been very low and life expectancies high compared with most developing countries. The lower numbers of Indians can be attributed to the earlier stage (1960 approximately) at which Indian fertility started to decline, and its faster rate compared with Fijians whose fertility showed a slight downward trend after 1966 (1977:9–10). It is clear that the population is dominated demographically by Indians and Fijians, with

78   *The Pluralist Dilemma in Education*

TABLE 5 Total Populations by ethnic groups for 1966 and 1976 censuses (with 1977 comparisons)

Ethnic group	Census 1966 No.	%	Census 1976 No.	%	Estimates 1977 %
Chinese*	5 149	1.08	4 652	0.79	0.80
European	6 590	1.38	4 929	0.84	0.70
Fijian	202 176	42.41	259 932	44.20	44.40
Indian	240 960	50.54	292 896	49.81	50.00
Part-European	9 687	2.03	10 276	1.75	1.70
Rotuman	5 797	1.22	7 291	1.24	1.20
Other Pacific Islanders	6 095	1.28	6 822	1.16	1.00
All Others	273	0.05	1 270	0.21	0.20
Total	476 727	100.00	588 068	100.00	100.00

Sources: *Census of the Population, 1976*, table 1 (Bureau of Statistics); 31 December 1977 estimates.
* Includes part-Chinese.

the former holding close to 50 per cent of the population but beginning to lose ground compared with the more rapidly increasing Fijians.

Socio-economic groupings

From table 6, the agricultural bias of the economy as a whole is apparent, with nearly half (47.3 per cent) of the workforce occupied as agricultural and related workers. The breakdown of the total workforce by ethnic group shows that Fijians, Indians, Rotumans and Other Pacific Islanders predominate in this occupational category. In contrast, Europeans, Chinese and Part-Chinese, and Part-Europeans are least represented, but predominate in the first four categories.

Broad categories and figures such as these conceal complex and often subtle sub-groupings within ethnic groups, and the association of these groupings with specific occupations. For instance, the Gujeratis, a small linguistic group within the Indian population component, have a virtual monopoly on middle-level commerce through owning or managing small to medium-sized retail and wholesale shops (Ali, 1976:414).

In the professional and related occupations group Fijians occupy a large number of positions as primary and secondary teachers, and also as professional nurses. Indians, too, rank high in primary and secondary teaching, as well as providing a large proportion of accountants. Further, Ali has pointed out (1976:414) that Indians surpass the number of European doctors, lawyers and other professionals. Europeans in this occupational group rank high as architects and engineers, teachers, workers in religion and accountants.

The agricultural and related occupations category also illustrates contrasts both within and between racial groups. The majority of Indians are sugar cane farmers, there being in June 1976 13 142 Indians with this occupation, comprising 80 per cent of the total; the remaining 20 per cent were Fijians (Ali, 1976:417). Figures from the 1976 census indicate that 43.3 per cent of Indians were cane farmers and 46.7 per cent field crop workers. Of the total number of Indians in the agricultural and related occupations category, then, 90 per cent are associated with a cash-crop economy. Historically, most of them are from the Tamil or Telegu linguistic and regional sub-division of India. In contrast, the majority of Fijians in the same category are villagers (65.3 per cent) practising subsistence economy. Only 25.4 per cent are specialized farmers and field crop workers.

Farming and rural settlement patterns provide a further contrast between Indians and Fijians and highlight another facet in the complexity of pluralism in Fiji. Both are closely related to geographical features of the country and the relationships between land mass distribution, climate and drainage patterns. Fiji consists of two main islands and over 300 smaller ones. In all, some 150 islands are inhabited. The climate of Fiji is tropical oceanic and is dominated by the prevailing south-east trade winds for the majority of the year. In consequence, the windward, southern and south-eastern sides of the islands experience a tropical wet climate with maximum rainfall, while the leeward northern and north-western sides experience dry winters and wet summers, conditions which are beneficial to sugar growing, the dominant cash crop (Norton, 1977:3–4). The rainfall also ensures that the main islands of Viti Levu and Vanua Levu have abundant streams and main rivers. Many are navigable and have river flats and adjacent lower lands which contain fertile, deep, easily worked soils.

The influence of landholding

Landholding laws and regulations in Fiji are designed to protect the rights of the indigenous Fijian population for whom land has a deep 'socio-psychological value which supercedes the needs of a market economy' (Ali, 1978a:5). As a result of this close relationship, most Fijians 'regard the unhindered ownership of their land as essential for their continued existence as a cultural/racial entity'. In consequence, safeguarded by the Constitution and by prior historical and legal rights, 82.16 per cent of the land is Fijian communally owned. Another 0.24 per cent is Rotuman communally owned (DP7, 1975:108). This total, amounting to almost 83 per cent of all land in Fiji is inalienable, and 'cannot be part of any commercial transaction whatsoever between Fijians and non-Fijians which will lead to any part of this land being sold as free-hold to non-Fijians' (Ali, 1978a:4).

Freehold land, other than Crown freehold, amounts to no more than

TABLE 6 Occupations of ethnic groups as percentage of total economically active population aged 15 years and over, for 7 categories of occupations.

Occupational Group		Chinese & Part-Chinese	Europeans	Fijians	Indians	Part-Europeans	Rotumans	Other Pacific Islanders	All Others	Totals	Group
1 Professionals, technical and related	number	151	875	5232	5497	321	268	162	143	12 649	Group 1
	%	9.3	45.5	7.0	7.3	10.5	9.9	9.7	32.9	7.8	
2 Administrative and managerial	number	90	344	237	803	101	19	25	37	1656	Group 2
	%	5.5	17.9	0.3	1.1	3.3	0.7	1.5	8.5	1.0	
3 Clerical and related workers	number	308	211	3748	6016	605	374	158	42	11 462	Group 3
	%	18.9	11.0	5.0	8.0	19.7	13.8	9.4	9.7	7.1	
4 Sales workers	number	446	94	1870	6376	183	148	94	11	9222	Group 4
	%	27.35	4.9	2.5	8.4	6.0	5.5	5.6	2.5	5.7	
5 Service workers	number	150	100	6792	3799	228	180	152	28	11 429	Group 5
	%	9.2	5.2	9.1	5.0	7.4	6.7	9.1	6.5	7.1	
6 Agricultural, etc., workers	number	147	98	43 217	30 683	548	1125	590	36	76 444	Group 6
	%	9.0	5.1	57.9	40.7	17.8	41.6	35.2	8.3	47.3	
7 Production, Transport, equip- and labourers	number	339	200	13 572	22 267	1083	589	493	137	38 680	Group 7
	%	20.8	10.4	18.2	29.5	35.3	21.8	29.5	31.6	23.9	
Totals in 7 Groups	number	1631	1922	74 668	75 441	3069	2703	1674	434	161 542	Total
	%	100.0	100.0	100.0	100.0	100.0	100.0	100.0	100.0	100.0	

Source: Based on *Census of the Population, 1976* tables 33, 34 (Bureau of Statistics, 31 December 1977 estimates).

8.15 per cent of the total (DP7, 1975:108). Of this, most of the first-class land was alienated before Fiji ceded to Britain in 1874, and is in European hands. Approximately 1.7 per cent of the freehold is owned by Indians (Ali, 1976:417). As this is clearly insufficient for cane farming, the remaining land required is leased from Fijians. Leasing arrangements have become the subject of complex litigation between Indians and Fijians, and have exacerbated tensions between the two groups.

In Ali's opinion (1978a:4), land is also a political issue:

> Land has also been a sensitive factor because it has been exploited and mani-
> pulated as an issue of politics by certain aspirants to political office who have
> placed victory at the polls above all else.

Some indication of the socio-psychological 'power' of land in the minds of Fijians is brought out in the institution of the Mataqali (pronounced matang-gali). This is the land-holding clan whose members were governed by a chief who is its social, political, and economic head (Bolabola, 1978:154). The Mataqali are patrilineal, but women do have land-using rights. The Mataqali exert considerable influence over economic life at the village and Fijian community levels.

The combined effect of geographical and land-holding factors has been to produce marked concentrations of Indians and Fijians in different parts of the two main islands of Viti Levu and Vanua Levu. Apart from urban areas such as Suva, the Fijians live in small, close-knit villages scattered along the river valleys. In contrast, the Indians live in separate homesteads on individual farms, which are located in the sugar cane areas in western Viti Levu and northern Vanua Levu. In addition, there are substantial numbers of Indians in the areas of south-east Viti Levu where rice growing and dairying are practised, and in the rice-growing valley of the Sigatoka River in south-west Viti Levu (1969:3). Such regional and geographical differences are important determinants of the access people have to mainly town-based resources of electricity, sanitation, medical help, social welfare, and education. In many of these resources Fijians are less well endowed than Indians.[1]

Language and cultural contrasts

A further differentiating factor between these two groups is language. The most commonly used dialect of Fijians is Bauan, but as there are other dialects officers of the Suva-based Curriculum Development Unit of the Ministry of Education, Youth and Sport are trying to develop a standard language which is a variant of, but based on Bauan. Their task is complicated by the fact that there is a broad linguistic division between the eastern and the western language groupings, in addition to the 200 or more other dialects in Fiji. Teachers in the field are thus encouraged to use the developing standard language, while not neglecting the dialect of the area in which they happen to be teaching. The two main Indian languages are the lingua franca, Hindustani (with the closely related Hindi), and Urdu. In addition there are a number of dialects such as Tamil, Telegu, Gujerati, and Gurmukhi (Coulter, 1967:155), which may be spoken in the schools belonging to their respective communities. Both Indians and Fijians have to master English as the common language of commerce and educational advancement.

The language and cultural differences have become institutionalized in several ways. In day-to-day social interactions within their own groups, Fijians and Indians speak their own languages. Some newspapers, such as the *Fiji Times*, are printed in English, but Indian newspapers are printed in the vernacular. The Fiji Broadcasting Commission transmits broadcasts in English, Fijian and Hindustani, prepared by separate departments for these languages. Other media, such as the Indian films screened in quite a number of cinemas, also help to maintain the cultural identification of Indians with India and the vernacular (Norton, 1977:12).

Religion also provides a basis of contrast between the two main racial/ethnic groups. Fijians practise Christianity, particularly Methodism and Catholicism. While some Indians are Christians, the great majority are Hindus, with a lesser number following Islam. it should also be noted that within the broad categories of Christian, Hindu, Moslem, there are a number of sub-groups which further diversify religious affiliations. However, these are only the 'official' religions. Coulter (1967:78) points out that, in the case of Fijians, Christianity 'is in part a veneer over native animism. The Fijian has a vague but strong belief in spiritual beings; he lives in great fear of evil spirits; he believes that isolated and uninhabited spots on his island are haunted.' Indians also have 'folk' beliefs in addition to their main religions. One of these is in the power of faith healers who live in various localities of Fiji. Religious differences are institutionalized in Fijian national holidays. Fiji Day, Dipawali (the Hindu Festival of Lights), the birthday of the Prophet Mohammed, and Christian holidays are all provided for in the yearly calendar.

A final difference between Fijians and Indians and other ethnic groups is to be found in the levels of education they attain. Europeans and Chinese constitute the majority in Forms 5 and 6 (Grades 11–12) and in post-secondary levels. Although sizeable proportions of Indians have had no education or have only achieved primary level, in comparison more Indians have achieved a higher level of education than Fijians, the majority of whom have achieved levels below Forms 1 and 2 (Grades 7–8). A major problem causing concern to educationists is the lower levels of performance by Fijians at the major secondary and tertiary examinations. As Ali has commented (1976:423):

In 1973, 338 Fijians passed the New Zealand School Certificate, compared to 843 Indians and 191 others; in the New Zealand University Entrance, 58 Fijians were successful compared to 232 Indians and 62 others. From the University of the South Pacific, of the 56 Fiji citizens who graduated with B.A. or B.Sc. in 1974, only 10 were Fijians; in 1975 out of a total of 81, 19 were Fijians.

In order to reduce the disparity between Fijians and others 'scholarships at the University level are offered to deserving Fijians to a total value equal to those offered to non-Fijians' (DP7, 1975:177). In other words, 50 per cent of all scholarships are reserved for Fijians while the remainder are given to members of all other communities (Ali, 1978b:150). This issue of preferential treatment for Fijians caused an outcry during the 1977 elections when the decision was made by the government 'to grant scholarships for the University of the South Pacific's Foundation Year science programme to Fijians who had passed the New Zealand University Entrance examination with at least 216 marks, while Indians were required to have a minimum of 261 marks' (1978b:150). This provoked a student strike on campus, and led to the matter becoming a major political issue during the election. As Ali has commented (1977:19), 'education is to Indians what land is to Fijians, the source of their existence.'

All the evidence cited above points to what appears, on the surface at least, to be a pronounced dualism between two basically homogeneous, monolithic racial/ethnic groups. However, the homogeneity in the case of the Indian community is more apparent then real. Coulter points out (1967:168–69) citing a number of authorities, that the Indians are not a unified community, as there are broad differences in languages, rules of marriage, religious rites, diet, and names.

> The ideological exclusiveness of the Muslim faith compared with the inclusiveness of Hinduism keeps members of those religions apart in Fiji as it does in India. There is almost total absence of intermarriage between northern and southern Indians since they don't speak the same language. . . Northerners, southerners, and Muslims have sufficient cultural differences to give their members the feeling of belonging to separate groups. The Punjabis, mostly Sikhs, and the Gujeratis, tend to stand aloof from the other Indians in the Colony.

The squabbles between the 'Dove' faction and the 'Flower' faction in the Indian National Federation Party at the time of the 1977 general election attest to the persistence of this aspect of Indian life, noted a decade earlier by Coulter (1967:171): 'The predominant characteristic of their political life is "rivalry, factionism, and schism" '.

Fijians, on the other hand, also appear to be a monolithic group, but even here there are important, if subtle, dichotomies: between east and west in language/dialects, and Polynesian/Melanesian backgrounds; between rural village community settlement and life, and the urban life to which more and more young Fijians are being attracted; between the vast majority of Fijians who are still subsistence farmers and the small minority who hold upper-status positions in government and the bureaucracy.

Historical context

Population movements

It is convenient to discuss other aspects of Fijian dualism within an historical context because, unlike other case studies, Fiji has no current *im*migration problem of the kind that has generated ideological discussion in Britain and Canada. The present demographic composition of the Fijian population was largely pre-determined in 1916 when the indenture system, which had brought Indians to work in the sugar cane fields, was abolished. 'Since the late 1930s the volume of migration from India has been small, and by 1966 only 6 per cent of Indian adults were born outside Fiji' (Norton, 1977:7−8). Today, immigration is strictly controlled because of the increasing Fijian population and a shortage of employment. Permission to work in Fiji is given to non-Fijian citizens only when there is no qualified local personnel capable of doing the job. A number of immigrants are selected transilients (Richmond, 1967) i.e., professional workers taking up contracts and appointments for a limited period.

Instead of an immigration problem, Fiji suffers from a net *em*igration problem, currently running at more than 0.5 per cent of the population each year, coupled with a modest rate of population growth. Inder (1977:59) notes that Canada has been the main destination for emigrating Fiji Islanders, especially for Indians and Chinese. The skill drain is causing considerable concern for the government as evident in the Seventh Development Plan (DP7, 1975:3). In 1974, for instance, emigration, particularly of skilled people, had reached a rate of 9600 per year. This represented 1 per cent of the population and a marked increase over the 1960s, during which the rate had not exceeded 1300 per annum (Inder, 1977:59).

Internal migration has also affected the present population pattern. Historically, as Norton notes (1977:8), it has influenced the distribution of Indians and Europeans:

> As Indians displaced Europeans in sugar cane farming and trading in the countryside, the latter increasingly moved to the towns, where they preserved their dominance in large-scale commerce and industry and in the highest ranks of the civil service.

Currently, another kind of population distribution is being generated by two characteristics of the labour market. The first is the gradual shift of emphasis on the part of Fijians away from their traditional reliance on village settlement and subsistence economy. As Norton notes (1977:10), such reliance no longer persists:

Many villagers seek occasional employment in towns and industrial centres as labourers or house servants, and some are engaged seasonally by Indian farmers. A large number of urban workers commute daily. In addition there is a growing number of commercial farmers within and outside the villages, either as individuals or organized in cooperatives or other schemes.

The second problem is the growing unemployment situation, particularly among young urban males of both major races, accentuated by the internal migration of Fijians from the villages to the main cities such as Nadi, Suva, and Lautoka. Paradoxically, this problem coincides with the skill drain which might be expected to result in increased employment opportunities. Instead, as the government notes (DP7, 1975:3), 'the fact that the stream of emigrants includes a disproportionate number of highly trained and skilled citizens makes it a mixed blessing'.

The political situation

Much of the ideological debate about Fijian society and the relationships between Fijians and Indians has been political in nature. Fiji achieved independence on 10 October 1970, and since that date has been an independent dominion within the Commonwealth. As set out in the Constitution, the form of government is a bicameral parliament consisting of an elected House of Representatives and a nominated Senate. The former has 52 representatives: 12 Fijian, 12 Indian, and 3 general members elected from the communal ('racial group') rolls, plus 10 Fijian, 10 Indian and 5 general members elected from national rolls, which have members of all races who vote together. The Senate consists of 22 members. Eight of these are appointed by the Great Council of (Fijian) Chiefs, seven members are appointed by the Prime Minister (currently a Fijian), six by the Leader of the Opposition (currently an Indian), and one by the Council of Rotuma.

An important arm of government is the Fijian Affairs Board. This is the authority under which the Fijian administration system described below functions. It comprises the Minister for Fijian Affairs and Local Government, eight members elected by the Fijian members of the House of Representatives, and two members elected by the Great Council of Chiefs. One of the Board's main functions is to make recommendations to the government on matters which it considers will benefit Fijians.

The system of Fijian local government and district administration comes under the Board's aegis. The latter is based on four districts each having a commissioner in charge. Local government is based on the village (*koro*) with a head (*turaga-koro*) who directs its activities. Several *koros* in a group constitute a district (*tikina*), and several districts make up a province (*yavusa*). Ali (1976:414) has suggested the consequences of this arrangement, which has been carried over from historical times into the present government:

In practice, the Fijian administration became a parallel government, and virtually a state-within-a-state. It was within the context of this administration that Fijians settled their differences: they came to compromises there about their own needs, after discussing their goals and ordering their priorities. They were then able to come to the national level in the Legislative Council [now the House of Representatives] with a degree of unity that was not apparent in the other communities.

This paints a favourable picture of Fijian local government and its relationship with the national level, probably coloured by Ali's pre-occupation with what he sees as pressures militating against Indians' legitimate claims to a greater share of political power and resources. However, despite the appearance of Fijian unity, other factors militate against the Fijian ethnic group:

All authorities on Fiji are agreed that the whole philosophy of native life, as enshrined and enforced in the Fijian administration by its regulations, is inimical to the best interests of that ethnic group, and that, if the separate administration is not abolished, it will continue to handicap the native people severely in competition with the Indians and other people in the islands. (Coulter, 1967:178).

Political parties

The present political party structure and organization also reflects historical racial and industrial rivalries. Until the 1977 general elections there were two main political parties, the National Federation Party and the Alliance Party. The former originated at the time of the 1960 sugar cane farmers' strike, and was formally constituted as the Federation Party by a group of radical leaders in 1964. The great majority of its members are Indians, and it has close associations with cane farmers' unions, which also include lawyers, merchants and farmers. From its beginning the Federation Party 'extended its influence by promoting objectives that tended to isolate Indians from the rest of the population. It directed its propaganda principally against the powers and privileges of the European minority and the communal election system alleged to protect them' (Norton, 1977:79). The party membership gradually expanded outside its original western and south-western cane-growing power base, to include the south-east and Suva region. 'Party officials and workers in the south-eastern towns were typically Indians outside multiracial society and of modest economic and occupational status in the lower middle class' (1977:83).

The ruling Alliance Party was launched five months before the 1966 election, but its roots stretch back to the Fijian Association, which had 'developed from a body created in 1956 to counter criticism of Fijian leadership by the European president of the Kisan Sangh [sugar cane farmers' union] and to oppose the strike of Indian cane farmers that he threatened to call if Fijians were not permitted to elect their political representatives' (1977:84). Effectively the Association was anti-Indian, and had a number of Fijian Ratus, or chiefs, in prominent positions of power. One of these, Ratu Mara, heir to the paramount chieftainship of Lau, became the present Prime Minister.

The Association gradually developed from a mainly Suva-based élitist organization into a national party during the early 1960s. As Norton notes (1977:85):

> [This was] a period when uncertainty about the political future accentuated distrust of Indians. Racial preoccupations submerged resentments against the chiefs as an administrative élite. The people championed the Association as an organization guarding against Indian domination.

Members of the Legislative Council and a group of young men newly returned from studies in England organized the Association into a political party in 1964. The political outlook of the young men 'was more aggressively racial than that of established leaders whose defence of the Fijians was tempered by long association with representatives of other races and colonial officials'. Ratu Mara was 'the strongest advocate of multi-racialism, and the initiative for guiding the association was mainly his' (1977:85–86). However, he was not without opposition, as the Alliance Party was originally 'a union of potentially hostile groups' (1977:92) set up to oppose the Federation Party, by principals from a number of organizations. These were the Fijian Association, the National Congress, the General Electors' Association, the Muslim Political Front, Fiji Minority Party (Moslem), Chinese Associate, the Rotuman Convention, and the Tongan Association (1977:90). The 1972 general election saw an increased racial polarization on political lines (despite inter-racial appeals), fewer signs of antagonism between the rival parties, and the apparent cordial relations between Prime Minister Ratu Mara, leader of the Alliance, and Siddiq Koya, Leader of the Opposition and Federal Party.

The ideological models of Fijian society and race relations also differ along political party lines, and provide the climate which affects the education system.

> The Alliance Party conceives Fiji as a society based on the accommodation of antagonistic racial interests by a balance of political power. The Federation Party conceives it in terms of a struggle by the people against their political and economic overlords. The former definition of society is upheld principally by the eastern chiefs and the Europeans, while the second is affirmed mainly by Indian leaders produced by cane farmer politics. The extent to which both Fijians and Indians are divided between the two positions partly corresponds to regional differences and inequalities. (Norton, 1977:77)

The education system

'The history of education in Fiji is largely one of private initiative and effort' (Fiji Education Commission, 1969:6). Despite much greater government involvement in, and expenditure on, public education in recent years, especially since the publication of the Fiji Education Commission's report in 1969, this statement applies to the current educational situation. It is part of the socio-historical background of an education system, which still reflects the racial and ethnic dualism that is such a pronounced feature of Fijian society. Despite attempts by the central government education authority to reduce the different provisions for the various racial and ethnic groups, the present pattern of education is not qualitatively different from what is was pre-1969. Then the missions and other private organizations, many with ethnic affiliations, played the major role in providing education in default of the government, which had neither the finances nor the teaching manpower to do so. In 1976, of a total of 642 primary schools, 3.3 per cent were operated by the Education Department; of 121 secondary schools, 6.6 per cent; and of 27 technical schools 11 per cent. Out of a total of 790 schools of all types in 1976, the Education Department exercised 'minority control' over only 32 or 4.1 per cent. The remaining 95.9 per cent were under a variety of other controlling agencies including local committees, religious groups, and commercial organisations.

One of the major themes in the history of education has been the pressure put on the government, largely by the Indian community, to take over committee schools and achieve multiracial schooling by catering for all races in the one school. For instance, in 1944 the Stephens *Report on Education in the Colony of Fiji* suggested that the government take over Indian committee schools, institute the use of English as the medium of instruction in all schools, and make education compulsory between the ages of 6 and 12 years. These suggestions were supported by Indians in the Lautoka and Rewa Districts on the grounds that the existing system of government financial aid had only intensified racial and religious divisions, and that it had led to wasteful competition between denominational schools in some areas, while other areas were starved of schools.

In 1969, one of the recommendations in the report of the Commission (1969:90) was 'That the Government should continue to encourage schools to become multi-racial in areas where this is practicable, on the basis of area plans drawn up by rural development committees'. At that time, Irene Narayan, then the Federal Party's member for Suva, moved in the Legislative Assembly that the government should take a step in the direction of making education free and compulsory throughout Fiji. This had been one of the Commission's recommendations (1969:90). She also emphasized the importance of universal education 'as a means to promote economic growth and racial harmony in Fiji' (Whitehead, 1975:208).

Since the Commission's report in 1969 only limited progress towards multiracial education has been made. As Whitehead notes (1975:292):

The Government places a high priority on developing a racially harmonious society and multi-racial schooling is frequently invoked as the principal means by which this is to be achieved. The subject remains controversial but slow progress is being made.

Moag (1978:134) cites a report by Rodger (1972) which claimed that in 1972 nearly half the schools in Fiji (305 out of 627) were uni-racial, i.e., having a totally Fijian or totally Indian enrolment. Of these, 137 schools served mono-racial areas. On this evidence Rodger makes the somewhat sweeping claim in conclusion (1972:9): 'Of the 490 (627 minus 137) which *could* be multiracial, therefore, 322 (65.5 per cent) *are* multiracial.'

As Moag (1978:134) and other writers have pointed out, claims like these need to be interpreted with caution. Figures such as the above can present a quite misleading picture:

> Many schools in the countryside have two or three students from the other communities on their rolls. In a survey conducted by this writer [Moag], supervising teachers provided figures indicating that over ninety percent of primary schools in rural districts are communal. The lowest percentage is in Suva, the capital, where nearly one third are multiracial.

Moag also suggests that the proportion of uni-racial secondary schools might be rising due to the founding of many secondary and junior secondary schools in outlying country areas. As H.C. Sharma rightly pointed out in the Fiji Senate in 1970, this does not make them multi-racial.[2] Nevertheless, evidence suggests that there has been a slight softening of Fijian attitudes towards racial mixing in schools to indicate that their thinking is turning somewhat towards multiracial schooling. In addition, resistance to multiracial schooling is weakening in urban areas, where a variety of secondary schools have been established, which are willing to take children from any race, just to fill their rolls (Whitehead, 1975:293).

A second major theme concerns the below-average academic performance of Fijian children compared with that of children from other races. Whitehead notes (1975:160) that even before the problem was officially recognized in the 1966 Department of Education annual report, concern had been expressed about the poor educational achievements of Fijian children. The problem also featured in Development Plan V of 1965–70 (Baba, 1978:2). and in the report of the Fiji Education Commission (1969:7). Examination results confirming the pattern have been published in each report of the Ministry of Education, Youth and Sport to date. As Baba notes (1978:2): 'Fiji is now in the eighth year of its independence and yet the so-called Fijian problem is still very much in evidence. . . . The evidence suggests that in terms of academic achievements in external examinations, the situation has not improved.' Hopkin (1978:116) has pointed out that this academic achievement imbalance along racial lines 'has had adverse effects on the government's attempts to maintain the racial balance in the modern sector which is thought desirable in a multi-racial country such as Fiji'.

The use of vernacular languages in schools is another closely related feature of education that has its roots in the Indian or Fijian racial composition of communal schools. 'The racial alignment of schools on the one hand is partly a result of the linguistic differences between the two communities and, at the same time, helps to perpetuate those differences' (Moag, 1978:134). The use of the vernacular as a medium of instruction for all subjects correlates with the racial, communal character of the school. 'The current pattern for communal schools features vernacular medium plus E.S.L. instruction for the first three years, with English medium beginning at Class 4. Many multiracial schools follow the same pattern with separate vernacular classes for the first three years' (Moag, 1978:134). These kinds of provisions were recommended by the Fiji Education Commission (1969:23) with the added proposal that the use of English as the medium of instruction should be encouraged to extend as quickly as possible, given the availability of suitable teachers, but should not be imposed in advance of local feeling. The Commission also recognized that there is no alternative to English as a medium of instruction at the secondary level, but that there should be provision for the continued study of Fijian, Hindi, Urdu, Tamil, etc., as cultural languages. The difficulties of finding enough literature in standardized Fijian was recognized, and a special recommendation was made to develop Fijian as a language and to sustain Fijian cultural arts (Fiji Education Commission, 1969:24–35). For some years both Fijian and Hindi have been available at the secondary level as optional examination subjects in the Fiji Junior examination, which takes place at the end of Form 4 (Grade 10). Surprisingly, there is a long-standing, 'striking imbalance' between the two languages: in 1976, 1742 candidates sat the Fijian examination, while only 543 sat the Hindi paper, reflecting considerable interest in Fijian language at the secondary level.

Teacher education

Teacher education reflects the dual system of control over schooling discussed above. There are four organizations providing pre-service courses for primary teachers. The largest, Nasinu Teachers' College, which was inaugurated in 1947 under the control of the Ministry of Education, was the only government organization until the establishment of the Lautoka Teachers' College in 1978. Two 'private' colleges have been operating since the colonial period: Corpus Christi, run by the Roman Catholic Mission, and Fulton Missionary College, administered by the Seventh Day Adventist Mission. Both these colleges are much smaller in scale and output of teachers than the government organizations.

Pre-service training for secondary teachers is provided by the University of the South Pacific, which was established as a regional university to serve the south Pacific area and not exclusively Fiji. The first preliminary courses began in February of 1969 as a preparation for south Pacific islanders wanting to study for degree and diploma courses. 'Prior to the initiation of the teacher education course at the University of the South Pacific in 1969, Fiji was completely dependent upon teachers trained overseas; this group included students from Fiji as well as expatriates' (Fiji Education Commission, 1969:31).

The major problem facing both primary and secondary levels concerns the quality of teachers. This too has been a legacy from colonial times, as to cope with the increasing numbers of pupils, untrained ('licensed') teachers have had to be employed where there was an insufficient number of trained teachers. This problem has been exacerbated subsequently by the increase in secondary schools, particularly in the period 1965–75. During that time enrolments also increased by 43.6 per cent at the primary level, and a dramatic 275.4 per cent at the secondary level (Hopkin, 1978:111). This put a great strain on the teaching service, and led to an increased number of untrained teachers with poor academic qualifications being placed in classrooms at both levels. The Fiji Education Commission noted in 1969 (pp. 30–31) that in the period between 1960 and 1968 the number of untrained primary teachers had increased from 391 to 679. The number of untrained secondary teachers in the same period increased from 87 to 199.

The Commission's comments in 1969 reflected its concern at the situation resulting from the dilution of the teaching service's quality by untrained or undertrained teachers: 'It became very evident to the Commission that, in many schools, inadequately prepared teachers are providing a low quality of education in Fiji. Even though many of these teachers are conscientious, their limited knowledge makes it impossible for them to be effective.' Despite the government's efforts at upgrading the standards and qualifications of teachers, the problem is still affecting the quality of the teaching service. In 1976, 5 927 teachers were employed in Fijian schools. Of these 1 128 or 19 per cent were untrained (Ministry of Education, Youth and Sport, 1978:2).

The teachers' organizations

The dualism so evident in Fiji is further institutionalized in the two teachers' organizations. These are the Fijian Teachers' Association (FTA) and the Fiji Teachers' Union (FTU). Originally, in the early 1930s, there was one union with membership drawn from all racial/ethnic groups. However, problems developed between Fijian and Indian members, partly because of geographical reasons. The Fijian teachers were mainly located in rural schools and the Indian teachers concentrated in urban areas. Neither group could understand the other's problems, with the result that the Fijians broke away in the 1940s and formed the Fijian Teachers' Association. Its membership is limited by its constitution to Fijians, part-Fijians, and teachers married to Fijians. Teachers from other ethnic groups are excluded. The current President, Esiteri Kamikamica, went to some pains to stress, in discussion, that the exclusive membership was not a racial matter, but was intended to spell out what being Fijian means, in terms of self-identity as an indigenous group, and what contribution Fijian teachers might make to their own community.

In contrast, the Fiji Teachers' Union is open to teachers from all racial/ethnic groups but tends to be dominated by Indians. It is also more 'political' in approach and until recently its President was a political figure such as a Member of Parliament or a lawyer, both of whom could also be part-time teachers. This is a bone of contention for the FTA, which has a more 'professional' approach and elects a non-political Committee and President. Both organizations tend to come together on issues of pay, teaching conditions and other 'gut issues' but are separate on fundamental issues of race and membership.

A final component in the pattern, noted by Whitehead (1975:278), is an environmental one:

> The precise nature of Fiji's education system has been determined by the geographical layout of the territory, the mixed racial composition and contrasting cultural backgrounds of the population, and by the legacies of British colonial education policy. The far-flung distribution of the Fijian islands has always posed a communication problem and necessitated the building of many small schools, while racial distinctions have given rise to segregated schooling and frequently to wasteful duplication of facilities.

Ideologies and ideologists

The government ideology

The basic issues underlying the government ideology concerning the nature of Fijian society have been promulgated by prominent government leaders. The Right Honourable Ratu Sir Kamisese Mara, the Prime Minister of Fiji, has consistently highlighted two themes in many of his speeches during the last decade. The first theme, frequently expressed in homely metaphors, stresses the multiracial nature of Fijian society. The second theme, which largely complements the first, is the need for national unity and nation-building.

Addressing those present at the *Fiji Times* centennial dinner, the Prime Minister commented: 'Here, in our multiracial community, where we are striving to maintain harmony and tolerance among our peoples, the press has a grave responsibility to ensure that it does not undermine these efforts either wittingly or unwittingly' (Mara, 1977:78). It was probably not a coincidence that his remarks were addressed to the press — a strong agency of ideology management — in a plea to have the ideology supported.

Religious occasions have been used to promote the ideology. During the Hindu Festival of Lights (*Diwali*) in October 1967 the same multiracial theme was stressed by the Prime Minister in an address to the Suva Merchants' Club. In this case, an attempt was made to specify and legitimate the ideology by spelling it out in more detail (1977:28):

> What we want is not a dull enforced homogeneity, but all the wealth of diversity, with each culture retaining its own individuality, but all blending together to form a variegated pattern — a kaleidoscope if you like — to enrich the whole.

In 1978, the same Festival was made the occasion for several public rehearsals of the ideology, by means of the mass media. The Governor General's Diwali greetings — reported in the *Fiji Times*, 30 October 1978 — included the opinion that 'We in Fiji have enjoyed a record of multiracial harmony and prosperity to which all sections of this multiracial, multi-religious community has [*sic*] contributed'. The Minister for Labour, Ratu David Toganivalu, spoke against any assimilationist tendency in Fiji, and came closer to multiculturalism in his plea for diversity (*Fiji Times*, 1 November 1978, p. 3), possibly as a counter to the newly proposed integrationist ideology by the F.T.U.:

> We don't want to lose what is distinctive in any of our cultures in Fiji. We can only enrich our whole culture by learning more about each culture.
>
> I don't have much sympathy with the idea that we should lose our Fijian or Fiji-Indian, or Chinese, or Rotuman, or Christian, or Muslim culture in one big mush that is lifeless and tasteless.

Expressions of the official ideology have not been necessarily confined to members of the ruling political party. During the constitutional negotiations that preceded independence there appears to have been a tacit agreement between the two main political parties to push for the good of Fiji as a whole over narrow factionalism. The Leader of the Opposition, S.M. Koya, supported Ratu Mara's plea to preserve multiracial harmony (Mara, 1977:6). At the time of Diwali in 1978, the Honourable Mrs I.J. Narayan, MP, further elaborated aspects of Fijian pluralism (*Fiji Times*, 30 October 1978, p. 28): 'In Fiji's multiracial, multi-religions [*sic*] and multilingual community we have a proud record of living in peace and harmony for the last one hundred years.'

Nation-building, the other main theme in the Prime Minister's speeches, is often coupled with the multiracial ideology. For instance, in a radio broadcast on the eve of independence on 9 October 1970, Ratu Mara stressed the need for the races in Fiji to work together harmoniously for the good of the whole (Mara, 1977:13). At an address at the opening of the Conference of Principals of Secondary Schools,

11 May 1976, the theme was given greater specification (1977:55):

> First of all, we are trying to weave the fabric of one nation from many varying strands — strands differing in race, language, culture and religion. Now, success in such handiwork is not achieved by trying to impose a dull uniformity on all the threads — indeed the very threads would reject it — and in any case what a drab picture would emerge. No. Success and the fullest exploitation of all our assets is to be achieved by the closeness of the weave and the blending of all the varieties, so that the inherent good points of all are fully utilized to provide a rich and varied texture.

Ratu Mara's weaving analogy recalls the richness of the metaphors used in describing the Canadian 'mosaic'. It seems to be almost impossible to bring out what one means by 'multiracial' without employing these kinds of literary devices, almost as if the multiracial concept defies description, or, possibly, is imperfectly understood by its advocates.

The concept of culture is another trap for the unwary, and is mentioned by Ratu Mara in relation to 'doing culture' in schools. In a speech opening Pacific Week at the University of the South Pacific in May 1976, the Prime Minister referred to the wrong approach to cultural studies in schools, and suggested that teachers were making a gimmick out of culture (1977:90):

> I get the feeling for example, here in Fiji, that Fijian culture is a subject with capital letters, set apart perhaps for two periods of the week when children are taught about the presentation of *tabua* and *yagona* and perhaps *meke*. And yet, I am surprised and disappointed to find that students are not taught planting, fishing, housebuilding and the like. These are all part of the total culture of the people. . . . What we would like to see our schools doing, and so far as it can our university, is teaching our local culture in all its facets.

Educational organizations

Multiracialism and nationhood may comprise the dominant ideology, but, with one or two notable exceptions such as the Fiji Education Commission, insufficient detail is provided to indicate how it is to be implemented in practice. Its report (1969:8) *Education for Modern Fiji* saw education as 'related to the aspirations of the people' — the nationhood theme. From the representations it received, the Commission was of the opinion 'that there exists in Fiji a common and strong desire to see established a system of education that will promote the cultural, social, economic and political development of the several races as a single nation'. Nation-building, as a collective responsibility, would be achieved through 'bringing together children of different ethnic origins from an early age to study under one common roof, and not by having separate communal schools'. In the school curriculum, history and geography should be pressed into service to build a sense of national awareness and pride, and to promote national unity.

The less materialistic aim of cultural and social development was seen to be as important as economic development for the country. 'A country without culture is a country without soul' (1969:11). But it is clear that the Commission had in mind the more aesthetic aspects of culture — Fijian language and literature, and folk lore — rather than the more technical connotations referred to by Ratu Mara above. According to the Commission (1969:11): 'In a multi-racial society, provision should also be made to promote cross-cultural studies. The strength of Fiji seems to lie in her rich variety of cultures; a meeting point of indigenous Fijian culture with those of Western Europe and Southern Asia.'

Members of the Ministry of Education, Youth and Sport have the task of re-stating and specifying the official ideology. This is often done at public gatherings of teachers and other educationists. Examples of the opportunities taken to spread or clarify some of the more practical implications of the official ideology are provided by the speeches of Hari Ram, the Deputy Secretary, Professional, in the Ministry. In a paper presented to a seminar of Education Officers in 1974 (Ram, 1974), Hari Ram presented Fiji's national and educational goals as the basis for discussion of the qualities needed in those who operate the education system. These goals are:

(i)   to develop Fiji into a progressive, peaceful and prosperous multiracial nation, with a diversity of cultures, and to promote cross-cultural understanding and tolerance;
(ii) to improve the country's economy with a particular regard to the need to reduce the gap between the rural and urban sectors of the population.

A second opportunity for the Deputy Secretary to legitimate the ideology was afforded by the 45th Annual Conference of the Fiji Teachers' Union (Ram, 1975:29):

> We have a large body of experience in multiracial education and our experience suggests that, by and large, children who have been educated in multiracial schools are better prepared for life in our society than those who have not. One of our important future priorities should be the enhancement of the multiracial character of our educational institutions wherever possible.

In the opinion of Krishna Datt, a past-President of the Union, such devices as the journal, reports of annual conferences, and even the President's yearly report, are all important ways by which official policy may be elaborated and the ideology converted into practical action. However, it is far from evident, from the literature on education in general and on teacher education in particular, just how much flow-on from the multiracial ideology to concrete practice is occurring in the schools and colleges.

Several members of the Curriculum Development Unit said that the interpretation of multiracialism was more a question of feeling one's way, rather than of following well-documented policy guidelines. Only very recently have the implications of multiracialism been spelled out, but in cultural terms that seem almost to constitute a counter-ideology and, consequently, will be considered as such in the following section. Logically, the development of harmonious inter-racial attitudes and relationships necessitates appropriate training, with an emphasis on affective domain education rather than on the cognitive domain. It is one thing to advocate multiracial harmony, but quite another to set up programmes that will implement it.

The examination system, into which Fijian education is still locked, militates not only against the above aims, but also against a full-scale development of the type of education necessitated by a multiracial ideology. The Ministry of Education, Youth and Sport, is aware of the problem, which is explicitly recognized in the Seventh Development Plan 1976–1980 (DP7, 1975:174):

> The old system selected and moulded a small group of academically superior pupils in a system of increasingly stringent examinations, with a majority of pupils falling by the way side on the way to the top. The new aim is to provide an appropriate and relevant form of education and training whether formal or non-formal, for every individual.

However, as Hopkin points out (1978:115), the external examinations still exercise considerable control over the curriculum:

> External examinations are set by the Education Department at Class 5, Class 8 (or Form 2) and Form 4; at Form 5 and 6 the School Certificate and University Entrance examinations are set by New Zealand and British authorities. . . . The educational results are unfortunate. Rote teaching methods predominate, little emphasis is placed upon creating learning situations orientated to students, 'academic' studies of the worst kind are pursued and an increasing number of students, teachers and the public are expressing dissatisfaction with the irrelevant curricula and orientation of schooling.

Perhaps the root cause of the mismatch between ideology and educational practice has to do with a lack of awareness of the connection between the education system in general, curriculum planning and development in particular, and the types of sociological and philosophical value judgements that have to be made about society. This, however, does not apply to all those who are involved in curriculum planning. The comments of Gurmit Singh, formerly Principal Education Officer (Curriculum) in the Ministry, and now Principal of Lautoka Teachers's College, show his awareness of the conceptual link between society and curriculum (Singh, 1978:123):

> A curriculum development programme has to take cognisance of the milieu in which it operates — in Fiji this is a particularly complex one. Socio-cultural, political and economic factors have, to date, rendered the programme particularly vulnerable to attack, and this has hampered progress. . . . If a clear conceptual framework which took the milieu into account were established, evaluation would be more effective, and the prospects for the successful development of the total curriculum programme and its component parts would be enhanced.

Counter-ideologies and ideologists

It is difficult to identify counter-ideologies and counter-ideologists in Fiji. This may be due, in part, to the relatively unformulated nature of the official ideology and to the fact that there are few theorists and other educationists who might evolve counter-ideologies. Consequently, these seem even more exploratory than the official ideology. Despite this difficulty, two tentative educational movements seem to be evolving. The first advocates an integrated society, but may be short-lived. The second is multiculturalism, which seems likely to become the dominant ideology of the future.

The political background

The ideological nature of the socio-political scene outside education needs to be noted. In the opinion of Dr Ahmed Ali (1977:4 & f.m.), allegiances to political party power matter most in Fiji, and tend to dominate other considerations. At the time of the 1977 general election, a major disruption occurred to the pattern of political dualism which we have seen to be a feature of Fijian government, with the emergence into the political arena of the Fijian Nationalist Party (FNP), which had been formed in 1976. Its leader, Sakiasi Butadroka, directed his appeal solely to Fijians, broadcast only in Fijian, and refused to provide Hindi and English translations of his speeches (Ali, 1977:4 & n.). His ideas were diametrically opposed to Prime Minister Mara's multiracialism. They stressed, among other things, that 'the interests of the Fijians will be paramount at all times', and that 'Indians should be repatriated to India after Fiji gained full independence' (1977:4–5). Other measures advocated were the return to Fijians of all land that had been illegally sold, and the provision of more opportunities for Fijians to catch up with other racial groups in such areas as business and commerce.

The efforts of the FNP revealed the power and depth of Fijian nationalism, and injected a strong element of anti-Indian racism into politics, features which run counter to the multiracial harmony so assiduously cultivated by the Prime Minister. They also had the effect, at least at the time, of setting up tensions between the Alliance Party and the National Federation Party which may have weakened the carefully institutionalized racial dualism in government. The emergence of Fijian nationalism in what appears to be more of a groundswell of public opinion, fostered for political purposes, than a clearly articulated ideology, demonstrates that the multiracial society model of Fijian society is not without its challengers.

The integrated model

The theme of the 46th Annual Conference of the Fiji Teachers' Union, held in May 1976, was 'Education and an Integrated Society'. The theme is an intriguing one since judging from the history of countries such as the United States, integration as a societal goal has followed assimilation in a form of conceptual evolution, and precedes multi-racialism, multiculturalism and so on. For Fijian educationists to be thinking about achieving an integrated society now, would appear to be a retrograde movement.

As set out in an editorial, (Fiji Teachers' Union, 1976:4–5), it seems that the Union itself is the instigator of this new counter-ideology, because of its concern 'with the way separate societies are being developed in Fiji. It is a matter of concern that communalism is on the increase.' The essence of the pluralist dilemma — individual autonomy versus the collective good — is appreciated by the Union, which states its opinion on this issue:

> The Fiji Teachers' Union affirms that in all societies, while there should be freedom and equality, social control is necessary so that the teachers can work confidently towards building a truly integrated society.

> The Union strongly reaffirms its determination to work for the formation of a truly integrated society in Fiji. And towards these objectives the FTU fully recognises the fundamental task of the teacher in the advancement of society and the development of the individual.

Dr Maraj, Vice Chancellor of the University of the South Pacific, gave a key address that was somewhat critical of the concept of integration and an integrated society (Maraj, 1976:9):

> When I saw your theme 'Education and an Integrated Society' I could not help asking myself whether too much was not being demanded and expected or even promised on the part of education. . . . I get the feeling that perhaps what is expected is that by reorganization, or a new pedagogy, or revised syllabuses and so on, we shall arrive at the Utopia of an integrated society.

The Vice Chancellor issued a number of cautions about the difficulties of the pluralism concept, and supported those 'people [who] have said that attention ought to be focussed deliberately on some of the strengths of pluralism rather than its weaknesses and if this is done people might come better to appreciate one another' (1976:12). To bring about a closer relationship between educational efforts and society, Dr Maraj also proposed that education should be much more concerned with community service.

The 46th Union Council of the Fiji Teachers' Union took up this issue and resolved to organize a symposium to find ways and means of promoting and administering such service to community programmes (Fiji Teachers' Union, 1976:4). It also proposed that the Ministry of Education, Youth and Sport should find ways and means of organizing programmes similar to the Pacific Week for the students of Fiji. The editorial considered that the symposium and the programmes are necessary in Fiji because of a number of 'prevailing conditions'. These are merely listed, without supporting evidence as if they are self-evident:

Firstly, the role of education in forming an integrated society is minimal.

Secondly, the desirability of an integrated society in the commonly accepted meaning equating integration with assimilation is being questioned.

Thirdly, education in itself has been seen in some societies to have led to disintegration.

Fourthly, the entire issue of education and an integrated society is a matter for much deeper and careful study and analysis.

Fifthly, intergration [*sic*] pertains largely to the affective domain.

And sixthly, we have not been able to use our human resources to promote and administer the 'service to the community programmes' that the Vice Chancellor of the University, Dr James Maraj outlined during his theme address at the 46th Annual Conference.

Multiculturalism

The concept of multiculturalism and the aim of education to achieve a multicultural society have begun to appear in the literature only very recently. In discussion, Dr Ahmed Ali, Director of the Institute of Social and Administrative Studies, USP, said that he would prefer to use the word multicultural, as it is accidental that race has become an issue in the Fijian situation, and the problem is much more subtle than a bi-racial situation. A great deal of the problem concerns control over power. Fijians, in his opinion, will share power but not relinquish it. Indians, on the other hand, see that they lack involvement in the decision-making process. 'A plural society is inherently a crisis in itself when seen in terms of resources and competition for resources.' Although multiethnic might be a preferable and more accurate term, Dr Ali would not use it, as outside people would not understand what it means.

The developing trend towards the use of multicultural is due in part to the officers of the Education Department, who consider this to be the most feasible way of implementing the official ideology of the multi-racial society. As Moag has suggested (1977:15):

The Fiji Government has often stated its commitment to a multiracial society. The Education Department supports this by encouraging cross cultural themes in all new curricula. Most recently, they are considering the implementation of a nationwide program in the teaching of Fijian language to Indians and Hindi to Fijians.

An outline of this approach has been stated publicly by Mr D. Rao, Principal Education Officer, in the 'lead' paper presented at a PEACESAT seminar 'Secondary Education of the Youth of Fiji', on 27 September 1978:

In our multiracial society, there is a wealth of diverse cultures. My government is presently engaged in promoting 'cross-cultural' studies at primary as
well as secondary levels. It is important that each ethnic group understands
and appreciates the culture and language of the others.[3]

Again, as in the Canadian situation, we can note the free juxtaposition
of the terms 'multi-racial', 'cross-cultural', and 'ethnic group' without
regard for the fact that *technically* they are not entirely compatible
when used together in some kinds of arguments.

The work of the Curriculum Development Unit in Suva appears to
have adopted a cross-cultural emphasis on the assumption — possible
simplistically — that the school curriculum reflects the multicultural
nature of Fiji. Implicit in this approach is the philosophy that increasing children's knowledge about each other's backgrounds through
cross-cultural studies will lead to an increase in racial tolerance. An
example of this approach is to be found in the programmes of geography, history and social science being prepared by members of the
Unit. According to Mohammed Kalaam, Senior Education Officer
(History), a cross-cultural interaction programme is being developed
for Form 5 (grade 11), to encourage children to arrive at their own
values. He pointed out that CDU programmes and development in
schools were not stressed until the 1970s; borrowed material from
Britain and New Zealand had been used instead. The Ministry of
Education, Youth and Sport opted for change in the 1970s. It decided
to include more local content, and to re-examine the official policy
which at times was multiracial. The CDU tended to re-interpret this
ideology as multiculturalism and develop the cross-cultural programmes. Much of its recent research work has been concerned with
producing an integrated social science programme for Form 1, rather
than separate syllabuses for history and geography.

The guidelines for the new programmes were set out in mimeographed circulars from the Ministry of Education, and grew out of discussions with the Education Advisory Council (Education Department
Fiji, 1972). In 1972, the decision was made to prepare two types of
vernacular/cultural studies syllabuses in Forms 1 and 2. Their
philosophy is set out in Section 11.2 of the 1972 circular:

Certain aspects of the course will aim specifically to enable children
(a) to develop an awareness of those aspects of culture which are common
     to all cultures;
(b) to understand the chief factors underlying variations in cultures;
(c) to understand the problems that could arise when groups of people with
     different cultures interact; and
(d) to develop religious tolerance.

When Gurmit Singh was Principal Education Officer (Curriculum) he
apparently favoured the multicultural ideology (Singh, 1975:46):

One of the greatest assets of a multi-cultural society like ours is the great store of diverse cultural patterns in thought and behaviours. The diverse cultural backgrounds of our students enable them to perceive elements in the environment somewhat differently and attempts should be made to use this hitherto unused diversity in perception to advantage.

It would seem that old ideas die hard, however, judging from the article 'The Changing Primary Curriculum in Fiji', which appeared in the following year (Singh, 1976:36) and states that the proposed basal readers in Hindi 'will be based on research, and Fiji's multi-racial society will be taken into consideration'.

More recently still, the multicultural emphasis is re-stated in a way that shows Singh's keen awareness of key issues in curriculum development (Singh, 1978:121):

> To date the progress made in producing and using new materials has been uneven. . . . Progress made in different subject areas reflects the socio-cultural factors that exist in a multicultural community such as Fiji, and not the competence of those responsible for the curriculum development programme.

Much of the discussion about the kind of education most suitable for Fijian conditions has centred on the desirability of children learning a second language. In passing, it should be noted that a similar concern is also a feature of discussions in Canada and Australia. It is the kind of issue that inevitably involves some consideration of the type of society for which children are being educated. This problem has been carefully analysed by Dr R. Moag, a former Visiting Fulbright Fellow in Linguistics at the University of the South Pacific (Moag, 1977:18):

> Fiji today is unquestionably multiracial and multicultural, but will it remain so? Doubtless the path of emphasizing English and developing a single unified culture is the cheaper course in monitary [*sic*] terms. But there is also a human side of life. People in many multicultural nations are now beginning to think that the benefits in human terms justify the higher monitary cost. They point to the values gained in terms of cultural richness and variety instead of the problems inherent in multiculturalism. . . .

> What kind of society this country is to have is a decision which must be made by the people of Fiji and their representatives, the government officials and policy planners, not by outsiders such as I. If the decision is for multiculturalism as well as multiracialism, as it seems from public pronouncements to be, then the type of second language program must be decided on and implemented very soon, before forces at work further erode Fijian and Indian cultures.

Moag's comments stem from the distinction he makes in the article between multiracialism and multiculturalism. By the former he means a society comprising people who represent more than one race, or combination of races, but in which there is only one language and one culture. When differences occur in these latter aspects, then the society is also multicultural. Moag's description of Fiji as multiracial and multicultural is thus quite logical in the context of this argument.

Tupeni Baba, of the School of Education, University of the South Pacific, has also adopted a cultural perspective to which he has added the idea of a multiethnic society. He is critical of the multiracial ideology, which he sees as mainly a politically expedient concept. In practice, the way it is being achieved is through a pragmatic government policy of institutionalized dualism and separation of the two main racial groups. One of the effects of this policy, noted above, has been the stress laid on producing sufficient qualified Fijians 'to occupy a "due share" of top and middle level positions in the public and private sections of the economy' (Baba, 1978:1). The 50:50 racial policy of allocating scholarships in the University of the South Pacific's Foundation year, however, could well be seen as blatant discrimination by non-Fijians. 'In any multi-ethnic community, the acceptance of any measure of affirmative action usually depends on the goodwill of other members of the community, a commodity which is not always inexhaustible, and which if eroded or lost, could hardly be regained' (1978:4).

Teacher training ideologies

The three major teacher training organizations apparently have not developed explicit ideologies. The Handbook of the School of Education in the University of the South Pacific makes no specific reference to wider considerations about Fijian society that might have guided its curriculum, apart from the general comment by the Head of School, Professor William Maxwell (1978:2) that 'all Societies face many problems'. There is no specific reference, however, to those that might face Fiji.

Nasinu Teachers' College in Suva is the larger of the two government training organizations, with a total student roll in excess of 400, balanced evenly between Fijians and Indians and including a few students from other groups. Among the objectives of the College (Nasinu Teachers' College Fiji, 1978:13), the only ones which relate in some way to the nature of Fijian society are:

> The College also aims to develop in all its students the capacity to understand self-respect and respect for each other; to think and act with responsibility and independence, and to appreciate the moral, religious and social values of the community in which they operate. The College seeks to foster qualities of integrity, tolerance, flexibility, imagination, and a sympathetic commitment to human welfare and the future of Fiji.

There is no over-arching philosophy of the nature of Fijian pluralism guiding the curriculum, but the College now has a programme of cross-cultural studies. This is a compulsory provision in the official syllabus. It involves one and a half hours per week for a whole academic year, with lectures, discussions, visiting lecturers, and activities that enable students to 'practise' different cultures. The overall aim is to learn about oneself and one's own culture in addition to learning about other cultures. In addition, the students are encouraged to organize themselves so as to learn about their own cultures informally, and outside class time.

Established in 1978, the Lautoka Teachers' College initially provided a one-year course for licensed teachers. Students took a compulsory social science unit for one hour per week, part of which dealt, incidentally, with cross-cultural aspects. This policy is being maintained, but on an incidental basis. Like Nasinu Teachers' College, Lautoka College also provides extra-curricular cultural activities, based on 'cultural nights' for each main group.

The abiding impression of the situation in Fiji, both historically and in the present, is the pronounced dualism through the society, with the Indian/Fijian relationships dominating all considerations in educational policy making. Yet the society is termed *multi*cultural or more recently, *multi*ethnic. Some explanation is offered for this in the last chapter of the book. It is clear, in comparison with a larger society such as Canada, that smallness of size does not bring about a reduction in the complexity of pluralism. The Fiji case illustrates most admirably the subtleties of the factors that must be taken into account when assessing the likely effects of pluralism. Culture is often thought to be the sole determinant of pluralism, but in Fiji locality, geography, loyalty to a political ideology, region of language affiliation in the country of origin, and other aspects must all be considered, and strengthen the case for analysing through a theory of ethnicity rather than culture. This issue is taken up in the final chapter.

Notes

1. The opinion of Tupeni Baba, School of Education, University of the South Pacific.
2. Fiji Senate Debates, December 1970, p. 107.
3. PEACESAT is a satellite communication network linking Fiji with other islands and countries within the Pacific Basin (including Hawaii and New Zealand at Wellington), through which regular fortnightly seminars 'on the air' are organized. Mr Rao's paper is in mimeographed form.

CHAPTER 5

The United States

The United States has long been the major source of innovations and trends in pluralist education. All of the important concepts have originated there, and it is to the United States that most educationists look for the most recent ideas. This chapter attempts to cover both past and present theories and concepts.

The socio-historical context

The current demographic pattern

Based on latest available data, the total population of the United States according to the 1970 census was 203 212 000 people. Table 7 classifies these according to race and by urban or rural residence. In 1973 the total population was 206 295 000 persons.[1]

TABLE 7 Population, by race and by urban or rural residence 1970

	Total (000s)	Urban	Rural
White	177 749	128 773	48 976
Negro	22 580	18 367	4 213
Indian	793	256	437
Japanese	591	524	68
Chinese	435	419	16
Filipino	343	293	50
Other*	721	593	127
Totals of racial groups	203 212	149 325	53 887

Source: *Current Population Reports* Series P-20 and unpublished data. (U.S. Department of Commerce, Bureau of the Census, 1976:21).
* Other: Aleuts, Asian Indians, Eskimos, Hawaians, Indonesians, Koreans, Polynesians and other races not shown separately.

With the exception of native American Indians each racial group shows a preponderance of urban dwellers, with Chinese (96.3 per cent) being the most urbanized, followed by Japanese (88.7 per cent), Filipino (85.4 per cent), Negro (81.3 per cent). Whites are comparatively less urbanized (72.4 per cent).

Both 'race' and 'ethnic origin' are determined for census purposes on the basis of self-classification by the person according to how he perceives his origin or classification to be. Using this criterion, table 8 gives figures for the major ethnic groups as at 1973.

TABLE 8 Population by ethnic origin, 1973

	Total (000s)	%
	206 295	
English	25 993	12.6
French	3 939	1.9
German	20 517	9.9
Irish	12 240	5.9
Italian	7 101	3.4
Polish	3 686	1.8
Russian	1 747	0.85
Spanish	10 557*	5.1
Mexican	6 293	(3.1)
Puerto Rican	1 548	(0.75)
Other	97 593	47.3
Not reported	22 902	11.1

Source: *Current Population Reports*, series P-20, no. 264, and unpublished data (U.S. Department of Commerce, Bureau of the Census, 1977:30)
* Includes persons of Central or South American, Cuban, and other Spanish origin, not shown separately.

Two racial or ethnic groups have tended to dominate educational thinking about disadvantaged children: the Negro and the Spanish groups. Table 9 gives details of the Black population by region and residence in 1975. Table 10 shows the residence pattern of people of Spanish origin.

In the thinking of most educationists in the field of education for the disadvantaged, the most important demographic feature is the concentration of both Negro and Spanish groups in metropolitan areas. Three-quarters of Blacks live there, and 83.9 per cent of Spanish speakers. Of the latter the greatest concentration in metropolitan areas, particularly the central cities, is of Puerto Ricans. In contrast, nearly a quarter of Mexicans live outside metropolitan areas. Educational and social deprivations of Blacks and Puerto Ricans are largely 'centre-city problems'. Major conurbations such as New York, Chicago, Washington, and San Francisco contain large concentrations of both racial/ethnic groups largely as a result of internal migration (Griffith et al., 1960:186–89):

> No single factor has had a greater effect on the status of the Negro in America and race relations in general than the great migrations of Negroes

TABLE 9   Black population in the United States, by region and residence, 1975 (percentage distribition)

Region	%
North	39
North-east	18
North Central	20
South	52
West	9
Residence	
Metropolitan areas	75
Central cities	58
Outside central cities	17
Non-metropolitan areas	25

Source: *Current Population Reports*, forthcoming report in the P-23 series. (U.S. Department of Commerce, Bureau of the Census, 1977:30)

TABLE 10   Residences of families of Spanish origin in 1976, (percentage distribution)

Residence	Total %	Mexican %	Puerto Rican %	Other* %
Metropolitan areas	83.9	76.8	97.4	90.8
Central cities	51.7	43.1	82.0	50.4
Non-metropolitan areas	16.1	23.2	2.6	9.2

Source: *Current Population Reports*, series P-20, no. 302, and unpublished data. (U.S. Department of Commerce, Bureau of the Census, 1977:30).
* Includes persons of Central or South American, Cuban, and other Spanish origin, not shown separately.

from the south to the north and west, which have produced a most profound displacement over a period of about two generations. . . . It is not only a regional shift but a move from rural to urban areas.

The Negro migration waves began in 1915, slackened during the depression period of the 1930s, accelerated again in the decade 1940–50, and are continuing in the current period (1960:190–91). In contrast, the migration to the mainland that has resulted in concentrations of Puerto Ricans in the major cities is a post-1950 phenomenon, so that 'a relatively new population has been added to the "high visibility" minority group' (1960:186). In addition, concentrations of Chicanos (Spanish-speaking persons of Mexican descent) have built up in the five south-western states.

Socio-economic, 'class' structure

Negroes and Puerto Ricans are two of the racial/ethnic groups that rank low in socio-economic status. Here their 'visibility' has played an important role (1960:186):

> . . . the rate of upward status movement has differed for the various minority and immigrant groups. It is in general in inverse ratio to darkness of skin. Immigrants from England and northern Europe rank highest in the scale of preference and status mobility, and Orientals, Mexicans, Puerto Ricans, Indians and Negroes are on the lower end of the scale. Negroes were among the early groups coming to the American continent, and they remain the group with perhaps the lowest rate of social mobility and with an almost chronic identification as a minority group.

Some indication of the socio-economic status of Negroes and other non-white groups is shown by table 11. It gives selected major occupational categories for these groups in comparison with whites, and clearly indicates that the former occupy the lower status occupations. Even though Negroes and others perform similar occupations to whites, they do so in lesser proportion in the case of high status categories, and are proportionally over-represented in low status categories.

TABLE 11 Employed persons, by selected occupational categories and race, 1976.

Category	White %	Black and other %
White collar workers	51.8	34.7
Professional, technical and kindred workers	15.7	11.7
Managers, administrators, excluding farm managers	11.4	4.4
Salesworkers	6.7	2.5
Clerical workers	18.0	16.1
Blue collar workers	32.6	37.6
Craft and kindred workers	13.4	8.7
Operatives	14.6	20.5
Non-farm labourers	4.5	8.3
Service workers	12.3	25.4
Farm-workers	3.3	2.3

Source: U.S. Bureau of Labour Statistics, *Employment and Earnings*, monthly. (U.S. Department of Commerce, Bureau of the Census, 1977:407)

The lower status of Negro and Spanish-speaking groups is shown by comparison of their annual incomes with those of whites. Figures for these (U.S. Department of Commerce, Bureau of the Census, 1974:383) show that the median income of white families in 1973 was US$12 595 compared with the median income of Negro and other families of US$7 596. That is, Negro families earn slightly less than two-thirds (0.6) of the white income.

The general status ranking of ethnic groups is illustrated by the earnings of a selected number of groups. Table 12 provides figures for the median family income in 1972, and it is apparent that Spanish-speaking (Hispanic) ethnics, and particularly Puerto Ricans, rank lowest.

TABLE 12   Median Family income by ethnic origin, selected groups, 1972

Total	*$11 233*
English	12 278
French	10 877
German	12 217
Irish	11 518
Italian	12 520
Polish	13 069
Russian	14 627
Spanish*	8 183
Mexican	7 908
Puerto Rican	7 163
Other	10 856
Not reported	9 886

Source: US Bureau of the Census, *Current Population Reports*, series P-20, no. 264, and unpublished data.
* Includes persons of Central or South American, Cuban, and other Spanish origin, not shown separately.

The relationship between socio-economic status and the urban concentration of the Negro and Puerto Rican groups is the subject of a report produced by the National Center for Urban Ethnic Affairs, which is based in Washington, DC (Baroni & Green, 1976). The report is based on a comparative analysis of 87 white, black and Hispanic centre-city neighbourhoods in 18 metropolitan areas. The neighbourhoods in this sample are all working class, of low and moderate income, have large concentrations of poor people, and are located in the older industrial cities of the north-east, mid-Atlantic and mid-west regions of the nation.

However, the problem for Blacks and Spanish-speaking groups is not exclusively a socio-economic one in such neighbourhoods, as there is the additional factor of discrimination keeping both groups in a subordinate position. Baroni and Green note (1976:iv):

> Black and Hispanic mean incomes are similar in spite of much higher levels of black educational attainment. This appears to constitute strong evidence in support of black claims of massive discrimination.

Historical context

Internal migration and its results

With the cessation of the major waves of immigrants from overseas in the 1800s and early 1900s, which have formed the basic stock of the American population, the more recent period, particularly post-World War II, has been concerned mainly with the results of internal migration. Its corollary has been the emergence of civil rights movements and legislation to ameliorate the condition of those minority groups, which have come to occupy the lowest ranks of the socio-economic scale through a discriminatory, sorting process of the kind described by Hunter (1974:14):

> Migrations throughout the United States of Puerto Ricans, Mexican Americans, Black Americans, and Native Americans brought on second-generation discrimination and the outright practice of open and legalized segregation. The Italians, Slavs, Greeks, and Jews who were looked down on by the Irish, Germans, and Scandinavians, who were in turn looked down on by the English or others of Anglo-Saxon origin — all looked down on, discriminated against, and segregated the color-visible groups — particularly Blacks (who also had been recently subject to slavery), Chicanos, Native Americans, and Puerto Ricans.

Paradoxically, this result is the antithesis of the idealism and reverence for universal human rights that had motivated the early colonizers of America.

One of the major concerns in education has been to find means through schooling to remedy the effects of this discrimination on children from minority groups. It has led to the adoption of a variety of ideologies and models aiming to conceptualize the forces at work and suggest educational strategies to cope with their effects. In this task, the fundamental idealism and optimism so characteristic of the American educational ethos has been marshalled to combat those discreditable tendencies in society which work against the ideals of the American founding fathers. An accompanying tendency has been to discard models and concepts as soon as they have been shown to be unsatisfactory, and to evolve hopefully more powerful ones. Such conceptual evolution in a search for *the* solution appears to have become one of the major characteristics of the American educational scene since the Second World War.

This is largely due to educationists' efforts to master what may be an intractable problem.

> A fundamental question hangs over the American scene, namely: Why is there racial and group discrimination and segregation in a nation whose traditions have been nurtured in the Judaeo-Christian ideal of the sacredness of the individual and whose political and social institutions have grown out of the democratic ideal of human freedom? (Griffith et al., 1960:187)

The same writers suggest that Gunnar Myrdal has given the best and clearest answer to this problem in a publication aptly titled *The American Dilemma: The Negro Problem and Modern Democracy (1944)*, by pointing to the 'conflict between the American ideal of democracy, fair play and justice, on the one hand, and American practices on the other'. A great deal of the constant search for new models and ideologies on the part of educationists may well be in response to the challenge of this dilemma. Their search is not being made easier by the lack of consensus at the national level over the treatment of racial and ethnic minorities. 'At no time in the history of American racial and minority group experience . . . could the nation be described as having a clearly-committed national policy on race which was thoroughly consistent with the democratic ideals expressed in the Declaration of Independence and the Constitution' (Griffith et al., 1960:187).

Changing definitions of the situation in minority group issues

A feature of the American experience has been the way changes have taken place historically in official definitions of racial and minority group issues (Griffith et al., 1960:182−85). They have set the background 'climate' for educational thinking and its related ideologies about pluralism. Until recently, probably at least as late as the mid-1960s, the race and ethnic minority issue was seen by sociologists, educationists, and in common parlance, in terms of a problem faced by one or the other racial or ethnic group. Terms such as the 'Negro problem', the 'Jewish problem', the 'Catholic problem' stressed this orientation, but also inferred 'that the groups were themselves the essential problem, due to fixed characteristics peculiar to them and to their backwardness. Consequently, much of the earlier ameliorative effort was inclined to be paternalistic in the form of action *for* the Negro and other dispossessed groups, although it was inspired by motives of justice and religious idealism' (1960:182−83). In education this approach generated a vast programme of compensatory schemes and projects with the underlying philosophy of catering for children from groups who were deprived or disadvantaged, largely due to their own fault.

In race relations changes took place in these ideas in the late 1940s, somewhat earlier than they occurred in education, and it is comparatively rare to find the group-oriented, paternalistic stance in recent literature. Griffith et al., (1960:183) comment:

> In place of group-centred definitions of the issues, there is now a new language of which the expressions 'problem of Negro-white relations', 'problem of Jewish-Gentile relations', 'problem of minority-majority group relations' are characteristic. . . . The essential problem lies in the relations between the interacting groups, and these aspects, in turn, have to do with the policies, practices and attitudes which define and sustain group status. Accordingly, the problem of race relations shifts from a group focus to a policy and practice focus.

A further 'subtle though significant change in definition' noted by the same authors is the 'widespread substitution of the term "human relations" for that of "race relations" ' (1960:183).

Perhaps the most important change, inaugurated by the passage of the federal Civil Rights Act in 1957, has been the emergence of a new stage in American race relations known as the 'Civil Rights Era' (1960:185). This generated the civil rights movement pushed by the Black communities, but also affecting Chicano and Puerto Rican groups whose youth were concerned to obtain improved education. The movement spilled over into schooling.

The civil rights movement was followed in the late 1960s and 1970s by a wider phenomenon involving 'white ethnics' in addition to racial groups. It is known variously as the 'new ethnicity', 'new pluralism', or the 'ethnic revitalization movement'. The essence of this has been described by Glazer and Moynihan (1975:2–3) as:

> A new social category . . . [marked by] a pronounced and sudden increase in the tendencies by people in many countries and in many circumstances to insist on the significance of their group distinctiveness and identity and on new rights that derive from this group character.

Historical models of society

Parallel with these evolving definitions of the situation there has also been an historical evolution of views about American society and its constituent groups, as Hunter notes (1974:12):

> America has perceived the character of its society and the roles of its different peoples in different ways. The historical choice open to members of disparate cultures or communities has been to assimilate and disappear into the mainstream of the American Anglo-Saxon character of society or to be isolated and relegated to second-class citizenship — or no citizenship at all, as in the case of the Native Americans.

The early period of American immigration and minority-majority relationships prior to World War 1 was characterized by an assumption that there was one American Anglo-Saxon culture to which all newcomers and indigenous ethnics should assimilate, through a process of 'Americanization' or 'Anglo-Saxonization' (Krug, 1977:6).

The fact that millions of immigrants rejected this approach led to the adoption of a more subtle form of assimilationist ideology, captured in what was probably the most striking and famous ideological metaphor in the literature about pluralism. This was the melting pot concept, first introduced in 1909 by the British writer, Israel Zangwill, in his play *The Melting Pot*.

This concept gained considerable currency, even though, as subsequent events have clearly demonstrated, it was largely a myth.

> [It] denied the supremacy of the Anglo-Saxon culture and rejected the demand that the immigrant cultures assimilate into it. Instead, Zangwill wanted *all* cultures — those of the native population and those of

immigrants — to fuse and melt in order to create a superior new and uniquely American culture. (Krug, 1977:6)

However, while many immigrants found the concept attractive and tried to 'melt', for very many others it was of dubious value (Gollnick, Klassen & Yff, 1976:3). Firstly, for many immigrants the privilege of melting or assimilating into American society was purchased at the cost of leaving behind their customs, dress, language, even to the extent of trying to get rid of their accents and Anglicizing their names. Secondly, the concept was applied selectively in practice, and discriminated against some sections of American society (Hunter, 1974:244):

> For one thing, it rejected as unmeltable many ethnic groups, including Native Americans, Blacks, Spanish speakers, and Orientals. The concept assumed that only the dominant white Anglo-Saxon Protestant culture was worth saving, and it was expected that those who wished to be absorbed by the melting pot had to surrender their own cultural heritage as the price of admission.

In the outcome, however, as Glazer and Moynihan (1963:v) concluded 'the point about the melting pot is that it did not happen'. This was partly due to historical and social forces which produced an early counter-ideology of cultural pluralism, first introduced by Dewey in 1916 and taken up some eight years later by Kallen (1924). Hunter (1974:15) describes the underlying reasons behind the genesis of the concept:

> Ethnic groups — rebuffed socially, exploited economically, ignored and disenfranchised politically — began to develop within-group institutions, agencies, and power structures for services within community areas. . . . Movement among these communities increased as education, economic development, political coalition, intermarriage, and cooperative mechanisms were needed to cope with external forces attempting domination.

> What resulted was the continual development of a different concept of nationality; a concept accommodating and dignifying subnationalities and contributing cultures. This move toward a central tendency which defined a new kind of national ethos and cultural mosaic characterized the rise of the concept 'cultural pluralism'.

In his first formulation of the concept of cultural pluralism, Kallen (1924:41) maintained that by the 1920s there was an American culture which was noble, rich, and attractive. It was also pluralist with its 'roots in the founding of America, its basic political documents . . . the frontier tradition, the way in which the American people settled on this continent, and the values they developed'. Cultural pluralism, Kallen maintained, was intrinsic to what he called 'the American Idea'. One of the implications of this was the 'Americanization' that would occur in the course of the history of immigration. He did not see this process as assimilationist, however. It seems that Kallen differentiated between external aspects of ethnicity, which could be changed, and internal or intrinsic aspects which would remain unchanged, even though the process of Americanization occurred (1924:79):

> The general notion of 'Americanization', appears to signify the adoption of the American variety of English speech, American clothes and manners, the American attitude to politics. 'Americanization' signifies, in short, the disappearance of *external* differences upon which so much race prejudice often feeds.

Krug has suggested (1977:6) that Kallen underestimated the strength of the process of Americanization, by showing that many immigrants' adjustment to America went beyond mere acceptance of the external values and mores listed by Kallen to many of the deep-seated intrinsic ones. It is important to appreciate that Kallen's ideas were essentially a counter-ideology born of the anti-immigrant legislation and climate of the early 1920s.

> [His] erudite philosophy of cultural pluralism was, on the one hand, aimed at the majority ideology of assimilation and pure Americanism. On the other hand, Kallen wished to refute the doctrine of the melting pot, which had gained great currency, especially among the liberal intellectuals of the day. (Newman, 1973:68)

Kallen himself (1956) modified his ideas by adopting a more comprehensive idea of Americanization. This meant that both native-born and foreign-born Americans would accept an 'over-arching culture' based on the 'American Idea'. Such an over-arching culture was pluralistic because it reflected the components of a pluralist society.

Kallen also appeared to take a situational view of persons' adaptation to the cultural diversity within a pluralist society, by maintaining that people can live in several cultural environments because of the fluid nature of pluralism. Despite this, as Krug points out (1977:7), Kallen did not equate cultural pluralism with 'separatism or tribalization' of American society. On the contrary, 'Unity in Diversity' was the phrase he often used to answer his native-born critics.

In one respect, Kallen did not advance beyond those who advocated the melting pot or full assimilation into American society and culture. Like them, he did not deal with the role of Blacks, Latinos, and other racial minorities in his conceptual framework of cultural pluralism. To be fully applicable to the present American situation. Kallen's ideas would have to take these neglected groups into account.

The concept of cultural pluralism, like other concepts now in use — such as multiculturalism, multicultural education, and ethnic studies — has been given varying and often conflicting interpretations and definitions, but a full treatment of these is beyong the scope of this book. In fact, all the above concepts 'are often used interchangeably or to convey different but highly ambiguous meanings' (Banks, 1977b:2). However, it is necessary to consider cultural pluralism in a little more detail as its underlying philosophies, however imperfectly understood, have provided the impetus for the other concepts now used in discussions. Previous chapters of this book have shown that these concepts are often used in a very imprecise way, and this lends support to Pacheco's contention (1977:16) that

> Analysis and clarification is necessary if such discussions are to be fruitful; otherwise, we have terms that are only rhetorically useful and function as slogans, serving to call attention to a problem or an issue, while remaining so ambiguous and vague that almost any behavior would seem to fall under their rubric.

During 12–14 May 1971, the Conference on Education and Teacher Education for Cultural Pluralism was held in Chicago. Its purpose 'was to take steps to make the cultural diversity that characterizes American society a major asset instead of being a problem or becoming a threat' (Stent, Hazard & Rivlin, 1973:1). One of the outcomes was a working definition of cultural pluralism, produced by the National Coalition for Cultural Pluralism, which was formed at the conference (1973:14). This group defined cultural pluralism as

> a state of equal co-existence in a mutually supportive relationship within the boundaries or framework of one nation of people of diverse cultures with significantly different patterns of belief, behavior, color, and in many cases with different languages. To achieve cultural pluralism, there must be unity with diversity. Each person must be aware of and secure in his own identity, and be willing to extend to others the same respect and rights that he expects to enjoy himself.

Elaborating on this definition, Hazard and Stent (1973:14–15) add a number of important riders and qualifications. Cultural pluralism should be regarded on an international scale, transcending national boundaries. The concept 'must include basic ideas of equal opportunity for all people, respect for human dignity, and the power to control the significant environmental and psychological forces impinging on people. . . . Cultural pluralism includes recognition, acceptance, and support of all cultures. It includes gut-level respect for human dignity and human differences.'

There has also emerged a heightened awareness among non-white communities about the need for group identity which has largely overshadowed the drive towards integration that was a major concern of the conference (1973:16):

> To function effectively in a pluralistic relationship, each group needs to define its own cultural base and develop a pervasive sense of cultural identity, as well as cultural unity. In order to accomplish this cultural unity, the racial and ethnic groups separate prior to negotiating back into pluralism. After separation, subsequent negotiations with others may proceed from genuine strength rather than traditional stereotyped cultural positions.

Social justice as a treasured American concept may then take on real meaning in practice, as each group may define and demand equality of opportunity and constitutional protection. Cultural pluralism as a philosophy and
strategy is all-encompassing and means co-existence of these separated, and
significantly distinct groups.

This concern with social justice and a fair share of socio-economic
resources for all groups in society, without their paying a price in terms
of assimilating or integrating with the mainstream, dominant group, is
stressed in a passage by Bruce Gaardner of the United States Office of
Education, quoted by Stent, Hazard and Rivlin (1973:16–17). It
emphasizes how great a difference there is between the modern concept
of cultural pluralism and the earlier versions of Dewey and Kallen,
which were mainly concerned with the co-existence of different cultural
groups in American society within the over-arching cultural matrix
arising out of their 'Americanization':

> Cultural pluralism is not an assimilative posture; it is a negation of assimi-
> lation. It is a posture which maintains that there is more than one legitimate
> way of being human without paying the penalties of second-class citizenship,
> and that this pluralism would enrich and strengthen the nation. Social
> justice, alone, means a fair share of the pie; as a goal in the United States it
> has usually meant an assimilative attitude. Cultural pluralism, on the other
> hand, calls unavoidably for a pluralistic viewpoint; it demands the same fair
> share *plus the right not to assimilate*.

The above views of cultural pluralism provide excellent examples of
the tendency noted by Pacheco (1977:16–17) for there to be 'widespread confusion between goals and concepts, and more than one
author suggests that we implement the *concept* of cultural pluralism
with little further specification. Common to the rhetoric of such arguments is a confusion between *descriptions* of American society as
culturally pluralistic and *prescriptions for* cultural pluralism as the
most desirable form of social organization.' There is also the tendency
to make logical slides in such a way that cultural pluralism appears, by
implication, to be synonymous with other concepts, some of which
emerge in the course of the argument, yet remain undefined and
apparently taken for granted, as if commonly understood.

Such confusion and lack of logic arise, in part, from what Pacheco
sees as simplistic notions in educationists' thinking about pluralism,
coupled with ignorance of the two different streams of thought in the
social sciences about the nature of pluralist societies. The first has
generated a long tradition of scholarship and is based on the ideas of
Alexis de Tocqueville, an early nineteenth-century historian and political scientist. This became known as *democratic pluralism*, and
developed into one of the most influential models of American society
since that date (Pacheco, 1977:18):

> As a descriptive theory, it refers to a model of social organization in which

there is a balance of power between competing and overlapping religious, ethnic, economic, and geographical groupings. Each group has some interests which it protects and fosters and each has some say in shaping social decisions which are binding on all groups that make up society. Common to all groups is a set of political values and beliefs which serve to maintain the entire social system through accommodation and resolution of conflicts via appropriate channels.

The second tradition does not originate from American theorists but from writers describing and analysing colonized societies in Asia and Africa in the early twentieth century. This tradition, usually known as the *theory of the plural society*, concentrates almost exclusively on the phenomenon of culture. In what has become one of the influential works in this group, Furnivall (1948) showed that in the former colonies of Burma and the Dutch East Indies various racial/ethnic groups formed a medley but did not mix. In this kind of milieu each group maintained its own religion, culture and language, mores and customs.

> As individuals they meet, but only in the market-place, in buying and selling. There is a plural society with different sections of the community living side by side, but separately, within the same political unit. Even in the economic sphere, there is a division of labour along racial lines. (1948:304)

Consequently an even greater source of confusion for educationists is their reluctance to utilize theoretical ideas, relying instead on conventional wisdom and man-in-the-street definitions of technical concepts. The following criticism of the American scene is equally applicable to all the other case studies in this book (Pacheco, 1977:18):

> First, most educationally-related analyses have not drawn on this well-developed tradition of theoretically-oriented scholarship on pluralism. With few exceptions, contemporary educators are either unaware of the theoretical tradition or do not perceive it as relevant and useful. Most discussions, therefore, lack theoretical considerations and are overly programmatic in nature. Second, in being programmatic, they often reveal a fact/value ambiguity, i.e., they confuse prescriptive conceptions of society as it ought to be with descriptive accounts of how it actually is . . . . A clear distinction should be maintained between language which purports to describe society and language which advocates social change to some ideal form of society not yet achieved.

The various interpretations placed on the basic model of pluralism and related processes of assimilation have not assisted clarity. In the 1940s and 1950s the notion of the 'multiple melting pot' was in vogue. This was first introduced by Jo Reeves Kennedy (1944) and popularized by Will Herberg (1955). Greeley explains (1971:24):

> In this view the old immigrant groups were collapsing, but three super-ethnic groups based on religion were replacing them. One would, therefore, no longer think of oneself as German or Swedish or Irish or Romanian, but rather as Protestant, Catholic or Jew.

In the 1960s the work of Eisenstadt (1965) and Gordon (1964) achieved prominence in social science literature about pluralism. They hypothesized two kinds of assimilation. Acculturation, or cultural assimilation, involves members of immigrant groups in learning the customs, manners and general style of the new society — such aspects as dress, reading materials, job choice, political and social values and so on. The second kind, structural assimilation, involves members of immigrant groups in making more permanent relationships, such as intimate friendships and marriage with members of other groups. Eisenstadt and Gordon suggest that acculturation may be taking place among immigrant groups but not structural assimilation.

Finally, there are the theories of such writers as Glazer and Moynihan (1963, 1975) and Gans (1962) who 'tend to view ethnic groups as essentially interest groups, which came into being because of common origin and cultural background and continue in existence as the most appropriate units through which their members can seek greater political, social and economic power for themselves' (Greeley, 1971:25).

The historical role of education

To a large extent educational provisions in America have matched the historical developments in immigration and models of society. In the early period of assimilationist ideology and mass immigration at the end of the 1800s and beginning of the 1900s, Elwood P. Cubberley, a leading educator of that time, 'demanded that public schools lead the way in the process of assimilation of the children of the immigrants and teach them "the Anglo-Saxon conceptions of righteousness, law and order and popular government" ' (Krug, 1977:6). Of the same period Karier (1975:255) comments:

> Throughout the first half of the century, schools were organized to educate the immigrants away from their un-American traditions, and the children of immigrants away from the ways of their un-American parents, and toward Anglo-Saxon standards. The new conditions in America necessitated state intervention. . . . The children were to be shaped to fit the Anglo-Saxon standard. . . . The shapers and molders of this assumed meritocratic system ideologically reflected the collective values of the emerging middle class which, itself, had largely been nurtured on liberal enlightenment social philosophy.

In the period that culminated in the 1924 Immigration Act, which provided a quota system that was unfavourable to southern and south-eastern Europeans, there was considerable controversy in education over the nature-nurture debate. This led some supporters of the effect of genetics (nature) on intelligence to throw their influence behind the act in an endeavour to curb the entry of 'inferior hereditary stocks' such as, so it was claimed, southern and south-eastern Europeans. The most recent manifestation of what, to Karier (1975:277), is a misleading paradigm, has been the furore caused by the hereditarian views of Jensen and Eysenck in the 1960s and 1970s. Like issues of immigration, ethnic relations, and education for the disadvantaged, it is instructive to understand the broader social context which surrounds such debates and infuses them with a passion and intensity out of all proportion to their intrinsic contentiousness. In the case of the nature-nurture controversy:

> Close scrutiny of the social context of this continuing debate leads one to suspect that while on the surface the discussion seemed to justify a given course of action, at the same time, it more often obscured the more potent reasons for that action. For example, while the hereditarians stressed the genetic defects of southern Europeans and thus justified discriminatory immigration restriction (1924) on hereditarian grounds, their argument, at the same time, obscured the movement of powerful economic and social groups interested in closing the gates for decidedly economic and social reasons. It was in the economic interest of the larger industrialists to close the gates. (Karier, 1975:277)

A strong emphasis on environmentalism (nurture) took place in the 1930s and the post-war period, particularly in relation to the educational provisions for Blacks. The Brown decision of 1954 was an important legal landmark in this period, and was built on the argument by environmentalists (anti-hereditarians) that Blacks were intellectually equal to others in society. There followed the period of educational reform in the 1960s with a major emphasis on programmes for deprived, largely Black, Puerto Rican and Spanish-speaking children. This also coincided with the post-Sputnik (post – 1957) curriculum reform movement generally, with its tremendous boost in educational spending to improve the quality of American education. It will also be recalled that the 1960s ushered in the Civil Rights era.

However, the Brown decision occurred in a social milieu that, like the earlier Immigration Act in 1924, also had its economic aspects, derived from the post-World War II concern to improve American social and industrial efficiency. Many commentators warned that this could only be achieved by 'giving the Black a fairer deal' (Karier, 1975:335). One effect of this concern was to produce a social milieu more favourable to Blacks than might otherwise have been the case:

> This recognition that discrimination was socially and economically inefficient by liberals, businessmen and others would no doubt play an instrumental role in defining the social milieu from which the Brown decision emerged. From purely an economic standpoint, equal educational opportunity was not necessary for Blacks as long as they were regarded merely as a source of unskilled labor. It was necessary, however, to fully educate Blacks if they were to be used as skilled laborers and consumers.

In a review of federal and state educational legislation and policies, Giles and Gollnick (1977:115–16) note that since 1945 some provisions had been made by the United States Congress to:

authorize activities to promote and encourage a greater degree of inter-cultural understanding among American citizens through education. However, it should be strongly emphasized that prior to the passage of the Ethnic Heritage Program in 1972, Title IX of the Elementary and Secondary Education Act (ESEA) of 1965, no specific provisions were made by the Congress to promote or encourage the study of American cultural, ethnic or racial minority groups by children in U.S. elementary and secondary schools.

Prior to 1972 the Congress was concerned mainly with the foreign relations of the United States, and the two acts passed in 1958 and 1966 reflected both this concern for intercultural understanding and the political climate at the height of the Cold War period, as Giles and Gollnick suggest (1977:116). In 1958 the National Defense Education Act was passed, and in 1966 the International Education Act. The former, through Title VI, authorized the Secretary to 'make grants or contracts with institutions of higher education for developing language and area study centers and programs . . . funds were to be used to encourage persons assisted under this act to enter the teaching professions at any level or perform other services of a public nature'.

Legislation that had an impact on children's schooling was contained in Title IV of the Civil Rights Act of 1964 and Title VII of the Emergency School Aid Act (ESAA) of 1972, both of which authorized activities providing for the study of Black history and culture. The former 'authorized short-term institutes for special training which included topics related to the culture and heritage of black Americans . . . [and] were designed to improve the ability of teachers and other elementary and secondary school personnel to deal effectively with problems occasioned by desegregation' (1977:116–17). The latter went further in being also concerned with the curriculum used by children in elementary and secondary schools. The programmes of instruction which the curricular materials were designed to support also included treatment of the language and cultural heritage of American minority groups. Again, it is pertinent to see these developments within their wider political context. As Giles and Gollnick state (1977:117):

> All of the above education laws were politically motivated. They were designed either to promote U.S. foreign policy objectives or to facilitate school desegregation and integration and racial harmony on the domestic scene.

A further major piece of federal legislation was the first national Bilingual Education Act, passed in 1968 as a result of organized pressure and demands on the school system by Mexican Americans and Puerto Ricans. This Act is alternatively known as Title VII of the Elementary and Secondary Education Act (ESEA). Casso (1976:7) refers to the 'bilingual/bicultural education renaissance' that has taken place in the United States in response partly to 'current opinion that the essential role of public education is the development of a responsive citizenry for the twenty-first century'. The renaissance is 'founded on notions of (a) equality of educational opportunity and (b) accountability in public education'. More specifically, the Act also reflected a series of decisions in the law courts, which found that the exclusive use of English in schools serving largely non-English speaking communities was an infringement of school children's rights to equal educational opportunity. In addition to provisions designed to alleviate this situation, Section 701 of the Bilingual Education Act also recognizes that provision has to be made for the cultural diversity of children in schools catering for such minority communities.

The Bilingual Education Act reflected the climate of the times and the socio-political atmosphere of the 1960s. Like other legislation it also reflected hard-headed economic business interests. In the earlier periods of melting pot and assimilationist ideologies it was perceived as a disadvantage to speak languages other than the dominant English. In the 1960s and 1970s, characterized by new ideologies such as concern for human and civil rights, self-determination, equal opportunity in education, and by the influx of Cuban refugees and other Spanish-speaking minorities, it was deemed educationally and economically advantageous to do so. The non-educational reasons are noted by Casso (1976:8):

> . . . it is well to note here that some of the impetus is due to the moving of international companies into Latin America, the growth of multinational companies, and the shift of the oil monopoly to the Middle East. Without a doubt, success for the merchant, lawyer, engineer, architect, educator, financier, economist, communicator and government representative in these new societal, international dynamics depends on familiarity with the culture and language of another country.

Ideologies and ideologists

The background to the current ideologies and the types of ideology managers involved is similar to that of the Acts discussed above. The National Education Association (NEA, 1977:10–12) traces this background and comments:

> Out of the racial and ethnic turmoil of the sixties, there developed among social scientists, civil rights advocates, leaders of ethnic groups, and educators a growing awareness of the need for a multicultural vision of our society.

Federal government initiatives

Such a vision may have inspired the efforts to establish a federal ethnic heritage programme through legislation in Congress. Moves in this direction were initiated in 1969 by Congressman Roman Pucinski who introduced the Ethnic Heritage Centers Studies Act as an amendment to the Elementary and Secondary Education Act (ESEA) of 1965. At the preliminary hearings, the Congressman 'defined the bill's dual purpose: of providing opportunities for the study of one's own background and of the multi-ethnic composition of our society as a whole' (NEA, 1977:11). However, Congressman Pucinski was defeated in the 1970 Senate elections and Senator Richard Schweiker introduced a similar bill into the Senate in January 1971, under the slightly different title of Ethnic Heritage Studies Program. A major theme in the Senator's advocacy was stability (1977:11):

> We now see many Americans in a fluid state, with few community ties, and a lack of any firm roots to provide stability for their lives. What was seen as an opportunity for unlimited growth has instead resulted in insecurity and a loss of the important values of community, identity, tradition, and family solidarity.

An important feature of the Senate Committee report was the concern to define the term 'ethnic' for purposes of programme grants (1977:12). 'The report made it clear that Mexican, Indian, Black, Puerto Rican, Asian, and other groups of people sharing a common history, culture, or experience in America, were to be included as well as various European immigrant groups.' The Ethnic Heritage Studies Program Act was passed in May 1972, and signed into law as a new Title IX of the Elementary and Secondary Education Act of 1965. It included the following statements of purpose and policy (1977:12):

Purpose
- To afford students an opportunity to learn more about the nature of their own heritage and to study the contributions of other ethnic groups to the Nation.
- To reduce educational disadvantages and social divisiveness caused by ignorance or misunderstanding of multicultural influences in the lives of individuals and communities.
- To realize the educational gains that can result from understanding the contributions of cultural pluralism to a multiethnic Nation.
- To encourage citizens of our pluralistic society to have intercultural awareness.

Policy
In recognition of the heterogeneous composition of the Nation and of the fact that in a multiethnic society a greater understanding of the contribution of one's own heritage and those of one's fellow citizens can contribute to a more harmonious, patriotic, and committed populace, and a recognition of the principle that all persons in the educational institutions of the Nation should have an opportunity to learn about the differing and unique contributions to the national heritage made by each ethnic group, it is the purpose of this title to provide assistance designed to afford to students opportunities to learn more about the nature of their own heritage and to study the contributions of the cultural heritage of the other ethnic groups of the Nation.

Giles and Gollnick note (1977:126) that 'the effects of the provisions of Title IX are not as far reaching as those of Title VII', and a comparison of these two Acts shows this to be the case. The same authors also suggest (1977:126):

Clearly then the role of federal legislation related to ethnic and cultural diversity in the public schools falls into two categories. First it addresses the needs of schools in culturally diverse educational settings. In these cases ethnic identity has been supported to address the special needs of the non-white ethnic minorities with first languages other than English. Secondly, the Ethnic Heritage Studies Act speaks of the educational needs of a multicultural society and world.

Of key importance are the phrases 'multi-ethnic nation' and 'multi-ethnic society' incorporated into the statements of Purpose and Policy in Title IX. 'Cultural pluralism', 'pluralistic society', 'heterogeneous composition', and a stress on the importance of ethnic groups' heritage are also present. It is clear that the ideology behind Title IX is pluralistic and in no way assimilationist. However, it seems that some commentators read into the statements intentions that are then rephrased in their ideological terminology. For instance, it is puzzling why, concerning this legislation, Giles and Gollnick (1977:128) maintain that 'although the goal of educating all Americans for life in a *multicultural* society has been stated as a national policy, it appears that very little has been done by the federal government' [italics added].

Further information about the intentions and progress of Title IX was obtained from Dr Carl Epstein, who is the Education Program Specialist in the Ethnic Heritage Studies Branch of the Division of International Education, part of the United States Office of Education, Washington. During discussion, it became clear that Dr Epstein is very keen that ethnic studies should get beyond the trappings of food fairs, festivals and dancing, and that in-depth attitudinal studies should now be undertaken. It is necessary to get closer to various ethnic groups to find out why they act as they do, and what will facilitate inter-group discussions.

Carl Epstein explained that there was a time when people felt that ethnic studies was a means of dividing people, i.e., that it was more a divisive than unifying element in society. Michael Novak (1971) has since pointed out that it was a unifying factor that goes beyond the idea of the melting pot. The third generation has become more conscious of ethnicity than their fathers or their grandfathers. At present there is a preoccupation among many ethnic groups and individuals with finding out their identity and origins — the 'roots syndrome'. This is colouring the approach to ethnic studies.

Every state, through its schools, is mandated to include some form of ethnic studies in the curriculum. Most schools have put in multicultural studies, this term being used interchangeably with multiethnic studies.

Carl Epstein would not equate the two terms, or define multiethnic in multicultural terms. In his opinion, the latter is a somewhat broader concept than multiethnic.

Multiethnic is the term and approach stressed by Title IX, as there is so little funding to go around for the whole country. This is borne out by the Guidelines for Applications for Grants in 1978, which state that the appropriation for the fiscal year 1978 is expected to be $2 300 000. The programme expects to award 50 major grants averaging approximately $46 000. Also, 'contingent upon receipt of eligible competitive applications, support may be given to establishing two regional clearinghouses for the dissemination of information on ethnic studies. The amount of the award for these clearinghouses is expected to be about $100 000 each. In addition, the program expects to award approximately 15 mini-grants not to exceed $15 000 in size' (Health, Education and Welfare, 1977:A2).

The Guidelines also stress that any programme or research carried out should have *multi*ethnic impact: even if a monocultural or monoethnic programme is developed it should have an impact beyond the specific group concerned. This is primarily to get more ethnic groups involved, and thus bring about more understanding, not merely for people in one ethnic group, but for people in other ethnic groups and other areas.

Conservative responses to the socio-historical context

Policies of the National Education Association play a major part in shaping the direction of the nation's education through its publications and regular, national conferences. At its Thirteenth Annual Conference on Civil and Human Rights in Education, held in 1975, the following resolution was adopted by the Ethnic Studies Special Interest Group in support of multicultural education (Gollnick, Klassen & Yff, 1976:10):

> A recognition and awareness of the individual's ethnic/cultural heritage is a positive first step in the implementation of an effective process that:
> a.   Enables the individual to accept and respect his or her cultural heritage and that of people of other backgrounds;
> b.   Speaks to both the multicultural dimension and unity of our society;
> c.   Involves individuals, schools and community in common concerns, problem solving processes, and the creation of goals;
> d.   Forms a basis for understanding the nature of equal educational opportunity.

As Gollnick et al. comment of this NEA position based on a multicultural model of society (1976:10):

> It is education that recognizes and values the culturally pluralistic nature of this society. It is education that encourages people to accept and respect both their own cultural heritage and that of people of different cultural

backgrounds. It prepares people to function both within their own ethnic community and within other ethnic communities while participating fully in the common American culture.

However, in addition to this emphasis, the NEA has also adopted a multiethnic perspective, as is evident from the sets of multiethnic education in-service training aids in the form of practical, tested curriculum resource materials on display at its Washington headquarters. This apparent revision of the ideology may be little more than a response to the Ethnic Heritage Studies Program Act, and recognition that teachers who want to implement it are likely to be attracted by materials that contain a multiethnic theme, if only on the label.

A similar body, the American Association of Colleges of Teacher Education (AACTE), comprises more than 860 collegiate and university organizations in the United States, Guam and Puerto Rico, in which over 90 per cent of the educational personnel in America are trained (Hunter, 1974:v). In 1972 the Commission on Multicultural Education, which had been set up in 1971 by the Association in the aftermath of the Kent State and Jackson State tragedies, published what has become a much cited and influential statement of policy in the area of pluralist education. The pamphlet, *No One Model American* . . . states:

> Multicultural education is education which values cultural pluralism. Multicultural education rejects the view that schools should seek to melt away cultural differences or the view that schools merely tolerate cultural pluralism. . . . Multicultural education recognizes cultural diversity as a fact of life in American society, and it affirms that this cultural diversity is a valuable resource that should be preserved and extended. . . .
>
> Education for cultural pluralism includes four major thrusts: (1) the teaching of values which support cultural diversity and individual uniqueness; (2) the encouragement of the qualitative expansion of existing ethnic cultures and their incorporation into the mainstream of American socio-economic and political life; (3) the support of explorations in alternative and emerging life styles; and (4) the encouragement of multiculturalism, multilingualism, and multidialectism. While schools must insure that all students are assisted in developing their skills to function effectively in society, such a commitment should not imply or permit the denigration of cultural differences.

The model and related theory of American society on which these recommendations are based is evidently cultural pluralism. Its basic ideas have been set out by the AACTE in the same publication, using language that comes close at times to being rhetoric, with many of the high-flown phrases that seem to be an indispensable part of writings on this subject.

> To endorse cultural pluralism is to endorse the principle that there is no one model American. To endorse cultural pluralism is to understand and appreciate the differences that exist among the nation's citizens. . . . Cultural

pluralism is more than a temporary accommodation to placate racial and ethnic minorities. It is a concept that aims toward a heightened sense of being and of wholeness of the entire society based on the unique strengths of each of its parts.

Cultural pluralism rejects both assimilation and separatism as ultimate goals. The positive elements of a culturally pluralistic society will be realized only if there is a healthy interaction among the diverse groups which comprise the nation's citizenry. Such interaction enables all to share in the richness of America's multicultural heritage. Such interaction provides a means for coping with intercultural tensions that are natural and cannot be avoided in a growing, dynamic society.

Several important publications have flowed from the AACTE or organizations closely affiliated with it in an attempt to spell out the practical implications of the *No One Model American* . . . ideology (e.g., Hunter, 1974; Gollnick, Klassen & Yff, 1976; Klassen & Gollnick, 1978). The first of these publications, edited by Hunter, links multicultural education with another current American preoccupation — competency-based teacher education. From many of the contributions it is apparent that there is lack of consensus about what multicultural education and cultural pluralism really mean.

Asa Hilliard, Dean at the San Francisco State University, and one of the Black contributors to Hunter's (1974) publication makes a number of necessary qualifications about the uses of the term multicultural in order to overcome 'one impediment to the development of better teacher education which is the general fuzziness of terms and constructs which we use' (Hunter, 1974:41). To him, multicultural is a term used to define a society 'made up of a number of cultural groups based upon race, ethnicity, religion, language, nationality, income, etc.'. Multicultural education 'is used to mean learning about various cultural groups. Ethnic studies programs and cultural appreciation studies are examples.' Multicultural teacher education, according to Hilliard, 'means the focus in teacher education which is designed to help teachers to function effectively with pupils in a culturally diverse society. . . . The fundamental assumption here is that teachers can improve their teaching of school subjects to their own or other cultural groups if the appropriate attitudes, cultural experiences, and self-understanding are present.'

Hilliard also makes the important criticism that much of what passes for multicultural education obscures the central problems of inequality, racism, and discrimination, which many educators seem unable or unwilling to tackle (Hunter, 1974:43 – 44):

> For some educators multicultural education is simply a matter of infusing regular school content with material which deals with different customs, dress, food, or other matters which fall under the label of cultural appreciation. This is a very limited perspective and will contribute little to the solution of the fundamental problem of inequity. The main reason is that it leaves out

consideration of individual and institutional racism or other prejudice as part of the foundation for victimization. As painful as it may be to deal with racism and other prejudice, it is impossible to approach problems realistically while ignoring these matters.

Like most associations of this type AACTE publishes a regular bimonthly *Journal of Teacher Education*. Some issues are devoted to a single area of concern, and the issue for May – June 1977 covered multicultural education, pursuing the theme which the AACTE has stressed consistently. Tómas Arciniega made it clear that the function of the issue was to develop the specification of the Association's ideology (Arciniega, 1977:2):

> We reaffirm and support our commitment to cultural pluralism as it is very eloquently stated in the original commission's "No One Model American" statement. . . . What remains unclear is how best to organize and operationalize the noble precepts of cultural pluralism in educational form and practice. This underscores the need for a more systematic effort to broaden dialogue.

The overall standards of teacher education in America for those organizations affiliated to AACTE come under the control of the National Council for Accreditation of Teacher Education (NCATE), which collaborates closely with the AACTE. On 15 January 1970 the Council adopted a series of standards which were prepared by the Evaluative Criteria Study Committee of AACTE. They were subsequently revised by the Council's Committee on Standards during the two-year period 1975 – 77. After appropriate consideration and discussion by relevant educational and public bodies, the final revision was made in April 1977 and adopted on 16 May 1977, to become operative on 1 January 1979.

In the curricula for basic programmes proposed by NCATE (1977:4) there is explicit recognition of the need to cater for multicultural education, and the down-to-earth approach advocated by Asa Hilliard is again evident:

> Multicultural education is preparation for the social, political, and economic realities that individuals experience in culturally diverse and complex human encounters. These realities have both national and international dimensions. This preparation provides a process by which an individual develops competencies for perceiving, believing, evaluating, and behaving in different cultural settings. Thus, multicultural education is viewed as an intervention and an on-going assessment process to help institutions and individuals become more responsive to the human condition, individual cultural integrity, and cultural pluralism in society. . . .

This statement is in marked contrast to another statement, which appears to advocate an earlier, more naïve view of multicultural education. It was developed at a conference sponsored jointly by NEA and the Council on Interracial Books for Children. Again, the inflated rhetoric is obvious (NEA, 1977:3):

This is reality: Ours is a multicultural society. Our population includes U.S. citizens of European, Asian, African, Central and South American, Caribbean and Native American descent. All of these groups have contributed to the total cultural fabric of our society. Our laws, music, art, language, and literature reflect the values of this diversity. Our public educative process is obligated to reflect this reality. All people have the right of access to materials that express the rich multilingual, multicultural nature of our society. Our heritage of freedom of speech and freedom of inquiry demands this. The goals of a democratic society require it.

Ideologies underpinning research

An important group of organizations operating in the United States forms a network of educational laboratories, research and development centers, and similar bodies affiliated with the Council for Educational Development and Research (CEDaR). An example of one such organization is the Northwest Regional Educational Laboratory (NWREL).

NWREL has a division of Multicultural Education directed by Dr Felipe Sanchez Paris, comprising the Indian Reading and Development Program (Dr Joe Coburn, Director), the Center for Bilingual Education (Dr Francisco C. Garcia, Director), the Multicultural Inservice Training Program (Dr George Banks, Director) and the Non-Sexist Curriculum Development Program (Dr Barbara Hutchison, Director). One of the major tasks of the Bilingual Education group is to advise schools in the north-west area how to comply with the mandate requirements of Title VII (ESEA), the Bilingual Education Act. Like many programmes in the west and south-west of the United States, a major concern is with Spanish-English bilingualism.

The multicultural ideology of the Division was elaborated during discussion by Dr Paris, who clarified the situation that has apparently developed in the United States, where two competing sets of ideas about pluralism have emerged. The first is concerned with the issue of desegregation, based on criteria of race, sex and national origin. A preferred term by 'non-realists' is integration. Desegregationists advocate a heterogeneous racial, national, and sexual 'mix' in school populations. This approach is contrary to the pride and exclusiveness of some ethnic groups, who want to control their own education. Other ethnic groups, on the other hand, prefer desegregation, maintaining that the 'mix' in schools promotes better learning among educationally marginal children in lower socio-economic and academic levels, as research has shown that they try to emulate children in higher levels. Desegregation (integration) ideas are usually catered for by a multicultural approach to education.

The segregation position, in contrast, advocates a policy of positive or affirmative discrimination. This encourages separatism, and attempts to build up the various ethnic groups' pride, self-esteem and cultural worth. Groups are encouraged initially to maintain their cultural, political, and social autonomy and group awareness. Once these are established and secure as a base, ethnic groups can choose to enter the wider field from a position of strength rather than weakness, which would undermine their efforts to achieve justice and their rights. In education the segregationists advocate separate schooling for the various ethnic groups and oppose bussing. This cluster of ideas is usually associated with multiethnic or multiracial models of education.

Both are rejected by Paris on the grounds of their basic weakness as long-term policies. They may be acceptable in the short term as strategies for ethnic groups to achieve social, economic and political power quickly, but both are possibly socially destructive in the long term. The Québecois movement in Canada is an example of a dysfunctional type of multiethnicity in terms of the nation or socio-political system as a whole, as it tends to perpetuate or harden segregation and separatism and thus weaken the cohesion of the society. It is also very insular. Adherence to the symbols and achievements of one minority group can only be destructive in the long run; those who claim that they cannot receive anything of value outside their own culture are being ethnocentric and shortsighted.

Multiculturalism, according to Paris, is more a long-term ideology, on the other hand. A group that espouses it is able to appreciate aspects of other groups, such as their values, customs, languages, and other cultural features. Multiculturalism also produces the type of climate in which ethnic groups are outward looking and able to communicate with each other instead of being inward looking and insular. However, for the former to occur in a situation of socio-political and economic parity, proportional representation from cultural groups is needed in politics. In the opinion of Dr Paris, the American system has moved from *laissez-faire* to a form of governmental quasi-socialistic control, in which it is much more difficult for the lower economic groups and new ethnic groups to get power. For instance, Spanish-speaking people in America form the second largest language and ethnic group, but have virtually no power in political terms. This type of situation has been the cause of significant opposition among some ethnics to Title VII, the Bilingual Education Act. The basic philosophy of this legislation is one of culture maintenance and culture restoration. This works against the significant number of those ethnics who see their main chance of survival and advancement in terms of obtaining fluency in English through total emersion in the language and a functionalist approach to English language development. The opposing theoretical view stresses that cognitive achievement and development are best achieved in the language native to the child, and in the home setting and its language.

The separatist tendencies which such a view might encourage, however, are obvious, and for true multiculturalism to flourish bilingualism should be seen more in transitional terms. The American Indian educational provisions are an exception to this as they do allow for some culture restoration and culture maintenance programmes. Dr Paris commented that what should be aimed for are multicultural goals for society rather than a multicultural society. The distinction is as subtle as it is intriguing.

Other programmes listed in the CEDaR Directory are concerned with bilingualism/biculturalism. This concern was generated in educational research and development by Title VII, the Bilingual Education Act and, in some cases, the geographical location in predominantly Spanish-speaking areas of the R & D centre or laboratory. Biculturalism is the apparent underlying ideology in these cases. Fewer programmes refer to multiculturalism or cultural pluralism. Despite the emphasis of Title IX, little reference is made to 'ethnic' issues and multiethnicity as a basic ideology. It is also worth noting that the great majority of R & D programmes in the United States are heavily psychometric and opera-tionalized, incorporating clearly specified aims and objectives so that outcomes can be precisely measured in quantitative data which will indicate quite clearly to funding agencies what has been achieved through the research. The more speculative, conceptual mapping or model building exercises are comparatively rare.

The National Council for the Social Studies (NCSS) is one of the national organizations in the United States that have played a leading role in generating conceptual and pedagogical approaches to pluralistic education. Subject associations are important knowledge managers in education. Their ideologies often reflect concern to protect their academic fields or subjects from encroachment by other subjects — a form of academic boundary maintenance — but can also reflect considered judgements about the nature of society and the education process. In the case of the NCSS there is a certain ambivalence of attitude towards the problem of pluralistic education. It basically appears to favour a multicultural approach, but also supports almost a counter-ideological position in multiethnic studies. The latter is discussed in the following section.

Counter-ideologies and ideologists

Reactionary views

As in Great Britain and Canada, countries with a strong Anglo-conformist tradition, there is an ideological climate which is assimila-tionist and fostered by some reactionary educators and administrators in the United States. Rather than generate new ideologies, they hold views that run counter to the official government ideology in Titles VII and IX discussed above and the general multicultural emphasis fostered by such organizations as AACTE and NCSS. They hark back to old ideologies and concepts (Casso, 1976:25):

Shored up by its educational institutions, U.S. society in general has clung to and furthered the melting pot concept. . . . Most administrators, counselors, teachers, and teacher educators have been trained under the melting pot theory, which is now being challenged. The changing of many deep attitudes and long-standing practices will be necessary, and in the process, rough spots will, naturally, be encountered.

In short, as Giles and Gollnick observe (1977:119): 'The cultural base of the American education system has traditionally been a very narrow one which centered around an Anglo conformity, value-oriented approach.' Such views are both implicit in much teaching material and many textbooks, as well as quite explicit in what is advocated. As Gollnick, Klassen and Yff point out (1976:11):

> Historical assertions, for example, have been greatly distorted in textbooks and public literature because most social, political economic, and historical events have been presented from an Anglo-American perspective and value system. Few educators have been trained to recognize these historical distortions or to be sensitive to the self concepts of students from cultural backgrounds different than their own.

Another reactionary tendency is more negative in that it ignores the pluralism in American society or plays it down. This may, even be a more subtle and effective counter-ideological strategy than overt attacks on pluralism: at least one can pinpoint statements in textbooks and show how they are reactionary. A bland dismissal of the problem gives little to counterattack. The tendency has been noted by Krug (1978:8):

> The existence, the dynamics of ethnic groups in America, the role of ethnic ties in city, state, and national elections, are mostly ignored or even disdained, not only by secondary schools but in education, history, and political science departments in many institutions of higher learning.

The US Commission on Civil Rights, established by Congress 'to provide hearings, studies, data and recommendations on the rights of U.S. citizens and areas where these rights may have been infringed upon', began an exhaustive educational research on Mexican Americans in 1968 (Casso, 1976:14). In its report, published in 1974, the Commission describes the effects of the Anglo-orientation of schooling on Chicano children, and illustrates how even school organization, the curriculum and related assumptions about the status of Chicanos produce devaluation of their culture and discrimination in education, reflecting basic assimilationist and Anglo-conformist thinking by default (Casso, 1976:14):

> Entrance into public school brings about an abrupt change for all children, but for many Mexican American children the change is often shattering. The knowledge and skills they have gained in their early years are regarded as valueless in the world of the schools. The language which most Chicano

children have learned — Spanish — is not the language of the school and is either ignored or actively suppressed. Even when the Spanish language is deemed an acceptable medium of communication by the schools, the Chicano's particular dialect is often considered 'substandard' or no language at all . . . with little or no assistance, Mexican American children are expected to master this language [English] while competing on equal terms with their Anglo classmates.

Teachers and teacher educators oppose pluralist education programmes such as bilingualism/biculturalism on a number of grounds. Firstly there is an unwillingness to accept the fact that the public schools have failed to socialize into the American culture many of those children who are linguistically and culturally different from it. Second, there is fear and opposition to change. Third, there is a fear of job displacement on the part of regular teachers at a time in the United States (as in Australia, Britain and Canada) when there is a surplus of monocultural teachers. Fourth, there is a strong negative feeling toward anything foreign: a ubiquitous phenomenon in all societies. Finally, as Casso (1976:25–26) comments: 'As far as the growth and acceptance of bilingual/bicultural education is concerned, it is beset by an added feature — a 200-year old history of a monolingual, monocultural, and ethnocentric thrust in the public schools.' These grounds have even been used by a former president of the New York City local branch of the American Federation of Teachers to state the opposition of some teachers to bilingualism/biculturalism in schools, and to negate its ideology (Casso, 1976:27; Wright, 1973).

The mass media

As in Great Britain and Canada, some representatives of the press have played an active role in negating the current ideology and advocating a return to assimilationist thinking. The following examples are taken from those cited by Casso (1976:27–31). Not all of them are one-sided, for instance the *New York Times* of 12 March 1975, in an article entitled 'Issue and Debate', presented both sides of controversy over bilingual/bicultural education. Stephen Rosenfeld wrote a column, 'Bilingualism and the Melting Pot', which originally appeared in the *Washington Post* on 27 September 1974. He was critical of the legislation passed by Congress, and felt that bilingual/bicultural education was objectionable for two reasons (Casso, 1976:29):

> First, it is not clear how educating children in the languages and culture of their ancestral homeland will equip them for the rigors of contemporary life in the United States . . . [Second] Bilingualism springs from a very different idea of America than what the public institutions of this country have accepted in the past.

Andrew Tully, also a Washington columnist, followed Rosenfeld's article with another, entitled 'Education Is Raped', which was widely syndicated in many papers including the *Albuquerque Journal* which is the leading newspaper in New Mexico. This state's population includes minorities of which the largest groups are Mexican Americans and Native Americans, many of whom support bilingual/bicultural education. Isolated as the two columnists may appear to be, they are widely influential as their columns are syndicated across the country. Thus they not only influence education policy makers in the Executive and Legislative branches of the federal government in Washington but also others throughout the country (1976:29). The *Albuquerque Tribune* also attacked the concept of bilingual education in May 1975, when the Civil Rights Commission released its major document on bilingual/bicultural education — *A Better Chance to Learn: Bilingual Bicultural Education*. The *Tribune* sided with the assimilationist melting pot ideology (1976:30−31):

> However lofty its motives, the U.S. Civil Rights Commission is giving impractical advice by urging bilingual education for the millions of children who enter U.S. schools without being able to speak English. As should be obvious, this approach to education could handicap a child — perhaps permanently — by offering him a crutch that won't hold up in the work-a-day world in which he must live in later life.

Reactionary social theories

A sizeable number of academic writers are not sympathetic to the concepts of cultural pluralism or bilingual education. Others are cautious about their theoretical merits. Among the former, John Higham (1975:283) argues that 'cultural pluralism is "morally objectionable"', because it limits the autonomy and freedom of young men and women of the second and third generation of immigrants'. Gunnar Myrdal, also argues against cultural pluralism, maintaining that it is reactionary and divisive, and that the 'new ethnicity' is a romantic aberration (1974:62). In a more philosophical analysis, Wolff, Moore and Marcuse (1965:47−50) argue that an over-emphasis of the concept of cultural pluralism can divert attention from major social problems, in terms of the unequal distribution of, and access to, the resources desired by all members of society.

Theorists in the second group are not so negative, and mostly base their arguments on sociological and philosophical analyses of the types of pluralism. For instance, Arturo Pacheco, of Stanford University, distinguishes between the concept of cultural pluralism as 'a theory of society — a particular form of social organization' and multicultural education as 'a form of educational practice — a specific practice within one institution of society which may or may not be congruent with cultural pluralism, depending on how that theory is defined' (1977:19−20).

Pacheco divides the types of multicultural education programmes

into two major approaches — *compensatory* and what we can call
functional, i.e., 'its goal is to produce students who can function in a
culturally plural society, one in which there is parity between various
cultural groups' (Pacheco, 1977:20). The compensatory approach has
two variants. The first necessitates designing special programmes or
units of work for those pupils who are considered to suffer from disadvantages due to their home cultures being different from that of the
school. Its underlying assumption is that if these disadvantages are
remedied and the special needs of such children met, their educational
progress will improve. The second variant of the compensatory
approach maintains that multicultural education has value for all
students, and not just for those from minority groups. 'The thrust of
these programmes is heavily psycho-social in nature, stressing awareness, tolerance, understanding, and pride in one's cultural identity,
whatever that may be'. Both variants of the compensatory approach
stress that *cultural* differences are the root of the problems children
from minority groups face at school, but that they are remediable
through education.

The functional approach also has two variants. The first is based on a
recognition of the lack of socio-economic parity between the various
cultural, minority groups in society. 'It attempts, through a variety of
structural arrangements in the school, to aggressively support the right
of a cultural group to maintain itself, it perceives that parity of power
and decision making among groups is crucially important, and it
assumes that the school has a critical role in bringing cultural pluralism
about in the greater society'. In this variant such problems are looked at
in a number of cultural groups. The second variant concentrates only
on two, making it essentially a bicultural/bilingual programme.

However, Pacheco admits that even this approach is basically compensatory to assist the transition of minority children into the mainstream, and comments (1977:20):

> . . . all the above models are severely limited. We must question the relation-
> ship between multicultural education reform efforts in the context of the
> school and the more ambitious goal of cultural pluralism, which addresses an
> alternative social structure.

Pacheco also touches on a matter taken up in the final chapter of this
book — the adequacy of theories such as cultural pluralism and multiculturalism to fully conceptualize all the forces at work in a pluralist
society. The concept of culture itself has been, and continues to be, a
seductive trap for the naïve. It is part of the 'hydra' noted by Troper in
Canadian thinking, able to change its head at will, and accommodate
virtually every direction thinking takes in education, except that which
has to do with real issues of power and control. Pacheco's incisive
summary of the key issues relates not only to the United States, but also
to all the case studies considered in this book:

Cultural pluralism, as an alternative theory of society, also must undergo a radical reanalysis. Like programs in multicultural education, it often assumes that culture is the major factor in addressing the problems. Other sociohistorical factors must be taken into account and integrated into the theory. Most central is the phenomenon of class and its role in the American socio-economic system. We know that schooling systems are inherently conservative and often reflect the social structure of the greater society, where class stratification continues to play a major role in the maintenance of the present socio-economic structure. If we neglect or omit these economic factors from our analyses and proposals for change, cultural pluralism may very likely turn out to be, as Thomas R. Lopez, Jr., suggests, a political hoax which diverts us from confronting the history of political-economic oppression and exploitation which has had, perhaps, a more important role than has culture in the structural organization of American society.[2]

Freeman Butts (1977:18) also has cautioned against making too enthusiastic claims for cultural pluralism. Some balance in favour of a degree of 'civism' — the claims of the wider society or community — is necessary. His remarks are especially pertinent to the discussion of the AACTE statement given above:

> A careful reading of the full AACTE statement will reveal not only the obvious concern for the pluralistic communities, but also virtually no reference to the common elements that bind the different groups together. In this respect, AACTE and many other enthusiastic adopters of multicultural education have forgotten or little noticed a major tenet that the father of cultural pluralism always insisted upon — the fundamental principles of *political* democracy that must underlie the diversities of *cultural* pluralism.

Writing in the context of the Canadian debate about pluralism, Findlay makes broadly similar points about the weaknesses of the multicultural approach (1975:223):

> The pluralistic idea contains the seeds of its own confusion . . . important social problems can be obscured or ignored because they are not expressed through any cohesive group. . . . In a pluralist approach, society-wide interests may never be defined or dealt with.

Progressive social theories

Not all criticisms of cultural pluralism, bicultural/bilingualism, and multiculturalism are as reactionary as the above examples. There is a group of what might be termed progressive theorists, who propose models that are alternatives to pluralism. Others in this group attempt to make extensions or elaborations of the multicultural approach, without completely negating its basic premises, in particular by adding the dimension of ethnicity.

Among the former is an early model proposed by Despres (1968), building on the work of such theorists as Furnivall (1939:446–69) and M.G. Smith (1957; 1965). Despres (1968:13) distinguishes two ideal types of society on a continuum of 'sociocultural integration'. One is the 'heterogeneous society': one that 'contains local cultural sections'. The United States, in Despres opinion, is such a society:

> It contains many cultural groups that are integrated in varying degrees in local communities (e.g., the Irish, the Polish, the French Canadians, etc.). We usually think of these as ethnic groups. There are practically no institutional structures that serve to integrate each of these groups, separately, at the national level.

Following this model, Australia is also a heterogeneous society. In contrast, groups in a 'plural society' are culturally differentiated and locally integrated, but also 'participate in institutional structures which serve to maintain their cultural differentiation at the national level'.

In a more recent formulation, Despres (1975:187−207) proposes a framework for the comparative study of ethnic phenomena. In this discussion he employs the concepts of the polyethnic society and polyethnic system. While he does not apply these terms to an analysis of the United States, it seems from the argument that they would be applicable, but are in need of further refinement. Their major utility would appear to be in an analysis of power relationships and social stratification. As Despres concludes (1975:204):

> . . . significant relationships are more than apparent between factors affecting the competition for resources and the persistence, corporate organization, and differential incorporation of ethnic populations. . . . The precise nature of these relationships and the extent to which they are determined by material factors, which presumably admit of political alteration, remain to be closely investigated.

Michael Novak is one of a group of theorists who want to extend the concept of multicultural America by adding new dimensions of ethnicity, in Novak's case with a quasi-religious humanitarian emphasis (Novak, 1976:185−86):

> We in North America, I believe, are engaged in a great experiment. Trying to live out in advance for the rest of the world a way in which multicultural differences and diversity can be lived humanely and civilly and democratically. If we cannot do it here, how would it be done elsewhere. . . .

Novak believes that the turn to the 'new ethnicity' — a phenomenon of the seventies — is a 'new, great international issue' for reasons that are rational rather than emotional or a 'gut reaction based on ignorance, lack of travel, on self-protection'. One explanation he gives for the occurrence of this phenomenon is that

> ethnicity is always associated with power, with differential power, power unevenly distributed. It is associated with temporal diversity because different cultural traditions are at different points in their development, particularly at points in their development with respect to the conditions of modern society. (1976:186)

Andrew M. Greeley, another leading theorist in the United States, also develops an ethnic perspective. His book (Greeley:1971), is about the religious and ethnic pluralism resulting from the immigration of white ethnic groups to America between 1820 and 1920, and which has produced one form of diversity in American society. 'Ethnic pluralism is part of the very fabric of American urban life' (1971:13); ethnic diversity 'is alive and well' (1971:15). From this perspective, 'the critical problem then for those who wish to expand the area of trust and love in human relationships is not to eliminate diversity but to understand how diversity can be integrated in some form of unity' (1971:16).

Greeley also comments on the rise of ethnic diversity, with its underlying power conflict dimension and its implications for research. These have obvious relevance for education (1971:16):

> The emergence of a multi-ethnic society in the United States in a relatively brief period of time is one of the most astonishing social phenomena of the modern world . . . it [is] not at all unreasonable to suggest that the study of ethnic diversity in the United States can be extremely helpful in understanding the fundamental problem of human diversity.

An important and influential group of social and political theorists have advanced theories about ethnicity and described case studies in a collection edited by Glazer and Moynihan (1975). This collection has become something of a 'bible' for workers in the field of ethnicity, and a strong counter-argument against those academics and laymen who continue to denigrate the subject as academically disreputable, or who use outmoded dictionary definitions to deny the modern validity of the term ethnic. Glazer and Moynihan suggest that ethnicity 'seems to be a new term' (1975:1) and suggest that its only relatively recent appearance in dictionaries reflects the fact that the emergence of the phenomenon of ethnicity itself is recent. However many of its manifestations might well be missed or taken for granted by observers of social life, (1975:2–3):

> to see only what is familiar in the ethnicity of our time is to miss the emergence of a new social category as significant for the understanding of the present-day world as that of social class itself. For in the welter of contemporary forms of group expression and group conflict there is both something new and something common: there has been a pronounced and sudden increase in tendencies by people in many countries and in many circumstances to insist on the significance of their group distinctiveness and identity and on new rights that derive from this group character.

According to modern theorists, the term 'ethnic group' refers not only to subgroups or minorities of the wider society, but also to 'all the groups of a society characterized by a distinct sense of difference owing to culture and descent' (1975:4). Glazer and Moynihan consider that whereas ethnic groups were 'formerly seen as *survivals* from an earlier age, to be treated variously with annoyance, toleration, or mild celebration, we now have a growing sense that they may be *forms* of social life that are capable of renewing and transforming themselves' (Glazer and Moynihan, 1975:4). An extra element in the emergence of this new phenomenon is that ethnic groups can act as interest groups in a way that is probably more effective than interest-defined groups. Glazer and Moynihan comment (1975:7−8):

> As against class-based forms of social identification and conflict — which of course continue to exist — we have been surprised by the persistence and salience of ethnic-based forms of social identification and conflict . . . we might hazard the hypothesis that ethnic conflicts have become one form in which interest conflicts between and within states are pursued.

Glazer and Moynihan suggest that there are two related reasons for this development (1975:11):

> The first had to do with the strategic efficacy of ethnicity in making legitimate claims on the resources of the modern state . . . the second . . . has to do with the social dynamics that lead to such claims and concerns the fact and the nature of inequality. . . . Men are not equal; neither are ethnic groups.

The inequality between ethnic groups leads to ethnicity being used as *one* of the means of advancing group interests. As Glazer and Moynihan point out (1975:18):

> . . . there is some legitimacy to finding that forms of identification based on social realities as different as religion, language, and national origin all have something in common, such that a new term is coined to refer to all of them 'ethnicity'. What they have in common is that they have all become effective foci for group mobilization for concrete political ends challenging the primacy for such mobilization of *class* on the one hand and *nation* on the other.

Counter ideologies in education

Probably the most important ideological and programmatic development in the social studies and related curricula in recent years is the emergence of a multiethnic perspective, which draws, in part, on some of the ideas discussed by Glazer and Moynihan. This emergence does not seem to be an ideological negation of the general ideology of multiculturalism which is the most common in American education. Indeed, the Ethnic Heritage Studies Program Act, Title IX, uses the term multiethnic to describe American society. However, the latest development seems such a significant departure from, and extension of, the philosophy of this programme, as to constitute a counter-ideology.

Professor James Banks (1977a) has developed a typology of ideologies relating to ethnicity and pluralist education, which can be summarized below:

1. The cultural pluralist who is ethnocentric and stresses a strong ethnic identity and alliance,

2. The pluralist-assimilationist who believes that while ethnic groups have some unique cultural characteristics, all groups in America share many cultural traits, and
3. The assimilationist who believes in one common culture for all and supports the melting pot concept.

From the cultural pluralist perspective 'the United States is made up of competing ethnic groups, each of which champions its economic and political interests. The individual is expected to develop a commitment to his/her ethnic group, especially if that group is "oppressed" by more powerful groups within society' (Gollnick, Klassen & Yff, 1976:6). Sizemore (1969: 249–279) has taken a similar view: that holders of the cultural pluralist ideology assume that an ethnic group can attain inclusion and full participation within a society only when it can bargain from a powerful position and when it has 'closed ranks' from within.

Despite its association with the term culture, cultural pluralism of the kind the above writers advocate is not the ideology on which the concept of multicultural education is based; rather this concept is based on the pluralist-assimilationist ideology. Banks clarifies the ramifications of this connection (1977a:238):

> The pluralist-assimilationist believes that the curriculum should reflect the cultures of various ethnic groups *and* the common culture. Students need to study all of these cultures in order to become effective participants and decision makers in a democratic society. The school curriculum should respect the ethnicity of the child and make use of it in positive ways. However, the students should be given options regarding their political choices and the actions that they take with regard to their ethnic attachments. The school should not 'force' students to be and feel ethnic if they choose to free themselves of ethnic attachments and allegiances.

One of the first formal moves towards the multiethnic perspective occurred in 1976 with the publication by the National Council for the Social Studies of the Curriculum Guidelines for Multiethnic Education. They were produced by an NCSS Task Force of five educationists working on Ethnic Studies Curriculum Guidelines. Professor Banks was a member of the Task Force and also its Chairman. The Task Force worked in conjunction with the NCSS Ethnic Heritage Advisory Council. At the initial joint meeting of these two bodies, a number of principles were agreed on to set the boundaries for the Guidelines (NCSS Task Force, 1976:6). Among these are:

2. The Guidelines should focus on *ethnic pluralism* and not on *cultural pluralism*. Cultural pluralism suggests a type of education which deals with the cultural contributions of all groups within a society. Consequently, that concept is far too broad and inclusive to set forth effectively the boundaries of an area encompassing both the contributions of ethnic groups and the problems resulting from ethnic discrimination in American society.

The programme outlined in the Guidelines (p. 8) and reiterated in several of Professor Banks' other writings, is to encourage the development in all members of society of what he terms 'ethnic literacy', i.e., a solidly based understanding of ethnicity and ethnic groups. Banks (1977b:4) considers multiethnic education (and the implications it has for teacher education) to be a specific form of multicultural education, it is also concerned to promote change in the education system:

> Multiethnic education is concerned with modifying the total educational environment so that it is more reflective of the ethnic diversity within American society. This includes not only the study of ethnic cultures and experiences but making institutional changes within the educational setting so that students from diverse ethnic groups have equal educational opportunities and the institution promotes and encourages the concept of ethnic diversity.

In Banks' opinion ethnic studies programmes form a part of multiethnic education, and are mainly concerned with the 'scientific and humanistic study of the histories, cultures, and experiences of the ethnic groups within a society' (Banks, 1977b:4). Ethnic studies uses a comparative and interdisciplinary approach, which cuts across subject matter lines.

Banks sets out a programme for curriculum reform which advocates proceeding even further beyond multiethnic education, as a necessary method of helping teachers 'to reconceptualize the ways in which they view and teach about American society'.

> Most schools and college courses are currently taught primarily from Anglo-American perspectives. These types of courses are based on what I call the *Anglo-American Centric Model* or Model A. . . . Ethnic studies, as a process of curriculum reform, can and often does proceed from Model A to Model B, the *Ethnic Additive Model*. In courses and experiences based on Model B, ethnic content is an additive to the major curriculum thrust, which remains Anglo-American dominated. . . .

> However, I am suggesting that curriculum reform proceed directly from Model A to Model C, the *Multiethnic Model*. In courses and experiences based on Model C, the students study historical and social events from several ethnic points of view. Anglo-American perspectives are only one group of several and are in no way superior or inferior to other ethnic perspectives. I view Model D (the *Multinational Model*) types of courses and programs as the ultimate goal of curriculum reform. In this curriculum model, students study historical and social events from multinational perspectives and points of view.

The Multinational Model reflects yet another educational ideology that seems to be emerging in the United States. This is international education, in which President Carter has taken an interest with the establishment of a Congressional Committee, under a leading educationist, to examine the need for, and likely future developments in international education in the United States. Only time will tell whether this too will set off another evolutionary stage in the curriculum and further counter-ideological speculation about the nature of American society and its place in the world. It is significant that this move coincides with the post-Vietnam period of uncertainty and reassessment in American foreign policy.

Another interpretation could be that even pluralist ideologies are coming under reassessment. As Jarolimek warns (1979:208):

> We must not allow pluralism to flourish to the extent that it will shatter any sense of common identity that is essential to the political and social health of the nation. If this happens, it will lead to civil strife and conflict, as it has in every place in the world where pluralism, rather than unity, has been emphasized. . . .

Notes

1. Based on US Bureau of the Census, *Current Population Reports*, Series P-20, and other unpublished data.
2. Thomas R. Lopez, Jr., 'Cultural Pluralism: Political Hoax? International Need?', *Journal of Teacher Education*, 1973:277–81 (Winter).

CHAPTER 6

Hawaii

'Hawaii is different' is a catchphrase that a visitor to Honolulu frequently hears. Not only is it used with pride to stress the many unique features of Hawaii, but it crops up in conversation with government officials and other knowledge managers to justify policies that differ from those on the American mainland, or to bolster an assertion that the mainlanders do not really understand what is going on in Hawaii. James Banks takes a similar view of this distinctiveness (1978:178):

> Politically, Hawaii is part of the United States. It became the nation's fiftieth state in 1959. Hawaii also shares many cultural, political, and economic characteristics with the United States mainland. Sociologically, however, Hawaii is in many ways distinct from the rest of the nation.

Eleanor Nordyke (1977: Introduction) stresses other factors, but reaches the same conclusion:

> Hawaii is unique. It is the only state in the country where all racial groups are minorities and where the majority of the population has roots in the Pacific islands or Asia instead of Europe or Africa. Waves of immigrants of different ethnic groups have arrived in Hawaii over more than a century. With the passing of each generation, the racial identity and distinct cultural patterns have been diluted by intermarriage and culture-mixing.

As a case study Hawaii is valuable, both in its own right — Hawaii *is* different — and as a way of pointing up the features of mainland policies in a different context. This chapter briefly discusses some of the major features of Hawaiian pluralism. The implicit question to be kept in mind is: how significantly different is Hawaii from the mainland, and what problems, and solutions to these problems, has this produced?

The socio-historical context

The current demographic racial and ethnic pattern

In 1970 the total population of Hawaii, according to the United States census final count, was 769 913 persons. According to preliminary estimates for mid-1976 there were 886 600 persons in Hawaii (State of Hawaii, 1977:9). These included approximately 56 000 members of the armed forces and 67 000 of their dependents. The figures excluded 78 500 temporary residents who were present in 1976.

The state of Hawaii actually comprises eight major islands of which the largest is Hawaii. The much smaller Oahu is the island which contains Honolulu and by far the greatest bulk of the population.

In 1975 81.5 per cent of the population lived on Oahu. In Honolulu, with 42.2 per cent of the island's people, the *de facto* population density per square mile was 4 500 persons (1737/Km²) while the average for the whole island was 1 251 persons per square mile (483/Km²). The remaining 18.5 per cent of the population was distributed unevenly over the other islands. Niihau is small and privately owned; 95 per cent of its small population are full or part-Hawaiians. Maui has a population that has been growing rapidly since 1970, with a *de facto* density in 1975 of 53 persons per square mile (21/Km²) Hawaii is also attracting residents, and in 1975 had a density of 20 persons per square mile (8/Km²). A further distribution pattern for the state as a whole is basically urban: 83.5 per cent of the population is concentrated in urban areas, the remaining 16.5 per cent is distributed in rural areas. This is despite the continuing plantation economy, which, though declining, still plays a major role in the whole economy.

The ethnic composition of Hawaii can be seen in two ways, depending on the sources used for the data. Table 13 gives the composition by ethnic groups according to the definitions used by the census.

TABLE 13   Ethnic stock in percentages for spring 1976

Ethnic stock* according to census definition	Number	%
White	279 128	33.7
Hawaiian	98 177	11.9
Negro	9 416	1.1
Chinese	47 482	5.7
Filipino	109 127	13.2
Japanese	235 257	28.4
American Indian	1 893	0.2
Korean	13 048	1.6
Other and unknown	33 871	4.1

Source: *Data Book 1977: A Statistical Abstract p.26.* (State of Hawaii, 1977).
* Based on a sample of 38 815 persons. Excludes persons in institutions or military barracks or on Niihau.

A more detailed breakdown of ethnic composition is obtained when definitions of ethnicity are adopted from the 1969–71 Hawaiian Health Surveillance Program Survey (HSPS). Table 14 gives the breakdown of ethnic composition according to these criteria, based on a sample survey of 11 861 households on the six major islands, in spring 1976.

TABLE 14   Ethnic stock according to HSPS definition

Ethnic stock according to HSPS definition	Numbers	%
Unmixed	615 784	74.4
Caucasian	230 080	27.8
Japanese	219 823	26.6
Hawaiian	10 933	1.3
Filipino	83 790	10.1
Chinese	35 861	4.3
Korean	10 731	1.3
Samoan	4 460	0.5
Negro	7 637	0.9
Puerto Rican	3 184	0.4
Other & unknown	9 285	1.1
Mixed	211 612	25.6
Part-Hawaiian	135 287	16.4
Non-Hawaiian	76 325	9.2

Source: *Data Book 1977: A Statistical Abstract p.9.* (State of Hawaii, 1977).

Another picture of the ethnic diversity of Hawaii is obtained from the mother tongue spoken by the various groups. Table 15 gives data based on replies to the question 'What language, other than English, was spoken in this person's home when he was a child'. The tabulation was made from a one per cent sample of the 1970 census, and the results are thus subject to considerable sampling variation.

From the above, it is indisputable that there is considerable ethnic and racial diversity in Hawaii, which appears greater when language variation is taken into account. The many dialects in the Filipino language, for instance, make planning for the education of Filipino children a formidable one, as it is not solely a question of devising programmes that cater for one 'Filipino language'. The racial pattern is somewhat distorted by the inclusion of figures for the armed forces and their dependents within those for Caucasians. If they are excluded the percentage proportions of major ethnic, racial groups are: Japanese 30.2, Caucasians 21.5, part Hawaiians 18.2, Filipinos 10.8 (Schmitt & Kawaguchi, 1977:1). There is also a marked 'racial mix' in the population which is an accepted feature of Hawaiian society. According to Schmitt and Kawaguchi (1977:1), the HSPS survey of 11 861 households showed that over one-quarter of the household population was of mixed race, chiefly part Hawaiian. Since 1955 more than one-third of all marriages were interracial (Nordyke, 1977:63).

TABLE 15   Mother tongue spoken, based on a one per cent sample, 1970

Mother tongue	No. of Persons
English	447 200
German	5 700
Portuguese	9 300
Spanish	13 300
Other European languages	10 400
Chinese, Cantonese, or Taiwanese	26 900
Korean	6 200
Japanese	116 900
Ilocano, Tagalog, or other Filipino tongues	50 200
Hawaiian	18 700
Other Polynesian, Melanesian, Micronesian**	4 200
Other languages	13 200
Not reported	46 100
Total population*	768 300

Source: *Data Book 1977: A Statistical Abstract p.28* (State of Hawaii, 1977)
* Final Census count for 1970 was 769 913.
** Includes Samoan, Tahitian, Tongan, and other Polynesian languages except Hawaiian.

The present population composition is largely the result of immigration, which has been taking place since 1900 but which has been most marked since 1965. As David and King point out (1972:i) 1965 'is a logically convenient date to separate recent immigrants from longer-term immigrants' because on 3 October of that year the United States Immigration Act of 1965 was enacted. The Act, which was put into full effect in 1968, abolished the national origin quota system and permitted a larger number of immigrants to enter from Asia, based on an annual limit of 170 000 immigrants from the Eastern Hemisphere. It also established a new preference system, and redefined relatives of residents as non-quota immigrants. 'This policy had the effect of changing the profile of immigration. In proportion to its population, Hawaii received more legal immigrants than any other state in the country' (Nordyke, 1977:79).

Nordyke notes some of the consequences of this immigration (1977:33–47). By 1900 Caucasians represented only 18.7 per cent of the population, but by 1960 their number had increased to 32 per cent. By 1970, Caucasians and part-Caucasians had increased to 39.2 per cent of the total population. It should be noted, however, that this growth is partly due to the presence of armed forces, who consist primarily of whites and their dependents. The remainder has been caused by census definitions of race, and the recent large in-migration of Caucasians from continental United States. Almost one-quarter of Hawaii's total population in 1970 had moved from the mainland in the period since

1965. Most of these new residents were white. Between 1960 and 1970 the numbers in this category showed an estimated net increase of 35 845.

Increases have not been confined solely to white residents, however. Blacks have shown the highest average annual growth rate. Most of them have been military personnel and their dependents, who in 1970 numbered 7 517, or one per cent of the population. The numbers of Filipinos in Hawaii have also increased dramatically, particularly since the national origin quota system was abolished by the Immigration Act in 1965. They formed the largest percentage of alien immigrants to Hawaii during the early 1970s. Many have relatives in Hawaii. From 1961 to 1965 there were 2 777 immigrants from the Philippines. Following the liberalized quotas, 33 117 Filipinos arrived between 1966 and 1975. This represents an average of about 3 000 persons each year. The relaxation of federal immigration laws also led to an influx of Koreans, who 'have become the second largest annual foreign immigrant group and have added 6 224 persons between 1969 and 1975. Koreans in Hawaii have had a relatively high rate of out-marriage; a low crude birth rate, and a slightly higher crude death rate and older age composition than other ethnic groups' (Nordyke, 1977:47).

Socio-economic structure

The demographic pattern and ethnic variance discussed above are closely related to other patterns produced by socio-economic factors (Lee, 1976:8):

> Ethnicity, crisscrossed with social class, is creating the social stratification pattern which ascribes differentiating roles to individuals in the various ethnic groups. Arranged in a hierarchical order — some ethnic groups occupy more super-ordinate status-roles, while other ethnic groups occupy more subordinate status-roles'.

Evidence for the above assertions can be found in statistics relating ethnic groups to educational attainment, occupational levels, and income pattern.

Educational attainment is closely related to socio-economic status. In general, the higher the level of education one attains the higher one's position in the occupational ranking. Lee (1976:5) comments on the patterns shown by the figures:

> . . . the percentages of their ethnic subpopulations who had some years of college education were moderately high for the Caucasians, Chinese, Japanese and Koreans; moderately low for the Filipinos and Hawaiians; and extremely low for the Puerto Ricans and Samoans. Post-graduate training also figured good percentages of their ethnic subpopulations for the Caucasians, Chinese, Japanese, and Koreans; and low percentages of one percent and less for the other ethnic groups.

Inversely proportional to their low percentages in the higher educational levels — the Filipinos and Puerto Ricans had the highest percentages with eight years of schooling or less, 52.3 percent and 46.8 percent, respectively, followed by the Samoans, 34 percent. The high ratio for the Filipinos might be attributed to their recent immigrant status and their alien subpopulation comprising 45.1 percent of the State total alien population. . . . Of interesting note is the fact that the Hawaiians, of native status, and the Puerto Ricans, despite their three-fourths of a century residency in the State, had relatively low educational status.

Employment status and occupational levels of ethnic groups in Hawaii show a similar pattern. It is apparent that 'males in the Caucasian (including 25.3 per cent in the military), Chinese, Filipino, Japanese, Korean, and Puerto Rican groups exceeded by 10 per cent or more the State ratio of 42.1 per cent; the Hawaiian and Samoan male subpopulations had low participation rates, 29.8 per cent and 22.7 per cent, respectively' (Lee, 1976:5). Status rankings or occupational levels conform closely to educational attainment.

More of the Caucasians, Chinese, Japanese, and Koreans of both sexes were proportionately in the top professional, technical, and managerial occupational levels than in the bottom laborers and service workers levels. . . . 15 percent or less of the Caucasians, Chinese, Japanese, and Koreans were in the laborers and service workers occupational groups as compared to over 40 percent for the Filipinos and Samoans, and over 25 percent for the Puerto Ricans and Hawaiians in these lower occupational levels. (1976:6)

Not surprisingly the figures for family income before taxes, based on 1970 HSPS findings, indicate a similar variation between ethnic groups that matches the pattern in educational attainment and occupational status. The annual median incomes for the Chinese, Japanese and Koreans were high — above the state median of $11 650 and the national median of $9 867. Although not evident from the table, the civilian subpopulation of Caucasians also had a high annual median family income — $14 077 — which is comparable with the incomes of Chinese, Japanese and Koreans (1976:7). The other ethnic groups — Hawaiians, Filipinos, Puerto Ricans, and Samoans — had median family incomes below the state norm.

In summary, it is clear that the pluralistic nature of Hawaii is objectively a complex one, and not confined solely to race and ethnicity. Socio-economic, educational, occupational divisions and rankings are also evident and produce a structural stratification dimension, that has to be taken into account in any analysis. On all four measures — educational attainment, industry group, occupational ranking, family income — there is a clear division between Caucasians, Chinese, Japanese, and Koreans, who rank consistently high or occupy high status occupations, and Filipinos, Hawaiians, Puerto Ricans, and Samoans, all of whom occupy lower ranking on all the measures. In other words, Hawaii is clearly ethnically stratified due to such polarization of groups. This situation has obvious implications for controlling power and resources, including those of education. As Banks comments (1978:178):

> Interethnic relations in Hawaii suggest that, within an ethnically stratified society, ethnic groups that lack a sense of political efficacy, that are disproportionately represented in the lower classes, and that perceive themselves as economically, culturally, and politically oppressed, are likely to focus hostility on ethnic groups which are perceived as powerful and successful. This is likely to happen regardless of the racial or ethnic group memberships of the powerless groups and the groups that are perceived as powerful.

Historical context

> The demographic history of the past 200 years in Hawaii reflects the depopulation of the Islands by the native Hawaiians, the government policy for deliberate and gradual repopulation by immigrant national groups, the intermarriage and development of a multiethnic society, and the recent expansion of the population by foreign immigrants and by in-migrants from the continental United States. (Nordyke, 1977:58)

Following the period of initial western contact by European and American explorers, traders and later missionaries during the late eighteenth and first half of the nineteenth century, the plantation era was instigated. This was to last for nearly 100 years (Lind, 1967:7):

> . . . [it] markedly altered the racial complexion of Hawaii's population and set the stage for an unprecedented experiment in race relations. Peoples of sharply contrasting ethnic and racial origins . . . were imported in varying numbers to supply laborers for the expanding plantations of Hawaii, but with little thought for the complex processes of ethnic interaction which were thereby initiated.

In order of their arrival, the major ethnic groups recruited for sugar and pineapple plantation labour were Chinese, Portuguese, Japanese, Puerto Ricans, Koreans, Spaniards (most of whom subsequently emigrated to California), and finally Filipinos (1967:26–31). One of the results of this era has been a partial stratification by race of Hawaiian society.

> During most of the sixty-year period prior to World War II, when sugar and pineapple production dominated Hawaii's economic life, a fairly distinct barrier of social distances separated the proprietary whites from the large mass of nonwhite laborers on the plantation, and a further isolation of the ethnic groups at the lower levels of the plantation occupational hierarchy also emerged. (1967:9)

However, this structure did not become rigid, because avenues of escape for dissatisfied plantation workers were available in the growing trading and commercial centres. Social mobility has been a feature of

148   *The Pluralist Dilemma in Education*

the system, as the successive waves of immigrants imported every few decades or so loaded the bottom levels of the social scale and helped earlier arrivals move up the scale. 'Thus, the labor demands of the plantation system itself helped to undermine the static ethnic stratification ordinarily associated with it' (Petersen, 1969:867).

The second major influence on the present ethnic and racial composition of Hawaii has been the introduction of American political and military forces. This started in the mid-nineteenth century as a means of protecting American commercial interests, but became much more apparent after 1920 and accelerated during World War II. One effect was to generate some 'racial' tensions between servicemen and local non-Caucasians which have persisted. However, in Lind's opinion (1967:11) 'the preponderant influence has been toward the preservation of the Island pattern of race relations, and in the areas of normal association outside the military reservations, it has been the newcomers who have found it desirable "when in Hawaii to do as the Hawaiians do" '.

The third influence on Hawaii's pattern of interethnic relations has been the marked increase in tourism and temporary visitors chiefly from the American mainland in the post-World War II period. This has also produced a service and entertainment economy. A further influence from the mainland discussed earlier has been the influx of immigrants and in-migrants, i.e., those from mainland United States. The latter have increased markedly and now outstrip the immigrants. 'In 1975 there were 34 969 new residents from other states, and 9 012 from abroad. . . . Migration accounted for more than half the civilian population growth in Hawaii between 1970 and 1975' (Nordyke, 1977:80). The influx of in-migrants and residents has become a contentious political issue. 'The continued inflow of population from the United States mainland and abroad resembles a running faucet. City planners and legislators have been drafting measures to cope with resultant increased population and migrant problems, but they have not attempted to close the open tap' (1977:81).

The racial and ethnic groups making up the Hawaiian population have adopted varying forms of settlement location and strategies of adjustment to life in the islands (Lind, 1967:45–61). Hawaiians are still partially located in 'rural havens' or in small communities associated with cattle ranches in the less accessible parts of islands such as Hawaii, Maui and Niihau. On the most populated island, Oahu, Hawaiians, and part-Hawaiians even more so, have been attracted to the major urban centre of Honolulu. Since 1950, they have tended to move into 'suburban and peripheral areas outside the city proper' (1967:48).

Historically, the other major ethnic groups have followed different types of strategies (1967:49):

> In contrast with the Hawaiians and Part-Hawaiians, the immigrant labor groups have gravitated chiefly to either the plantations or the cities and

towns, with a limited number of intermediate movements to small farming areas or to military or tourist centers. With the plantations chiefly responsible for their introduction to the islands, the workers almost without exception found in the camps in the midst of the cane or pineapple fields their initial and sometimes their permanent places of residence in Hawaii, but most of them have also utilized the city as another area of adjustment to Island life.

Groups such as the Portuguese, Puerto Ricans, and more recently the Filipinos, have tended to remain more concentrated in or near the plantations. On the other hand, the Chinese, Koreans, and Japanese have been more attracted to life in the major cities. Haoles, i.e., the Caucasian (excluding Portuguese) segment of the population, differ markedly from the other ethnic groups. Historically, Haoles were the original 'invaders and the promoters of both commercial and plantation enterprises in the Islands' (1967:53), but despite these activities they were attracted to Honolulu. Today, Oahu accounts for nearly 90 per cent of the Caucasian population of Hawaii, mainly located in Honolulu or its suburbs and nearby naval or military establishments.

Despite the different settlement preferences of the various ethnic groups in Honolulu, Lind (1967:53−61) notes several features that make it different from other mainland cities, even though historically it did have distinctive areas and immigrant 'camps' virtually exclusive to various ethnic communities. 'Probably the first impressive fact about the ethnic communities in Honolulu, as compared with those of most cities in continental United States, is the relative absence of sharply marked boundaries between them' (1967:54). Most formerly separate and distinctive ethnic or racial 'islands' have also lost these characteristics as the boundaries between them have fused, or as members of other ethnic groups have moved into the area and made it more cosmopolitan. This has occurred in the better-class neighbourhoods and suburbs as each ethnic group improves its economic status and is able to move up the social scale and disperse out of the poorer community or 'ghetto' where it first settled. An exception to this cycle has been the Haoles, who have always been better placed economically. 'The one distinguishing trait of the European and American settlements in Honolulu is their location in the better residential areas of the city' (1967:59).

Two other historical aspects of Hawaiian society have a bearing on present day interethnic and interracial relationships. They are the economic or occupational life of the ethnic groups, and their degree of assimilation or fusion into one 'people'. Lind (1967:83) sums up the former after considering various factors about the changing Hawaiian economy and the degrees of success members of the ethnic groups have had in finding occupations and trying to advance their status:

Obvious inequalities, based in part upon the order of arrival, the length of residence in Hawaii, and the cultural traditions which each group has perpetuated, still exist and will continue for some time in the future, but the differences become less apparent with each passing decade. . . . It is also evident, however, that the trends toward the equalization of occupational participation occur only in stages and usually involve a considerable number of separate steps.

The implication of Lind's analysis of the economic situation is that the gradual equalization of opportunity and availability of avenues for upward social mobility will reduce 'racial' tensions between the various ethnic groups. However, he notes (1967:71) a considerable unemployment rate in the 1950s (8.4 per cent) following the decline of the artificial wartime prosperity. His analysis at this point is not pressed to the logical conclusion, namely, that unemployment might exacerbate tensions.

A further economic shift during the forties which had far-reaching consequences on race relations following the war was 'the sudden transformation of Hawaii from a region of minimal labor organization to one of the most highly organized areas in the United States' (1967:71). Prior to this time the general organization of plantation labour was paternalistic, with recreational and social clubs, or religious groups arranged on racial lines. Less than one-twenty-fifth of the gainfully employed were unionized (1967:73).[1] Again Lind does not elaborate on this statement, and we are left to infer that with increased unionization, the organization of labour at least on the plantations became less paternalistic, and race relations improved.

Lawrence Fuchs (1961:436) provides some evidence that in the post-statehood period since 1959 some non-Haoles succeeded in getting into top executive positions in Caucasian firms. For a time Oriental businessmen tended to regard such persons as 'window dressing', but this tendency gradually disappeared. Nevertheless, there was a history of Haole domination of top posts in commerce and industry, and of little social mixing between Haoles and Chinese or other ethnic groups. Evidence also suggests (1961:441) that 'discrimination against Filipinos in employment in Honolulu and other cities continued throughout the 1950s, although it was probably not nearly as widespread as claimed by Filipino respondents in interviews'. Another ethnic group affected was the Hawaiians and part-Hawaiians. These 'still found it difficult to compete for status, wealth and power on the terms imposed by the dominant Haoles and Orientals' (1961:443). A further trend noted by Fuchs is what might be termed the 'roots syndrome'. Chinese, Japanese, and Filipinos and Hawaiians more recently, are becoming conscious of their cultural backgrounds and roots. In 1959, something of a 'psychological rebirth of the Hawaiian people' was taking place (Fuchs 1961). Whether this trend has led to cleavages between the various ethnic groups during the 1960s and 1970s — the period following the publication of Fuchs' book — remains to be established.

Lind's analysis of the factors leading to the fusion of the islanders into one people takes in such aspects as education and assimilation, political status and participation, place of living, births and deaths as assimilative indices, interracial marriages, and biological fusion. Some of the evidence seems inconclusive in supporting Lind's general thesis: the gradual assimilation and amalgamation of ethnic groups. However, his overall conclusion tends to point in this direction (Lind, 1967:115):

> It is reasonable to assume, and evidence from this and other sources support the proposition, that assimilation or the spiritual fusion of Hawaii's people moves more rapidly than amalgamation, but both processes are moving irresistibly forward. The peoples of Hawaii are becoming Hawaii's people.

Ideologies and ideologists

It is very difficult to establish a clear-cut distinction between ideologies and counter-ideologies in Hawaii because the research data do not divide neatly into these types of categories. This may well be due to the subtle complexity of power relationships in the islands' education system, a feature well described by Shiho Nunes, formerly Associate Director of the Hawaii Curriculum Center and Manager of the Hawaii English Project (Nunes, 1977:13):

> The influence networks which obtain in Hawaii's educational system form a fascinating arena for study . . . We know, for example, that a relatively few legislators hold the key to educational decisions in our state legislature but that their support depends on a number of shifting factors in which personality plays a large part. We know that the board is often frustrated on policy issues about which they differ strongly with the legislature and/or the Governor's office and that the pressure points to apply on these issues lie outside the school body. We know that the decisive power is exercised by a relatively small number of people in an informal power structure outside of the formal decision structure, but that this power varies according to the nature of the decision. We know that the members within this group vary greatly in the degree of influence they wield, and that their influence is not necessarily associated with social or economic status.

The conventional wisdom

It seems popularly held that there are few, if any, racial tensions or prejudices between the various ethnic groups. In general conversation, the subject is tacitly avoided, or one is cautioned quickly that it is 'not done' to refer to Hawaii as a multiracial state or to use racial criteria to describe the society. 'Multiracial' as a descriptive term is generally not found in the literature.

This does not mean that such tensions are absent; they are in fact there, but the official and semi-official views for 'public' consumption paint a much more idyllic picture, one rather similar to that implied by Andrew Lind's conclusions discussed above. It is ideologically assimilationist and anticipates the evolution of 'one people'. In its most poetic form, it looks forward to the making of a Hawaiian who is 'raceless', as the following description, written in 1974 by the newspaper columnist Sammy Amalu, suggests (cited in Nordyke, 1977:55):

> A Hawaiian is a child born of this soil or bred of its bounty. A child who has known the mountain rain wet upon his cheeks, who has sipped of our sweet waters. A child who has worn our blossoms upon his neck and who has known tears when he has had to live away from our hills and our valleys. He is not of any one blood or of any one race.

Government and official ideologies

The pre-selection campaign for the Governorship and associated Senate positions took place in 1978. Candidates' speeches reported in the media provided some general information on ideologies at this official level. Two themes emerged in speeches by Governor Ariyoshi. The first concerned Hawaii's ethnic diversity, the second referred to environmental issues and the quality of life. Typical of the former is the statement reported in the article 'Report on Rally for Governor Ariyoshi' (*Honolulu Star-Bulletin*, 25 September 1978, p.1):

> In his brief speech Ariyoshi harked back to his campaign theme of ethnic diversity. 'You are a very unique people . . . look at the diversity which surrounds me tonight. It's that same diversity that unites us in a spirit of togetherness. That's Hawaii'.

That apparently contradictory catchphrase, 'Unity in Diversity', which the statement echoes, is a favourite one with politicians in countries around the world. Associate Professor Chattergy of the College of Education, University of Hawaii, believes that Governor Ariyoshi's ideology is indicative of a humanistic approach to people, i.e., that one should not mistrust them. An ideology of ethnic diversity implies the cultivation of harmonious human relationships between the people of Hawaii.

The Governor's second major theme related to a current preoccupation of Hawaii's leaders — that the islands are under threat from environmental and demographic pressures. This can be interpreted as a form of conservationist concern to resist or mitigate change that might radically alter the lifestyle status quo. In the final analysis it leads to an assimilationist stance towards newcomers, who must adapt, rather than create change. Renaud (1972:6) suggests that government concern over this issue may be psychologically motivated at a fundamental level that has its roots in a Hawaiian ethos: 'The traditional Hawaiian way of life appears to have a high psychic value for many locally born residents and others as well.' Governor Ariyoshi's position on this issue was reported in the article 'The Gubernatorial Campaign Issues' (*Honolulu Star-Bulletin*, 22 September 1978, pp.A14–15):

I am well on record as advocating, and acting on, the premise that we must control growth in Hawaii if we are to protect this fragile treasure of Hawaii, socially, economically and environmentally.

Running concurrently with the election compaign was a protracted Constitutional Convention. This produced a number of statements which provided insights into the quite contrary views of Hawaiian society held by some prominent politicians. Majority leaders at the Convention were reported as saying that a struggle had developed between those members of the local-dominated Democrat Party, who were elevated to power by the political 'revolution' of the 1950s, and those Republican Party 'landed gentry' who had been deposed. A number of interpretations of the struggle were put forward, one even suggesting that the locals' resistance to change was a form of paranoia and non-acceptance of the fact that Hawaii is multi-ethnic. Others saw the struggle as a conflict between locals and newcomers to the islands, or between a special interest group trying to preserve the status quo and its established power base and a large number of other people who do not have such an advantage, for example, mainland Haoles and Filipinos. This last was one reason for the charge that the struggle was essentially a form of racism.

One delegate, Lawrence Kono, suggested that the 1960s, when 90 per cent of the Hawaiian State Legislature was of Japanese and Chinese ancestry, have long gone. The new, emerging reality, reflecting a radical shift in the population base and the awakening of the aboriginal Hawaiian culture consciousness, is that the Japanese/Chinese political influence will diminish as the mainland Haole, Hawaiian and Filipino influences replace it. This possibility brought out a genuine fear among conservatives that mainland Haoles would capture more power than the locals. What Kono objected to, however, was the assimilationist view adopted by some locals, that newcomers should suppress their cultural identities and adopt the prevailing norms.

The possibility of power confrontation also shows itself in a generational split that has developed in Hawaii, according to Professor Arthur King, head of the Curriculum Research and Development Group at the University of Hawaii Laboratory School. Many of those who are over 40 years old in Hawaii are assimilationist, and adopt the melting pot ideology. They are a generation of Anglo-Saxon 'Americans' and locals who are traditionally achievement-oriented, and who extol the virtues of 'doing one's own thing' and 'making it' in commerce and industry. Many Chinese in this group are millionaires, or at least very well off. Japanese-Americans of this generation dominate the State Legislature.

Opposing this group are those who are in the 30–35 age bracket. They have been affected by the 'roots syndrome' and believe in the importance of their ethnic heritage. As a form of counter-ideology, they place considerable emphasis on the economic and social situation affecting them and their group, and on the discrimination that brought their ancestors to Hawaii. The views of this group — many of whom are counter-ideologists — are not so strident as was formerly the case, as their economic situation is ameliorating to some extent. Members of this group tend to see themselves as 'hyphenated Americans'.

Statistical support for the apparent presence of a generation gap is provided in a survey carried out by Dannemiller (1977) for the Commission on Population and the Hawaiian Future, a body set up by the government. The anti-mainlander feeling came out in data which showed that more respondents were in favour of reducing immigration from the mainland and other countries than were against, although the relative degree of agreement to limiting mainland in-migration was noticeably lower than for limiting foreign immigration. There was a clear division between those who had lived in the islands for less then twenty years, and those who had lived there for over twenty years. The majority of the former disagreed with the policy alternative about limiting numbers of people coming from the mainland; a majority of the latter agreed with the policy alternative.

A closely related phenomenon both in ideology and practice is to emphasize the 'local boy'. According to Dr King, the attitude of former Governor Burns was to encourage non-Caucasian immigrants to avoid domination of the islands' structure by whites (Haoles). The new Japanese/American government's policy is to keep immigrant foreigners out. The Government and Legislature are controlled by the descendants of earlier immigrants, and have adopted an approach which promotes locals, i.e., people from Hawaii who are non-Haole, and localist interests. Local values are stressed and outside values de-emphasized. This approach also appears to conform to public sentiment, but in Dr King's opinion could lead to tensions between 'in' and 'out' groups. It is obviously assimilationist as diversity is discouraged, and for the newcomer to succeed in Hawaii he must conform to its values and attitudes.

Whatever his ethnic group and country of origin, he also has a number of economic, educational and other barriers to overcome, according to David and King (1972:i). For instance, many Samoan immigrants have less than a high school education. Like some recent immigrant groups, e.g., Filipino, Koreans, and Japanese, they also have problems with the English language, and this, combined with low level of education, limits their employment opportunities. If Samoans face a major problem of unemployment, for the Filipinos there is a problem of under-employment for some professionals and probably tensions associated with a change of occupation for many others, e.g., farmers and fishermen being employed in service industries.

United States' citizenship requirements have severely limited employment opportunities for immigrants, although recent legal decisions have indicated that these limitations will be eased in time. The more restrictive element, however, is the 'residency' rule operating in Hawaii. According to Christensen (1972:77–82):

> Hawaii has maintained and continues to retain several statutory residence requirements which undoubtedly have a 'chilling effect on the right to travel'. Examination for and admission to the practice of the professions, county and state employment, employment by public utilities, and appointments to government bodies are among the activities prohibited to new residents of Hawaii.

It would appear that the 'golden local' also has legal backing to protect his interests. More importantly, it enables control to be exercised in an assimilationist way over those who may be accepted into professions. The implication seems clear: conform to local rules or not be accepted.

Ambivalent ideologies about Hawaiian society

One interpretation of the above evidence is that there is some ambivalence at the official political level about the nature of Hawaiian society. This is also the opinion of Helen Nagtalon-Miller, Project Coordinator for the Disadvantaged Minority Recruitment Program, School of Social Work, University of Hawaii at Manoa (1977:15). She finds supporting evidence for the ambivalent attitude in the Hawaii State Plan that was being considered in 1977, and was published in newspapers throughout the state to encourage public discussion. Among its suggestions are:

> CULTURAL HERITAGE: Hawaii's most valuable asset is its people and the various cultural and ethnic groups in the islands. Historical sites, artifacts, customs, traditions, and language are part of Hawaii's multicultural heritage. Hawaii's cultures are also viewed as dynamic entities that transmit values, beliefs, identity, and knowledge through the generations, act as a mutual benefit association, and promote socialization. . . .

> It is important to realize that without a strong desire by Hawaii's people to maintain their cultural and ethnic ties, on an individual and family level, there is little that government can do to support the influences of cultural and ethnic groups.

The ideology is apparently multiculturalism, of the cultural pluralist variety described by James Banks. There seems to be official support for the desirability of ethnic and cultural diversity as a benefit to society, but it would seem to be half-hearted and qualified support. Nagtalon-Miller goes on to suggest that elsewhere in the Plan an opposite point of view is evident:

> SOCIO-CULTURAL ADVANCEMENT: Society places a high value on self-reliance for each individual. Satisfying employment and adequate income should provide each individual with the opportunities to fulfill his or her needs and aspirations. Basic needs include adequate food, clothing,

shelter, health care, and a purposeful life. Education, social services, culture and leisure provide the basis for personal well-being. Society, through its government, assumes responsibility for the protection of civil rights, community values and public safety.

'Clearly', suggests Nagtalon-Miller, 'this is a statement of the Anglo-American-Puritan ethic prevailing in the community which does not include within it other cultural values sharing the Hawaiian scene, such as the *'ohana* system of the Hawaiians and the similar extended family systems of those with Asian backgrounds.' The ambivalence seems obvious.

Social welfare and educational ideologies

The state of Hawaii has a centralized school system, administered from Honolulu by a Department of Education (DOE) which is dominated by persons of Japanese-American and Caucasian ancestry (Howard, 1974:222). The Superintendent, Charles Clark, is a local Haole. The DOE makes policies within the school system, and is guided by the official ideology in such matters as curriculum selection, staffing and school organization. Some development is undertaken in collaboration with organizations such as the Curriculum Research and Development Group (CRDG) of the University of Hawaii. The Department also has its own Curriculum Development and Technology Section, recently renamed the Curriculum Materials and Services Development Section.

Judging from an edition of the College of Education's journal devoted to curriculum research and development, such collaboration has been productive. As Hinze *et al.* note (1977:4):

> . . . we are convinced that Department of Education/University of Hawaii cooperation in curriculum improvement activities can be maintained over long periods of time. The common goals held by both state education agencies provide enough cohesive force to overcome the differences that occasionally arise.

Programmes are developed by each organization either unilaterally or in collaboration. These include the Hawaii English Program (Elementary and Secondary); the Multicultural Awareness (Social Studies) Project; the Japanese Language and Culture Program. The latter is initiated and developed by CRDG. A number of other programmes are listed in the Kalihi-Palama Directory. Recurring themes are the need to improve skills in English as a second language for adults and children, multicultural awareness development in order to improve interpersonal-intergroup relationships among students, and culture-learning by children from ethnic groups in order to enhance their self-image.

A major programme developed unilaterally by the DOE is the Hawaii Bilingual/Bicultural Education Project.[2] This is a 'federally funded, experimental project to demonstrate a successful model for aiding the education and social development of Hawaii's limited-English speaking students'. The organization administering the Project is the Community and Support Services Branch of the Office of Instructional Services of the Hawaii State Department of Education. Its purpose is 'to assist limited-English speaking students to learn academically through their native language, to gain proficiency in English and participate successfully in regular classrooms, and to develop positive self-images and respect for their native language and culture'. The major emphasis is on elementary grade students who come from homes where Ilocano, Samoan, Korean, Cantonese, and Japanese are spoken.

Bilingual aides are employed to assist the regular classroom teachers, in teaching mathematics and language arts to those speaking limited-English, using their native language as the medium of instruction. The aides also 'assist in the development and evaluation of bilingual learning materials and present culture learning activities. They also aid the student with special language problems and participate on request in parent conferences.'

The basic ideologies behind the project seem assimilationist and compensatory. In the opinion of Associate Professor Virgie Chattergy the Education Department's approach to bicultural/bilingual projects has been heavily influenced by the mainland experience with Chicano students. The mimeographed description of the project makes it clear that Anglo-conformity and compensation are emphasized although the importance of home language is recognized:

> The primary purpose of the program is to help limited-English speaking students acquire competent English language skills to succeed in school. They are instructed in their native language to assure their continued development in mathematics and language arts, and to promote retention and fluency in their native language. . . . The program is designed to accelerate the learning of English. . . .

The emphasis in the above programmes is either a limited form of multiculturalism or bilingual/biculturalism. The former group stresses interpersonal and intercultural awareness skills, though it is not clear whether this reflects the Governor's humanistic ideology of group harmony mentioned above or the presence of interethnic tensions in schools. The group of bilingual/bicultural programmes heavily emphasizes adjustment to Hawaiian culture, or 'American culture in its Hawaiian setting', and thus have an assimilationist implication.

However, the notion that there might be tensions in schools is disputed by the DOE Superintendent, Charles Clark, whose pronouncement on this issue is forceful. In a DOE publication, *The News of the School* (vol. 8, no. 3, November 1976) Clark is reported as refuting charges of racism in Hawaii's public schools by a political candidate by referring to them as a 'bunch of hogwash'. The Superintendent noted at a news conference that 'Hawaii's population in general is composed of more than 50 per cent minorities and that 77.8 per cent of Hawaii's children are minority group children . . . [they] are assigned to schools on a geographical basis and . . . [the] school populations reflect the communities from which the students come'. Clark also stated that the federal regulations forced the DOE to categorize students by ethnic group and thus may, in themselves, cause some racial problems.

> We are not going to let this happen in Hawaii as long as I am superintendent. We would like to see every child continue to get equal opportunity . . . and there isn't any state in the nation that provides equal opportunity for all its children as Hawaii does because of our unique statewide system. The Board of Education and the Legislature see that funds are allocated equally to every place so that every child gets an equal education.

In the opinion of Associate Professor Mike Forman, of the Department of Linguistics at the University of Hawaii, ethnic group categories do exist and are known; it is not creating categories and racial problems by mentioning them. Racism and intergroup tensions do exist in schools according to David and King (1972:51). Pointing to the problems of Filipino immigrants, they note that ethnic group leaders reported that immigrant children who learn standard English may be ridiculed by children who speak the island dialect (i.e., 'pidgin' English). Recent immigrant children are frequently called 'PIs' (Pacific Islanders) by Hawaiian-born Filipino children. A police officer reported that an increasing number of recent immigrant children have been taking knives to school to protect themselves from non-immigrant children. Forman also commented that the DOE policy of making federal funds available on an equal basis to each child contravenes specific regulations in the Act forbidding this practice. Hawaii was the last of the 45 eligible states to apply for and accept money under the provisions of the Title VII Bilingual Education Act, and the bilingual education provided would appear to be a token in minimal fulfilment of the Title VII mandate. What is provided is based mostly on the transition approach, and is thus fundamentally assimilationist.

Something of the reluctance of the DOE to apply for Title VII funds in response to the beginnings of pressure from the community for bilingual education can be gauged from a 'leaked' in-house memorandum, 'Some Considerations Relative to Designing and Implementing a Bilingual Program for the State of Hawaii'. This was sent by Thomas M. Hale, in charge of the section of DOE responsible for TESOL programmes to Dr Clarence Masumotoya, in charge of Federal Grants, as an apparent attempt to drum up an argument to counter the pressure from the community. Among other things, it states:

> (1) The following thoughts may assist you, in responding to the Superintendent regarding DOE's participation in acquiring funds for a bilingual project —

1. A major aspect to consider is the fact that Hawaii is not a multilingual or even a bilingual community. . . .

* * * * *

(4) Although a monolingual community, Hawaii is also a bi-dialectical community, in spite of the vast sums of money and effort expended in an attempt to make it mono-dialectical.

Regardless of the somewhat involved logic of the above, it is apparent that the main thrust of the argument is assimilationist.

Such views and antipathy to dealing with mainland or federal authorities are not the prerogative of DOE bureaucrats. Jean King, a candidate for the 1978 elections, had this to say on the 1975 Federal Voting Rights Act's requirement to have election material available in a language other than English, where sufficient numbers of non-English speakers were in the community to warrant such a provision (*Honolulu Star-Bulletin*, 26 September 1978, p.A.17): 'For Hawaii, it doesn't make sense and is a waste of taxpayers' money. We should continue to follow through on Lieutenant-Governor Doi's efforts to get the federal government to either change the requirements or exempt Hawaii.' The underlying attitude is similar to Clark's on racism, and is widespread in Hawaii. There cannot be discrimination because 'Hawaii is different' and federal laws therefore do not apply. It is also assimilationist in intent: voters must learn English to vote, regardless of their ethnic backgrounds.

Thus, for several reasons, the official commitment to bilingualism/biculturalism implied by programmes in the Kalihi-Palama Directory needs to be treated with some caution. Even the claim that some programmes use bilingual teacher aides, counsellors, interpreters or other personnel is suspect. Although a variety of languages is referred to, e.g., Ilocano, Tagalog, Visayan, Japanese, Chinese, Korean, Samoan, Vietnamese, etc., the degree of expertise in these languages possessed by the bilingual person may not be at all adequate. For example, a Japanese cleaner or janitor who knows a little Ilocano might be listed to make it appear that an interpreter is available to fulful the federal requirements. He obviously would not be at all competent.

Superintendent Clark's more recent comments on Hawaiian education do not specifically mention bicultural/bilingualism or multiculturalism. His address to principals at the annual superintendents' seminar, setting the tone and direction for the coming school year, was reported in the *Honolulu Advertiser*, 22 August 1978, p.A7, under the title '4th R (reasoning) added to schools' literacy drive'. It reflects the growing climate of concern in education for basic literacy, and the toughening of standards for matriculation. In Clark's opinion: 'Schools should concentrate their resources on teaching students the three Rs and the culture, history and government of Hawaii and the U.S.; on challenging students to do their best; and on helping students develop a positive self-concept.' In referring to '*the* culture . . .' (italics added), Clark may be implying that only one version needs to be taught, while the cultures and histories of other ethnic groups can be neglected. If this is the intention, it is obviously assimilationist.

Ideologies in curriculum development and teacher education

The working relationship between the Department of Education and the CRDG is one justification for including the Group in this section. Dr Mike Hamnett of the East-West Center Culture Learning Institute was doubtful about seeing the Group's role in counter-ideological terms. Further, the theoretical basis of its curriculum research and development activities is a justification for seeing the Group's role as supportive of the current ideology.

Professor King, Director of the Group, provided the information that the theme of the cultural materials it has produced is 'All cultures in all times'. Most recent developments are to write materials in two languages and to 'ethnicize' themes and booklets, with Japanese being the most common second language. Research into how people learn differently is being carried out, but, rather surprisingly, a class-based model is being used to explain the differences between the various ethnic groups.

A major feature of the Group's work is to produce materials and kits *and* provide a course of training in their use as an indispensable part of the programme. Over 90 per cent of teachers are signing up for the materials and training programmes, and seem highly motivated by this type of strongly controlled in-service training. However, it is not an approach that appeals to those in teacher education organizations, who are wedded to doctrinaire progressivism, and are resistant to what they would see to be a reactionary movement including the theory developed by King and his colleagues from which the Group takes its direction (King, 1977:6). 'Interestingly the theory found support among the majority of school board members, state legislators, and general citizens.'

The Hawaiian State Department of Education has used various federal funds to undertake the development of several major multi-cultural projects. One of them, the Hawaii Multicultural Awareness Pilot Project (HMAP), is funded under the Emergency School Aid Act (ESAA), and carried out by the CRDG under contract with the DOE. Forman and Mitchell (1977:26) describe the main features of the programme:

> HMAP is designing and pilot-testing multicultural programs which are intended to help accomplish the following: (1) enhance the students' understanding and appreciation of their own cultural heritage, (2) increase students' intercultural understanding and appreciation, (3) increase students'

cross-cultural communication skills, and (4) provide students with the necessary knowledge and skills to live successfully in Hawaii's pluralistic society (including those features and institutions common to all).

. . . The developers are well aware that other approaches are also needed if the harmful effects of minority group isolation and alienation are to be eliminated in Hawaii. However, the provision of multicultural curriculum materials suitable for Hawaii's unique multicultural situation seems a necessary, if not sufficient, condition for achieving that end.

Details provided by the authors of what has been produced to date indicate that the approach seems to be what Gay has termed Stage 1 of multicultural education (1977:6) typical of mainland programmes in the 1960s. So far the HMAP has produced units for inclusion in the grade 4–6 social studies programmes, materials for inclusion in the grade 7–8 social studies programmes to provide a multicultural perspective, and in high school 'a semester course in modern Hawaiian history which will give full play to the roles of Hawaii's various ethnic groups' (1977). One feature is the translation of programme materials into the various native languages represented among those groups presently immigrating to Hawaii (Forman & Mitchell, 1977:27).

It seems apparent that the College of Education's basic approach to teacher education in Hawaii is broadly similar to that followed by colleges on the mainland. Each department follows its own direction, as do individual professors, who tend to follow their own inclinations and academic preferences, and prescribe their own books as student reading. Students have considerable autonomy in choosing a programme from a wide range of 'bitsy' courses available. There is little sense of an overall pattern to the whole teacher education curriculum or of it being wedded to a cultural theme or ideology that really caters for local Hawaiian needs. This lack of pattern is exacerbated by the current preoccupation, particularly in west-coast colleges, with competency-based education programmes. These are too often incapable of going beyond slogans and 'vocationalisms', and tend to fragment learning and reduce it to absurdity by neglecting the complexity and *gestalt* of the learning process. They also produce a negative, 'loser' effect on children and teacher education alike.

When all these comments are seen in the context of the sociopolitical, economic, and cultural situation, it is hard not to concur with the opinion that the major craft of teacher education in Hawaii is really impervious to its complexity. Coping effectively with its cultural differences is proving a baffling task for the majority of teacher educators. Some of these, it seems, have developed ideologies more as 'proposal language', for applications for federal and other grants, rather than as guiding philosophies at the levels of school, classroom and teacher education.

Counter-ideologies and ideologists

Parts of the counter-ideology about Hawaiian society have been alluded to in the above sections — anti-localism, preference for mainland influences, even multiethnicity. Much of this is vague and covert, and expressed through personal opinions in casual discussion. Here we attempt to identify the more overt counter-ideologies, but it is clear from the covert sources that there is a significant 'underground' body of dissatisfaction with the status quo and the dominant ideology. For whatever reason, these are not surfacing apart from very guarded and highly qualified criticisms.

Academic observers and theories

Typical of these broad criticisms are the counter-ideologies proposed by academic theorists. Some of these are attached to the University of Hawaii, others to the East-West Center Culture Learning Institute. For instance, according to Dr Franklyn Odo, Head of the Permanent Ethnic Studies Programme at the University of Hawaii, the 'golden local' syndrome — even a local Haole who is different from a mainland white — is a myth. It was 'spawned out of the logic of multicultural progress in Hawaii', and enables an official ideology of multiculturalism to be held simultaneously with a policy of assimilation. This is a neo-colonial mentality, dependent upon tourism and the military presence, which results in a labour force that is powerless to control production or mount effective criticism against the controlling forces. Ethnic groups in Hawaii, according to Dr Odo, are part of a very subtle situation in which there is considerable room for cultural flexibility. Ethnic minorities are large enough to preserve their continuity but not their old traditions. Despite this, each still maintains a strong sense of group identity.

Whether this is a strong enough basis for mounting political action and developing a coherent counter-ideology with programmatic and social change implications is debatable. Dr Mike Hamnett is of the opinion that the various ethnic programmes provided by the University and described below may be the first foundations of a counter-ideology that could lead to greater political awareness on the part of Hawaii's ethnic groups, and even to political action.

Hamnett maintains that he has observed local trends similar to those which became major features of the Black power movement and Black Revolution on the mainland in the 1960s. The stress in such programmes as Philippine studies and south-east Asian studies at the University seems to be on the historical, ethnic heritage features of respective groups. In the political arena, some of the people who have been involved with the ethnic heritage approach are using the data obtained from historical studies as symbols to group and motivate people, give them a common cause, and provide the basis for a common identity to struggle for scarce resources. One would have to trace through, person by person, to see whether it is the same people, e.g., the ethno-historians, who are politicizing the ethnic heritage and making it symbolic, or different people who see the other, political way of competition for scarce resources as the name of the game in Hawaii. It may well be that this other group is taking the symbols provided by the University's ethnic studies programmes and turning them into focuses for action, or ideologies of some sort.

According to Mike Forman, it seems apparent that a counter-ideological movement of the kind suggested by Hamnett does exist in Hawaii. For instance, there are strong grounds for believing that more discrimination exists in the schooling provided for some ethnic children than is apparent from the official programmes publicized by the DOE, or from the disclaimers to the contrary of Superintendent Clark. Less than 3 per cent of the teachers employed by the Department are Filipinos, yet 16 per cent of the school population comes from this ethnic background. This produces tensions in class, for instance, Ilocano-speaking or English creole-speaking kindergarten children quickly learn to keep their mouths shut when a Japanese teacher is taking them. The Oahu Filipino Task Force on Education has been set up, and acts to counter discrimination of the sort described above. It has adopted a pluralistic, multicultural approach, and already it has filed lawsuits with the Office of Civil Rights Against Discrimination.

The need to politicize ethnicity and use it as the basis for action to counter discrimination is not confined to Filipinos. Alan Howard (1974) gives an account of a major project conducted in the late 1960s by a team he directed from the Department of Anthropology at the University of Hawaii, which made an intensive study of 'Aina Pumehana, a Hawaiian-American community some forty-eight kilometres from Honolulu. It aimed to 'analyze the cultural, social, and psychological contexts within which the behaviour of interest to social action agencies took place'. As a possible solution, Howard advocates a brand of cultural pluralism, after rejecting both assimilation and resistance as 'simplification strategies' (1974:240). The main tenor of the argument is that diversification in the society should be encouraged but abuses of power by the ruling élites should be curbed, in order to limit the scope of the 'public domain' in society (1974:243):

A strategy of cultural pluralism, since it aims at limiting the power of the ruling élite, will almost certainly involve a degree of resistance and doing battle. . . .

It would mean striving to increase the material resources available to Hawaiian-Americans, thus altering the situational variables affecting their lives, while allowing cultural patterns to work themselves out. It would also require demanding of the power élite that the Polynesian-Hawaiian lifestyle be accommodated by the current institutional structure, including the schools.

It is interesting to speculate whether this type of 'manifesto' from an academic writer has played any part in the emergence of the Hawaiian consciousness referred to above.

Programmes within the University of Hawaii

Although the programmes appear on the surface to be conventional and even in line with the official ideology, within the context of what appears to be happening in Hawaii, they may well be the harbingers of a counter-ideology. Courses of English as a Second Language are available as an academic programme to all eligible applicants. Members of this programme also provide consultancy services for local organizations and teachers. A conventional ethnic studies programme is provided for University of Hawaii students and interested members of the community, consisting of academic classes in ethnicity; ethnic programs, e.g., dances, films, speakers, etc.; holiday celebrations; moral support for immigrants; and ethnic identity courses.

'Operation Manong' based at the University is a novel programme to bring students in community work into contact with Samoan, Filipino and Korean youth in the city. It is particularly concerned with cross-cultural communication and heritage, through tutorials, recreational and cultural assistance. 'Manong', according to Mike Forman, is derived from the Spanish for 'brother', which is a respectful term of address among Filipinos, but also can be used as a subtle term of reproach in reference to others.

The need to keep the overall context in mind applies with equal force to the innovatory programme introduced into the College of Education's Department of Curriculum and Instruction by Virgie Chattergy, backed by the financial support of a large grant of US$108 000 from the Federal government. This has given Dr Chattergy considerable autonomy and 'leverage' to overcome the general apathy towards, and even suspicion of, multicultural education in the Department.

According to Dr Chattergy, this general suspicion may be the result of the developing attitudes of the American Association of Colleges of Teacher Education. The Association held a meeting of deans of colleges in Washington in December 1977 and it appears that the deans had difficulty in understanding multiculturalism. They were either wary or suspicious of ethnic studies, which were seen as the outcome of the civil rights movements. The deans emphasized that a human relations philosophy should be stressed instead. Dr Chattergy believes that this was an example of an AACTE power group changing the rules of the multiethnicity model to reduce the sharpness of the ethnic revitalization movement in schools, and of curriculum development. The new AACTE approach to multiculturalism represents an important institutional change with obvious implications for education in Hawaii and throughout the United States.

Her own approach to multicultural education is best conveyed by a working draft position paper, prepared on behalf of the Department for a PEACESAT transmission on Multicultural Education, which took place in October 1978.

> Philosophically, multicultural education must focus on the developing individual and the dynamics involved in his interactions which may be transcultural and transethnic. It is the development of the thinking and feeling individual who happens to be a member of a particular ethnic group.

> Pedagogically, multicultural education operationalizes the concept of cultural pluralism, within the school setting. It legitimizes diversity by incorporating into the curriculum, the contributions of diverse cultural groups, their ways of perceiving, explaining the environment, expressing fear, joy, sorrow and other expressions of survival and adaptation. It allows for a rational and intellectually honest approach to a comparative study of the human condition which makes us alike in some ways and different in other ways.

It will be obvious how closely this interpretation of multiculturalism matches the official, early ideology of the mainland ideologists. But, within the different situation of Hawaii, it may still be tantamount to a counter-ideology. Hawaii *is* different. The implications of this are taken up in the final chapter.

Notes

1. Lind cites these data from a publication by the United States Department of Labor, *Labor in the Territory of Hawaii* (Washington: US Printing Office, 1940), pp. 199, 202.
2. Mimeographed details were supplied by Dr Ted Rodgers of the College of Education, whose asistance is gratefully acknowledged.

CHAPTER 7

Australia

This chapter gives a concise review of the ideologies and provisions for ethnic education in pluralist Australia, drawing selectively on the wealth of material now available. As in Canada, for better or worse, multiculturalism has become the dominant ideology, generating a flourishing output of official, semi-government, and academic publications. For years Australian education has adopted overseas philosophies and practices, some years after they were current in their countries of origin — usually the United States or Britain. The adoption of multiculturalism is no exception, and details about Australia arouse a distinct sense of *déjà vu*. We have seen it all before in Canada, and the United States, even to the slogans and metaphors that are now being used in Australia to convey the ideology.

The socio-historical context

The current demographic pattern

The Australian population reached 14 million in January 1977, and the estimated total on 30 June 1977 was 14 074 000. 'In 1976, people born overseas made up 20 per cent of population, about the same as 1971 but an increase on earlier censuses' (*Year Book Australia*, 1979:10). Exact percentage figures for 1976 were: Australian born, 79.8 per cent; overseas born, 20.2 per cent (1979:10). From the point of view of identifying those 'migrants' (adults and children) for whom special educational, social welfare and other provisions may be needed, it is useful to know the percentage of persons born overseas and the percentage born in Australia of one or both parents born overseas. Figures provided by the *Report of the Committee on the Teaching of Migrant Languages in Schools* (1976:4−7), based on the 1971 census, show that out of a then total population of 12 755 638, 20.22 per cent of persons were born overseas, and a further 19.43 per cent were born in Australia of one or both parents born overseas. This makes a total of 39.6 per cent of the population either born overseas or with one or both parents born overseas. Of this total, over half were derived from non-English speaking countries.

The significance of these proportions should not be overestimated. It is frequently stated by those who support multiculturalism in Australia that well over a quarter to a third of the population are either migrants or children of migrants with the implication that they are culturally different from the rest of the population. The figures suggest otherwise. In 1971 the proportion of the total population from the United Kingdom, Eire, New Zealand, Canada, United States and the Republic of South Africa was 9.6 per cent. These are all people from backgrounds broadly similar to the Anglo-Australian mainstream culture. Only 10.6 per cent of the population came from countries which are non-English speaking, and these people *may* have backgrounds that are culturally different from the Australian culture to a significant degree. Even if we accept that a certain proportion of the children enumerated in the 1971 census were born in Australia of immigrant parents, the percentage of those in the total population from culturally different backgrounds is likely to be much smaller than conventional wisdom has it.

Taft (1978:98–99) arrives at somewhat similar conclusions. At least 80 per cent of the population of Australia is of English-speaking or Anglo-Saxon derivation and can be assumed to have a broadly matching Western culture. The remaining 20 per cent constitutes the 'multi' in multicultural. We would be more certain about the real significance of this figure if data were available to indicate how many people in Australia are living now in ways that are significantly different from the rest of the population. But this kind of data is not available, and any assessment of numbers of people who are culturally different must be very speculative indeed.

What is indisputable is the great variety of countries from which migrants have come, producing a rich diversity of cultural traits and backgrounds in Australia. The details are based on 1971 census data relating to the origin of immigrants and their children (1976:4–7). Nearly 100 individual countries are listed, and this number would be well exceeded if the countries grouped in such categories as 'other countries in Asia', and 'Other East European countries' were listed separately.

A feature of the migrant population in Australia is the change that has taken place in the countries of origin. The percentage of persons with birthplaces in the British Isles has declined in relation to 'other foreign-born' persons. Within this latter category, persons from Eastern Europe, Southern Europe and West Asia show a relative increase. The most striking decrease is the percentage of persons born in New Zealand.

> Immigration has contributed substantially to Australia's postwar population growth. In the postwar years, some 3.35 million migrants have arrived, of which an estimated 80 per cent settled. They and those of their children born in Australia have been responsible for about half of Australia's postwar population growth. (*Year Book Australia*, 1979:21)

The rate of immigration has been uneven, however, and particularly since 1971 there has been a progressive reduction in the overall levels of net migration. During the four-year period 1949—52, Australia experienced very high gains from immigration. Some reduction occurred during the next decade, and the level of net migration in that period was continued in the following decade 1961—70. The years 1969—70 saw a peak of 185 000 net migrants. However, five years later, in the years 1975—76, the intake fell to a record low of 52 000 (1979:98—99, 121).

A feature of the demographic pattern in Australia, which has played an important part in making provisions for the education and social welfare of indigenes and immigrants alike, is the uneven geographical distribution of the population and its concentration in major conurbations.

> For historical, climatic and economic reasons the population of Australia is concentrated in capital cities and other major towns, mainly on the south and east coast of the continent. In June 1976, 69.7 per cent of the population lived in the six State capital cities and five other major towns of 100 000 or more persons. Of these, only Canberra is located inland.

Sydney and Melbourne are the two major centres with 3 094 400 and 2 672 200 people respectively (1979:100—101). In particular, the schooling of immigrant children has posed severe problems in these two cities. Large numbers of migrants are also concentrated in the heavy industrial areas of Whyalla in South Australia. As the Committee on Community Relations has pointed out (1975:16):

> The heavy concentration of non-English speaking migrants in urban areas emphasizes the extent to which Australian industry and manufacturing industry is dependent on migrant labour and high-lights the social problems of urban growth. Migrant workers in lowly paid occupations are further disadvantaged by the cumulative harmful social effects of low quality housing, poor schooling and inadequate public facilities in congested inner city urban areas. The Henderson Poverty Inquiry Report stated that 'all groups of recent migrants had a higher proportion of poor people than the population as a whole'.

Assertions such as these need to be treated with caution, as it is all too easy to assume that all the states and major towns in Australia have similar concentrations of migrants, and similar 'migrant ghetto' problems. This is far from the case. For instance, although there are migrant groups in Hobart, the quality of their lives is different from that of migrant groups in Melbourne or Sydney, who are often assumed to be the norm in any discussion of migrants' problems.

Socio-economic, 'class' structure

The above comments are closely related to the positions that migrants occupy in the socio-economic structure of Australia. The following extended comments are taken from a detailed analysis by the Committee on Community Relations (1975:14—15), based on data from the Borrie Report, table III. 14, and statistical data provided by Professor Zubrzycki of the Australian National University:

> From Professor Zubrzycki's data it is apparent that: . . . of Australia-born males employed in the workforce, 18.3 per cent were 'craftsmen', British Isles migrants 26 per cent, Greeks 17.5 per cent, Italians 27.2 per cent and Yugoslavs 29.4 per cent. In the male workforce as a whole 'craftsmen' were represented by 20.3 per cent which included a significant number of other migrant skilled or semi-skilled workers not listed. This further confirms that the skilled labour component of the Australian workforce was significantly contributed to by migrants. It was also evidence of the concentration of non-English speaking Southern European migrants in these categories.

> The data also showed that a considerably larger number of Greek, Italian and Yugoslav migrants were employed as 'labourers' or in 'personal service' — approximately 31.9 per cent, 28 per cent and 31.3 per cent respectively, compared to the Australia-born component of 17.8 per cent, British Isles 16.9 per cent and the total male workforce percentage of 18.7. As these were essentially unskilled elements in the workforce, it also demonstrated that certain migrant groups were disproportionately represented as compared to others. 1971 Census data, showed that over 66 per cent of migrants from Southern and Eastern Europe were classified as unskilled or semi-skilled.

However, this picture is partially relieved by the presence of some migrants in higher occupational levels, which suggests that caution should be exercised before claiming, on the basis of the above data, that Australia's policy of directly recruiting migrants is generally aimed at obtaining cheap unskilled labour (Committee on Community Relations, 1975:15).

Migrant language groups

A major feature of the demographic pattern is the diversity of migrant languages spoken in the home or in informal situations. They are also used instead of English in the workplace when numbers of migrants from a similar background are present. Inability to speak English and difficulty with it is a recognized contributing cause of the lower ranking position of many non-English-speaking migrants in the occupational structure. It is often an excuse used by employers to retrench migrant workers at times of economic downturn (1975:20).

Making provisions for the training of both adult migrants and their children in English language skills is the responsibility of each state's education system, with federal assistance. It is made very difficult by the geographical concentrations of migrants described above. In particular, the situation faced by two states, New South Wales and Victoria, is accentuated by the patterns of concentration and dispersion of non-English language groups in primary and secondary schools. Immigrant children's language difficulties are of major concern in the education system, and both the dominant states have had to cope with disproportionate numbers of children from non-English-speaking homes in their schools.

The diversity of migrant groups is also reflected in the language groups, details of which will become available if, and when, data based on Item 19 in the 1976 Census are published. However, it should be noted that the details will probably show only a fraction of the possible languages and dialects spoken in migrant homes.

Indigenous racial groups

Australian Aboriginals and Torres Strait Islanders form a small but nevertheless important part of the demographic pattern of Australia. On 30 June 1971 there were 115 953 persons identifying with these races (*Year Book Australia*, 1979:104). Details are not provided, but Aboriginals and Torres Strait Islanders are of various degrees of full and mixed blood.

The distribution of these persons within each state varies considerably. Major cities like Sydney and Melbourne have numbers of Aboriginals living in depressed, slum and inner city areas. Some major country towns such as Alice Springs in the Northern Territory, Darwin, Mildura, and Bairnsdale in Victoria have Aboriginals living in fringe settlements. Some Aboriginals are artisans and small shopkeepers in country towns. In Queensland, where a major proportion of full-blood Aboriginals live, government-controlled reservation settlement is more common. Other Aboriginals in outback areas live on, or in close association with, cattle or pastoral stations and mission settlements. The 500 key tribal affiliations to which Aboriginals can belong lead to further diversity among these people (Tindale, 1974) — a point which is not generally recognized.

Historical context

Official policies towards immigrants

The arrival of immigrant settlers to Australia has always been a major feature of its history. Professor Borrie's (1948:33) comments about the very early period of immigrant settlement might equally apply to more recent times, although the sources of immigrants have changed:

> The demographic history of Australia from the foundation of the first settlement at Sydney Cove (1788) to the emergence of a federal Commonwealth (1901) . . . is the chronicle of the inpouring of thousands of immigrants, the great majority of them from the 'lower' and 'middle' classes of the British Isles.

The 'inpouring' of immigrants has been accompanied by regular shifts in official government thinking and policies about migrants. Their demographic foundations were laid largely in the pre-war period. This saw successive waves of British immigrants, many of them assisted by the British government, that continued through the 1920s under the Empire Settlement Act of 1922 and were only checked by the depression of the 1930s, which caused many British to return home. These waves were superimposed on the strong Australian nationalism which had continued since its evolution in the 1890s, coupled with an ' "old approach" to the assimilation of immigrants [which had] persisted with the tenacity of an unchangeable dogma' (Kovacs & Cropley, 1975:119). The result was a view of the type of immigration required for Australia's needs that persisted into the post-war period. As Jupp has noted (1966:5):

> This picture of an essentially British-Australian people, recruited partly with government assistance and fitting into a prosperous and relatively egalitarian society is the ideal on which subsequent immigration policies have been based. Even while launching the greatest planned influx of foreigners in Australian history, the Minister for Immigration, Mr Calwell, hoped 'that for every foreign migrant there will be ten people from the United Kingdom'.

This ideal had two important consequences. Firstly, the composition of the Australian population was predominantly of British origin. Secondly, this produced an official ideology which was assimilationist and Anglo-conformist. Immigrants were expected to fit into the Australian social and economic situation as quickly as possible. In extreme cases official feelings were even anti-migrant (1966:6):

> Apart from the Italians, who were officially discouraged after 1925, the only important foreign element arriving between the wars were the Jewish refugees of 1938 to 1940. Their entry was strongly opposed by the conservative side of Australian politics. The term 'reffo' was coined as one of abuse and continued to be used about the non-Jewish refugees who came after the war.

Immigration resumed in the immediate post-war period with the establishment of the Labour Government's Department of Immigration in 1945, with Arthur Calwell as Minister for Immigration. Planned immigration started in 1948, following the conclusion of the United Kingdom Assisted Passage scheme in 1947, and the start of Australian efforts through the International Refugee Organization to bring in refugees from the displaced persons (DP) camps of war-torn Europe.

A cluster of ideas contributed to the continuation of the assimilationist, Anglo-conformist official and public ideology of the following period (1966:7–8). The danger Australia had faced during the war from Japan revived the 'old myth of "populate or perish" as the response to the Yellow Peril'. This and the nationalistic sentiments of the Australian Labor Party were reflected in Calwell's determination to 'build Australia's population and industrial potential . . . [thus] in the immediate post-war years migrants were chosen because they could work and would contribute as much to Australia as they were likely to demand from it. The British were chosen as skilled workers and had someone in Australia to accommodate them' (1966:7–8).

Refugees and displaced persons, on the other hand, were chosen not only for their potential as industry fodder, but initially for reasons that were blatantly assimilationist, i.e., to be as physically like Australians as possible. This would assist their absorption into the community and arouse less antagonism than would the introduction of 'foreign'-looking immigrants. As Calwell himself (1972:103) was to comment later about the Balts and other Nordic types:

> Many were red-headed and blue eyed. There was also a number of natural platinum blondes of both sexes. The men were handsome and the women beautiful. It was not hard to sell immigration to the Australian people once the press published photographs of that group.

Pity those intending immigrants who did not match the Nordic image! 'If one were Scandinavian or British one could be assisted, but if one came from further south, more restrictions were placed in the way of migrating to Australia' (Appleyard, 1972:19). Other desirable groups of people were those from northern European countries close to Britain, such as the Netherlands, Germany, and Austria. Only when supplies of available migrants from these countries dried up, as they too experienced manpower shortages, were southern European countries like Italy, Greece, Yugoslavia tapped (1972:20).

Several organizations and programmes were set up in these early days to effect the 'organized assimilation' of immigrants into Australia, and to promulgate the official ideology. These moves took place under the Liberal government, which was elected to power in 1949, when it became apparent that many immigrants were not assimilating quickly or willingly enough, and when the government was faced with the type of situation described by Jupp (1966:9):

> Many East Europeans were almost destitute on arrival. They could not speak English, and had suffered great hardship and social dislocation. The new government saw this as a social problem. Like all Australian governments in the past, it wanted the smoothest and quickest assimilation of foreigners that was possible. Mr Menzies turned to the existing social work and religious groups for help. The problem was two-fold. The refugees had to be made welcome and the Australians had to be sold the idea of foreigners in their midst. On this basis the Good Neighbour movement was formed in 1950. A federal association of existing welfare groups, Good Neighbour stressed the 'handshake and cup of tea' approach. The Immigration Department set up the Commonwealth Immigration Advisory, Publicity, and Planning Councils.

Throughout the 1950s and 1960s the official ideology and policies towards immigrants continued to be assimilationist. Government leaders such as Harold Holt were able to say of this period at the major Citizenship Convention in 1965, 'You will remember that there was anxiety lest our assimilation purpose should fail and leave us with colonies of migrants, alien to our way of life and unassimilated, giving rise to a continuing social problem' (1966:102). This convention was dominated by an emphasis on naturalization which 'is taken as sealing the act of assimilation' despite the fact that many migrants choose to become naturalized for purely personal reasons or for convenience (Jupp, 1966:145; Kovacs & Cropley, 1975:113). Bill Snedden was appointed Minister for Immigration in December 1966. His three-year term of office was notable for at least one statement (cited in Cigler, 1975:23):

> We must have a single culture — if immigration implied multi-cultural acti-vities within Australian society, then it was not the type Australia wanted. I am quite determined we should have a monoculture, with everyone living in the same way, understanding each other, and sharing the same aspirations. We don't want pluralism.

The underlying philosophy is clearly Anglo-conformist and assimi-lationist. It is to this Minister's credit that, according to Martin (1976a:27), 'his active interest brought a new focus and stimulus to the Commonwealth's concern with the question of child migrant educa-tion'. However, his motives for this interest may have been coloured by a desire to assist migrant children to assimilate more readily.

The late 1960s saw some signs of a shift in the official thinking under this Minister's direction, with a recognition that migrants after all did have important cultural contributions to make and should not be expected to abandon their culture altogether. The shift is apparent in both official terminology and statements. For instance, the Depart-ment of Immigration decided to adopt a policy of integration and appointed an Officer in Charge of Integration. One incumbent of this position, John Rooth, wrote (1968:61; also in Kovacs & Cropley, 1975:128): 'We should not merely tolerate but also respect and, on occasions, encourage cultural differences. . . . As members of minor-ity groups they can make invaluable contributions to our Australian way of life while retaining their ethnic identity.'

The shift was virtually bowing to inevitable forces in society rather than an innovative policy that might generate new ideas and approaches. Official organizations such as the Good Neighbour Council with its essentially English approach were shown to be more and more ineffec-tive. In Jupp's opinion (1966:150) ' "Organized assimilation" has failed because it was impossible'. Its successor integration, was a result of 'rather halting moves towards interactionism', i.e., the theory that 'there must be sufficient interaction between native-born and immi-grants for each to influence the other' (Smolicz, 1972:50). However this policy, while more innocuous than assimilation, was not always very meaningful, in Smolicz's opinion. It nevertheless became official government thinking, as evident in the comments by the then Minister for Immigration, Phillip Lynch, at the 43rd Annual Summer School organized by the University of Western Australia in 1970 and devoted to Australia's immigration policy. Addressing the conference, Lynch pointed out (1972:10): 'The earlier desire to make stereotype Australians of the newcomers has been cast aside. The use of the word "integration" instead of " assimilation" is not mere semantics — it is the outward sign of a fundamental change in attitude of the Australian government and people.' Whether this attitude really permeated related official organizations, such as the education system, is questionable. In 1971, Smolicz, on the basis of empirical evidence, could still ask 'Is the Australian School an Assimilationist Agency', and find scant evidence to suggest that it might not be. Smolicz was also of the opinion that 'While fine phrases about integration and respect for the cultures of new arrivals are frequently heard from public platforms, such pronouncements remain empty gestures as long as action does not follow words' (1972:50).

The rather vague ideology of integration guided official policy until the change of government in 1972 and the vigorous, new-broom approach of the Minister for Immigration A.J. Grassby, in the Labor government. His advocacy of multiculturalism is clearly the foundation stone of the current official ideology, and is constantly being reiterated by Grassby in his capacity of Commissioner for Community Relations under the following Liberal government, which was elected in 1975.

The White Australia policy

Almost hidden away in the literature on immigration is an ideology that virtually forms a 'chapter' in itself. This is the White Australia policy. Until very recently it excluded as residents non-Europeans (non-Caucasians), apart from very small numbers of students temporarily resident in Australia often under such schemes as the Colombo Plan, and those engaged in previously established business or having professional skills deemed essential for Australia. 'The effectiveness of "White Australia" may be measured by the fact that in 1961 there were more residents born in Latvia than in China or India and more born in Estonia than in Indonesia. Even so, many from Asian countries were Eurasians, White Russians or Dutch' (Jupp, 1966:3).

The policy had its origins in the political and economic situation of the mid-1800s, when Chinese emigrants fleeing catastrophes in China managed to establish themselves in many countries around the Pacific seaboard. A number came to Australia as identured unskilled labour. The situation was exacerbated when gold was discovered in Victoria and tens of thousands of Chinese flocked to the goldfields, leading to grievances from 'white' miners, some violence, and restrictive legislation by the Victorian government in 1855. The second half of the nineteenth century saw restrictions placed on Chinese in various industries and for a variety of excuses: they were anti-working class solidarity and unionism, 'a servile and degraded class incompatible with the safe possession of national liberty' (Parkes, quoted by Johnson, 1962:11), who depressed working conditions and wages; and so on.

> Coupled with these major arguments went all the crudities and excesses of unrestrained racism. This could be social, ranging from emphasis on the different allegiances, dress and living conditions of the Chinese, to tendentious and plainly exaggerated attacks on their morality. . . . Their assimilation was presumed to be impossible and so never tried. (1962:11)

Besides prominent anti-Chinese politicians of the day, such ideology management was also carried out by Australian nationalistic journals such as the *Bulletin*. It found fertile ground in misapplied ideas about evolution current at the time, originating from Darwinian theories. With the expansion of Asian immigration to include Japanese and Chinese in the last decade of the nineteenth century, a 'conscious pursuit of "White Australia" ' emerged, which culminated in the Immigration Restriction Act of 1901 passed by the New Federal Parliament whose underlying motives were both racial and economic (1962: 12–13). It is possible that the name of the policy derived from the style of parliamentary debate at the time. Johanson notes (1962:14): 'One member, who was also a Presbyterian Minister, spoke of "the noble ideal of a White Australia — a snow-white Australia if you will. Let it be pure and spotless".'

The White Australia policy was firmly adhered to during the succeeding years. 'Until the late thirties, as observers noted, . . . [it] was regarded as "the indispensable condition of every other policy" and "firmly rooted in sentimental, economic and political ground" ' (1962:24). However, racist implications were played down in the 1930s and 1940s, with more apologetic reasons, such as Australia's inability to assimilate Asians, and national defence taking their place. In the post-war period moves were initiated by some politicians and in particular the churches to modify the extreme provisions of the policy, and to substitute an immigration quota system. These moves were adamantly opposed by the Returned Servicemen's League (RSL), which 'unreservedly insisted on the continuation of the policy', the Australian Natives' Association, and Arthur Calwell, who 'pursued the "White Australia" line with unrelenting consistency', even to the extent of deporting a small number of Asians who had fled to Australia during the war to escape the Japanese (1962:26).

In 1958 the Migration Act passed by the Liberal government consolidated or repealed previous legislation and provided for new immigration procedures. In this Act (since superseded):

There is no reference to race or nationality; and the dictation test is abolished. Anyone can be admitted if he has an entry permit. But whether the permit is granted is wholly at the discretion of the Minister and his officials. Nothing is said in the Act as to the grounds on which permits will be granted or refused. (1962:28)

The following years saw a rigid, and at times cruel and unnecessarily hard application of the policy, which had the effect of restricting the entry of Asians to a comparatively very small number — i.e., some 1785 in the period 1940—60 (Rivett, 1962:33—42). In a defence of the policy in 1959, A.R. Downer, Minister for Immigration, clearly favoured the Anglo-conformist view. 'My principal concern is that we should exercise our imaginations in the acutest way to attract both overseas capital and the types of peoples here who can most readily be absorbed, so that we can mould Australia into an Anglo-European community embodying all the best of the Old and the New' (1962:158): Sir John Latham, formerly a leader of the Nationalist Party, Chief Justice of the High Court, and Australia's first representative in Japan, favoured a 'general homogeneity of population', but denied that the policy of excluding Asians had been based on colour prejudice or any idea of racial superiority. Instead, he claimed (Latham, 1961:3—8) that it was solely due to the recognition of

difference . . . in political, social and economic outlook, in religion, in history and tradition, in customs, in manner of living — in nearly everything. Difference in race — European or Oriental — is accompanied as a general rule, by these differences.

Opposition to the White Australia policy increased during the 1960s, and its more rigid provisions underwent progressive liberalization. Major reforms took place in March 1966, instituted by Hubert Opperman, Minister for Immigration in the Holt Liberal government. Within a few years of these the government was admitting approximately 10 000 non-European and part-European immigrants per annum, 'without incurring any significant outcry or generating any racial tensions' (Mackie, 1977:10). In 1971 Phillip Lynch, then Minister for Immigration, proclaimed a new policy on non-European immigrants. In this the emphasis was placed on 'maintaining a cohesive community'. However, as Mackie comments (1977:11) the general result may have been assimilationist in intent.

The main stress was put on avoiding substantial 'undigested minorities . . . very different from the host community', particularly if they were determined to perpetuate that difference to the extent of disputing the government's efforts to achieve national integration and social cohesion. In short, the ultimate goal was presented as something very close to assimilation, though that word was carefully avoided by Mr Lynch.

The year 1971 saw the final demise of the White Australia policy and its later variants as far as official Labor Party thinking was concerned. The annual federal conference of the Australian Labor Party at Launceston altered the party platform to expressly require 'the avoidance of discrimination on any grounds of race or colour of skin or nationality'. This was the basis for later policies introduced by the Labor government.

The Racial Discrimination Act was passed in the autumn session of the Australian Parliament in 1975, when its principles were subscribed to by all the major political parties. The Act outlaws acts of discrimination on the grounds of race, colour, descent or national origin, and which deny fundamental rights and freedoms. However, despite the apparent unanimity between the political parties, Hansard records of the debate about the Racial Discrimination Bill, as analysed by Kalin (1978:32—41), make it clear that many parliamentarians still hold attitudes which are strongly Anglo-conformist and ethnocentric. A further nail was placed in the coffin of the White Australia policy at the 31st National Conference of the Australian Labor Party held in February 1975. The section on immigration (Australian Labor Party, 1975:43) sets out the following official Labor Party policy towards immigrants:

> Labor recognises the valuable contribution being made by migrants to Australia's economic growth, prosperity and culture. Labor supports an immigration policy administered with sympathy, understanding and tolerance. The policy should ensure a smooth and harmonious transition for migrants into the Australian community.

Educational provisions for immigrants

Not surprisingly, educational provisions for immigrants have reflected the major ideologies during the pre- and post-World War II periods. In the former, the Anglo-conformist, assimilationist assumptions of the time made any special provisions for immigrants unnecessary. Children and adults were more or less left to sink or swim, to 'pick up' English and a knowledge of Australia, and to assimilate as rapidly as possible into the homogeneous Anglo-Australian culture. The fact that the great majority of immigrants were of British origin — they spoke English, and therefore were thought to suffer no problems of adjustment (a fallacy also common in the post-war period) — led to their assimilation being regarded as needing no special attention.

The first twenty years of the post-war period

In the first twenty years of the post-war period assimilationist ideas dominated the educational scene. The attitudes of such organizations as Commonwealth and state bureaucracies, political parties, trade unions, churches and voluntary welfare bodies were, overall, indifferent to the migrant presence (Martin, 1976a:2):

> This indifference was based on the conviction that the success of migrant adaptation depended 'fundamentally, not on structures and policies, but on

the goodwill of *individual* migrants and *individual* Australians' and 'that it would be contrary to the prevailing egalitarian values and detrimental to assimilation for migrants, as migrants, to be given unique privileges or consideration of any kind'. (Martin, 1972:14)

A number of 'educational motifs' regarding migrant children dominated the period from 1950 to the mid-1960s, but these need to be seen in relation to the general crisis in education during the period and also to the issue of Commonwealth-state relations. Migrant children of Displaced Persons were seen as a problem; their movements were unpredictable, and they tended to disrupt normal teaching work, especially when they arrived unannounced in schools adjacent to migrant hostels and holding centres. More specifically, the problem was seen basically in terms of their lack of familiarity with English. Martin (1976a:3) comments 'As the General Secretary of the Victorian Teachers' Union put it: "The normal class teaching is affected by the inability of the New Australian children to speak, write and understand English to a satisfactory standard." ' A migrant child — or New Australian child, to use the then current descriptive term — was even defined as one experiencing difficulty with English for the purposes of the Haines Committee's Survey, which enquired into the teaching of English to non-English speaking pupils in state primary schools in South Australia in 1956. The interim report of this Committee is notable historically for mentioning the desirability of training teachers for work with non-English-speaking children, or at least of selecting teachers with sympathy and understanding (1976a:4). Despite this and its other sympathetic recommendations, as well as subsequent surveys, interest in, and provisions for, migrant children in South Australia were small. Presumably as a result of either complacency, apathy, or holding the assimilationist ideology (among other possible reasons), the administrators:

> . . . succeeded in defining the changes that were needed in such a limited way that the necessary adaptations could be made without causing more than a ripple on the surface of the existing system: provision of a few extra staff in problem schools and the production of some assignments through the use of already available resources and according to familiar procedures. (1976a:6)

In 1960, the Commonwealth Immigration Advisory Council (CIAC) published its first and only report, based on a nationwide enquiry on pre-school children, school children, young children, young workers, social participation and delinquency. Its methodology, statistical procedures and interpretation of information were immediately shown to be faulty by the sociologist and expert on migration, Dr Charles Price. What is noteworthy about the survey, as Martin explains (1976a:10), is the light it throws on the prevailing perspective towards migrant children; one which the Chairman of the Special Committee undertaking the enquiry, Mr Justice Dovey, speaking at the Australian

Citizenship Convention in 1960, implied reflected the views of 'literally thousands of Australians throughout the length and breadth of this land'. According to Martin, its findings claimed:

> . . . migrant children have adjusted well, are above average in scholarship and present no problem of absorption (i.e. non-conformity); such problems as do arise with either parents or children result from lack of knowledge of English and evaporate when English has been mastered, which, for the children, happens 'fairly quickly'; parents should therefore be encouraged to speak English in the home; 'national groups' among school children, though not a 'major problem', are undesirable because they hinder 'the children's integration in the school community and their progress'.

Martin adds the felicitous comment about the enquiry's role: 'The Dovey committee acted as a gatekeeper and legitimating agent: it screened out information that ran counter to prevailing views and ideologies and confirmed the wisdom of current policies' (1976a:10).

By the mid-sixties, as Martin notes, 'there was increasing evidence of a quickening of interest in the question of the schooling of migrant children (1976a:11). The interest, however, was in terms that were quite familiar to teachers and reflected basically assimilationist, Anglo-conformist thinking. Moreover, it was also teacher-dominated: 'The emphasis on learning English, discipline and conformity remained in subsequent contributions to the subject of migrant education, and the pre-eminence of the teacher's definition of the situation was mostly taken for granted' (1976a:13). An interesting corollary of this factor relates to the complete lack of materials for teaching English — another recurring theme in migrant education. These materials were demanded by teachers not only to teach migrant children English and keep them occupied in class, when they could not take part in regular work, but also to alleviate their own (i.e. the teachers') anxiety. This was due to the fact that teachers were totally unprepared or trained to cope with non-English-speaking children. Their very presence 'threatened the teachers' competence to carry out the classroom role for which they *had* been trained' (1976a:14). The use of materials from overseas and some experimental books was, at best, an ineffective stopgap.

The educational bureaucracy and administrators in each state were unable and largely unwilling to assist teachers' attempts to cope with migrant children. They could devote little time to thinking about their special problems, and remained dissembling and largely unresponsive to the demands of teachers, who were backed by teachers' unions and surveys of primary and secondary schools. The bureaucratic tactics are described by Martin (1976a:19):

> In defending their position, the administrators had on their side a major weapon: their control of information. So long as the state departments refrained from collecting adequate data on the distribution of migrant pupils, their knowledge of English, their scholastic performance and their

learning and psychological difficulties, teachers and outside observers were
severely handicapped in challenging official complacency. The other states
may have expressed themselves less forthrightly, but Dr Wyndham spoke for
them all when he asserted the authority of the bureaucracy to control the
supply of information:

> We deliberately refrain from collecting any statistics in regard to school
> pupils from overseas. Once they are enrolled in school, they are, from our
> point of view, Australian children. (Commonwealth Department of
> Immigration, Australian Citizenship Convention, *Digest*, 1963:21)

We might add that the administrators' ideology was obviously assimilationist, and had a number of parallels with the bureaucratic attitude in
Great Britain which, it will be recalled, also entailed a refusal to collect
statistics, albeit at the instigation of teachers' unions.

The late 1960s and early 1970s

Demographically this period saw a major decline in the absolute
numbers and proportions of children from northern and eastern
Europe and a corresponding increase in numbers from southern
European, and a variety of Middle Eastern and Asian source countries.
This coincided with 'an explosion of interest in education in general and
a shift in orientation among educators from a system-centred to a child-
centred philosophy, with an attendant increase in school and teacher
autonomy'. Coupled with this was the realization, backed by criticism
of the migrant programme and evidence from the Henderson Poverty
Survey published in 1970, 'that failure to take account of the special
situations and problems of migrants was causing severe personal and
social damage' (Martin, 1976a:20–21).

One tangible result was the introduction of the Commonwealth Child
Migrant Education Programme (CMEP) in 1970. The state education
departments also began to introduce various programmes, with
Victoria taking the lead. The Department there appointed a coordinator and advisor on migrant education in 1967; inaugurated a
series of four-day teacher training courses in teaching English as a
second language in 1968; and set up advisory committees on primary
education in 1968 and on secondary education in 1969. The Department's Psychology and Guidance Branch established its own working
committee and started producing teachers' notes on the cultural background of particular migrant groups.

In New South Wales the first survey of migrant children in primary
and secondary schools was carried out in 1968 and a second in 1969.
However, poor questionnaire design and other methodological weaknesses limited the usefulness of the data. Yet, despite the interest these
surveys caused and pressure from a number of public groups and individual schools, the question of migrant education did not become the
major concern it had in Victoria, virtually the 'only state where any
serious attempt was being made to deal with the education of migrant

children or the problems of schools with large numbers from non-English speaking background' (Martin 1976a:32–33). But even in Victoria, the major solution took the form of some 33 full-time and a number of part-time teachers taking children in withdrawal classes for English as a second language. Some teachers were receiving in-service training in this approach.

Developments at the Commonwealth level gained momentum in 1971 with the passage of the Immigration (Education) Act. This provided more support for expanding the adult education programme than for child migrant education. However, the Child Migrant Education Programme had to be expanded during the period 1970–75 due to increasing demands from schools and a recognition that far greater needs existed than had been anticipated when the programme was started. Under the scheme, which still operates, training courses for teachers are held in each state. Training normally consists of a four-week in-service course conducted under the auspices of the Commonwealth (and even this has been scaled down in Victoria in the last year or two).

Although such schemes were innovative and went some way towards remedying the deficiencies in migrant education, there were still criticisms on the grounds of inadequate teaching materials, lack of accurate statistical data about the numbers of migrant children in schools, and a serious limitation on the numbers of children that could be catered for. There was also a general apathy among teachers many of whom had attitudes towards migrant children that ranged from patronizing to uncaring. Martin (1976a:42–43) cites one department official's comments:

> The general philosophy has been that 'they pick it up'; so its a 'sitting next to Nelly' idea; you pick it up and that's that. [There are] any amount of schools now where although we made a survey and found that there are x number of migrant children — quite enough to justify a migrant teacher — they still don't apply for a teacher.

Supporting evidence for these attitudes was provided by the 1974 Inquiry into Schools of High Migrant Density in New South Wales and Victoria. As Martin comments (1976a:57–58):

> There were some positive findings, but the report shows clearly that response to the presence of migrant children in these schools has been minimal. Apart from CMEP,
>
> > the usual school programs are designed for Australian children and make no concessions to the particular needs and backgrounds of migrant pupils (Australian Department   of Education, *Report of the Inquiry into Schools of High Migrant Density*, 1975:6).
>
> . . . . Teachers were not adequately prepared to work in schools of this kind and there was much indifference and even intolerance towards migrant children. . . The heart of the Committee's final 'overview' is that most of

these schools continue to function in a 'narrow' assimilationist mould' and try 'to make the migrant children into a pattern which was determined before any migrant pupils were enrolled in the schools (1975:21–22, 29).'

Despite these adverse tendencies, it would be erroneous and simplistic to imagine that there were no positive developments in migrant education during the late 1960s and 1970s, or that the picture was as negative as the above might suggest. However, as Martin notes (1976a:46): 'It is much more difficult to pin down the way in which changing perspectives on the nature of Australian society and the place of migrant and other ethnic groups within it have influenced approaches to the education of migrant children in recent years.' Demographic changes since the end of the sixties resulted in an increasing diversity of migrant children in schools, with a relative decline in the numbers of the Greek and Italian children; the emphasis changed to migrant children's problems in secondary as well as primary levels, with a need for language enrichment courses rather than the elementary English emphasis that was the original thrust of the CMEP (1976a: 46–47). The late sixties also witnessed a ferment in Australian educaional thinking, which came under the influence of not always clearly understood progressive educational philosophies.

But probably of more crucial importance, according to Martin (1976a:47–48), were the structural changes that occurred in the early 1970s. These consisted of the creation of a variety of government, semi-government, and private organizations which were invested with the power, or took it upon themselves, to investigate migrant problems, publish findings (occasionally polemically), and press for decisive action. This was in direct contrast to what had happened in the 1950s and 1960s, when the main instigators of action were individual teachers and a few other educators with first-hand knowledge of the problems of migrant children in the schools. They had attempted to formulate their own theories, approaches and remedies, but in general 'these efforts were spasmodic, lacking in continuity, dependent on the enterprise of a few individuals and easily snuffed out. They contributed as little to cumulative understanding of the situation of migrant education as did the few official enquiries of the period' (1976a:62). The changes are welcome, but overdue, and seem like reactions with hindsight rather than rational planning for the future.

It is possible to advance a further interpretation, however, and one which is more in line with the theoretical framework of this book. The late 1960s and, more particularly, the 1970s have seen the emergence of individuals and organizations of many kinds with the express function of creating and managing the public knowledge about migrants and migrant education. This came about for several reasons: firstly, the issues of migrants and migrant education became academically 'respectable'; secondly, the new Labor Government, elected in 1972, found it politically expedient to become involved in these issues, which in any case fitted in with its social welfare and educational philosophies; and finally, ideas from the United States, Canada, and, to a lesser extent, Great Britain, diffused into the conventional wisdom of Australian educational thinking, after the customary few years knowledge lag.

In short, the 1970s have been years not only of structural change that encouraged the emergence of new ideas but also of the deliberate creation of ideologies, some of which have generated policy and action outcomes. Inevitably, these developments have had a catalytic effect in encouraging a smaller number of counter-ideologies and their proponents. Especially after the election of a Labor government, a major feature of the 1970s is the dialectical interplay between ideologists and counter-ideologists.

Ideologies and ideologists

Origins of the official ideology

The current official ideology in government and most educational circles is multiculturalism. A multicultural model for studying plural societies in social studies syllabuses had been advocated by this writer as early as June 1968, in a series of the *Age* newspaper articles[1], and developed in subsequent publications (e.g. Bullivant, 1972, 1973b). These ideas, however, were ahead of their time. It took an influential public figure, in the person of A.J. Grassby, Minister for Immigration in the Labor government, to bring the term multicultural into the public arena in 1973 through the publication *A Multi-cultural Society for the Future* (Grassby, 1973a). However, apart from the title, the concept does not appear elsewhere in the text, and one is left to *infer* the kind of society the Minister envisaged.

We are given a number of vague but nevertheless important clues to the Minister's thinking. A theme which recurs in subsequent publications is the 'Family of the Nation': a phrase Grassby preferred to use because of 'an aversion to the technical jargon in the literature'. The preferred concept (1973a:5) 'is one that ought to convey an immediate and concrete image to all. In a family the overall attachment to the common good need not impose a sameness on the outlook or activity of each member, nor need these members deny their individuality and distinctiveness in order to seek a superficial and unnatural conformity. The important thing is that all are committed to the good of all'.

Other ideas he proposed were: Australia should offer (1973a:1) equal opportunity for all; it has been 'no small achievement' that Australia's 'national fabric' has been woven from 'rather ill-assorted strands', [a favourite metaphor we have encountered elsewhere] 'but without suffering the major upheavals marking the history of other societies' (1973a:3); Australia is one of the 'most cosmopolitan societies on earth'

(1973a:4). Grassby's vision of our society in the year 2000 'foreshadows a greatly increasing social complexity, in which the dynamic interaction between the diverse ethnic components will be producing new national initiatives, stimulating new artistic endeavours, and ensuring great strength in diversity'.

Ethnic groups in society also came in for consideration (1973a:8–9). Indeed, despite its title, the whole paper seems to be about ethnic pluralism rather than about multiculturalism.

> The dynamism in an ethnically diverse society seems somehow related to the group life within that society. . . . The corporate life of ethnic groups represents a great deal more than the simple totality of their individual members' lives and activity. To an extent, they have created their own national image. They have brought with them a common history and culture, an ideology different from the Anglo-Saxon. They perceive different goals and pursue them in their own traditional ways. In short, they lead a way of life which, while in living touch with its ancient forms and impulses, is imperceptibly coming to terms with — or at least learning to co-exist with — that of many other ethnic groups in our society and of course with the 'old Australians'. Such pluralism is not operating within a time scale, but looks ahead far into the future.

Grassby was at pains to explain that pluralist views did not constitute advocating a 'sort of communal apartheid', with attendant undesirable consequences such as hostile segregation of part of the population (1973a:11).

In a subsequent publication *Australian Citizenship Policy : Our Objectives* (Grassby, 1974b), the multicultural vision is missing. This was a paper tabled in the House of Representatives on 6 December 1973, and harks back to an earlier ideology — integration — though the new 'homely' concept is still employed:

> I put forward the following submission, not as a definitive proposal, but as a basis for discussion that may lead to clearer definition of the Department's role in the integration of migrants and of the role that should be played by the community at large. . . .
> 1. To develop a cohesive 'family of the nation' in which citizenship, however acquired, confers equality of opportunity and treatment on all who hold it, without distinction or preference based on race, colour of skin, religion, political opinion, national extraction or social origin. . . .

Yet another forward looking number of ideas emerged in *Credo for a Nation* (Grassby, 1974c). As well as stressing the by now familar themes of cultural diversity, the family of the nation, and the need to develop Australia's linguistic resources to avoid the narrowness of monolingualism, Al Grassby also stated his personal commitment to Australia's ethnic heritage. He advocated practical measures of support for the 2300 ethnic organizations in Australia covering people from over 70 countries as part of a nationwide ethnic heritage programme (1974: 11–13), Such a programme would be 'vital to the full development of the 750,000 migrant children currently [i.e., 1973–4] attending Australian schools. It will give them, their fellow pupils and their teachers a new insight into the histories and cultures to which they are heirs, and which they will share with all Australians . . . these children [are] the cultural bridge which we will cross to create the new Australia.'

The trans-Pacific influence is quite evident in this new thinking, which is far from coincidental. The reports of the Canadian Royal Commission on Bilingualism and Biculturalism (1967, 1970) were available in Australia; the American Ethnic Heritage Program, Title IX (ESEA) was passed in 1972, and details were just percolating into the Australian educational scene. Al Grassby was also in direct communication with leading administrators in the United States; in fact, Dr Carl Epstein, of the Ethnic Heritage Studies Branch, visited Australia in 1975 and held discussions with the Minister. In this instance, then, ideas from overseas came relatively quickly into Australia and had an earlier effect on ideologies than would have been the case if they had percolated more slowly with the usual knowledge lag.

The Labor government was forced to relinquish office at the end of 1975, and Grassby subsequently became Commissioner for Community Relations, heading the office established by the Racial Discrimination Act of 1975. In this capacity he has had no less influence on knowledge management and ideologies in education than in his previous position. The output of articles and papers from his office continues unabated, and invitations to address educational conferences and seminars provide opportunities to promote the multicultural ideology and introduce new concepts, despite the fact that their original meaning might differ widely from Al Grassby's.

The central role of Grassby as an ideologist in the Australian context is significant and indisputable, and his ideas have undoubtedly exercised a major seminal influence on the directions that conceptual mapping (however naïve) about the nature of Australian society and its education system has taken since 1973. This impetus has not played itself out, despite the apparent revisionism of the Liberal government's Minister for Immigration and Ethnic Affairs, to be discussed below.

However, despite the fact that Grassby's vision of a multicultural and polyethnic Australia, and personal drive to achieve it, are an excellent example of his own dictum — 'Nations are not built on cautious policies, or by timid men' (Grassby, 1974c:9) — it is more often than not impossible to discover the real substance of his often rhetorical ideas. One wonders whether they go much further than support for fostering the preservation of 'cultures', ethnic heritages and languages along Canadian and American lines. One can only assume that this is the case, judging from the vision he proposed at the conference on the theme 'Towards a Multi-Cultural Tasmania', one of several conferences around the country during that time of enthusiasm for the new bandwaggon. In his address, Grassby (1977:17–19), enthusiastically refers to:

> . . . a revival of interest in the folk cultures of the people of England, as opposed to the pomp and pretence of imperialisms in the past. At the grassroots, the English County Organization in Sydney is doing wonders in showing the customs, cooking and background of the people, from countries [sic] as diverse as Durham and Devon. The eternal Scots have never faltered in their attachment to ethnic culture and identity in that culture. . . .

At this conference, Grassby employed yet another concept, 'polyethnic', without elaborating on its meaning. However, the concept was not entirely novel in the Australian context. It was given probably its first public exposition, *but as a counter-ideology*, by this writer at the Australian UNESCO Seminar on Teacher Education for International Understanding, (Bullivant, 1977a). 'Polyethnic' was quickly taken up by Grassby, who has come to bracket the two terms together — Australia is a multicultural and polyethnic society. This usage appears in the foreword he has written to each book in the series, 'Making Australian Society', published by Nelson for classroom and teacher use. The term is gaining currency in other quarters too, which shows how quickly an ideology and its related concepts can be disseminated at the grassroots level of educational practice by a leading ideologist, who is alert to the possibilities of concept, even though its precise application is unclear.

Revisionist tendencies in government ideology

With the transfer of political power to the Liberal government at the end of 1975, some revision in official ideology appears to have occurred, but was followed by a renewed commitment, with detailed specification, of what has now become the official orthodoxy, even though it originated from the previous Labor government. The initial revisionism was brought out by the Minister for Immigration and Ethnic Affairs, M.J.R. MacKeller, in his comments on the Immigration (Education) Bill 1973 (CPD MR85:1664, 27 September 1973). They were assimilationist in tone and concentrated heavily on the familiar theme that all migrants had to do was to learn English. But the Minister did at least give token recognition to the fact that migrants have made other contributions to Australia. In an address to the Stable Population Forum held in Adelaide, Mackellar (1976:6) commented that 'very few would dispute that migration has enriched our culture and our society as well as expanding our contacts with other countries. In our geographic situation such stimuli are essential' (1976:6).

However, his more recent policy statement is explicitly integrationist. It appears in the Ministerial Statement to Parliament on Immigration Policies and Australia's Population. (MacKellar, 1978) Among other details of the new immigration policies, it sets out nine principles upon which the government intends to act (Mackellar, 1978:2−3). Of these the following are most relevant:

3. The size and composition of migrant intakes should not jeopardise social cohesiveness and harmony within the Australian community.
4. Immigration policy should be applied on a basis which is non-discriminatory. . . . The principle of non-discrimination means that policy will be applied consistently to all applicants regardless of their race, colour, nationality, descent, national or ethnic origin or sex. . . .

9. Policies governing entry and settlement should be based on the premise that immigrants should integrate into Australian society. Migrants will be given every opportunity, consistent with this premise, to preserve and disseminate their ethnic heritage.

The Minister's further comments on monitoring the programme (1978:6) indicate that it 'will be undertaken to ensure that the composition of migrant intakes sustains cohesion and harmony in Australian society'. In short, the Australian community appears to be seen in essentially monocultural terms and migrants should not 'rock the boat' (Principle 3; also comment on p. 6). The policies adhere to the principles established by the 1975 Racial Discrimination Act, but monitoring the intake implies that non-discrimination will not be allowed to let in migrants who cannot 'fit in', i.e., conform. However, even these ideas had a limited currency, as further developments in government thinking took place later in 1978 — a year in which the Liberal government found it expedient to take an increased interest in migrants' affairs. As Stockley suggests (1978:23), this was motivated partly by a concern to woo the ethnic vote, and partly because the Prime Minister himself had taken a personal interest in ethnic issues.

Multiculturalism: the official ideology

In a striking parallel with the way a basically similar ideology was developed and finally presented in Canada, a major change of direction occurred in Australia at the end of 1978, when Prime Minister Fraser presented to Parliament the *Report of the Review of Post-Arrival Programs and Services to Migrants* (the Galbally Report). The review had been commissioned by the government on 1 September 1977, to 'examine and report on the effectiveness of the Commonwealth's programs and services for those who have migrated to Australia, including programs and services provided by non-government organizations which receive Commonwealth assistance, and shall identify any areas of need or duplication of programs or services' (Galbally 1978:1).

The Prime Minister made much of the fact that the report was the first to be available in ethnic languages (Fraser, 1978:1), and stated that the government agreed with the general conclusions of the review. 'It agrees Australia is at a critical stage in developing a cohesive, united, multicultural nation. It agrees there is a need to change the direction of its services to migrants and that further steps to encourage multi-culturalism are needed' (1978:3). Of relevance to Australian education, and among other recommendations of the Galbally Report adopted by the government, are the provision of extra funding for special instruction in English as a second language together with better planning and assessment of English teaching to migrants (1978:9); the establishment of a special programme of 'multicultural resource centres' as a means of supporting self-help activities by ethnic groups, with the corollary that this effectively means the phasing out of the Good Neighbour Councils (1978:11 – 13); and special provisions for workers to be employed by ethnic communities to work in child-care centres and pre-schools 'to foster a multicultural approach and to help bridge the gap between school and home' (1978:14).

In the light of its interpretation of the philosophy, the government made what appears to be a major commitment to multiculturalism (1978:15 – 16):

> The Government accepts that it is *now* essential to give significant further encouragement to develop a *multicultural attitude* in Australian society. It will foster the *retention of the cultural heritage of different ethnic groups* and *promote intercultural understanding* . . .

> For students training in professions, we will encourage introduction of *components on cultural backgrounds* of the major ethnic groups.

> Because of the *lack of information on multicultural developments in Australia and overseas* we will establish an Institute of Multicultural Affairs, which among other activities would engage in and commission research and advise government bodies on *multicultural issues*.

> In accordance with the recommendation of the Review, The Australia Council will be asked to reassess its financial assistance to the *arts of ethnic communities*, to ensure that such arts are given more equitable support. [italics added]

One creation of the Galbally Committee, the Australian Institute for Multicultural Affairs, is very significant within the framework of analysis adopted for this book. It is a major knowledge and ideology managing agency, empowered to develop an awareness among members of the Australian community of its diversity of cultures, to encourage an appreciation of their contribution to the Australian society, and to promote tolerance, understanding and cohesion throughout the society. To these ends the Institute's functions include the commissioning of research into multiculturalism and related issues; the preparation of material on cultural and racial backgrounds and other factors affecting migrant settlement for use in professional training courses; the provision of advice on multicultural and migrant issues to government departments and other bodies to help them in preparing programmes and policies appropriate to a multicultural society (Galbally, 1978:108 – 109).

Strong reservations must be held about the Institute's capacity to carry out these functions in an objective, non-political way. The chairman of its council is Mr Frank Galbally himself; its director is a former press secretary to the Prime Minister, Malcolm Fraser. One of the first exercises carried out by the Institute was a *Review of Multicultural and Migrant Education* (Institute of Multicultural Affairs, 1980) in mid-1980. To some observers, this was with the purpose of providing information for the Liberal Party's political platform for the Federal elections in October of the same year, and, indeed, some of its points can be traced directly back to recommendations in the Review. With the re-election of the Liberal Government and assured continuation of the Institute, a subsequent development can only give cause for concern among those who wish to see the official policies on multiculturalism and multicultural education being subjected to some non-political scrutiny and control. This development is the apparent decision to establish within the Institute a research group, whose members range from professorial to lecturer rank. Its function is to conduct research and studies and furnish reports to the Minister (*The Australian*, October 25–6 1980, p.18). Whether this group will come to replace commissioned research workers from outside organizations, who might have less of a vested interest in promoting the official ideology, remains to be seen.

On the surface the government's commitments add up to a significant package, and one can usefully compare its contents and general philosophy with those of the very similar package in Canada. Such an undertaking would be enlightening but beyond the scope of this chapter. But even as they are explained above, some of the commitments must give cause for concern and the reflection, based on comparative evidence from overseas, that in buying the multicultural 'poke' from the Galbally Committee, the government may well have got a very queer 'pig' indeed. Grounds for this concern are apparent when one consults the original report, which the Prime Minister has endorsed and commended so enthusiastically, and quoted unreservedly. This is to be regretted as, on the subject of culture and multiculturalism at least, some of its pronouncements are naïve at best, and ill-informed and wrong at worst. As Stockley has suggested (1978:23): 'Galbally is a clever lawyer and he has produced an astute Report tailored to what the Fraser Government wanted.' Other aspects of the Galbally Report are discussed in the section on counter-ideologies below.

Official views of the Department of Education

Another government body to evolve its own views about the nature of Australian society is the Department of Education. It has now endorsed the multicultural ideology, after a period when there appeared to be a certain ambivalence in its thinking about migrant problems.

Transfer of responsibility for migrant education from what was in those days known as the Department of Labour and Immigration to the Department of Education took place on 12 June 1974. This period was one of intense speculation and political 'power politics' regarding the scope of the new arrangement and the financial allocations to make it viable. These are not of central concern here, but were a factor in the 1974 Maquarie Conference which is discussed below. Of more concern here is the expression of the Department's ideology by the Minister for Education, Senator J.L. Carrick, in a letter to the organizing committee of the June 1977 Hobart Conference, 'Towards a Multi-cultural Tasmania' (Bostock, 1977a: appendix D, pp. 135–38):

> . . . the Government's policy on education is directed to an appreciation and understanding of the cultural diversity in present-day Australian society. . . .
>
> If education is to provide an understanding of the variety and spread of ethnic groups in our society, there must be changes in curriculum, new materials will need to be developed and most importantly, teacher education adapted so that teachers may become sensitive and properly attuned to the major changes that have taken place.

It will be noted that this view is pre-Galbally vintage, so it is not really surprising that in referring to several reports then before his Department the Minister presented more conventional views (1977a, pp.136–37).

> Each of these documents includes reference to the need to develop multi-cultural education and to maintain migrant languages and culture not only in the interests of migrants themselves but as measures designed to achieve *integration* through improved tolerance and understanding on the part of the community generally. (italics added)

Views of semi-government educational bodies

The Schools Commission

The 1970s were notable for the many committees, commissions, inquiries and permanent organizations that were established by either the Labor or Liberal governments. Each of these has promoted the multicultural ideology. The first organization was the Schools Commission, set up by the Labor government when it came to power in 1973. The evolution of its thinking illustrates clearly the influence of the socio-historical context. The Interim Committee for the Australian Schools Commission (1973) published its report, *Schools in Australia* in May of that year. It contained a scant 11 lines on migrant education (1973:107) prefaced by the comment that 'The Committee has not been able to undertake a detailed investigation into the educational problems of migrant children, although it believes that the Schools Commission should do so'. (See more detailed discussion in Bullivant, 1975.)

The Interim Committee's recommendations for migrant education reflected its twin principles of discovering the needs of disadvantaged schools and pupils (the 'needs principle') in order to inject into their education differential financial inputs and so bring about the second principle — 'equality of outcomes'. The whole thinking of the Interim Committee about migrant children, as well as about other deprived sectors of the education system, was wedded to the then highly influential educational ideology of providing compensatory education for those who are disadvantaged. Fundamental to this thinking was the now discredited assumption which held that one could effect social change and the eradication of underprivilege by improving the quality of schooling for the disadvantaged, even to the extent of radically altering the social structure itself.

By the time of the publication of the Commission's Report for the Triennium 1976–78 in 1975 all this had changed (Schools Commission, 1975). In this interim, Al Grassby's ideology had become official orthodoxy, the educational disadvantage and deprivation movement had come under sustained attack in the United States and Great Britain, from which new thinking on pluralism was emerging, and new political masters were in power with the election of the Liberal government in 1975. Chapter 8 of the report, 'The Education of Migrant Children', reflects some of these changes. It opens with the resounding 'Australia is a multicultural society', and proceeds to advocate a variety of new approaches relating to second language learning and the whole curriculum in answer to the question 'How best should the education of all Australians reflect the cultural variety that is present in the society?' (1975:119). Among the Commission's prescriptions for the schooling of migrant children (which also include improved TESL provisions and condemnation of the withdrawal system) those relating to the need to help such children maintain their ethnic self-identity are enlightened (1975:125):

> . . . the *multicultural reality* of Australian society needs to be reflected in the school curricula — languages, social studies, history, literature, the arts and crafts — in staffing and in school organisation. While these changes are particularly important to undergird the self-esteem of migrant children they also have application for all Australian children growing up in a society which could be greatly enriched through a wider sharing in the variety of *cultural heritages* now present in it [emphasis added].

Committee on Multicultural Education

Further specification of the Commission's ideological position on multicultural education is provided in *Education for a Multicultural Society* (1979), the report prepared by the Committee on Multicultural Education which the Commission had set up in response to the recommendation of the Galbally Report. This Committee had been convened in what, some observers would say, was indecent haste in order to meet the unrealistic 3 months deadline that the Galbally Committee had specified (Galbally, 1978:108).

As we know from overseas experience, the lure of money to spend would have been a powerful inducement for haste. Following its acceptance on May 30, 1978 of the Galbally recommendations the government, through the Minister for Education, issued guidelines to the Schools Commission allocating $1.5m to be spent on migrant and multicultural education. It also appointed the Committee on Multi-cultural Education on June 30, 1978, 'to advise the Schools Commission on the detailed distribution of the additional funds to be made available for multicultural education' (Committee on Multicultural Education, 1979:2).

The Committee's recommendations for the allocation of $.05m which had been provided under the Multicultural Education Program in 1979 were in fact forwarded to the Commission before 31 July 1978, in order for them to be included in its report of that date to the government (Schools Commission, 1978). The Committee's final report (1979) was presented to the Schools Commission on 5 January 1979, and bore many of the hallmarks of a hastily prepared document in its tacit acceptance of much that passes for conventional wisdom about the nature of culture and the whole multicultural education approach in Australia. More importantly, the report is locked into an approach to the teaching of community languages which, by the Committee's own admission (1979:3–4), is not its decision but the government's, stemming from the Galbally Report:

> The fact that the Government had decided that the funds to be made available in the first year of the three year program were to be used for the foster-ing of the teaching of community languages had a considerable influence on the work of the Committee and on the recommendations made in relation to 1980 and 1981.

In other words, educational decisions are being made for what appear to be political reasons, and regardless of whether the fostering of the teaching of community languages is a sound approach to multicultural education. The rationale behind this emphasis, which appears to have been accepted without question by both the Committee on Multi-cultural Education and the Galbally Committee, is that 'Australia should seek to become a society where the preservation of the identity of cultural groups and interaction among them is encouraged. . . . Australian society should promote a degree of cultural and social variation' (1979:8–9).

The evidence from the United States and Canada would seem to suggest that this emphasis on multicultural education is discredited. Even so, the Schools Commission's Committee has committed the development of Australian education to this approach for the next three years. We need only reiterate the comment of Professor Jean Burnet about the Canadian experience to emphasize the thoroughly wasteful, and politically ideological, nature of the decision:

> If it [multiculturalism within a bilingual framework] is interpreted . . . as enabling various peoples to transfer foreign cultures and languages as living wholes into a new place and time — multiculturalism is doomed.

There are thus grounds for doubting the assertion by the Committee on Multicultural Education (1979:13) that 'the current emphasis on education for a multicultural society is not just another educatioral "bandwaggon" '. All the evidence of the historical development of ideologies in Australia, and overseas, suggests that it is, and not the least for the Schools Commission itself which has been appointed to administer the government's multicultural education programme at least into the 1980s. The elaborate network of committees and advisory superstructure proposed by the Committee involves the Schools Commission at every point, rather than the Curriculum Development Centre in Canberra which is already developing programmes in multicultural education and which, one might have thought, would have been more involved in the new development. The Schools Commission has now been ensured of a continued role in Australian education at a time when rumours strongly suggested that it would follow the fate of other Labor Government innovations and be disbanded by the Liberal Government. The Schools Commission came into being within a socio-historical climate and ideological fervour bred of the 1960s' emphasis in education on equality of opportunity and compensatory programmes. That bandwaggon exhausted itself in the late 1970s in the same way as it did in the United States and Britain; now the Schools Commission appears to have jumped on the next one in line — multicultural education. It is thus hardly surprising that the Commission (1978:104−5) has been unable to reach any agreed interpretation of the multicultural commitment, and even admits contributing to confusion in schools and curriculum development.

The Committee on the Teaching of Migrant Languages in School

The Committee on the Teaching of Migrant Languages in Schools was set up in November 1974 by the Labor government 'to bring together up-to-date information about the extent of the teaching of languages of migrant groups in government and non-government schools . . . to seek and collate views about desirable courses; . . . to make suggestions about possible lines of action' (Committee on the Teaching of Migrant Languages in Schools, 1976:11). The Committee presented its report in March 1976, but the tabling of the report in Parliament was delayed until 8 December 1976, and then left in limbo for some six months. One suspects that this was due, in part, to the fact that the Galbally Committee had been set up by the Liberal Government, which might not have wanted to pre-empt its findings by those of a Committee established under the preceding Labor Government.

In a style with which we have become familiar, the Report on the Teaching of Migrant Languages opens confidently (1976:3): 'Australia is now a cultural mosaic'. A long list of immigrant languages is provided to validate this claim. More specifically the Committee goes on to stress (1976:3):

> This changed composition of the Australian population has affected the nature of Australian society. Immigrants of non-English speaking background have brought with them their language, *their cultural heritage*, their social structure and their value system, and these differ not only from the dominant culture but also vary considerably among migrant groups. Because of the existence of these alternative life styles in its midst, Australian society is becoming progressively diversified *and increasingly aware of its multicultural nature*. [italics added]

We might question the bland assumption that *Australian society* is becoming increasingly aware of its multicultural nature, but the moral is clear: this Committee, too, has been influenced by the current ideology. The considerations and recommendations for educational practice outlined in the body of the report indicate that the outcomes of this Committee extend well beyond rhetoric. In particular, it is refreshing to have recommendations about language teaching, which tends to be treated as a separate issue, bracketed with a recognition of the importance of culture learning, intercultural study as part of every child's education, bilingual education programmes (despite their acknowledged difficulties), greater cooperation between day-schools and part-time ethnic schools.

The Curriculum Development Centre (Canberra)

One of the most visible and influential organizations to manage the current educational knowledge in Australia is the Curriculum Development Centre, which was established as an independent statutory body by legislation passed with some delays in the period following the official announcement of the Centre in June 1973. In the beginning, the only project to bear upon migrant education was the Social Education Materials Project (SEMP) funded for the National Committee for Social Science Teaching. The booklet detailing the aims of the project stresses the need for materials to take account of the characteristics of Australian society. Among these are its multicultural nature and the fact that its population has been multiethnic since its inception. Among the units produced in the materials is, somewhat incongruously, one on *Race and Ethnic Relations*. It examines three groups — Aborigines, Ethnic Groups, and Papua-New Guineans — in an endeavour to achieve its major objective 'that students develop positive attitudes towards others in our increasingly multicultural society' '(Tonkin, 1976:3).

One of the Centre's most recent developments is the project on education for the multicultural society, which is backed by substantial government funding. This is used to pay for the CDC's own work in this area, and is also disbursed as small grants to schools or community groups involved in education for a multicultural society. Such grants are 'aimed at building up expertise in the area of education for a multicultural society, e.g., programmes in bilingual education, community languages, Teaching English as a Second Language, ethnic studies' (Adams, 1978). The scope of this CDC venture indicates that its view of multicultural education is somewhat eclectic. In the application form for the small grants, their purpose is set out:

(a) These grants are aimed at building up expertise at the school and community level in course design, development of teaching materials for community language and culture courses and for the development of courses in particular subject areas, e.g., health education, the expressive arts, career education, etc., for schools which have a multicultural population and for community groups.

(b) It is intended that some grants should be reserved to assist schools, community groups and others to write up completed projects, or nearly completed projects in such a way that the material could be made quickly available to schools, community groups and others throughout Australia through the Curriculum Information Service of the Curriculum Development Centre.

It is obvious that the CDC casts its net very widely indeed, but the overall effect of this decentralized approach to multicultural education could well compound the difficulty of achieving consensus about its aims, and exacerbate the problem of deciding what the concept really means. Attracted by the lure of funding, many diverse groups and individuals are likely to place their own interpretations on 'multicultural', if only to the extent of using it as 'proposal language'. Welcome as this initiative is at encouraging grassroots participation in curriculum development, the experience of the School Commission's very similar innovation scheme indicates clearly that it is open to abuse and cynical manipulation when money is in the offing. Comparisons are inevitable with the weaknesses of the Federal funding agencies in the United States.

A further major CDC innovation occurred in mid-1980 with the publication of *Core Curriculum for Australian Schools* (CDC, 1980). In this 'the multi-cultural composition and interests of our population' appears as one of a number of changes in Australian society to which schools must respond (1980:6). Among the list of 'fundamental learnings for all students' are included (1980:15):

focus on general, universal elements in culture for present and future life, i.e., *the common culture*; acknowledge the plural, multi-cultural nature of our society and seek a form of cultural-social integration which values interaction and free communication amongst diverse groups and sub-cultures, i.e., *the common multiculture.* [italics added]

The aims almost foreshadow the concept of pluralistic integration which we discuss in the last chapter, but the neologism 'common multiculture' seems a contradiction in terms, and could well compound the terminological confusion that afflicts thinking about pluralist education. It remains to be seen whether the phrase will join those others that are part of the rhetoric of multicultural education.

Education Research and Development Committee

An equally influential and wide-ranging knowledge managing organization is the Education Research and Development Committee, established in 1970 with the brief of advising the Minister for Education on research and developments in education. It stimulates research by funding selected research projects, and thus exerts control over the types and direction of educational research in Australia. Projects that entail curriculum development and the production of materials are referred to the CDC, thus linking one important knowledge managing agency with another.

This link is particularly important for the Priority Area Advisory Group (PAAG) on Multicultural Education. This is one of four groups with the task of mapping their respective areas, and recommending to ERDC

'a program within ERDC terms of reference which forms a coherent and co-ordinated research thrust on problems which have been identified as not thoroughly researched and of high priority. . . . The group has conceived that its task embraces the clarification of the concept of a multi-cultural or poly-ethnic Australia and the education appropriate for bringing it into being' (Falk, 1977:55).

Even in the work of this group it has not been possible to escape the inherent ambiguity, evident in the above quotation, that is a recurrent theme in this book, namely, whether the group is dealing with a theory of society or a philosophy of educational practice. The assumption that any form of education can bring a particular kind of society into existence, or change society, is highly questionable.

Ideologies held by teachers' organizations

Predictably, given the natural tendency of the Australian education system to follow whatever ideology happens to be fashionable overseas, some teachers and their organizations have been quick to endorse multiculturalism and multicultural education. A flurry of conferences on these issues has occurred, and many teacher education organizations have set up, or applied to have accredited, courses on multicultural education. However imperfectly understood and interpreted, the multi-cultural perspective has been enthusiastically taken up.

The immediate reaction to the events of 1973 was the National Seminar for Teacher Educators, 'The Multi-Cultural Society', held at Macquarie University on 28–31 August 1974. This seminar was recommended by the Committee on Migrant Education of the former Immigration Advisory Council, and organized by the Australian Department of Education in co-operation with the Australian Department of Labor and Immigration. The approach of the Seminar was to consider in turn three themes: The changing nature of Australian society; Consequences for the child in the classroom; and Teacher education: what next? The majority of those taking part were teacher educators. Of the 75 participants only a handful were from ethnic backgrounds, an imbalance criticized by some participants as a form of tokenism to placate ethnic groups.

By general consensus, the Seminar was not an outstanding success, although its proceedings were published with commendable speed afterwards. The concepts of pluralism and multiculturalism baffled most participants (as they appeared to baffle the Minister for Education), and led to heated arguments. Proponents of teaching English as a second language (TESL) argued strongly, and at times dogmatically to the exclusion of any other perspective, that — perhaps extended a little — their approach was all that was necessary for the education of migrant children.

The address by the Minister for Education, Kim E. Beazley, read in his absence by a member of the Department, gave an indication of the official views of the government at the time on teacher education and the general problem of migrant education. It was not conducive to getting proceedings off to a smooth start or to advancing the thinking of those present (National Seminar for Teacher Educators, 1974:37–38):

How can teacher education best produce a corps of sensitive, intelligent teachers properly attuned to the minds of migrant children in our society? The organ of one of our national groups recently suggested the essence of the problem, and I quote:

'To live in a multi-cultural society requires an education which is broad and flexible. Curricula must be developed which give all children an understanding of the variety of ethnic groups in our society and which allow all groups to appreciate the special contribution that their own ethnic culture can make.'

Unfortunately it is expressed in the turgid academic prose which is fast cutting off educators from the rest of the community, but which at least testifies to their assimilation to Australian academic educational tortuousness of expression. When you get its meaning after reading it three times it is valid.

Kim Beazley went on to express his own interpretation of what the quoted passage means.

> Let us start off with the assumption that children need to understand something of the religion, the literature and the history of migrant peoples, which is what the passage says in other words. An education system opening doors of understanding to other cultures cannot fail to be the richer for those insights. The treasures of the Renaissance in Italy, the story of the liberation of Greece, the music of Austria, the art of Holland may possibly become as intellectually exciting to Melbourne teachers as the pigskin folk festival Collingwood versus Footscray. . . . Teachers need a practical readiness to deal with school and classroom situations in which a very high percentage of their pupils will come from a non-English-speaking background, a more democratic or a less democratic background than Australia's; that some of them have a far greater respect for parents, for life, for art, for literature, for music and for culture than exists in the Anglo-Saxon tradition; and a religious faith far more deeply held and far more pervasive in their outlook than the Australian 'way of life', to quote the jargon, demonstrates.

Despite this inauspicious opening, the plenary sessions of the Seminar generated a number of important recommendations that have since become part of the on-going debate about teacher education for multiculturalism: the encouragement of an integrated approach to teacher education by weaving components about the multicultural society into the whole curriculum, or teaching compulsory core units of languages and comparative ethnic studies; the desirability of employing migrant teacher aides; the importance of in-service teacher education rather than pre-service training which was seen as too short and too filled with foundation and methods courses to give more than a superficial exposure to the problems of children from migrant backgrounds.

Ideological confusion in education

Since 1974, a number of conferences have followed this somewhat inconclusive one, some devoted to multicultural education, others to the multicultural society. Despite their frequency, as yet no unanimity has developed about the meaning and scope of multicultural education, and in this respect Australia is similar to the other cases. Rosita Young of Macquarie University has described the situation in New South Wales prior to 1977 as being characterized by five major, overlapping components: multicultural programmes, ethnic studies programmes, community language programmes, bilingual programmes, English as a second language programmes (Young, 1977).

Dr Jean Martin (1976b), addressing the Conference 'Education in a Multicultural Society' suggested that two approaches were apparent in school curriculum. 'One was to focus on aspects of "ethnic cultures" which fitted in with existing ideas about worthwhile knowledge, by stressing aspects of "ethnic cultures" harmonious with the existing education process or different in acceptable ways: this approach emphasized safe, neutral aspects of cultural pluralism, such as music, food preferences and cooking habits, traditional (folk) culture and religious observances'. The second approach was more phenomeno-logical and challenged the assumption that Western knowledge was paramount and immutable, and learned primarily through intellectual understanding. Instead knowledge is situationally determined and can be learned 'through the senses and emotions, by sensitive communi-cation with other people through verbal and non-verbal means. This approach suggested that schools need not only be concerned with preparing children for future occupations and encouraging rationality, responsibility and intellectual values' (Young, 1977:3).

Three other conferences of teacher educators have also shown how confused the situation is in Australia. Despite the title of the Australian UNESCO Seminar on Teacher Education for International Under-standing (Coffey, 1977) it would appear that most participants saw this largely as intercultural education and/or an extension of intercultural relations between the various ethnic and cultural groups that make up Australian society, i.e., multicultural education 'writ large'. Inspection of the offerings showed that they involved such themes as migrant cultures, racism, Aborigines, and teaching about different lifestyles and cultures mainly in Australia, some few overseas.

However, Dr Malcolm Skilbeck, the Seminar Director, saw the seminar as marking a watershed in the development of thinking about intercultural education, with important implications for social and cultural policy (Coffey, 1977:101):

> The reality of the multicultural society, of intercultural awareness, cannot be addressed adequately except through the engagement with the lived experi-ences of our fellow citizens. Now I take that as being one of the messages of the multicultural or intercultural or polyethnic emphasis . . . we cannot possibly talk about the future directions that education should take in rela-tion to our society, or teacher education in particular, unless we are prepared to have that society speak for itself about its own identity, about its own feelings and about meanings . . .

The South Pacific Association of Teacher Educators (SPATE) held its annual national conference in Melbourne in May 1978, on the theme 'Critical Issues in Teacher Education'. Nine broad issues formed the framework for discussion: an indication that either there is ferment in Australian teacher education, or it is groping around in the dark for a dominant theme. In all of these, teacher education for the multicultural society was really not featured at all except as a peripheral concern in a few papers.

Further evidence that multiculturalism in education may still be at the level of rhetoric and pious hopes was forthcoming during the Australian Council for Educational Administration's National Confer-ence in 1978. Its theme was 'Administering Education in a Pluralist

Society'; yet from conference papers and participants' impressions it would seem that multiculturalism is not such a preoccupation at this level as the conference title suggests.

Other educational organizations have been quick to adopt the multi-cultural label, even though it seems scarcely to match their practice. For example, the Victorian Association for Multicultural Education, VAME, subscribes to a policy which puts considerable emphasis on the teaching of English as a second language to migrant children and adults, and on children's first language maintenance in schools. Little or no account is taken of other aspects of the curriculum or the need to cater for Anglo-Saxon children. This emphasis was more apparent in the organization's former name, the Victorian Association of Teachers of English as a Second Language — and from both this and its present pressure-group approach on matters relating to language, it would seem that the term 'multicultural' in its present title is largely rhetorical.

The multicultural ideology has also been endorsed by the Australian Labor Party during its political campaigns for the May 1979 election for the state of Victoria, and the October 1980 Federal election. Its policy is set out in *Education for a Multicultural Society* (Button, 1979), and *inter alia* commits the Labor Party, if elected, to setting up intensive English language centres that would provide intensive tuition on arrival; to providing funds to subsidize improvements in teacher training and for instructional material in non-profit ethnic schools. It also endorses the recommendations of the Galbally Committee but points to its inadequacies and suggests where these might be improved. 'The ALP seeks a socially cohesive society, where differences in cultural heritage contribute to the overall vitality of national life' (1979:1).

Admirable as its aims are, it seems quite apparent that the Labor government's strategy is to provide 'more of the same' rather than make a radical reappraisal of the whole concept of multicultural education. Like many official bodies advocating this approach, it sees multi-cultural education largely in terms of catering for migrants and ethnic groups in a basically compensatory way. But they form barely a fifth of the total population of Australia: if multicultural education for a multi-cultural society is to mean anything it must cater for the total society in all its aspects rather than for a special segment of it.

Ideologies of organizations at the ethnic interface

As in countries overseas, there are in Australia several organizations whose express purpose is to liase with members of ethnic groups at what can be called the ethnic interface. Two of these organizations are the Good Neighbour Council and the Australian Ethnic Affairs Council (AEAC).

The Good Neighbour Council of Victoria

Some indication of the complexities inherent in the pluralist society can be obtained from the reaction to them of the Good Neighbour Council of Victoria. Its recent views were put by its President and its Director (GNC, 1978:6—7). According to the President, 'The work of the Council has been characterised by an openness to the issues posed by the multi-racial, multi-cultural nature of Australian society. . . .' (1978:6). The Director comments:

> Australia now has a multi-racial, multicultural *population*. But having such a population is not the same as having a multi-racial, multi-cultural *society*. . . .
>
> Today, we see that the only option open to us is to make of all these various racial and cultural elements in our midst a multi-cultural society. That this is the only option open to us is underlined by a mass of recent sociological research on 'ethnicity'. . . .
>
> The challenge that confronts us then is to build a society which allows and nurtures ethnic pluralism, and which at the same time is also cohesive. . . .
>
> The emphasis given by this Council to promoting a multi-cultural society is not only consistent with the Charter of the Good Neighbour Movement, but also grows out of the Movement's commitment to the *genuine* integration of the new settler. (1978:7—8).

The Director's analysis is a far cry from the type of naïve, paternalistic, handshake-and-cup-of-tea philosophy typical of the immediate post-war period. Echoes of it are certainly evident in the 'movement's commitment to the genuine *integration* of the new settler' [italics added], but the ideology is clearly multiculturalism, even though the references to other models and interpretations of pluralism seem to suggest either counter-ideological overtones or confusion over the meaning of ethnicity and culture. The reference to racial dimensions is a significant one, as it could indicate an awareness of the growing problem in Australia of discrimination on the grounds of racial differences — something which many official organizations ignore or gloss over.

The Galbally Report, to which the Liberal government is now committed, made a number of comments about the present effectiveness of the Good Neighbour movement, and could find no valid reason to recommend that it should continue to be funded by the Commonwealth government (Galbally, 1978:79). As a result, the Good Neighbour Council will be disbanded or its resources combined with organizations set up by ethnic communities to meet their own local needs. This decision culminates several years of pressure-group opposition by ethnic groups to the continuation of the G.N.C.

The Australian Ethnic Affairs Council (AEAC)

The Australian Ethnic Affairs Council was established on 31 January 1977 to advise the Minister for Immigration and Ethnic Affairs on a variety of issues relating to migrants in Australia. Most of the work of the Council is done through three committees: Settlement Programs, Multi-Cultural Education, Community Consultation & Ethnic Media. Comparisons are inevitable with very similar organizations established .n Canada to promulgate the official ideology, and to work on behalf of the various ethnic groups in Canada.

The overall ideology of the Council was expressed by its Chairman, Professor Zubrzycki, (Zubrzycki, 1977:62):

> We are to serve Australia, the whole nation, all of us, whatever our native tongue. The task is stupendous for we must make up our minds, whether we are to look backwards on what used to be rightly called British civilization in Australia or, whether we are to have a future as a multi-lingual, multi-racial, multi-cultural society.

The first two committees referred to above are to be responsible for policy formulation in their respective areas. The third committee has 'to come to grips with the difficult task of communicating with ethnic groups and ethnic media'. However, Professor Zubrzycki saw this work as going much deeper than the mechanical organization this would entail. 'The problem is how to organise the relationships between the various groups to enable each to maintain their own life while contributing to the good of society and the broader social frame' (1977:63) — the dilemma of pluralism in a nutshell, with social engineering overtones.

The Council puts out regular newsletters and press release sheets, and in August 1977 published its submission to the Australian Population and Immigration Council on its Green Paper, *Immigrant Policies and Australia's Population* (AEAC, 1977). The title of the submission, *Australia as a Multicultural Society*, indicates the underlying ideology. The argument owes a great deal to the personal vision of the Chairman. Broadly, it sees three key social issues confronting Australia today as the outcome of its imigration policies (AEAC, 1977:5). These are social cohesion, equality, and cultural identity.

> The crux of our argument is that Australia is already a society of multiple cultural identities, or a multicultural society, and that equality can best be promoted (perhaps can *only* be promoted) through policies that harness it to cultural identity. Both are means and both are ends: equality depends on and strengthens multiculturalism; multiculturalism depends on and strengthens equality. They are 'ends', however, only in the sense that they are the touchstones that guide our thinking and proposals, not in the sense that we see 'an equal society' or 'a multicultural society' as a tangible final social condition.
>
> We shall treat equality *as equal access to social resources.* . . .
>
> **Cultural identity**. Cultural identity is the *sense of belonging and attachment to a particular way of living* associated with the historical experience of a particular group of people. Multiculturalism exists where one society embraces groups of people with different cultural identities.

Professor Zubrzycki made probably the most apposite comment when he stated (1977:8) that 'In Australia at the present time different concepts of multiculturalism jostle for attention and different practices vie for resources'.

The Council's recommendations for the education of children (1977: 11 – 13) endorse the basic implication 'that policies and programs concerned with education for a multicultural society apply to *all* children, not just children of non-English-speaking background, and have ramifications throughout the curriculum'. Despite this its 'proposals for policy', which represents 'the minimal response that seems to us compatible with the value of equality, on the one hand, and cultural identity, on the other' are almost exclusively concerned with English language teaching (TESL) bilingual education, community language education, and the support of ethnic schools. Only one out of six proposals has more general application (1977:13):

> Schools should be given incentives to develop ethnic studies programs and to infuse the curriculum in general with the reality of the pluralist nature of Australian society, with the object both of enhancing the self-esteem of students of ethnic origin and giving *all* children a more authentic view of the nature of the society than the present mono-cultural education provides. It is important to note the interdependence of these two processes: the sense of identity of ethnic children will be defensive and inward looking unless other children accept the validity of ethnic cultures and identities.

One cannot help but wonder why the multicultural nature of Australia, so stressed in the earlier sections, now becomes pluralist, and why self-esteem apparently replaces self-identity. These are by no means synonymous. One must also be quite sceptical about the Council's emphasis on education for cultural identity, when, by its own admission (1977:11) 'we know little about the association between the child's achievements and his sense of *cultural identity*'.

Counter-ideologies and counter-ideologists

The academic debate

It is precisely this kind of concern that has led a group of theorists (including this writer) to press for clarification of the muddled terminology inherent in the official ideology, and on theoretical grounds to negate the 'received tradition' and its models of society. To this end such theorists claim to use more precise and up-to-date models and theories, which reflect modern developments in such disciplines as cultural anthropology, anthropology of education, sociology, and social psychology. Some appreciation of the grounds for their ideological attack can be obtained from the criticisms that can be made about the AEAC recommendations.

It seems clear that Professor Zubrzycki sees multiculturalism, in the form approved by the Council, as a panacea for the alienation and state of anomie that can afflict individuals in modern, industrial societies such as Australia. 'Ethnic pluralism can help us overcome or prevent the insecurity, homogenisation and loss of personal identity of mass society' (1977:17). The slide from cultural to *ethnic* pluralism is interesting and an example of the confusion between ethnicity and culture that bedevills the whole document. That ethnic (self-) identity need have nothing to do with culture, is a cornerstone of modern ethnic theory that seems to have escaped members of the AEAC. However, the double bind ethnic groups are in has also escaped them. Many may not wish to maintain their ethnic distinctiveness — the Dutch are an excellent example of this decision. Alternatively, if they do follow the injunctions of the Ethnic Affairs Council and similar bodies, in maintaining such distinctiveness they may risk being identified and labelled as 'different' by members of the majority ethnic group, the Anglo-Australian *Staatsvolk*, with all the prejudice and discrimination that such a socially ascribed boundary between groups can generate. The evidence from all pluralist societies is overwhelmingly that this tendency is ubiquitous, and is not to be negated by pious hopes of 'equality', 'cohesion', and 'cultural identity'. When socio-historical forces are such that ethnic groups are seen as an economic, social, or political threat, cultural niceties and democratic idealism are abandoned in the fight for survival. The decision of the Queensland Storemen and Packers Union in 1979 to close its books to Vietnamese labour, who, because they are willing to work hard, are seen as a threat to Australians' jobs, is a good example of this tendency (*Australian*, 13–14 October 1979).

The naïvety of the conclusions of the Ethnic Affairs Council can be now appreciated as little more than highly rhetorical special pleading (AEAC, 1977 17):

> We believe, therefore, that *our goal in Australia should be to create a society in which people of non-Anglo-Australian origin are given the opportunity, as individuals or groups, to choose to preserve and develop their culture —* their languages, traditions and arts — *so that these can become living elements in the diverse culture of the total society, while at the same time they enjoy effective and respected places within one Australian society, with equal access to the rights and opportunities that society provides and accepting responsibilities towards it. . . . Multiculturalism means ethnic communities getting 'into the act'.*

In his frequent public speaking engagements, Professor Zubrzycki has become an untiring and dedicated apostle of the new doctrine. The words 'equality', 'cohesion', and 'cultural identity' have almost become a ritual invocation — as if their very repetition will offset all the counter-arguments and pleas for greater conceptual clarity and realism that his pronouncements can generate in an audience.[2] In a public lecture in September, 1979 one may detect a note of doubt creeping into Zubrzycki's views, as if events after the publication of *Australia as a Multicultural Society* have begun to shake his faith in the absolutism of its doctrines.[3] The title of the lecture, 'Limits to Multiculturalism', itself gives some indication of this doubt, and the content too suggests that Professor Zubrzycki may now realize that the dangers of ethnic stratification, conflict and resource competition and misallocation are very real in Australia:

> Cultural differentiation of the kind envisaged in my Council's document on multiculturalism in Australia, or in the Swedish experiment, in the long run, may be incompatible with the doctrine of equality. Thus, the political goal of multiculturalism by which is meant the promotion of flourishing ethnic communities, may interfere with the political goal of equality, which has been the principal aim of modern democracy ever since the French Revolution. This to me presents an indication of one possible limit to multiculturalism.

Not for the first time, we can note the confused thinking on this issue, with free association being made between political, ethnic, cultural, and structural aspects of society — the American and Canadian muddle all over again. It is quite clear that Professor Zubrzycki uses cultural pluralism synonymously with multiculturalism, as 'a condition where many separate, distinct groups exist side by side'. This inevitably leads to political concerns inherent in cultural pluralism (a legacy of de Tocqueville) being brought into the notion of multiculturalism, which in the sense of respect for ethnic groups' traditions, languages, customs and heritage need have little to do with political concerns.

What Professor Zubrzycki and the Australian Ethnic Affairs Council have apparently failed to appreciate, as the Canadian experience makes clear, is that such cultural features are two-edged. On the one hand, they are retained and nurtured as good in themselves and as being worthy of preservation. In this sense the ethno-cultural contribution makes for a more diverse, interesting and colourful culture for all — *but only in the sense of life-style*. However, cultural features are also used as a basis for reinforcing ethnic group identity and politicizing ethnic group aspirations for better treatment by the *Staatsvolk*, equality of opportunity and access to social rewards and economic resources. The dilemma is that the more cultural aspects are cultivated to enhance the quality of a common life-style, the more they are likely to be made foci of efforts to attain better life chances.

However, it is not entirely clear whether the issue has much to do with cultural features at all, according to the implications of Professor Zubrzycki's analysis in the same lecture.

> I suggest that ethnic groups have been produced by structural conditions, which are intimately linked to the changing technology or industrial production, to distribution of goods, to methods of transportation and the like. More specifically, ethnicity, defined in terms of frequent patterns of association, identification of common origins — as in the work of Greeley in the

United States, or Jean Martin in Australia — is crystallized under conditions which reinforce the maintenance of kinship and friendship networks. These are common occupational positions, residential stability and concentration, and dependence on common institutions and services. These conditions in turn are directly dependent on the ecological structure of cities, which in turn is directly affected by the process of industrialization.

Where the concept that Australia is a multi*cultural* society can be deduced from this basically sociological, structural type of analysis, that employs ethnicity theory is very puzzling. One can only suggest that the label 'multicultural' is being maintained because it has now become part of the conventional wisdom, and sanctified by due political process (as in Canada), regardless of whether or not it fits the facts, i.e., it has become official rhetoric.

Professor Zubrzycki may not be unaware that his recent views could be interpreted as a departure from the official ideology. As if to reassure both himself and his audience Professor Zubrzycki embarked on further reformulation of the ideology, by adding a new dimension, that of 'holism', which he saw as being another desirable state for Australian society to achieve in the long term.[4] Asked when this might be, Professor Zubrzycki could give no closer estimate than 'a matter of years, decades, if not generations'. On this basis, 'holism' would seem to have limited validity, and is little more than a ritual incantation to bolster a flagging ideology and restore the spirits of the faithful. However, it seems that the rhetorical appeal of the term has obscured its technical implications. Professor Zubrzycki's views are cast in the dated mould of Parsonian 'grand theory', and could even be criticised for being unconsciously assimilationist, along lines similar to Gouldner's (1971:209) criticism of Talcott Parsons whose views were 'the product of an inward search for the world's oneness and a projection of his vision on that oneness'. The fact that Professor Zubrzycki is almost a chronological and theoretical contemporary of Talcott Parsons may explain a great deal of the Australian Ethnic Affairs Council's lofty visions of multiculturalism.

Not only are they inherently contradictory but they include ambiguities about the true nature of Australian society, which are not clarified by continuing to refer to Australia as 'a multilingual, multiracial, multicultural society' (A.E.A.C. News Release, March 21, 1980), as if in an attempt to cover all options. Why all these aspects cannot simply be encapsulated into the one, more comprehensive term multiethnic is surprising, and can only be put down to academic resistance to the term of the kind noted in other countries.

One central issue that no amount of rhetoric can gloss over is the contradiction between the aim of encouraging ethnic groups to preserve their cultural identity and the aim of achieving 'social cohesion'. As the Schools Commission's Committee asserts (1979:7):

Any action which encourages only the identity of groups and thus their continued existence may lead to a situation where separate groups compete with each other for economic, social and political power.

However, the Australian Ethnic Affairs Council and the Australian Population and Immigration Council seem to be now fully aware of the contradiction, which appeared in the former's (1977) publication. Their current views appear in the joint position statement 'Multiculturalism and its Implications for Immigration Policy' prepared for the Minister for Immigration and Ethnic Affairs, and presented to Federal Parliament for discussion on 7 June 1979. The two Councils state their concern (1979:14), but appear to do little more than pass the buck in what is the central issue of the pluralist dilemma — how to balance ethnic diversity and aspirations with national unity and the common good:

A major cause for concern is whether the creation of a network of ethnic organizations and the formalisation of group differences will adversely affect national unity. . . .

This is a delicate subject, but also a crucial one. It would certainly be legitimate for Government in a multicultural society to prevent the formation of divisive institutions that threatened national security.

The pluralist dilemma appears in various guises throughout the remainder of this publication, and the two Councils are quite restrained in their claims for what multiculturalism can and cannot achieve. However, the Minister was more rhetorical (1979:4):

I might paraphrase the overall objective as being freedom within citizenship. The goal is to ensure the cultural and personal freedom of the individual consistent with the obligations of Australian society and its institutions. Cultural diversity can help the strengthening of a cohesive Australia in which the dignity and freedom of all Australians are revered, protected and encouraged.

As in Canada and the United States, academic counter-ideologists in Australia attempt to negate the official ideology on the grounds that it misuses such key concepts as race or culture. The latter is obviously of crucial importance in an ideology such as multiculturalism, where the interpretation of what it means hinges on understanding the meaning of culture. Regretably, committees empowered to formulate a new ideology are often composed of laymen with no expertise in such disciplines as cultural anthropology or anthropology of education, or who are politically 'safe' and unwilling to use technical definitions that might reveal the ideology's inherent defects.

It is thus hardly surprising that many dated, and even wrong, notions and definitions relating to pluralism have been adopted by the Committee on Multicultural Education, and this must cast doubt on its capacity to make the recommendations it has. The same criticism can be levelled at the Galbally Committee. Both committees have made simplistic assumptions about the nature of culture and multiculturalism similar to those which characterized the early phase of thinking in the United States. This applies particularly to the definitions of culture that have been adopted. The Galbally Committee uses that of Tylor (1871) (cited as Taylor, 1891) which is now completely dated and of little use for a technical understanding of the phenomenon. The interesting feature of this definition, which a Committee composed of laymen would hardly be likely to know, is that Tylor proposed it as a form of counter-ideology at a time when Darwinian ideas were prevalent. Tylor's definition is an overstated, enumeratively descriptive attempt to stress all those aspects of the human condition that are non-biological. It was very much the product of its socio-historical context and to use it in a context that is completely different is tantamount to nonsense.

The Committee on Multicultural Education appears to have adopted, without reservation, the 'most common, popular usage in education which equates culture with a social group's heritage, i.e. traditions, history, language, arts and other aesthetic achievements, religion, customs and values' (1979:68). This is another enumeratively descriptive approach very close to the definition of Tylor and it suffers from the same limitations. In the opinion of at least one leading theorist, Bidney (1967:27), to equate culture with a group's heritage is 'a serious error', but it is one that has been perpetrated by non-anthropologists for years. It easily leads into the kind of specious argument adopted by the Committee on Multicultural Education to support its case (1979:5):

> Australia has always been a multicultural society. Even before the European settlement the continent was inhabited by the Aboriginal groups each with their own distinct and different languages and cultures.
>
> With the English colonization of the continent and thereafter, people from different cultures arrived and settled. . . .

This is not the place to criticize all of the simplistic notions contained in the above statement apart from saying that they are typical of the layman's thinking in this highly complex area. If culture contains language, according to the popular usage adopted by this Committee, it seems hardly necessary to separate out languages and cultures in the above statement. In saying that 'people from different cultures arrived and settled', the Committee has fallen into a common trap, discussed by Schneider and Bonjean (1973:123), of saying that people come from or belong to culture. They do not; they belong to or come from social groups. Culture provides the 'programme' which enables groups to survive. 'Culture programmes action systems' (1973:123).

As will be apparent from the discussion in the following chapter, confusion over the meaning of culture enables those responsible for educational planning and advice to obfuscate the central issue that pluralism generates social and cultural conditions leading to differential allocation of power, social rewards and economic resources among ethno-cultural groups and individuals constituting a pluralist society. In essence simplistic interpretations of culture enable policy makers to give the appearance of advocating something that will redress such discrimination and imbalance when, in effect, they are proposing policies that have very little bearing on such issues. For instance, the Galbally Committee (Galbally, 1978:4) adopted four guiding principles, of which the first two are most relevant in this discussion.

(a) all members of our society must have equal opportunity to realise their full potential and must have equal access to programs and services;
(b) every person should be able to maintain his or her culture without prejudice or disadvantage and should be encouraged to understand and embrace other cultures.

These two principles are unexceptional, although the concept of 'embrace other cultures' is a little puzzling. However, when seen in relation to the Committee's conceptualization of multiculturalism, it does not seem that its thinking has advanced much beyond the simplistic 'let's-all-understand-each-other' approaches we have noted overseas. As will be apparent from the discussion of *five* models of multicultural education in chapter 8, only one has the underlying philosophy of equal opportunity for all; it is not the one that the Galbally Committee appears to have espoused. This concern is exacerbated by its interpretation of multiculturalism and allied concepts, and in particular the definition of culture that has been adopted (Galbally 1978:104):

9.2   Our ethnic groups are distinguishable by various factors. For our purpose *we need only identify the two major relevant varying attributes of ethnicity* as culture and race.

9.3   It is desirable to define *our concept of culture*. We believe it is a way of life, that 'complex whole which includes knowledge, belief, art, morals, law, customs, and any other capabilities and habits acquired by man as a member of Society' [f.n. Taylor (*sic*) Primitive Culture, London, 1891 (*sic*)]. *The concept of race is clear. . . .*

9.6   . . . Provided that ethnic identity is not stressed at the expense of society at large, but is *inter-woven into the fabric of our nationhood* by the process of *multicultural interaction*, then the community as a whole will benefit substantially and its democratic nature will be reinforced. . . .

9.11   In broad terms, however, it can be said that our schools and school systems should be encouraged to develop more rapidly various initiatives aimed at improving the *understanding of the different histories, cultures, languages and attitudes* of those who make up our society. This greater understanding can be achieved in a range of ways — for example through greater allocation of resources to the teaching of *histories, cultures and languages* (both English and other languages), through development of bilingual teaching. . . . [italics added]

Detailed criticism of the above principles is superfluous, as it would only be a repetition of that made about the multicultural ideology in other case studies. Indeed, the similarity of ideas, even to the use of the weaving metaphor, is quite striking. 'The concept of race is clear' is a mind-boggling statement, which shows little knowledge of the vast and contentious literature on this subject, and the degree of polemic, political propaganda, and sheer malicious distortion the concept has generated. Coupled with total neglect of any consideration of the Australian Aborigines, it illustrates how limited the committee's concept of multicultural Australia is.

The recommendations for multicultural education are often naïve. As British (e.g. Stenhouse), Canadian, and American research has shown, there is little, if any, correlation between increased understanding (cognitive gains) of different cultural life-styles and improvements in intercultural/interracial attitudes (affective gains). This applies particularly to teaching the histories of various groups (including the 'great men of the past' approach) which research has shown does not lead children to develop tolerant intergroup attitudes or worthwhile personal values.

Such an approach indicates a limited understanding of the curriculum needed for multicultural education if one takes as a yardstick the positive recommendations from Canada and the United States described in earlier chapters. One notes in particular a complete absence of any reference to those areas of intra- and inter-group social relationships for which school subjects adapted from sociology, anthropology, economics, and political science would be most suitable. The concern to teach the past histories and cultural glories of the socio-cultural groups from which migrants come is in line with the fashionable ethnic heritage approach to migrant education but, as overseas research demonstrates, is of singularly little use in helping children from ethnic groups to understand their role and relationships within the Australian socio-cultural context.

In the recommendations of the Galbally Report on the development of multiculturalism and multicultural education, there are regretably many ideas similar to those which characterized the efforts of educationists in the United States, now known to have been misdirected. These led to the challenge from the multiethnic perspective and attempts by various theorists to develop more rigour in the thinking on multicultural education. It is depressing that the Galbally Committee appears to be advocating that Australian education should be locked into this wasteful evolutionary process by starting at the point where American development started, instead of learning from their mistakes.

The Committee has also chosen to ignore those theorists who have undertaken the detailed conceptual mapping of the nature of Australian society, culture, and related components (e.g. Bullivant, 1976, 1977a, c, 1979b; Cox, 1974; Martin, 1971, 1972, 1976a, 1978; Smolicz, 1971, 1972, 1974b, 1976a; Taft, 1975a, b, c, 1977b; Wiseman, 1974). Instead, it has claimed wrongly that 'There is very little information available on multicultural developments in Australia and overseas' (Galbally, 1978:108). What may be nearer the mark, but politically unpalatable, is that a great deal of theoretical literature in Australia has been counter-ideological, and thus unlikely to be countenanced by a Committee intent on pushing a politically motivated ideology. A simpler, but equally unpalatable explanation is that the Galbally Committee was composed of people who are not experts in the technical and theoretical disciplines needed for the study of pluralism in its various manifestations, and thus were unlikely to be au fait with the literature available.

One perspective that has been developed to generate better conceptual models that may enlighten the power dimension in Australia is that of the multiethnic (Wiseman, 1974) or polyethnic society (Bullivant, 1977a, c, 1979b, 1981). Both are concerned to take into account modern theories on ethnicity, culture and race (e.g. Banton, 1967, 1977a & b; Despres, 1968, 1975; Glazer & Moynihan, 1975; Schermerhorn, 1970). A common feature of these theorists is that they see culture as being only one of the factors responsible for the phenomenon of ethnicity and the 'new pluralism'.

Dr Naomi White, a leading counter-ideologist in Australia, takes a similar perspective to dispute the usefulness of a naïve cultural emphasis (White, 1978). She has developed fresh insights into the concept of ethnicity, which call into question the efficacy of the culture-based ideas of the Schools Commission Committee on Multicultural Education and the Galbally Committee. In particular, White has demonstrated that a sense of ethnicity can exist without shared culture or a geographically located community. As with the other theorists discussed above, White is not content to accept the conventional wisdom about culture and multiculturalism, and has pushed for a degree of analytic rigor uncongenial to those who hold the orthodoxy view. At least this might lead to more practical and less rhetorical solutions.

Finally, and somewhat unexpectedly, similar thinking using ethnic concepts appears in the annual Buntine Oration, delivered by Barbara Falk in May 1978 to the Australian College of Education — an institution not known for anything other than a conservative, establishment view of education. The title of this important contribution to the debate was 'Personal Identity in a Multi-Cultural Australia'. It employed a philosophical and historical analysis and was an attempt to focus on the question 'Is the concept of a multi-cultural Australia a paradox or a contradiction?'. Barbara Falk's answer is based in part on the recognition that 'polyethnic societies . . . have always been unjust in the sense of not offering equal opportunity for access to resources to all ethnic groups' (1978:9).

> . . . an Australian multicultural society could be a possible ideal to strive towards, only if we see the individuals in all ethnic groups, including the dominant group, as capable of both retaining and transcending their ethnicity. If we do not believe this and cannot devise institutions of society to make this belief real, we are pursuing a mirage, and we will perish in a desert in which we will have . . . no secure personal identity . . . no social structure embodying our common values, and no symbolism in which to express a shared reality. (1978:14)

Other counter-ideologists have adopted more conventional sociological theories and a structural analysis. For instance, Dr Tanya Birrell (1978:135), has stated the essence of the major weaknesses of the concept:

> [The multicultural model] neglects basic questions of social structures, power and the operation of social institutions. It does not take into account the issue of how much social cohesion is required to maintain social arrangements nor does it include consideration of the existing cleavages, structured inequalities and types of conflict among the host population itself. In other word, multiculturalism, while posed as an organizing principle for the whole social *structure*, rests on the assumption that attitudes and individual actions are the major issue in achieving a fairer society.

Birrell proceeds to a close analysis of many of the weaknesses of the multicultural model, and arrives at the somewhat pessimistic conclusion (1978:140):

> the issue seems to be one of how ethnic diversity can be accommodated and supported at the primary group level while easing the disadvantages to immigrants from the Anglo-Saxon institutional dominance. Although I am arguing that the multicultural model does not help much here, and may in fact add to the problem by offering unrealizable solutions, that is not to say that another approach will present a solution either. Essentially, this problem of diversity and equality is not remediable, at least not in the short term.

The doyenne of Australian sociologists, the late Dr Jean Martin, has consistently taken a stance which challenges the conventional wisdom in Australia about migrants. In 1971, which was a period when assimilationist and integrationist thinking was still the vogue in Australia, Jean Martin examined the evidence for the existence of ethnic or other forms of pluralism in Australia, and showed that the treatment of migrants involved devaluation, dispersal and non-recognition on the part of Australians. This resulted, in her view, in 'emasculated pluralism' (Martin, 1971:106), and the situation where migrants are seriously disadvantaged compared with the rest of Australia. In her Meredith Memorial Lecture, (Martin, 1972) these ideas were further developed together with the notion that significant structural pluralism and sector inequality between ethnic groups existed. This was a relatively new approach at the time, and this lecture was used as the base line from which 'The Changing Nature of Australian Society: Pluralism Today' could be examined. In this paper, (Martin, 1974) Dr Martin showed how Australia was becoming more pluralist, with a growing acknowledgement that it was no longer homogeneous. Dr Martin stressed that greater equality of options and access to resources and services on the part of migrants were most pressing needs and called for the provision of institutionalized pluralism where ethnic groups wanted it by structural changes in society and the channelling of resources to ethnic communities.

Dr J.J. Smolicz of the University of Adelaide has also been a leading exponent of conceptual clarification about the nature of Australian society, working within a theoretical framework of humanistic sociology based on the work of Znaniecki. Dr Smolicz was one of the first to challenge the assimilationist approach to the education of migrant children in 'Is the Australian School an Assimilationist Agency' (Smolicz, 1971). A later paper (1975b) attempted to construct a general conceptual model for the study of cultural interaction between immigrant groups and the host society. However, it seems from Smolicz's more recent work (Smolicz, 1979) that he has come to terms with the current ideology and supports multiculturalism, despite his adoption of ethnicity as a conceptual framework. This seems evident from his assertion that 'The focus of this book is very clearly upon the *cultures* of the ethnic groups', while recognizing that there are other dimensions to ethnicity that might be used for analysis (1979:xviii).

A group of theorists and workers in education for migrant children with a strong social action emphasis is based at La Trobe University in Melbourne. It uses a 'task force' orientation to carry out action research work in neighbouring schools with high migrant densities. A major outcome of this group's thinking is embodied in a major publication, (Claydon, Knight & Rado, 1977). Its approach is radical in challenging much of the 'conventional wisdom' about the education of migrant children. An important component in the work of this group, but also continuing in its own right, is the Multi-lingual Project directed by Dr Marta Rado since 1971 (Rado, 1978).

Radical counter-ideologies

The action-oriented organizations to be discussed below all subscribe to an ideology which Dr Martin has suggested moves thinking beyond even multiculturalism to 'the still more radical claim that the question at issue is one of "ethnic rights, power and participation" ' (1976a:46). This ideology has arisen from growing ethnic political consciousness in Australia, and can be compared with its American equivalent — the new pluralism, and the ethnic revitalization movement. In Australia, the 'ethnic social movement' is concerned to politicize ethnicity and press for structural reforms to achieve ethnic rights.

One of the earliest and most active organizations is the Ecumenical Migration Centre (EMC) in Melbourne. This is an experimental project of the Victorian Council of Churches, and is involved with southern and eastern European migrants in the inner suburbs of Melbourne. It operates through an outreach, casework, welfare and streetwork programme. Through its Clearing House on Migration Issues, its publication of the periodical *Migration Action*, and its documentation and abstracts service it brings together and makes available a vast amount of often otherwise inaccessible information about migrant issues.

The Centre acts as an important catalytic agency, stimulating the expression and publication of ethnic grievances, and encouraging their presentation to official investigating committees or commissions at state or federal levels. Although it subscribes to the ideology of the multicultural society, the Centre appears to do so in a polemical way that differs from the ideologists by stressing the rights and access ethnic groups have to the social and economic resources of Australia.

In its concern for action the EMC is joined by another organization, the Centre for Urban Research and Action (CURA) which is also based in Melbourne. This was originally the Fitzroy Ecumenical Centre. As its name implies, CURA is also action-oriented, and an indication of its concern in conjunction with the EMC is their joint publication *Ethnic Rights Power and Participation: Towards a Multi-Cultural Australia* (Storer, 1975). This publication is a collection of the talks and background papers prepared for a series of seminars held at the Fitzroy Ecumenical Centre between April and June, 1973. The important point is that, *for the time*, the concepts of ethnic rights, power and participation and even multiculturalism, were a radical departure from the current ideology of integration. Even the sub-title, *Toward a Multi-Cultural Australia*, would have been innovative for that period. The focus of the seminars was inspired by an earlier conference arranged by Australian Frontier at which the view was expressed that (1975:5):

> The need for various ethnic groups to work together for what might be termed migrant rights was seen as a crucial factor if migrant people were to receive justice. The kind of problems which migrants face in regard to health, social welfare, housing and employment were seen to be solvable only if migrants *themselves* could present a well documented case, and present it with some force. This would require a united front by the migrants. A paternalistic approach would be completely ineffective and even destructive for all involved.

The themes of the publication give the reasons why the work of the EMC and CURA is sufficiently different to constitute a counter-ideological movement. As Storer notes (1975:5):

> Concepts of *rights, dignity* and *justice* rather than consensus is [*sic*]

discussed; *multi-culturalism* or *ethnic pluralism* rather than homogeneity, assimilation or integration is stressed; and the transfer of power rather than the use of existing power structures or processes is sought.

Similar concepts are the background to one subsequent publication arising out of research conducted by CURA, *'But I wouldn't want my wife to work here . . .': A Study of Migrant Women in Melbourne Industry*. However, in a recent research study carried out for the Ovens-King Area Committee of the Victorian Country Education Project (CURA, 1979), CURA seems very close to subscribing to the current multicultural ideology, despite its recognition that

> The specific and practical content of multiculturalism as a policy is often lost in the rhetoric associated with a new concept. Multiculturalism is not a just solution to some of the problems of migrants. Rather, it represents a rejection of assimilation as unjust and undesirable.

However, the implications of the reasons why 'multiculturalism is not a just solution' seem to have escaped the authors of the report, or maybe they were concerned to go with the tide of the now official orthodoxy of multiculturalism expressed in the Galbally Report. In fact, so much emphasis is placed on the Italian community in the Ovens-King research (despite the presence of Yugoslavs, Spaniards, Germans, and Dutch) that perhaps a more apt ideology in this instance might have been biculturalism/bilingualism.

Many ethnic organizations have played a prominent role in trying to move thinking into the more radical new movement of ethnic rights power and participation. One of the leaders is the Australian Greek Welfare Society. An Ethnic Communities Council has also been established in Victoria following a meeting on 16 July 1974 of some 150 people representing 33 organizations. Like its New South Wales counterpart (see Jegorow, 1978:69), the Council in Victoria has among its objectives:

> 2. Ensuring the rights of ethnic minorities including effective participation in decisions which affect them, and access to Government funding.
>
> 3. Promoting action oriented research into the social conditions of ethnic minorities in the Australian society.
>
> 4. Encouraging the development of ethnic organizations concerned with the social and cultural life of their communities.
>
> 5. Participating actively in the development of a culturally pluralistic society in Australia and relating to relevant community organizations and structures. (Storer, 1975:88)

We might note that, although both these Councils subscribe to the principles of multiculturalism, the innovative feature of their thinking lies in the emphasis on ethnic rights and the setting up of new structures more representative of ethnic diversity in Australia, so that these rights can be respected and fulfilled.

An organization more concerned with education is Migrant Education Action (MEA) in Victoria, which has a counterpart in New South
Wales (Merry, Zangalis & Zangalis, 1978). This body arose out of the
campaign by ethnic and other organizations starting in April 1974,
which culminated in the massive, and at that time radical Education
Action Conference in Melbourne on 20–22 September 1974, attended
by 600 delegates. The delegates present called for English language
education for all migrants; adequately trained teachers; multicultural
and multilingual curricula in schools; and effective representation of
migrants in educational affairs. Again, although supporting the multicultural ideology, the Migrant Education Action group is committed to
structural and organizational reforms of the education system to make
it more responsive to the needs of migrant children, and acts as a
pressure group putting such views to the state and federal governments.
One of its recent campaigns was to mount a Conference on the Teaching of Migrant Languages in Schools, in Melbourne on 29 March 1977,
which was followed by a public petition supporting migrant language
maintenance in schools and other related provisions. The MEA is still
committed to obtaining an equal share of educational resources for
migrant children by an action-oriented programme.

Implications of the Australian case

This chapter on the Australian experience can serve as a summary of the
theme pursued through the case studies in this book. The situation in
Australia mirrors a great deal of what has occurred overseas, and this is
to be expected if the logic of the theoretical framework for our analysis
holds good. Dr Jean Martin, using a very similar kind of framework
with which she analysed Australian responses to the migrant presence
between 1947 and 1977, has come to very similar conclusions to those
stated or implied by the counter-ideologies referred to above (Martin,
1978:216):

> The proposition that we are, or are in the process of becoming, a culturally
> pluralist society has a specifically ideological aspect. First, it has been created
> by established institutions looking for a way to accommodate ethnically
> diverse populations with the minimum of change on their own part. Second,
> ethnic minorities themselves have had little share in formulating the idea
> (despite the fact that individual ethnics and some ethnic associations have on
> occasion been involved), while the experience of ethnics in establishing a
> structural base for their own lives — through kin, informal networks and
> formal associations — does not surface as relevant public knowledge (and,
> so far as the vital political orientation of much ethnic group life is concerned,
> is actively suppressed). Third, the thesis of cultural pluralism rests on the
> unspoken assumptions that ethnic culture can be sustained without ethnic
> communities and that a culturally diverse society is something different from
> a structurally pluralist one, assumptions that defy the weight of historical
> experience.

Notes

1. Subsequently edited and published as *The Study of Cultural Change: A Classroom Approach* (Melbourne, ACER, 1974). Professor J. Zubrzycki of the Australian National University has also claimed to have introduced the term in 1968.
2. For example, the Meredith Memorial Lecture, La Trobe University, Melbourne, 3 May 1978.
3. Centre for Migrant Studies Public Seminar, Monash University, Melbourne, 17 September 1979. These and following comments are taken from a transcript of the tape recording of the lecture.
4. With acknowledgement to Dr Frank Lewins, also of the Australian National University, who uses the term 'holistic multiculturalism'.

CHAPTER 8

The Ideology of Pluralism in Comparative Perspective

EPILOGUE — Every relationship of 'hegemony' is necessarily an educational relationship.

Antonio Gramsci

With the benefit of hindsight it seems apparent that much of the educational debate in each case study has been generated by a search for *the* ideology of pluralism. Multiculturalism is merely the latest ideology in that search, and it is instructive to trace the common features in the case studies that provide the socio-historical context of its evolution. A major advantage of the comparative perspective is to highlight aspects of social and political life that might go unnoticed if seen only as isolated instances. But when they recur ubiquitously in a number of otherwise separate cases, there are grounds for considering whether some common factors are involved. This chapter is an attempt to isolate them.

Common features in the case studies

In each case study, details of the socio-historical context are provided which clearly show that members of ethnic groups are disadvantaged socially and economically. Looked at in class or structural terms, they occupy the lower strata of the socio-economic system, perform labouring or blue-collar jobs, and in other respects are tangibly discriminated against. Historically, in each case there has been some weakening of prejudice and discrimination on the part of the *Staatsvolk* towards members of minority ethnic groups. This may have been more apparent than real, however, because there is evidence to show that considerable resistance still exists towards pluralist accommodation, even though, on the surface at least, the ideology of multiculturalism that has evolved in all the case studies would suggest otherwise.

Interpretations of socio-economic disadvantage

It is generally agreed in Britain that the most pressing need in education is to alleviate the serious disadvantages of children from coloured minorities. These are highlighted by close concentration of New Commonwealth immigrants in some stress areas, which makes their presence highly visible, particularly when it coincides with notoriously disadvantaged urban areas and 'centre-city problems' that also apply to lower working-class, 'white' Britons. Urban areas in Canada reveal similar problems of socio-economic discrimination on racial grounds, and this has led to the kind of bitter denunciation of white attitudes by Black educationists and social scientists that have been cited above. In the United States, Puerto Ricans, Chicanos, and Blacks are still among the most disadvantaged, while in Hawaii, the situation is clearly one of ethnic stratification. In Fiji, the pattern is more subtle, for it is not apparent which ethnic group is disadvantaged. In terms of having access to freehold land, and real political power, the Indians are disadvantaged, while Fijians suffer from lower educational achievement and are economically disadvantaged. The Australian pattern mirrors that of Canada, with members of ethnic groups continuing to occupy positions in the lower socio-economic levels of the social structure.

With the possible exception of Fiji — and even in this case it is possible to consider the Fijians as the dominant ethnic group politically — each case study provides evidence of continuing ethnocentrism and prejudice on the part of the *Staatsvolk*, which are historically of long standing. In Britain, such attitudes are claimed to extend even to members of the established church. In Canada, the situation is such that some changes in government policy towards multiculturalism have recently been foreshadowed by John Munro, the Minister for Multiculturalism. In his opinion, because of the emerging racial tensions and violence in some Canadian cities, much of the funds for multiculturalism should be devoted to projects aimed at decreasing bias and discrimination (Mallea, 1977:5). Despite the reduction of the Black Power militancy that characterized the 1960s, evidence suggests that discrimination and prejudice against Blacks, Puerto Ricans and Chicanos in the United States still exist. There is also a continuation of assimilationist and melting pot thinking from some reactionaries. In Australia, considerable prejudice and ethnocentrism still exist towards Aborigines and migrants judging from the regular reports coming from Al Grassby's Commission for Community Relations. A major target for union discrimination and violence is the Vietnamese immigrant.

The Fiji case is notable for the openness and candour with which prejudice and ethnocentrism have been expressed and debated at the government level. It merits more detailed description. In October 1975 Sakiasi Butadroka introduced a motion in Parliament urging that Indians or people of Indian origin be repatriated to India. This triggered off some ill-feeling between the political parties, heightened Indians' fears about their future, and in the parliamentary debate that followed revealed the depth of Fijians' feelings about the Indian presence. Ali notes (1976:427) that one of the most significant contributions to the debate came from the then Minister of Information, Ratu

David Toganivalu. As reported in the *Fiji Times* of 15 October 1975, he said in part:

> Ethnic feeling of rivalry is very real. One must be very honest in saying that all Fijians consciously, but mainly unconsciously, feel at times in terms of what is expressed in the motion; this is how we feel at times; at certain moments, in times of anger, this is what we say. It is helping that I should say this, because you really cannot take positive steps to further the national course unless and until the two major races living in the country are completely and utterly frank with each other.

In Ali's view, the Indian sense of insecurity will continue until Indians gain a greater say in politics, commensurate with their role in society and their contribution to the economy. But this is unlikely to occur, given the present voting system and the dominance of the Alliance Party. According to Ali, the sense of insecurity also derives from:

> the prevalence of communal loyalties in many aspects of life in Fiji. Until these diminish, and some of these will always remain as long as consciousness of 'race' persists, it is unlikely that the potential for racial tension will disappear. Feelings of insecurity and suspicion will endure, and will need accommodation and management to prevent their reaching conflict proportions. . . . (1976:429)

Establishing the causes of prejudice and ethnocentrism in each case study is beyond the scope of the research on which this book is based. Evidence suggests that they are the product of multiple causes, not a single one, let alone one that is racial in origin (using the term in its strict legitimate sense). Schermerhorn's (1970:6) comment on this issue deserves to be repeated:

> If research has confirmed anything in this area, it is that prejudice is a product of *situations*, historical situations, economic situations, political situations. . . .

If this interpretation is accepted, it seems clear that measures to reduce prejudice and ethnocentrism can only succeed if they tackle such situations. One major question to be answered is why this nettle is not grasped. A possible answer can be found in the vested interests and motives of the knowledge managers and ideology makers.

The knowledge/power managers

The *Staatsvolk* may hold general, diffused prejudiced attitudes towards other ethnic groups, but translating them into educational policies is in the hands of knowledge/power managers, who can be identified with some certainty in each case study. They influence the curriculum and legitimate their decisions by appeal to ideologies of pluralism, which they either create themselves or take over from ideologists who may not be directly involved with education. In turn, both groups are opposed by counter ideologists and knowledge/power managers who subscribe to their views and endeavour to foster what they believe to be more powerful ideologies of pluralism.

To see this situation in terms of conspiracy theory as an attempt by knowledge/power managers to control the life chances of children from ethnic minority backgrounds is tempting but obvious too facile, as evidence suggests that the motives of the knowledge/power managers range widely: personal advancement, political opportunism, bandwaggoning, sheer idealism. Often, these accompany general ignorance of educational and sociological issues. The complexity of the situation is well illustrated by Burnet's (1976:205−6) description of the way Canadian ideologists and managers were involved in the creation of the ideology of multiculturalism within a bilingual framework:

> The public servants who devised the policy and the politicians who adopted it were of course not concerned simply with acknowledging a sociological phenomenon. Some were English Canadians who wanted to play off the other ethnic groups against the separatists in Quebec; some were members of the other ethnic groups who felt that their turn at the pork barrel had come; some were politicians whose dominating interest was remaining in office. But some were idealists, who envisaged a Canada in which peoples of all ethnic origins and all ethnic identities would be much more equal than at present, and who felt that there was likelihood of achieving this through acceptance and even celebration of ethnic differences than through denial of them, and through collective action than through individual social mobility.

A variety of knowledge/power managers exists in Britain. In Hawaii, there are strong 'influence networks' which reflect its special characteristics (Nunes, 1977:13):

> Basically, the networks probably do not differ significantly from others, but it seems that the insularity and ethnic makeup of the Islands and the close familial and friendship ties that prevail impart a marked quality of pervasiveness which is unique. Just about everybody knows or is related to somebody who know or is related to somebody who occupies a position of influence.

The smaller context of Fiji has not led to simpler influence networks, as might have been expected. In that country, instead, the pronounced Fiji/Indian dualism, which tends to dominate a great deal of the political debate, may obscure the fact that a certain amount of knowledge/power is controlled by expatriate New Zealand, Australian and even American academics working quietly in the university and teachers colleges.

As might be expected, the situation in the United States is complex. It is also highly visible, as much of the argument about ethnic rights, power and participation has been conducted in open law courts, or through federal legislation and the various Titles making educational provisions. These have stimulated considerable knowledge/power management through the many curriculum research and development projects which have been set up with federal funding. Other federal bodies exert influence more directly on what happens in schools by suggesting guidelines for teacher education. The American Association of Colleges of Teacher Education is in this position, and its decisions have obvious impact on both pedagogy and the curriculum. The recommendation by the College Deans in 1977 that a human relations emphasis in multicultural education be adopted is an excellent example.

The overall picture of knowledge/power management in the United States has been summed up by Nathan Glazer (1977:103):

> It is clear the situation is still in flux. We have a mixed set of programs required, suggested, aided, proposed, with authority and funds flowing from federal, state and local levels, and divided among legislatures, courts, and education authorities, operating by means of law, order, and regulation. We have in addition a host of voluntary organizations representing distinctive ethnic groups, local alliances of ethnic groups, groups of educators, each proposing programs, developing curricula, bringing pressure on textbook publishers and local school systems. In short, we have a distinctively American buzzing confusion, and it is not easy to describe concretely and realistically what is going on.

In Australia, a basically similar situation can be seen. There are various knowledge/power managers, dominated for the present by the Galbally Committee, Schools Commission and the Curriculum Development Centre. Lured by the vision of government funding in a socio-historical context of declining school numbers and reduction in demand for teachers, other bodies such as teachers colleges and university departments of education have quickly jumped on the bandwaggon constructed by the Galbally Committee. In principle, Jean Burnet's comments about the Canadian experience might just as well have been said about Australia so many are the similarities in the dynamics of knowledge/power management.

Ideological and educational confusion

With so many knowledge/power managers, ideologists and counter ideologists with vested interests in pluralist education, it is little wonder that every case study demonstrates considerable confusion over how to make provisions for its ethnic groups and other features of pluralism. In Britain the situation is 'muddled' (Madeleine Blakeley) and the curriculum is in a 'mess' (Denis Lawton) although there is quite a bit going on with various people 'beavering away in small areas' (Blakeley). There are competing ideologies about the nature of the problem in British education but, when these are translated into educational practice, the types of approaches also reflect lack of agreement about catering for pluralist education. Some of them take into consideration the problems of socio-economic disadvantage experienced by children from coloured minorities while most concentrate on the ethnic traditions, heritage and other aspects of the country of origin. Meanwhile, the Department of Education and Science, through its HMIs, regards the problem of ethnic pluralism very largely as being part of the general problem of disadvantaged groups: a variation on a long-established theme in British education that children's education is related to their status in an essentially class-structured society. Currently this is being given ethnic connotations.

Against this background, it is not clear in which sense the current drive towards multiculturalism and multicultural education is being urged — substantively or normatively. One gets the impression that British society is being ideally conceptualized as becoming multicultural in the future though competing multiracial interpretations lead to a great deal of confusion. 'Race' is often used synonymously with 'group' (e.g., 'people belonging to different races') or with culture, so it is quite problematical what multicultural education really means. The variety of interpretations illustrated in chapter 2 points to confusion and not consensus on this matter.

These issues can be viewed in the light of the appeal of the former Secretary of State, Shirley Williams, for the needs of British society as a whole to be given more consideration. This puts the universalistic claims of the state against those of the relatively small number of ethnic groups in the country — the problem of 'civism' versus 'pluralism' in Butts' terms (1977). The situation is one that favours a continuation of the attitudes towards ethnics shown by the *Staatsvolk* as little is being done to alter the basic 'situational' causes of prejudice and discrimination referred to by Schermerhorn. It is hardly surprising that the curriculum in Britain is in a 'mess' or 'muddle'. Part of this may stem from historical reasons resulting from the type of educational philosophy in the post-World War II phase to put the individual before society by adopting a child-centred approach to education backed by various kinds of 'progressive' ideologies. Coupled with this are the new individualistic claims of ethnic groups for more pluralist education to suit *their* needs, which have been taken up by a number of sympathetic knowledge managers and ideologists. Not surprisingly, their efforts appear to be resisted by a majority of educationists, even though on the surface at least, multiculturalism has the blessing of the Secretary of State.

The lavish funding and organization promoted in Canada to put into operation the ideology of multiculturalism within a bilingual framework would lead one to expect that the education system has few problems, and is set on a course of action that is concerned to assist children from ethnic backgrounds. However, the reverse is the truer picture. Educational aims and programmes reflect the competing interests of those knowledge/power managers listed above (Burnet, 1976:205−6) and often statements on education are little more than platitudes, which have led one commentator (Holmes, 1978:248) to exclaim in exasperation — 'the school has to come to terms with this contradictory nonsense'.

Its success may be judged from the results of two surveys carried out in recent years. The first was carried out in Ontario, probably the most advanced and energetic province in the field of multicultural education. After commending the government's announcement of its policy on multiculturalism, McLeod comments (1975:29):

> However, the fact of the matter is that in classroom after classroom in the province immigrant children and children whose mother tongue is not English or French are being subjected at this very moment to continued programs of Canadianization based on the concept of and belief in assimilation. There is an irony to these programs, for the teachers of them often think that by teaching them they are doing something for multiculturalism.

The second survey was carried out by a review team based at the Centre for the Study of Curriculum and Instruction, Faculty of Education, University of British Columbia. It was a comprehensive survey of ethnic and multicultural content in prescribed elementary and secondary social studies curricula used across Canada during the 1974—75 school year. Some conclusions of this survey clearly suggest a situation of continuing *Staatsvolk* dominance (Werner, Connors, Aoki & Dahlie, 1977:55—57):

> There is an overwhelming British and French cultural perspective within most curricula. Other ethnic groups are interpreted in terms of one or both of these dominant groups. Typically, the choice of ethnic groups to be studied does not reflect the character of Canadian multiculturalism. . . . From examining curricula, one would conclude that Canada's population consists primarily of Indians, Inuit, British, and French. Those minorities which represent one-quarter of Canada's population are conspicuously absent.

In the United States there are also confused aims, as well as claims and counter-claims about various ideologies and programmes. In contrast to the situation in Britain, the multiracial perspective appears to have been abandoned completely. This is consistent with the historical evolution of ideologies and thinking about minority relations in the United States, where it is clear that multiculturalism and multi-ethnicity are the two ideological perspectives currently being espoused, with an intercultural (international, multinational) perspective looming on the educational horizon.

Multicultural education is seemingly more favoured at present, as the ethnicity model is still something of a newcomer to social scientific thinking, and most teachers and teacher educators are unfamiliar with its ramifications. But multicultural education has a number of subtle traps, so that it is easy to slip into what is basically still an assimilationist position (Hunter, 1974:244—45):

> As we work for multicultural education, we must be wary of committing an

error analogous to that involved in acceptance of the melting pot ideology. This ideology assumed that the dominant social group remained unchanged while the minority groups melted in. It is equally invalid to assume that with multicultural education the minority ethnic group will remain unchanged while the dominant middle class does the adjusting.

What multicultural education really means is also far from clear, and in this respect the United States is similar to Britain and Canada. In a very detailed analysis, Gibson (1976:7–18) has described five approaches to multicultural education and for each delineates basic assumptions regarding underlying values, change strategies, intended outcomes, and target populations. The fifth approach 'stems from an anthropological perspective on both education and culture and, unlike the others, does not equate education with schooling or view multicultural education as a type of formal educational program' (1976:7). The other four approaches or models considered are: (1) Education of the Culturally Different or Benevolent Multiculturalism; (2) Education About Cultural Differences or Cultural Understanding; (3) Education for Cultural Pluralism; and (4) Bicultural Education.

> All four approaches tend to equate education with schooling and to overlook the educational processes occurring outside of school. All of the approaches include among their goals increased social justice yet, with the exception of education for cultural pluralism, they tend to overlook the larger socio-political context of formal education. For each of these approaches I have suggested several major shortcomings. In doing so, I do not intend to negate the value of ongoing multicultural education programs, but wish to emphasize the need for greater conceptual clarity, which in turn will enhance our ability to test underlying assumptions and to evaluate program success. (1976:14–15)

Many features of education on the mainland are also found in Hawaii, but with small variations that reflect the islands' subtle power dynamics and influence networks. The dominant ideology is multicultural education, as a multiracial perspective is totally rejected. However, in the opinion of James Banks (1978:179), the education system is strongly Anglo-centric, possibly due to the fact 'that many of the indigenous Hawaiian educational leaders have internalized Anglo conceptions of education and perpetuate these ideas with a highly centralized and bureaucratic school system'. Banks found that there are comparatively few developments in ethnic studies in Hawaii; the mainstream curriculum tends to be Anglo-centric, pays little attention to contemporary race relations, and, despite Hawaii's rich cultural heritage and diversity, tends to be little different from the common school curriculum in many mainland districts.

In Fiji, the education system is feeling its way towards a multicultural approach in the curriculum, as one interpretation of the hitherto dominant ideology of multiracialism. However, it concentrates on language, music, and other aesthetic cultural elements, along lines that were recommended by the Fiji Education Commission. Cross-cultural and vernacular elements are also included in the curriculum. Whether these can assist children to cope with the type of society in which they will live is debatable, because the basic causes of tension between the two major ethnic groups have virtually nothing to do with these types of cultural concerns. Also, as more and more Fijians leave the villages and adopt an urban socio-economic existence, they are likely to come into active competition with Indians who dominate much of the middle-level commercial activity. If this occurs, the power relationships between the two racial groups may worsen.

Australian educators appear to be at an early stage in trying to come to grips with the multicultural approaches advocated by the Galbally Committee and Committee on Multicultural Education. The former states: (Galbally 1978:106): 'There is still apathy if not obstruction among some educators to the development of multicultural education despite the fact that since 1975 the Schools Commission has encouraged the government and non-government school systems to direct additional funds to multicultural education.' The evidence suggests that most attempts to develop new programmes have opted for the 'benevolent' or folksy approach to multicultural education. They are unlikely to receive much sound guidance from educational theorists, to judge from the plethora of confused and confusing writings this latest educational growth industry has generated, with many trying to get on the bandwaggon they can only dimly perceive.

Opting for an alternative multi- or polyethnic approach is also fraught with difficulties given the generally conservative nature of much sociological and psychological thinking in the Australian educational system. Theories of ethnicity have yet to gain respectability among academics and until they do such theoretical advances are unlikely to be made in education apart from in the odd centres, such as that at Monash University, where they are being brought into in-service courses of teacher education. Whether even this approach will solve the dilemmas expressed by Barbara Falk and pointed out by Tanya Birrell is highly questionable. The real issue in Australia, as in other pluralist countries, is a realignment of basic social structures and institutions to give minority groups more access to ethnic rights, power and participation. But it is now well recognized that this radical solution can only be generated from forces within society. The school system and its associated teacher education cannot achieve anywhere near the degree of social change required through the curriculum. This in essence is the pluralist dilemma in education, but it is manifestly not being solved. Can we advance sociological explanations why this is so?

Ideologies of pluralism as ethnic hegemony

One possible interpretation is to see the various ideologies of pluralism as ways used by the *Staatsvolk* to legitimate their control over the knowledge/power that is the key to achieving better life chances on the part of ethnic minority groups. As a corollary, if this proposition is substantiated by the analysis that follows, we must ask how does the *Staatsvolk* get away with it. How can it appear to be doing a great deal through various educational programmes yet in reality achieve so little of consequence in alleviating the socio-economic disadvantages suffered by children from minority ethnic groups? A final consideration then should be to examine ways of reconciling the irreconcilable — the claims and counter claims that underlie the pluralist dilemma.

In political theory the concept of hegemony has been used since the 19th century to describe the controlling influence or authority of one nation over another. The concept is also used in Marxist theory, especially that of Gramsci (1971), to denote the predominance or authority exercised by one social class over another. This authority involves not only political and economic control by the dominant class over subordinate classes (in Marxist theory bourgeois over proletariat), but also control over ways of legitimating this dominance by influencing the consciousness of both the dominating and dominated groups. This control ensures that the former sees its possession of power as legitimate and that the latter accept it as normal. In short, hegemony by the dominants involves the construction of a social and cultural reality to seduce the dominated class into accepting it is *the* reality and taken-for-granted commonsense. 'The hegemony of a political class meant for Gramsci that that class had succeeded in persuading the other classes of society to accept its own moral, political and cultural values' (Joll, 1977:99). Ideologies bolster this social and cultural reality to create an 'ideological soil' in which hegemony can flourish (Gramsci, 1971:365–6). The role of intellectuals (i.e. our knowledge managers), as 'experts in legitimation' is 'in mediating the ideological and political unity of the existing hegemonic structure, rendering it acceptable to allied and subordinate groups, universalizing its dominance' (Merrington, 1977:153). Such a role is 'educative' and thus closely concerned with methods of organizing and directing the transmission of knowledge. 'Every relationship of "hegemony" is necessarily an educational relationship' (Gramsci, 1971:350).

This framework of analysis can be extended by adding an ethnic dimension to the class perspective of Marxism, without in any way distorting the basic tenets of the concept of hegemony. Indeed the correlation between disadvantaged ethnic groups and the lower socio-economic strata in the case studies strengthens the case for doing so. It does not weaken the argument by pointing to members of ethnic groups who are also members of dominant groups of ideologists or knowledge managers, as, for example, the Australian Ethnic Affairs Council. Almost invariably they are self-appointed spokesmen or not truly representative of their ethnic constituencies. Research has shown that erstwhile members of an ethnic group who 'make it' into the ranks of the *Staatsvolk* become more chauvinistic towards members of their former group than members of the *Staatsvolk* themselves (Beswick & Hills, 1969). The concept of ethnic hegemony can thus be justified to mean a situation in which members of the *Staatsvolk* control knowledge/power and thus the creation of socio-cultural reality, to justify their control over the major institutions of the state and socio-economic dominance. Knowledge managers of various kinds manipulate ideologies of pluralism, particularly through the state-controlled education system, to legitimate the distribution of knowledge and make it, and the view of the social system itself, acceptable to members of dominated ethnic groups. Paradoxically, there need not be anything conspiratorial on the part of dominant knowledge managers in performing this function, they might do so unintentionally and from the best of motives. There may even be in an ethnically pluralist society deep-seated socio-biological pressures that ensure the control over power for the dominant ethnic group, thus preventing internal dissension and conflict between ethnic groups that will weaken the collective survival capacity of the state, i.e., a form of survival imperative (see discussion in Bullivant, 1981). Whatever forces are at work to maintain control over knowledge/power, whether they are intentional or unintentional, the net result is the same — ethnic hegemony prevails. A number of hegemonic strategies assist this process.

Strategies of ethnic hegemony

Constructing specious models of society

Ideologists and knowledge/power managers endeavour to construct and use the model of the pluralist society which best suits their political and educational aims. A great deal of reification frequently occurs in which the existence of, say, the 'multicultural society' is taken for granted as if it were not only an existential reality, operating apart from and outside man, but also has features and characteristics upon which all are in agreement. 'As soon as an objective social world is established, the possibility of reification is never far away' (Berger and Luckmann, 1971:106). Attacks on the validity of such an objectivated society are turned aside by counter arguments which imply that as such a society 'exists' it must be 'real' or 'true'. The 'decisive question' rarely faced by such knowledge managers is 'that, however objectivated, the social world was made by men – and, therefore, can be remade by them' (1971:106).

A recurrent theme is the confusion that exists between the substantive (truth claim) and normative (ideal prescription) elements of the models. For example, in Fiji it is not always clear whether multicultural is being used to describe the society (truth claim) or as wishful thinking about what it might become (ideal prescription). If the latter, then the policy is misguided and rather naïve idealism because there *are* very obvious racial differences in Fiji, in the strict genetic sense of the term 'race'. They will not be extirpated by the expedient of giving the society the less contentious 'label' of multicultural, coupled with any one of the gustatory ('salad bowl'), textural ('social fabric', 'mosaic'), or relational ('family of the nation') adjuncts which we have seen to be an almost obligatory part of the rhetoric about multiculturalism. Truth must be faced: 'race' is used as a convenient scapegoat on which to pin antagonisms and rivalries about power and control that arise from socio-economic and historical forces. These should not be defined out of consideration by fiat but should be made part of education within a model of Fijian society that gives scope for such considerations. It is very doubtful whether multicultural, as currently conceived, is that model.

The official doctrine of multiculturalism within a bilingual framework in Canada is so obviously flying in the face of demographic reality that it can only be a normative ideology, and highly rhetorical. Canada is not *effectively* bilingual throughout the entire nation and a great deal of the current debate about the ideology revolves around the demands of ethnic groups to have multilingual education catered for in schools. The more the flight from French and French-speaking provinces continues, as the research evidence cited above indicates (Valpay, 1978), the more the ideology of bilingualism becomes 'a fading dream'. Yet the myth persists, reinforced by an expensive and highly organized government propaganda machine.

In the United States and Hawaii racial differences do exist in the strict genetic sense of the term but they have been virtually outlawed in official thinking. One of the replacement doctrines is multiculturalism which provides unlimited opportunity to gloss over the highly-charged issue of race in which the 'colour' factor looms large. Again, this cannot be wished away merely by changing the label for society. If 'Black is beautiful' is something more than a political slogan, changing the label is also an insult to those who want to maintain pride in their race. Australian Aborigines might have similar grounds for complaint against the doctrine of multiculturalism in the reports of the Galbally Committee and the Committee on Multicultural Education, both of which ignore the special problems of Aborigines. Yet, presumably, they too are part of the 'multicultural' society but are 'written out' of it in official thinking.

All the above uses of terminology are an excellent example of the way interested parties in the pluralist debate have dominated the construction of knowledge about the nature of their respective societies, so that what is ultimately constructed, in Martin's view (1978:23–3), is ideological to justify their particular interests. The case of Australian Aborigines is a particularly interesting example of the way knowledge about Australian society is subtly channelled into a mode of thinking by tacitly avoiding the Aboriginal issue and not 'confronting it' (1978:21). The creation of 'blind spots' is also a strategy of ethnic hegemony.

The British case is also interesting because of the obvious competition between models of society none of which seems to be an accurate truth claim. The assertion that Britain is multiracial, put forward by the National Association for Multiracial Education (NAME), or multicultural, as proposed by some educationists, just does not square with the demographic reality of Britain. Only 3 per cent of the population comes from racially different stock and only some 4 per cent (including those who are racially different) of the population has cultural variations. Such small percentages scarcely warrant the use of the term 'multi-'. To maintain the fiction that Britain is composed of many (multi-) groups who are racially or culturally different is simply question-begging and ideological.

The government in Britain, on the other hand, has adopted a more conventional view of the problems of coloured minorities which sees them as part of the wider problem of deprived social classes. The ideological solution of Labour, enshrined in the urban renewal scheme, is to improve the general social and economic milieu of all deprived groups, and thereby improve the life chances of coloureds. Mike Feeley, President of NAME, is justified in his concern that the 'special problems', i.e. those caused by racial or 'colour' differences will be lost sight of in this kind of treatment. It could well be that the Labour government came to a non-decision, in Bachrach and Baratz's terms (1970) and thereby ruled out the race question as an object of public knowledge.

The decision of the University of London's Institute of Education to pursue the multicultural line, even to the extent of setting up a Multicultural Education Centre, obviously has ideological implications. As we suggest in what follows about very similar developments in Australia, the adoption of multicultural is question-begging because it defines other interpretations out of consideration and analysis. How racial and ethnic dimensions — i.e., those unrelated to culture — can be brought within a multicultural model of society, without doing violence to the concept of culture is not clear. The danger is that important issues which are promoting dissension and conflict in British society will be defined away as objects of legitimate concern. The parallels with Canada, the United States, Hawaii, Fiji, and Australia are striking.

The statement that Australia *is* a multicultural society is similarly question-begging but on grounds somewhat different from those that apply to the British case. Clearly, with some one hundred or more national and linguistic groups represented by persons who form a proportion of the Australian population, there are *a priori* quantitative grounds for thinking that Australia *might* be multicultural. However, until we are told in which one of the very many senses the concept of culture is being used — and this is rarely made clear by those who so glibly use the term multicultural — we are not in a position to accede to the proposition that Australia *is* a multicultural society. This difficulty is compounded by the proliferation of definitions of multicultural and by the confusion produced by what are often quite idiosyncratic interpretations of the concept.

The recent views of Professor Zubrzycki illustrate these problems.[1] Multicultural is taken to be synonymous with cultural pluralism and simply means 'a condition where many separate, distinct groups exist side by side'. It is not at all clear whether this model is being used substantively or normatively:

> In order for such groups to exist with self-satisfaction there must be positive self-identity among members of the group, who see themselves as holding certain positive, favourable traits in common, and the positive acceptance of the group by outsiders, who see the group as contributing to the total well-being of the society. And here, I think, we find two meanings by and large, that describe this situation.
>
> At best, cultural pluralism means that the separate groups coexist harmoniously, that they are secure in their distinct, distinctive biological, religious, linguistic or social customs, and equal in their accessibility to natural resources, civil rights, and political power. . . .
>
> At worst, at the other extreme, multiculturalism means that the separate groups compete with each other for economic, social, and political power, that they regard each other suspiciously as threats to their own survival and their own well-being. . . .
>
> Now contemporary Australian society, I suggest, operates somewhere between these two extremes. But the social and political reforms of the last seven to eight years, particularly, are moving our society perhaps toward a form of cultural pluralism which may not be too far removed from that more ideal state. It is still significantly removed but perhaps, I would hope, is moving towards the more ideal state.
>
> This particular movement is real not because one fifth of our population are people born in non-Anglo-Australian countries or are sons and daughters of such people. That movement occurs because the nature of cultural pluralism in Australia has changed from being an undesirable social condition, that was to be overcome by citizenship training, to being today a desirable social condition in which differences are respected and the positive group identity is seen as necessary for individual mental health and social progress.

This type of analysis can be criticised on several grounds. The substantive, truth-claims being made about the present nature of Australian society are not backed by empirical facts, and are little more than thinly disguised normative statements. The claim that a movement has occurred from what Zubrzycki sees as an undesirable type of pluralism to a desirable one is far from 'real', and would probably be disputed by many members of disadvantaged ethnic groups. More importantly, the ideal state which is being predicted, i.e., separate groups existing harmoniously without competing with each other, is naïve in the light of historical evidence that competing for resources is what groups do after they have become established and able to operate at a level above the fight for bare existence. Here, the projection of Professor Zubrzycki's vision of Australia's 'holistic' oneness — like Talcott Parsons' inward search for the world's oneness — verges on the fanciful.

Obscuring the routes to a share of power

A further way of maintaining ethnic hegemony is to obscure the way by which a fairer share of knowledge/power can be obtained by ethnic groups. One way to do this is to place most emphasis on the importance of cultural and ethnic identity as the major feature in pluralism, rather than others that determine successful negotiations with the dominant groups in society. For instance, the above quotation implies that 'a condition where many separate, distinct groups exist side by side' is what constitutes the essence of cultural pluralism. But like the visions of romantic pluralists, that of Zubrzycki ignores the major features of cultural pluralism which Horace Kallen (1924) the founder of the term always insisted upon. These are not cultural nor related to ethnicity but are the 'fundamental principles of *political* democracy that must underlie the diversities of *cultural* pluralism' (Butts, 1977:18). It is to political aspects that one must look if 'harmony' is to prevail in the pluralist society. This is inescapable. Certain common institutions essential for the well-being and smooth functioning of the nation-state *as a whole* must be maintained: common language, common political system, common legal system, common economic market system and so on. Cultural pluralism can operate at the level of *private*, rather than public, concerns such as use of ethnic language in the home, religious observances, family rules of conduct, kinship loyalties etc. These will give a quality of life to the ethnic groups concerned and, hopefully, some of this will spill over into other ethnic groups to improve their quality of life. But, the idea that maintaining these aspects of ethnic life and encouraging the maintenance of ethnic groups almost in the sense of ethnic enclaves will assist their ability to cope with the political realities of the nation-state is manifestly absurd. Unhappily, many educational programmes that go under the banner of multiculturalism operate under the same assumption.

This problem is acknowledged by the Schools Commission's Committee on Multicultural Education (1979:7–9), but it also opts for the cultural emphasis in its view of cultural pluralism or multiculturalism, and slides to a normative consensus model of society which again dodges the whole question of political conflict and competition:

> Any action which encourages only the identity of groups and thus their continued existence may lead to a situation where separate groups compete with each other for economic, social and political power. It becomes important, therefore, to recognise that within the diversity of Australian society there is

nevertheless a common thread . . . in the acceptance by all communities, however diverse, of some common values. These are likely to include a belief in parliamentary democracy, in equality of opportunity, in educational and economic activity and the right to a private life and choice of occupation. . . . "Multicultural" when referring to society can be used in two senses. The first sense is descriptive: the term describes a nation which has a number of different ethnic groups represented in its population. The second sense is one which implies value and refers to desirable structures which should exist in society. The Committee uses the term in the second sense. The acceptance of this view implies that Australian society should promote a degree of cultural and social variation.

Professor Zubrzycki and this committee fail to see that the dilemma has to do with providing for equality of opportunity through various 'systems of opportunity and freedom' — common educational system, open socio-economic system, equal rights before the law, few barriers to upward social mobility — while at the same time providing for quality of private life. Melvin Tumin has put the dilemma in another way (1977:xiv):

> Equality of opportunity refers to what sociologists call life chances, that is, the chances of having the relevant talents and powers of an individual dis-covered, trained, recruited, and employed in the competition for making a living and for securing a place on the ladders of property, prestige, and power that characterize this society. Equality of opportunity does not refer to something that is quite distinct, though closely connected to life chances, namely life styles, or the distinctive ways in which individuals spend their lives, including their forms of worshipping, eating, dressing, speaking, asso-ciating, thinking about the world, recreating, educating their children, and working out family problems. . . . It is to the freedom to choose a life style that the question of cultural pluralism mainly refers.

The distinction between life chances and life styles is at the heart of the pluralist dilemma. It is the former that has to do with control over 'knowledge/power' but this fact is obscured by educational pro-grammes and models of society that stress life styles thereby coming to 'non-decisions' about the more important issues of equality of oppor-tunity through the various 'systems of opportunity and freedom'. Naïve, romantic pluralists contribute to the problem when they stress educational programmes and curricula that emphasize only life-style concerns. This is easy to do, as they appeal to the vision of society that stresses its 'niceness' and one-big-happy-family 'holism', rather than the competitive nastiness of the real world. This is far less romantic, but much more pertinent for education.

The vision can also be legitimated by appeal to a related ideology, that of 'democracy', which, if pushed to its logical conclusion would support giving children from ethnic groups equality of opportunity and better life chances. This apparent paradox does not deter knowledge managers from appearing to provide educational programmes aimed at aiding such children — but which in the outcome do not — while at the same time subscribing to the ideology of democracy. As Cynthia Enloe explains (1973:60–61):

> Democratic ideology goes undisturbed as long as ethnic communities are intent upon assimilation or as long as they are too politically underdeveloped to make their existence forcefully known to the obvious majority. While this blissful condition lasts, democrats can sing the praises of individualism and pluralism simultaneously. The conceptual trick is to acknowledge diversity of cultures within the society but assume that culture deals mainly with styles and cooking recipes and has relatively little impact on ambitions, moral judgements and public goals. If ethnicity is this shallow, then things that really matter to individuals will hardly be affected, and it will not impinge on important national decisions. In other words, the discrepancy between democratic ideology and ethnic reality is resolved by reducing ethnicity to style.

Denigration of rival models of society

The role of the counter ideologist and the knowledge managers that support him is to generate competing ideologies and models of society. This can sometimes be done with impunity but evidence suggests that alternative models are resisted, often with little theoretical justification, by ideologists and knowledge managers. Partly this can be due to academic conservatism and ignorance of theoretical developments, and partly, one suspects, because they threaten the hegemony enjoyed by the conservative knowledge/power managers. At the personal level this may only be another variant of academic one-up-man-ship, but when it is seen that such conservatives are often in positions of influence within the wider education system it is difficult to escape the conclusion that they are determined to preserve their interpretation of social reality at all costs.

It is difficult otherwise to understand the degree of virulence with which ideas that run counter to those of the conservatives can be attacked. Academic resistance to ethnicity theory was encountered in all the case studies. The following example is Australian, and, significantly, took place at a major national seminar held to discuss and formulate guidelines for training teachers in international understanding. It is somewhat ironic that the seminar, with its implied necessity for tolerance and enlightened viewpoints, was the setting for these comments on this writer's (Bullivant, 1977a) theoretical model to assist curriculum decision-making (Tatz, 1977:41):

> Marvellous word, ethnic. . . . The 'nic' part is reminiscent of those delightful American-Yiddish ('Yinglish'!) words: beatnik, peacenik, refusenik, (for Russian dissidents) and nudnik/noodnik (a nag, a drag, a pest, a monumental bore, a pain in the arse). And a phudnik is a nudnick with a Ph.D. Ethnic, for my learned friends, comes from the ecclesiastical Latin word *ethnicus* which means heathen: it also derives from the Greek word for

nation. Forgive me if I stick to words like race, racism, religious and cultural groups. I have had a gutful of the euphemism revolution.

Constructing alternative types of knowledge

At a more fundamental level, it is legitimate to speculate from the evidence in six case studies, that hegemony is being exerted by knowledge managers by a process which goes to the heart of the enculturation model developed in chapter 1. It is commonly accepted that schools 'process' pupils, but less recognized that they also process knowledge, and that this is probably a more crucial function. The first chapter demonstrated how control over all levels and aspects of the curriculum is a way of exercising hegemony over children from ethnic and disadvantaged backgrounds. This is achieved by controlling the types and quantity of 'knowledge' through the value-based operations of selection, organization and implementation that comprise the curriculum. As Edgar has suggested (1975), two broad categories of knowledge can be affected — 'recipe' knowledge, being what everybody should know for effective social interaction, coupled with knowledge of the intrinsic limits on one's range of possible action; secondly, role-specific knowledge which accompanies one's status or place in society, coupled with the limits one's objective situation places on using this knowledge. These two types of knowledge provide the basis for a person's 'social competence', consisting of those skills and competencies necessary for effective action in social situations, coupled with the knowledge or sense of one's own ability or power, which enables a person to see him/her self as being competent to exercise the skills and competencies, and thus take advantage of opportunities. On this basis, hegemony can be effected by varying the 'mix' of recipe and role-specific knowledge that is offered to ethnic minority children vis-a-vis others. In this case the 'mix' draws on a common, agreed-on stock of knowledge.

A feature of many programmes of multicultural and even multiethnic education throughout the case studies is the predominance of the 'naïve' or 'benevolent' approaches. In many cases these are of the 'additive' type, being merely tacked on to existing syllabuses, and often only intended to boost the education of children from ethnic backgrounds, rather than form the basis of a common course taken by all children in the school. Here we may have not only a skewed selection of knowledge which produces one kind of 'mix' for some children and another 'mix' for others, but the possibility that what is taken to be knowledge itself may vary as a basis for the mix. This possibility rests on the conceptual connection we made in Chapter 1 between culture and knowledge.

Definitions of culture, such as those utilised by the various Australian educational committees, are implicitly definitions of knowledge. The curriculum, a selection from the culture or stock of public knowledge, can thus draw upon a variety of 'committee constructions' (rather than social constructions) of knowledge, which, in turn will be characterized by the world view, competence, and ultimately hegemonic inclinations of the committees concerned.

This can be taken further. A related feature of many programmes noted in the case studies is the conceptual separation that is made between language and culture, as if these are separate, rather than two sides of one coin: culture the 'content' of the enculturation transmission, and language of various kinds (systems of both signs and symbols) the 'vehicle' which does the transmitting. Again, the opportunity is present for the exercise of hegemony. As Bisseret (1979) has demonstrated, languages of the classes in a stratified society vary one from the other, and often reflect the 'dominance relationships' (1979:3) between members of those classes. Conceivably the same mechanism may also operate in a society that is ethnically 'stratified', as many of the case studies in this book appear to be from the socio-economic evidence. Encouraging members of ethnic groups to maintain their own languages, while eminently worthwhile from the point of view of maintaining their cultural and ethnic pride and self esteem, may function as a method of setting up 'dominance relationships' in relation to the language of the "*Staatsvolk*", English. By controlling both 'content' and 'vehicle' its dominant knowledge managers ensure even tighter control of ethnic hegemony.

The rhetoric of multicultural education

Many of the features of pluralist ideologies find expression in the programmes of multicultural education that have become the most favoured approach in all case studies. Those who support them make a number of quite dubious claims about their efficacy:

(a) that by learning about his cultural and ethnic 'roots' an ethnic child will improve his educational achievement;

(b) the closely related claim that learning about his culture, its traditions and so on will improve equality of opportunity;

(c) that learning about other cultures will reduce children's (and adult) prejudice and discrimination towards those from different cultural and ethnic backgrounds.

Such claims are either made explicit or implied in programmatic statements for multicultural education. For example, the Australian Ethnic Affairs Council (1977:12) comments:

> Current criticism that the Child Migrant Education Program has been over assimilationist in its concentration only on English teaching . . . suggests a *link between the issues of equality and cultural identity in child education.*

The Committee on Multicultural Education (1979:9 et passim) also supports the idea that the identity of cultural groups within Australia should be fostered, and its cultural diversity recognized for the benefit of the education of children from culturally different backgrounds. Without specifying why it recommends (1979:13) that 'it is good pedagogy to recognize and use all students' cultural backgrounds'. The Galbally Committee (Galbally, 1978:105) draws attention to the 'trauma' it claims is associated with children who have lost their native language and much of their culture, and claims 'It is damaging psychologically and is an impediment to education thus preventing individuals from achieving their full potential'. Again, there is the implication that greater equality of opportunity will be encouraged by assisting children to retain their native language and culture.

However, as Nathan Glazer has pointed out (1977:18−21), there is little hard research evidence to support the causal relationship between the improvement of an ethnic child's identity, knowledge of his cultural background and heritage and an increase in his life chances. In fact, there are many examples of children from ethnic groups such as Jews, Armenians, Chinese and Japanese who have succeeded academically without the support of ethnic identity maintenance and learning about their cultural backgrounds.

Such assumptions have become part of the rhetoric and conventional wisdom of multicultural education. In the case of Australia this may be due to misreading American experience. To assume that the enhancement of ethnic life styles will automatically improve their life chances puts the cart before the horse. The rise of the 'new pluralism' or 'new ethnicity' in the United States, with its stress on recognizing the traditions, histories, heritage and other contributions of ethnic groups to American life, came *after* their achievement of relative economic gains through political and socio-economic means. It other words, the achievement of improved life chances has created a socio-historical context which now favours the ideology of the 'new ethnicity' with its stress on life styles for their own sake and as a source of cultural pride. It is scarcely coincidental that the same period has produced the film *Roots* and what might be termed the 'roots syndrome' which has affected other ethnic groups in America.

A closely related recommendation in the Reports of the three Australian committees endorses the value of all children in Australia learning about its cultural diversity. As the Australian Ethnic Affairs Council puts it (1977:11): '. . . policies and programs concerned with education for a multicultural society apply to *all* children, not just children of non-English-speaking background, and have ramifications throughout the curriculum'. The Galbally Committee states (1978:106) '. . . our schools and school systems should be encouraged to develop more rapidly various initiatives aimed at improving the understanding of the different histories, cultures, languages and attitudes of those who make up our society'. The Committee on Multicultural Education suggests (1979:11): '. . . general programmes or studies which aim at fostering in all students an appreciation of the dignity of the contribution made by the cultures which exist within Australian society'. Running through the supporting arguments to these recommendations is the idea that such programmes will not lead to divisiveness but will produce a supportive climate in society that will benefit everybody in it. No mention is made of class or power dimensions, rather these are defined out of consideration by the emphasis placed on culture as the main determinant of social life. The net result of this could even work against the life chances of children from ethnic backgrounds (Birrell, 1978:107):

> The ''one big happy family'' ideology ignores this reality of class and cultural dominance by those in a position to recruit and admit members to the elite. There is no apparent imperative to change the existing arrangements and lofty multicultural sentiments are hardly likely to effect such a change. Under such conditions, a conscientious maintenance of ethnic communities and social patterns may actually operate to the disadvantage of the ethnic group, at least in concrete respects. The persistence of ethnic identity and affiliation may be satisfying, but in continuing this affiliation members may lack the social knowledge required for mobility into positions controlled by the dominant groups as well as the access to 'old-boy' networks which seem to be important in patronage mobility. . . . The time and effort required to learn and maintain ethnic languages and customs could inhibit the acquisition of skills and knowledge which, while in absolute terms are no better than ethnically valued ones, are nevertheless more useful in securing jobs, promotion, influence and the like.

> Whether we like it or not, it remains the prerogative of the Anglo-Saxon hosts to decide what are the ''good'' elements of other cultural traditions and this prerogative stems from their grip of power primarily in the economic and political areas.

Ideologies of Pluralism as Political Symbolism

Having come back full circle to the central issue of control over power by the *Staatsvolk*, it must now be asked how this situation is maintained politically so that members of ethnic groups are lulled into believing that their best interests are being served by the educational and other programmes that operate under the ideologies of pluralism. In short, how does the *Staatsvolk* get away with it?

An outstanding feature of all the case studies is the broad similarity between the language in which their ideologies of pluralism are expressed. This might be put down to copying — a form of cultural diffusion from one country to another — or to intent. The latter explanation is favoured here. The ideologies of pluralism, for which we can take multiculturalism as the prime example, are expressed in a symbolic 'political language' which enables people's behaviour to be manipulated, their fears assuaged, and the provisions of government to be seen as beneficient. Such is the power of symbolism in human affairs (Edelman, 1971:2):

> The ability to manipulate sense perceptions symbolically permits complex reasoning and planning and consequent efficacious action. It also facilitates firm attachments to illusions, misperceptions, and myths and consequent misguided or self-defeating action.
>
> To explain political behaviour as a response to fairly stable individual wants, reasoning, attitudes, and empirically based perceptions is therefore simplistic and misleading. Adequate explanation must focus on the complex element that intervenes between the environment and the behavior of human beings: creation and change in common meanings through symbolic apprehension in groups of people of interests, pressures, threats, and possibilities.

Symbolic political language is used by government to communicate its view of social reality to the governed, through channels of communication and 'apparatus of hegemony' (Gramsci, 1971: 365–6), set up by the knowledge managers. In this way government both structures people's expectations of what it provides and their acceptance of what is provided, while at the same time legitimating its claim to authority and having people take that for granted. In the field of multicultural education and multiculturalism, for example, symbolic political language of the kind analysed by Edelman (1964, 1971, 1977) structures ethnics' perceptions of their inequality in terms of cultural or identity deficits, that can be remedied by education, rather than in terms of structural aspects of the political system that deny them access to knowledge/power. Because pronouncements such as those of the Galbally Committee are also couched in symbolic political language, they are accepted by ethnics as legitimate and beneficial. Such pronouncements structure their expectations into a mould pre-determined by government and within the limitations of the provisions it is willing to concede. Even such a deceptively innocuous organization as the Australian Institute of Multicultural Affairs conveys by the components of symbolism in its title a way of structuring peoples' expectations and acquiescence of its responsibilities. 'Australian' and 'Institute' are both symbolic terms indicating power. To challenge the Institute is to challenge the Australian nation. 'Affairs' is grandiloquent and connotes comprehensiveness. We can possibly appreciate the symbolism in the title by rephrasing it in a way that probably matches the organization's responsibilities more accurately but, of course, conveys none of its hegemonic connotations, namely, Centre for Cultural Studies.

Ideologies of pluralism as myth and metaphor

The power of symbolic political language is based on its use of myth and metaphor. When this is appreciated it becomes clear that while many government pronouncements apparently appeal to reason, in reality, due to their mythical and metaphorical content, they are essentially metaphysical and appeal to faith. In this guise they are unassailable by reason or empirical verification.

'The word "myth" signifies a belief held in common by a large group of people that gives events and actions a particular meaning; it is typically socially cued rather than empirically based' (Edelman, 1971:14). A myth is not necessarily a fiction in this sense (Edelman, 1977: 3 f.n.). Political events get translated into myths, not because of any inherent mythical quality in the events themselves but by the way people perceive them. Edelman (1971:15) suggests that there are polar opposite modes of apprehending any issue:

> . . . on the one hand, tentativeness in reaching conclusions and systematic care to check hypotheses against empirical observation and, on the other hand, apprehension through social suggestion, generating beliefs not susceptible to empirical check or revision. In the second mode, what is manifest and observable is denied and repressed, often through metaphorical ambiguity; for it is not socially sanctioned. What is mythical and unobservable is publicly affirmed and believed, for it evokes social support.

From this perspective it is possible to throw light on many of the puzzling features of the ideologies of pluralism encountered in the case studies: the omission of empirical, demographic evidence about the nature of, say, a society's racial composition; the translation of 'race' into 'culture'; recurrence of metaphors like the 'cultural mosaic', 'family of the nation'; appeals to the rhetoric of equality; the dogmatism and faith in symbols shown by those who denigrate opposing views; the faith of educationists in programmes for which there is little if any supporting empirical research evidence. All these can be accommodated within the myth of multiculturalism and multicultural education, even to the extent of rationalising away opposing viewpoints by incorporating them into the same mythical, believable construction of a 'multicultural society' in which 'unity' is reconciled with 'diversity', 'equality' and 'harmony' are considered to be achievable, all within a time span of 'years, decades, if not generations', probably the most banal of the claims made about the multicultural society. Indeed, this very banality is one of the ways by which myth can be recognized (Edelman, 1977:3): 'In politics, as in religions whatever is ceremonial or banal strengthens reassuring beliefs regardless of their validity and discourages skeptical inquiry about disturbing issues'.

Other ways of recognizing the 'meta-language' of myth, i.e. the 'second language, *in which* one speaks about the first' (Barthes, 1973:115), are also found in the ideologies of pluralism. Statements frequently proceed by analogy as mythical signification is never arbitrary (1973:126); the symbolism and metaphorical content are high, 'in general myth prefers to work with poor, incomplete images . . . such as caricatures, pastiches, symbols, etc.', (1973:127); myth often involves tautology in which its proposer takes refuge when at a loss for an explanation, (1973:152); 'myths tend towards proverbs' (1973:154). It would be quite feasible, but pointless, to content analyse the literature associated with the ideologies of pluralism in all six case studies to find examples of all these recognition markers of myth.

The Pluralist Dilemma in Education

The essence as well as the complexity of the pluralist dilemma may now be appreciated. From the point of view of adult members of ethnic groups within a pluralist society, programmes of 'multicultural' education that cater for their lifestyles and culture maintenance have an obvious attraction, which might even be shared by some of their children. However, the components that make up these programmes, their place in the school curriculum, and the way that curriculum is devised provide almost unlimited opportunity for the dominant knowledge managers from the *Staatsvolk* to exercise hegemony over the life chances of children from ethnic backgrounds. In short, the obvious popularity of the naïve multicultural approach in all case studies may be due to this very fact: they are ideal methods of controlling knowledge/ power, while appearing through symbolic political language to be acting solely from the best of motives in the interests of the ethnic groups themselves. There is a corollary to this in the neglect of or much less emphasis placed on programmes that might improve the life chances of children from ethnic backgrounds. Not only do these run counter to the dominants' goal of maintaining ethnic hegemony, but in any case they are very difficult to effect, and may have little success in the final analysis as life chances are determined by political, structural, economic, and historical forces within society. These cannot be greatly altered by schooling and education, although educational programmes that heighten the consciousness of ethnic children and increase their sense of power and social competence (Edgar, 1975) may increase their potential capacity to contribute to reforming society when adults.

Even to encourage the preservation and transmission of ethnic life-styles, languages, traditions and other aspects of the heritage risks placing knowledge managers in a Catch 22 situation. Such aspects can function to heighten ethnic identity, group cohesion, and politicise ethnic groups' aspirations to the point where they may try to establish separate institutions and live as separate ethno-cultural groups within the society in the true sense of the model of cultural pluralism proposed by Despres (1968). Idealism of this kind is as misplaced as many programmes of multicultural education, as control over the central resources of the state is in the hands of the *Staatsvolk*, and must stay there for the benefit of the majority. Of necessity, ethnic groups must strive within the system to get their share of these resources, through the rules of the game set down by the *Staatsvolk*, unless they can change them by political processes. Is there a model that can conceptualize these issues and avoid the trap of reification, or of degenerating into more myth?

The integrated poly-ethnic society — a pluralist compromise

The more logical description of pluralist societies such as Australia — one already adopted officially in the United States — is multi-ethnic or poly-ethnic. The latter is preferable on albeit pedantic grounds of being better because it matches two Greek words, *polus* — much, many, and *ethnos* — nation. It is a term becoming increasingly accepted in recent anthropological literature on ethnicity (e.g. Despres, 1975). The term can also be used as the basis of a normative ideology or theory about pluralism, as the following discussion of Australia may illustrate.

Descriptively the term poly-ethnic society says no more than that it is made up of a number of ethnic groups, including the major or dominant ethnic group. We accept Schermerhorn's definition of an ethnic group (1970:12) as:

> A collectivity within a larger society having real or putative common ancestry, memories of a shared historical past, and a cultural focus on one or more symbolic elements defined as the epitome of their peoplehood. Examples of such symbolic elements are: kinship patterns, physical contiguity (as in localism or sectionalism), religious affiliation, language or other dialectical forms, tribal affiliation, nationality, phenotypical features, or any combination of these. A necessary accompaniment is some consciousness of kind among members of the group.

The combination of these two concepts — poly-ethnic society and ethnic group — enables us to take into account those features of the Australian society which the cultural perspective either ignores or provides only a tenuous theoretical justification for considering. They are:
1. The presence of ethnic groups observable in all their demographic social and cultural manifestations;
2. The facts and effects of ethnic identity and sense of community with no cultural or structural concomitants, i.e., the question of self-ascribed ethnicity;
3. The facts and effects of labelling by others of those who are racially different, with or without cultural or structural concomitants, i.e., the question of socially ascribed ethnicity;
4. The fact and effects of the use of cultural symbols and traditions as a means of politicizing ethnic aspirations.

The possibility that these different forms of group life and bases for personal identification will be used to demand political separatism must also be taken into account in any model that claims to be comprehensive. Here, the notion of *integrated* polyethnicity becomes important although it may appear to be a contradiction in terms. This can be overcome by thinking of a society that is integrated at one level but polyethnic at another, which was the way an early theorist conceptualized the plural society (Furnivall, in Barth, 1969:16):

> [A plural society] is a poly-ethnic society integrated in the market place, under the control of a state system dominated by one of the [ethnic] groups, but leaving large areas of cultural diversity in the religious and domestic sectors of activity.

The inevitability of some degree of political integration was a feature of cultural pluralism which was stressed by the founder of the concept, Horace Kallen, but many proponents of multiculturalism have chosen to ignore it. A very similar ideology of pluralistic integration has been proposed by John Higham (1975:242−43); this is probably the most objective assessment of what should realistically be aimed at in Western democracies. In particular, it attempts to reconcile the needs of ethnic groups while recognizing that there is a dominant culture which must be preserved:

> In contrast to the integrationist model, it will not eliminate ethnic boundaries. But neither will it maintain them intact. It will uphold the validity of a common culture, to which all individuals have access, while sustaining the efforts of minorities to preserve and enchance their own integrity. In principle this dual commitment can be met by distinguishing between boundaries and nucleus. No ethnic group under these terms may have the support of the general community in strengthening its boundaries. All boundaries are understood to be permeable. Ethnic nuclei, on the other hand, are respected as enduring centers of social action. If self-preservation requires, they may claim exemption from certain universal rules, as the Amish now do from the school laws in some states. Both integration and ethnic cohesion are recognized as worthy goals, which different individuals will accept in different degrees.

In the more idealistic, normative sense, a polyethnic society characterized by pluralistic integration, that endeavours to avoid extremes of ethnic hegemony by one ethnic group over another is all that should be aimed at for the future. The education system, curriculum development and teacher education would find much more to guide them from such a point of view: it does open the way to the consideration of questions relating to the distribution of power and access to resources experienced by ethnic minorities in society, as well as provide opportunities for them to preserve worthwhile aspects of their cultural and linguistic heritage. Regretably, however, these very features, while worthwhile educationally, could be interpreted by some as posing a threat or challenge to the dominance of educational and other knowledge managers who are concerned to maintain their vested interests and control over the distribution of power. In fact, the degree of opposition to the model proposed above could well be directly proportional to the level of threat it poses to the current ideology of multiculturalism. Similar resistance might apply to a supporting publication (Bullivant, 1981), which brings the argument into the practical level of school and classroom by proposing a core survival curriculum to reconcile the needs of the survival imperative of society with the individualistic claims of pluralism.

All these features must be accommodated somehow for the survival imperative affects all and brooks no compromise. Its major corollary is the fact that equality between human beings individually and nation-states as a whole is a natural or biological impossibility. The search for the utopia in which all shall be equal is a dream, impossible to achieve. Individuals and social groups *will* obey a fundamental law of survival and *will* strive to maximize their personal or collective advantages in the struggle to cope with, and attach meaning to, the environments in which they find themselves. At the same time, they will endeavour to search for some order and regularity in the dilemmas that surround them. Such is the human condition, one which, by similar reasoning, Robert Ardrey has been led to propose the idea of the just society (1970:3): 'one in which sufficient order protects members, whatever their diverse endowments, and sufficient disorder provides every individual with full opportunity to develop his genetic endowment, whatever that may be'. The search for order without disorder — the quest for utopia rather than reality — is at the heart of the forms of pluralist education discussed above. In the search, knowledge about the nature of pluralist societies has been distorted, reality replaced by ideology, truth claims by rhetoric and myth.

The task for educationists is to achieve a balanced form of pluralist education which recognizes the challenge of the survival imperative. Nathan Glazer has suggested how it might be done (1977:24):

> We should still engage in the work of the creation of a single, distinct, and unique nation, and this requires that our main attention be centered on the common culture. Cultural pluralism describes a supplement to the emerging common interests and common ideals that bind all groups in the society; it does not, and should not, describe the whole.

Despite all the seductions of the multicultural ideology such a task is essential for our very survival. The alternative for Western democracies could well be the kind of 'desert' Barbara Falk postulates as a possible outcome for Australia, in which we could have 'no secure personal identity . . . no social structure embodying our common values, and no symbolism in which to express a shared reality'.

Notes

1. Transcript of taped public lecture. Monash University, 17 September, 1979. Revisions of A.E.A.C. ideology to incorporate a poly-ethnic perspective were foreshadowed in December 1980.

Bibliography

Adams, I.J.W., 1978. 'Small Grants for Projects in Multicultural Education'. (Circular from the Ethnic Education Services Ethnic Education Centre). Mimeographed.

Ali, A., 1976. *Fiji Indians and the Politics of Disparity*. New Delhi : Indian Council of World Affairs. Reprinted from *India Quarterly*, October-December, 1976.

Ali, A., 1977. 'The Fiji General Election of March-April 1977'. A modified and abridged version of a Seminar given in the Institute of Pacific Studies, U.S.P., 29 April, 1977. Mimeographed.

Ali, A., 1978a. 'Fiji : Land, Policy and Politics'. Paper presented at the National Land Utilization Seminar, Suva, 9 September, 1978. Mimeographed.

Ali, A., 1978b. 'Ethnicity and Politics in Fiji'. *The Australian and New Zealand Journal of Sociology*, 14(2), pp. 149–153.

Allison, G.T., 1971. *Essence of decision : explaining the Cuban missile crisis*. Boston : Little, Brown.

Anderson, J.T.M., 1918. *The Education of the New Canadian : A Treatise on Canada's Greatest Educational Problem*. Toronto.

Appleyard, R.T., 1972. 'Immigration and National Development'. Pp. 13–28 in H. Roberts (ed.) *Australia's Immigration Policy*. Perth : University of Western Australia Press.

Arciniega, T., 1977. 'Multicultural Imperative. Guest Editorial'. *Journal of Teacher Education*, XXVIII(3), May-June, p. 2.

Ardrey, R., 1970. *The Social Contract. A Personal Inquiry into the Evolutionary Sources of Order and Disorder*. London: Collins.

Ashworth, M., 1975. *Immigrant Children and Canadian Schools*. Toronto: McLelland and Stewart.

Australian Department of Education, 1973. *Report on the Survey of Child Migrant Education in Schools of High Migrant Density in Melbourne*. Canberra : Department of Education.

Australian Department of Education, 1974. *The Multi-Cultural Society*. Proceedings of the National Seminar for Teacher Educators, Macquarie University, 28–31 August, 1974. Canberra : Australian Department of Education in co-operation with the Australian Department of Labor and Immigration.

Australian Department of Education, 1975. *Report of the Inquiry into Schools of High Migrant Density*. Canberra : Department of Education.

Australian Ethnic Affairs.Council, 1977. *Australia as a Multicultural Society*. Submission to the Australian Population and Immigration Council on the Green Paper, *Immigration Policies and Australia's Population*. Canberra : Australian Government Publishing Service.

Australian Institute of Multicultural Affairs, 1980. *Review of Multicultural and Migrant Education*. Melbourne: A.I.M.A.

Australian Labor Party, 1975. *Platform Constitution and Rules as approved by the 31st National Conference, Terrigal, 1975*. Barton : Australian Labor Party, National Secretariat.

Australian Population and Immigration Council and Australian Ethnic Affairs Council, 1979. *Multiculturalism and its Implications for Immigration Policy*. Canberra: Australian Government Publishing Service.

Baba, T., 1978. 'A Challenge to the Nation : The Fijian Education Problem'. A talk prepared for the Fiji National Radio Programme 'In my view', Wednesday, November 1, 1978. University of the South Pacific, School of Education. Mimeographed.

Bachrach, P. and Baratz, M.S., 1970. *Power and Poverty*. New York: Oxford University Press.

Bakker, M.L., 1977. 'The "Population Problem" in the South Pacific'. *South Pacific Bulletin*, 27(3), 3rd Quarter, pp. 7–13.

Banks, J.A., 1973. *Teaching Ethnic Studies : Concepts and Strategies*. 43rd N.C.S.S. Yearbook. Washington, D.C. : N.C.S.S.

Banks, J.A., 1977a. 'Cultural Pluralism: Implications for Curriculum Reform'. Pp. 226–248 in M.M. Tumin and W. Plotch (eds.) *Pluralism in a Democratic Society*. New York: Praeger.

Banks, J.A., 1977b, 'The Implications of Multicultural Education for Teacher Education'. Pp. 1–30 in F.H. Klassen & D.M. Gollnick (eds.) *Pluralism and the American Teacher Issues and Case Studies*. Washington, D.C. : Ethnic Heritage Center for Teacher Education, A.A.C.T.E.

Banks, J.A., 1978. 'Multiethnic Education Across Cultures : United States, Mexico, Puerto Rico, France, and Great Britain'. *Social Education*, 42(3), March.

Banton, M., 1959. *White and Coloured : the behaviour of British people towards coloured immigrants*. London : Cape.

Banton, M., 1967. *Race Relations*. London : Tavistock.

Banton, M., 1977a. *The Idea of Race*. London: Tavistock.

Banton, M., 1977b. *Rational Choice: a Theory of Racial and Ethnic Relations*. Working Papers on Ethnic Relations No. 8. Bristol : S.S.R.C. Research Unit on Ethnic Relations.

Baroni, G. & Green, G., 1976. *A Report on Relative Conditions in the White, Black and Hispanic Working Class Neighbourhoods of our Older Industrial Cities*. Washington, D.C. : The National Center for Urban Ethnic Affairs. Mimeographed.

Barrett, L.E., 1978. 'Rastafarianism as a Life-style'. Pp. 149–165 in V. D'Oyley (ed.) *Black Presence in Multi-Ethnic Canada*. Vancouver : Centre for the Study of Curriculum and Instruction, Faculty of Education, U.B.C.; Toronto : O.I.S.E.

Barrow, R., 1976. *Common Sense and the Curriculum*. London : Allen & Unwin.

Barth, F., 1969. *Ethnic Groups and Boundaries*. Boston: Little, Brown.

Barthes, R., 1973. *Mythologies*. Selected and translated from the French by Annette Lavers. St Albans, Herts : Paladin.

Berger, P.L. and Luckmann, T., 1971. *The Social Construction of Reality*. Harmondsworth : Penguin University Books.

Bernstein, B., 1970. 'Education cannot compensate for society'. *New Society*, 15(387), pp. 344−7.

Bernstein, B., 1971. 'On the classification and framing of educational knowledge', Pp. 47−69 in M.F.D. Young (ed.) *Knowledge and Control. New Directions for the Sociology of Education*. London : Collier-Macmillan.

Beswick, D.G. and Hills, M.D., 1969. 'An Australian ethnocentrism scale'. *Australian Journal of Psychology*, 21, pp. 211−23.

Bidney, D., 1967. *Theoretical Anthropology*. Second Edition. New York : Schocken Books.

Birrell, T., 1978. 'Migration and the Dilemmas of Multiculturalism'. Ch.8 in R. Birrell & C. Hay (eds.) *The Immigration Issue in Australia*. Melbourne : Department of Sociology, School of Social Sciences, La Trobe University.

Bisseret, N., 1979. *Education, Class Language and Ideology*. London : Routledge & Kegan Paul.

Bloom, B.S., 1971. 'Mastery learning and its implications for curriculum development'. In E.W. Eisner (ed.) *Confronting Curriculum Reform*. Boston : Little, Brown.

Bock, P.K., 1969. *Modern Cultural Anthropology: An Introduction*. New York: Knopf.

Bolabola, Cema, 1978. 'Changes in Fijian Leadership'. *The Australian and New Zealand Journal of Sociology*, 14(2), June, pp. 154−159.

Borrie, W.D., 1948. *Population Trends and Policies*. Sydney : Australian Publishing Company.

Borrie, W.D. (ed.), 1975. *Population and Australia. A demographic analysis and projection*. Canberra : Australian Government Publishing Service.

Bostock, W.W., 1977b. *Alternatives of Ethnicity. Immigrants and Aborigines in Anglo-Saxon Australia*. Hobart : Cat & Fiddle Press.

Boulter, H., 1978. NAME Conference. Chairman's Speech, April 2, 1978. Mimeographed.

Bourdieu, P., 1971. 'Systems of education and systems of thought'. Pp. 189−207 in M.F.D. Young (ed.) *Knowledge and Control. New Directions for the Sociology of Education*. London : Collier-Macmillan.

British Columbia Teachers' Federation 1978−1979. *Members Guide to the BCTF*. Vancouver : B.C.T.F.

Brown, R., 1976. 'Presentation'. Pp.7−10 in CCCM *Multiculturalism as State Policy Conference Report*. Second Canadian Conference on Multiculturalism, Government Conference Centre, Ottawa, February 13−15, 1976. Ottawa : Minister of Supply and Services Canada.

Bullivant, B.M., 1972. 'The Cultural Reality of Curriculum Development'. *Education News*, 13(9), pp. 14−16.

Bullivant, B.M., 1973a. 'Is there a hidden curriculum in curriculum development?' *Twentieth Century*, 27(3), Autumn, pp. 239−253.

Bullivant, B.M., 1973b. *Educating the Immigrant Child : Concepts and Cases*. Sydney : Angus & Robertson.

Bullivant, B.M., 1974. *The Study of Cultural Change : A Classroom Approach*. Melbourne : Australian Council for Educational Research.

Bullivant, B.M., 1975a. 'Challenging conventional wisdom about educational processes in a multicultural region'. *Papua New Guinea Journal of Education*, 11(2), October, pp. 44–55, 68–74.

Bullivant, B.M., 1975b. 'Implications of the Australian Schools Commission for the education of immigrants'. Pp. 122–134 in L.M. Allwood (ed.) *Australian Schools. The Impact of the Australian Schools Commission*. Melbourne : Australia International Press.

Bullivant, B.M., 1975c. 'Learning Cultural Realities through Intercultural Education : some Dilemmas and Solutions'. In D. Dufty & D. Harris (eds.) *Learning about one another*. Report of a Regional Seminar on Intercultural Education in the Asian-Pacific Region. Canberra : UNESCO.

Bullivant, B.M., 1976. 'Social control and migrant education'. *The Australian and New Zealand Journal of Sociology*, 12(3), October, pp. 174–183.

Bullivant, B.M., 1977a. 'A Polyethnic Perspective on Teacher Education for International Understanding'. Pp. 21–26 in G. Coffey (ed.) *Teacher Education for International Understanding*. The proceedings of the Australian UNESCO Seminar, Adelaide, April 17–20, 1977. Canberra : Curriculum Development Centre.

Bullivant, B.M., 1977b. 'Studying an ethnic school - towards a neo-ethnographic methodology'. *Ethnic Studies*, 1(3), December.

Bullivant, B.M., 1977c. 'Education for the Poly-ethnic Society'. *The Forum of Education*, XXXVI(2), June, pp. 27–31.

Bullivant, B.M., 1978a. *The Way of Tradition : life in an Orthodox Jewish school*. Melbourne : Australian Council for Educational Research.

Bullivant, B.M., 1978b. 'Educating for Inevitable Inequality : the challenge of pluralism for teacher educators'. Paper given to the South Pacific Association of Teacher Educators Conference, May 17–21, Melbourne. Mimeographed.

Bullivant, B.M., 1978c. 'Towards a neo-ethnographic research methodology for small-group research'. *The Australian and New Zealand Journal of Sociology*, 14(3), October, pp. 239–249.

Bullivant, B.M., 1979a. *Pluralism, Teacher Education, and Ideology*. The Report of the Survey of Teacher Education for Pluralist Societies, Parts 1 & 2. Melbourne: Monash University Faculty of Education and Centre for Migrant Studies.

Bullivant, B.M., 1979b. 'Curriculum Problematics in a poly-ethnic context'. Pp. 254–269 in P.R. de Lacey and M.E. Poole (eds.) *Mosaic or Melting Pot. Cultural Evolution in Australia*. Sydney: Harcourt Brace Jovanovich.

Bullivant, B.M., 1980. 'Riddles in intercultural communication. A view from structural anthropology'. In N. Asuncion-Lande (ed.) *Ethical Perspectives and Critical Issues in Intercultural Communication*. Washington, D.C.: Speech Communication Association.

Bullivant, B.M., 1981. *Race, Ethnicity and Curriculum. New Approaches to Multicultural Education*. Melbourne: Macmillan.

Burnet, J., 1975. 'The Policy of Multiculturalism within a Bilingual Framework : An Interpretation'. Pp. 205–214 in A. Wolfgang (ed.) *Education of Immigrant Students. Issues and Answers*. Symposium Series/5. Toronto : O.I.S.E.

Burnet, J., 1976. 'Ethnicity : Canadian Experience and Policy'. *Sociological Focus*, 9(2), April, pp. 199–207.

Button, J., 1979. Education for a Multicultural Society. Canberra : Office of Senator John Button. Mimeographed.

Butts, R.F., 1977. 'The public school as moral authority'. Pp. 5–29 in R.F. Butts, D.H. Peckenpaugh and H. Kirschenbaum *The School's Role as Moral Authority*. Washington, D.C.: Association for Supervision and Curriculum Development.

Calwell, A.A., 1972. *Be Just and Fear Not*. Melbourne : Lloyd O'Neil.

Canada Handbook, 1976. *Canada 1976. The Annual Handbook of present conditions and recent progress*. Ottawa : Statistics Canada.

Canadian Consultative Council on Multiculturalism, 1976. *Multiculturalism as State Policy. Conference Report*. Second Canadian Conference on Multiculturalism, Government Conference Centre, Ottawa, February 13–15, 1976. Ottawa : Minister of Supply and Services Canada.

Canadian Consultative Council on Multiculturalism, 1977. *A Report of the Canadian Consultative Council on Multiculturalism*. Ottawa : Minister of Supply and Services Canada.

Casso, H.J., 1976. *Bilingual/Bicultural Education and Teacher Training*. Washington, D.C. : National Education Association.

Central Office of Information, 1978. *Schools in Britain*. London : H.M.S.O.

Centre for Urban Research and Action (CURA), 1979. *Migrants and Education in a Rural Community. A Case Study of the Ovens and King Valleys*. A Research Report for The Ovens-King Area Committee of the Victorian Country Education Project. Melbourne : Centre for Urban Research & Action.

Christensen, S.K., 1972. 'The New Resident : Hawaii's Second-Class Citizen'. *Hawaii Bar Journal*, 5, pp. 77–82.

Cigler, M., 1975. 'History and Multicultural Education'. *Australian Historical Association Bulletin*, 4, pp. 23–29.

Claydon, L., Knight, T. and Rado, M., 1977. *Curriculum and Culture. Schooling in a pluralist society*. Hornsby, N.S.W. : George Allen & Unwin.

Clyne, M.G., 1968. 'The maintenance of bilingualism'. *The Australian Journal of Education*, 12(2).

Clyne, M.G., 1974. 'Language Contact and Language Ecology in Australia'. In M. Rado (ed.) *Bilingual Education*. Papers presented at the 3rd Language Teaching Conference, La Trobe University. Pp. 51–76.

Coffey, G. (ed.), 1977. *Teacher Education for International Understanding*. The proceedings of the Australian UNESCO Seminar, Adelaide, April 17–20, 1977. Canberra : Curriculum Development Centre.

Cohen, Y.A., 1971. 'The shaping of men's minds : adaptations to the imperatives of culture'. Pp. 19–50 in M.L. Wax, S. Diamond & F.O. Gearing (eds.) *Anthropological Perspectives on Education*. New York : Basic Books.

Coleman, J.S., 1972. *Policy research in the social sciences*. Morristown, N.J. : General Learning Press.

Cmnd. 6869 (Green Paper), 1977. *Education in Schools A Consultative Document*. London : H.M.S.O.

Cmnd. 7186 (Home Office), 1978. *The West Indian Community Observations on the Report of the Select Committee on Race Relations and Immigration*. London : H.M.S.O.

Commission for Racial Equality, 1978a. *Education Journal*, Vol. 1, No. 1, April-May.

Commission for Racial Equality, 1978b. *Education Journal*, Vol. 1, No. 2, June-July.

Committee on Community Relations, 1975. *Final Report*. Canberra : Australian Government Publishing Service.

Committee on the Education and Training of Teachers, 1978. *The Education and Training of Teachers in British Columbia. Report*. Vancouver : Department of Education.

Committee on Multicultural Education, 1979. *Education for a Multicultural Society*. Report to the Schools Commission. Canberra: Schools Commission.

Committee on the Teaching of Migrant Languages in Schools, 1976. *Report*. Canberra : Australian Government Publishing Service.

Commonwealth Immigration Advisory Council, 1960. *The Progress and Assimilation of Migrant Children in Australia*. First Report by a Special Committee of the Commonwealth Immigration Advisory Council. Canberra : Department of Immigration.

Commonwealth Institute, n.d. *Annual Report 1977*. London : Commonwealth Institute.

Commonwealth Institute, n.d. *A Teacher's Guide to Study Resources*. London: Commonwealth Institute.

Commonwealth Institute (Education Department), 1977. *Commonwealth Day in Schools*. London : Commonwealth Institute.

Community Relations Commission (CRC), 1976. *A Second Chance. Further Education in Multi-Racial Areas*. London : Community Relations Commission.

Conant, J.B., 1952. *Modern Science and Modern Man*. New York : Columbia University Press.

Connor, W., 1973. 'The politics of ethnonationalism'. *Journal of International Affairs*, 27(1), pp. 1–21.

Cook, R., 1971. *The Maple Leaf Forever : Essays on Nationalism and Politics in Canada*. Toronto : Macmillan.

Coulter, J.W., 1967. *The Drama of Fiji. A Contemporary History*. Rutland, Vermont & Tokyo : Charles E. Tuttle Co.

Council for Educational Development and Research, 1978. *CEDaR Directory*. Washington, D.C. : Council for Educational Development and Research.

Cox, D., 1974. 'Will Australia ever be a Pluralistic Society?' *Migration Action*, 1(1), pp. 5–7.

Cronbach, L.J. and Suppes, P. (eds.), 1969. *Research for tomorrow's schools*. New York : Macmillan.

Curriculum Development Centre (CDC), 1975. *Newsletter*, No. 1 (March). Canberra : CDC.

Curriculum Development Centre (CDC), 1980. *Core Curriculum for Australian Schools*. Canberra : CDC.

Dahlie, J., 1976. 'Ottawa report : A Note on the Second Biennial Conference of the Canadian Consultative Council on Multiculturalism'. *Canadian Ethnic Studies*, 8(1), pp. 89–93.

Dannemiller, J.E., 1977. Population Policy Alternatives and Demographic Correlates of Public Opinion. (Presented to the Commission on Population and the Hawaiian Future.) Mimeographed.

David, K.H. and King, W.L., 1972. *Review and Analysis of Problems of Recent Immigrants in Hawaii*. Honolulu : Evaluation Division, Office of Social Resources.

Davis, A.K., 1975. 'The Politics of Multiculturalism and Third-World Communities in Canada : A Dialectical View'. Paper presented to the Conference on Multiculturalism and Third World Immigrants, Edmonton, September, 1975.

De Lemos, M.M., 1975. *Study of the Educational Achievement of Migrant Children* (Final Report). Melbourne : Australian Council for Educational Research.

De Lemos, M.M. and Di Leo, P., 1978. 'Literacy in Italian and English of Italian High School Students'. *Ethnic Studies*, 2(2), pp. 1–12.

Department of Education and Science, 1971. *The Education of Immigrants*. London : H.M.S.O.

Department of Education and Science, 1972. *Statistics of Education*, Vol. 1. London : H.M.S.O.

Despres, L.A., 1968. 'Anthropological Theory, Cultural Pluralism, and the Study of Complex Societies'. *Current Anthropology*, 9(1), pp. 3–26.

Despres, L.A. (ed.), 1975. *Ethnicity and Resource Competition in Plural Societies*. The Hague : Mouton.

Dewey, J., 1916. 'Nationalizing Education'. *Addresses and Proceedings of the National Education Association*, 54, pp. 84–5. Washington, D.C. : N.E.A.

Dobbert, M.L., 1976. 'Another Route to a General Theory of Cultural Transmission: a Systems Model', Pp. 205–212 in J.I. Roberts and S.K. Akinsanya (eds) *Educational Patterns and Cultural Configurations*. New York : David McKay.

D'Oyley, V. (ed.), 1978. *Black Presence in Multi-Ethnic Canada*. Vancouver : Centre for the Study of Curriculum and Instruction, Faculty of Education, UBC; Toronto : O.I.S.E.

DP6, 1970. *Fiji's Sixth Development Plan 1971–1975*. Suva : Central Planning Office.

DP7, 1975. *Fiji's Seventh Development Plan 1976–1980*. Suva : Central Planning Office.

Ecumenical Migration Centre (EMC), 1974. *Migration Action*, 1(2).

Edelman, M., 1964. *The Symbolic Uses of Politics*. Urbana: University of Illinois Press.

Edelman, M., 1971. *Politics as Symbolic Action. Mass Arousal and Acquiescence*. Chicago : Markham.

Edelman, M., 1977. *Political Language. Words that Succeed and Policies that Fail*. New York : Academic Press.

Edgar, D.E., 1975. 'Adolescent Competence and Educational Ambition'. Pp. 3–13 in D.E. Edgar (ed.) *Sociology of Australian Education. A Book of Readings*. Sydney : McGraw-Hill.

Education Department Fiji, 1972. Curriculum Development Forms 1–4. Mimeographed.

Eggleston, J., 1977. *The sociology of the school curriculum*. London : Routledge & Kegan Paul.

Eisenstadt, S.N., 1965. *Essays on Comparative Social Change*. New York : Wiley.

Enloe, C.H., 1973. *Ethnic Conflict and Political Development*. Bosfon : Little, Brown.

Esland, G.M., 1971. 'Teaching and Learning as the Organization of Knowledge', Pp. 70–115 in M.F.D. Young (ed.) *Knowledge and Control: New Directions for the Sociology of Education*. London : Collier-Macmillan.

252   *The Pluralist Dilemma in Education*

Falk, B., 1977. 'The ERDC Multicultural Education Advisory Group'. *Ethnic Studies*, 1(3), pp. 55–56.

Falk, B., 1978. *Personal Identity in a Multi-Cultural Australia*. The Buntine Oration delivered to The Australian College of Education Nineteenth Annual Conference, Canberra, May 1978. Melbourne : Australian Council for Educational Research.

Fiji Education Commission, 1969. *Education for Modern Fiji. Report*. Suva : The Government Printer.

Fiji Teachers' Union, 1974. *Education for What?* Fiji Teachers' Journal, Term III.

Fiji Teachers' Union, 1976. *Fiji Teachers' Journal*, Volume 3.

Findlay, P.C., 1975. 'Multiculturalism in Canada : Ethnic Pluralism and Social Policies'. Pp. 215–224 in A. Wolfgang (ed.) *Education of Immigrant Students. Issues and Answers*. Toronto : O.I.S.E.

Firth, R., 1964. *Essays on Social Organization and Values*. London: The Athlone Press.

Fisk, E.K., 1970. *The Political Economy of Independent Fiji*. Canberra : Australian National University Press.

Foot, P., 1965. *Immigration and Race in British Politics*. Harmondsworth : Penguin.

Forman, S. and Mitchell, R., 1977. 'The Hawaii Multicultural Awareness Pilot Project (HMAP)'. *Educational Perspectives. Journal of the College of Education/University of Hawaii*, 16(4), December, pp. 26–28.

Foucalt, M., 1977. 'The political function of the intellectual'. *Radical Philosophy*, 17, pp. 12–14.

Fraser, M., 1978. Migrant Services and Programs. Statement by the Prime Minister, The Rt. Hon. Malcolm Fraser. Commonwealth of Australia. Mimeographed.

Fuchs, L.H., 1961. *Hawaii Pono : A Social History*. New York : Harcourt, Brace & World.

Fuller, M., 1974. 'Experiences of Adolescents from Ethnic Minorities in the British State Education System'. Pp. 173–192 in Philippe J. Bernard (ed.) *Les Travailleurs Etrangers en Europe Occidentale*. Paris : Mouton.

Furnivall, J.S., 1939. *Netherlands India : a study of plural economy*. Cambridge : Cambridge University Press.

Furnivall, J.S., 1948. *Colonial Policy and Practice - A Comparative Study of Burma and Netherlands India*. London : Cambridge University Press.

Galbally, F., 1978. *Migrant Services and Programs*. Report of the Review of Post-Arrival Programs and Services for Migrants (The Galbally Report). May 1978, Vol. 1; Volume 2 - Appendixes. Canberra : Australian Government Publishing Service.

Gans, H., 1962. *The Urban Villagers*. Glencoe, Ill. : The Free Press.

Gay, G., 1977. 'Changing Conceptions of Multicultural Education'. *Educational Perspectives. Journal of the College of Education/University of Hawaii*, 16(4), December, pp. 4–9.

Gibson, M.A., 1976. 'Approaches to Multicultural Education in the United States : some Concepts and Assumptions'. *Anthropology and Education Quarterly*, 7(4). pp. 7–18.

Giles, R., 1977. *The West Indian Experience in British Schools. Multi-Racial Education and Social Disadvantage in London*. London : Heinemann.

Giles, R., 1978. 'The need for an expanded concept'. *Education Journal*, 1(1), April-May, p. 3.

Giles, R.H. and Gollnick, D.M., 1977. 'Ethnic/Cultural Diversity as Reflected in State and Federal Educational Legislation and Policies'. Pp. 115–160 in F.H. Klassen & D.M. Gollnick (eds.) *Pluralism and the American Teacher Issues and Case Studies*. Washington, D.C. : Ethnic Heritage Center for Teacher Education, A.A.C.T.E.

Gjessing, G., 1975. 'Socio-archaeology'. *Current Anthropology*, 16(3), September, pp. 323–341.

Glazer, N., 1977. 'Public Education and American Pluralism'. Pp. 85–109 in J.S. Coleman et al *Parents, Teachers, and Children : Prospects for Choice in American Education*. San Francisco : Institute for Contemporary Studies.

Glazer, N. and Moynihan, D.P., 1963. *Beyond the Melting Pot*. Cambridge, Mass. : The M.I.T. Press and Harvard University Press.

Glazer, N. and Moynihan, D.P. (eds.), 1975. *Ethnicity : Theory and Experience*. Cambridge, Mass. : Harvard University Press.

Gollnick, D.M., Klassen, F.H. and Yff, J., 1976. *Multicultural Education and Ethnic Studies in the United States. An Analysis and Annotated Bibliography of Selected ERIC Documents*. Washington, D.C. : American Association of Colleges for Teacher Education and ERIC Clearinghouse on Teacher Education.

Goodenough, W.H., 1964. 'Cultural Anthropology and Linguistics'. Pp. 36–39 in D. Hymes (ed.) *Language in Culture and Society*. New York : Harper & Row.

Good Neighbour Council of Victoria, 1978. *Annual Report 1977–78*. Melbourne : The Good Neighbour Council of Victoria.

Gordon, M.M., 1964. *Assimilation in American Life : The Role of Race, Religion and National Origins*. New York : Oxford University Press.

Gould, J., 1964. 'Ideology'. Pp. 315–317 in J. Gould and W.L. Kolb (eds.) *A Dictionary of the Social Sciences*. London : Tavistock Publications.

Gould, J. and Kolb, W.L. (eds.), 1964. *A Dictionary of the Social Sciences*. London : Tavistock Publications.

Gouldner, A.W., 1971. *The coming crisis in Western sociology*. London : Heinemann.

Gramsci, A., 1971. *Selections from the Prison Notebooks of Antonio Gramsci*. Edited and translated by Q. Hoare and G.N. Smith. London : Lawrence and Wishart.

Grassby, A.J., 1973a. *A Multi-cultural society for the future*. Canberra : Australian Government Publishing Service.

Grassby, A.J., 1973b. *Australia's decade of decision*. Canberra : Australian Government Publishing Service.

Grassby, A.J., 1974a. *Foreign Languages in Australia*. Immigration Reference Paper. Canberra : Australian Government Publishing Service.

Grassby, A.J., 1974b. *Australian Citizenship Policy : Our Objectives*. Canberra : Australian Government Publishing Service.

Grassby, A.J., 1974c. *Credo for a Nation*. Immigration Reference Paper. Canberra : Australian Government Publishing Service.

Grassby, A.J., 1977. 'Australia's Cultural Revolution'. Pp. 17–27 in W.W. Bostock (ed.) *Towards a Multi-Cultural Tasmania*. Report of a Conference,

June 25, 1977. Hobart : Multicultural Conference Committee, University of Tasmania.

Grassby, A.J., 1978. 'Do we mean what we say?' Keynote Address. Pp. 10–16 in D.J. Phillips & J. Houston (eds.) *Our Multicultural Capital*. Report on the Community Conference held at The Canberra College of Advanced Education, March 4–5, 1978. Canberra : Multicultural Conference Steering Committee, Canberra College of Advanced Education.

Greeley, A.M., 1971. *Why Can't They be Like Us? America's White Ethnic Groups*. New York : Dutton & Co.

Green, T.S., 1966. *Education and Pluralism : Ideal and Reality*. Syracuse : School of Education, University of Syracuse.

Greenfield, T.B., 1976. 'Bilingualism, Multiculturalism, and the Crisis of Purpose in Canadian Culture'. *Canadian Society for the Study of Education Yearbook*, Vol. 3.

Griffith, J.A.G., Henderson, J., Usborne, M. and Wood, D., 1960. *Coloured Immigrants in Britain. An Investigation carried out by the Institute of Race Relations*. London : Oxford University Press.

Harman, G., 1978. 'Policy-making and policy processes in education'. Paper given at the Fourth International Intervisitation Program in Educational Administration. Conference Phase, Vancouver, B.C.; May 22–25. Mimeographed.

Head, W.A., 1978. 'The Blacks in Canada : A Revised Edition'. *Multiculturalism*, 1(4), pp. 17–19.

Health, Education, and Welfare, Department of, 1977. *Application for Grants under The Ethnic Heritage Studies Program* (CFDA No. 13.549). Washington, D.C. : Department of Health, Education, and Welfare.

Herberg, W., 1955. *Protestant-Catholic-Jew*. New York : Doubleday.

Higham, J., 1974. 'Integration vs. Pluralism. Another American Dilemma'. *The Center Magazine*, July/August, pp. 67–73.

Higham, J., 1975. *Send These to Me : Jews and Other Immigrants in Urban America*. New York : Atheneum.

Hilliard, A.G., 1974. 'Restructuring Teacher Education for Multicultural Imperatives'. Pp. 40–55 in W.A. Hunter (ed.) *Multicultural Education through Competency-Based Teacher Education*. Washington, D.C. : American Association of Colleges for Teacher Education.

Hinze, R.H., King, A.R., Jr., Krauze, D.L. and Nunes, S.S., 1977. 'Ten Years of Curriculum Research and Development in Hawaii : where have we been?' *Educational Perspectives. Journal of the College of Education/University of Hawaii*, 16(2), May, pp. 3–5.

Hiro, D., 1971. *Black British White British*. London : Eyre & Spottiswoode (also in Penguin Books).

Hirst, P.H., 1974. *Knowledge and the Curriculum*. London : Routledge & Kegan Paul.

Holmes, M., 1978. 'Multiculturalism and the School'. Pp. 241–256 in V. D'Oyley (ed.) *Black Presence in Multi-Ethnic Canada*. Vancouver : Centre for the Study of Curriculum and Instruction, Faculty of Education, U.B.C.; Toronto : O.I.S.E.

Holzner, B., 1972. *Reality Construction in Society* (Revised Edition). Cambridge, Mass. : Schenkman Publishing Company.

Hopkin, A., 1978. 'The Context of Education in Fiji'. *The South Pacific Journal of Teacher Education*, 6(2), pp. 109–118.

Howard, A., 1974. *Ain't No Big Thing. Coping Strategies in a Hawaiian-American Community.* Honolulu : The University Press of Hawaii and East-West Center.

Hunter, W.A. (ed.), 1974. *Multicultural Education through Competency-based Teacher Education.* Washington, D.C. : American Association of Colleges for Teacher Education.

Inder, S. (ed.), 1977. *Pacific Islands Year Book.* Twelfth Edition. Sydney : Pacific Publications.

Inder, S. (ed.), 1978. *Pacific Islands Year Book.* Thirteenth Edition. Sydney : Pacific Publications.

Innis, H.R., 1973. *Bilingualism and Biculturalism. An abridged version of the Royal Commission Report.* Ottawa : McLelland and Stewart, in co-operation with The Secretary of State Department and Information Canada.

Interim Committee for the Australian Schools Commission, 1973. *Schools in Australia : Report of the Interim Committee for the Australian Schools Commission* (The Karmel Report). Canberra : Australian Government Publishing Service.

Isajiw, W.W., 1977. 'Presidential Address : Olga in Wonderland : Ethnicity in Technological Society'. *Canadian Ethnic Studies,* 9(1), pp. 77–85.

Jarolimek, J., 1979. 'Born Again Ethnics: Pluralism in Modern America'. *Social Education,* 43(3), pp. 204–209.

Jegorow, W., 1978. 'Address to National Conference of Ethnic Organizations'. *Ethnic Studies,* 2(1), pp. 69–72.

Jencks, C. *et al.,* 1973. *Inequality. A Reassessment of the Effect of Family and Schooling in America.* New York : Basic Books.

Johanson, D., 1962. 'History of the White Australia Policy'. Ch. 1 in K. Rivett (ed.) for the Immigration Reform Group, *Immigration : Control or Colour Bar.* Melbourne : Melbourne University Press.

Joll J., 1977. *Gramsci.* Glasgow : Fontana/Collins.

Joint Working Party of the Community Relations Commission and A.T.C.D.E., 1974. *Teacher Education for a Multicultural Society.* London : The Community Relations Commission and the Association of Teachers in Colleges and Departments of Education.

Jupp, J., 1966. *Arrivals and Departures.* Melbourne : Cheshire-Lansdowne.

Kalihi-Palama Interagency Council, 1977. *Directory of Services available to immigrants in Kalihi-Palama, Honolulu.*

Kalin, K., 1978. ' "Where do we stop this discrimination business?" A Discussion of the Senate Parliamentary Debate on the Racial Discrimination Act, 1975'. *Ethnic Studies,* 2(2), pp. 32–41.

Kallen, H.M., 1924. *Culture and Democracy in the United States.* New York : Boni & Liveright.

Kallen, H.M., 1956. *Cultural Pluralism and The American Idea.* Philadelphia : University of Pennsylvania Press.

Kaplan, L., 1977. 'Survival Talk for Educators. Multicultural Education'. *Journal of Teacher Education,* XXVIII(3), May-June, pp. 55–56.

Karier, C.J. (ed.), 1975. *Shaping the American Educational State 1900 to the present.* New York : The Free Press.

Kneller, G., 1965. *Educational Anthropology: An Introduction.* New York : John Wiley.

Kennedy, R.J.R., 1944. 'Single or Triple Melting Pot? Intermarriage Trends in New Haven'. *American Journal of Sociology,* 49, January, pp. 331–39.

256   *The Pluralist Dilemma in Education*

King, A.R., Jr., 1977. 'Curriculum Theory and Educational Change Processes : Comments on the Role of Curriculum Theory in the Hawaii Curriculum, Research and Development Group'. *Educational Perspectives. Journal of the College of Education/University of Hawaii*, 16(2), May, pp. 6−8.

Klassen, F.H. and Gollnick, D.M., 1978. *Directory Multicultural Education Programs in Teacher Education Institutions in the United States, 1978*. Washington, D.C. : Commission on Multicultural Education, A.A.C.T.E.

Kohler, D.F. (ed.), 1974. *Ethnic Minorities in Britain : Statistical Data*. London : Community Relations Commission.

Kotler, G., Kuncaitis, V. and Hart, E., 1976. *Bibliography of Ethnic Heritage Studies Program Materials*. Washington : National Center for Urban Ethnic Affairs and the National Education Association.

Kovacs, M.L. and Cropley, A.J., 1975. *Immigrants and Society : Alienation and Assimilation*. Sydney : McGraw-Hill.

Krausz, E., 1971. *Ethnic Minorities in Britain*. London : MacGibbon & Kee.

Krug, M.M., 1977. 'Cultural Pluralism - Its Origins and Aftermath'. *Journal of Teacher Education*, XXVIII(3), May-June, pp.5−9.

Kuhn, T.S., 1962. 'The Structure of Scientific Revolutions'. *International Encyclopaedia of Unified Science*, 2(2), pp. 1−210.

Kuhn, T.S., 1970. 'Reflections on my critics'. Pp. 231−278 in I. Lakatos and A. Musgrave (eds.) *Criticism and the Growth of Knowledge*. Cambridge : Cambridge University Press.

Kuper, L., 1974. *Race, Class and Power*. London : Duckworth.

Kuper, L. and Smith, M.G. (eds.), 1971. *Pluralism in Africa*. Berkeley : University of California Press.

Latham, J.G., 1961. 'Australian Immigration Policy'. *Quadrant*, 18, Autumn, pp. 3−8.

Lawton, D., 1975. *Class, Culture and the Curriculum*. London: Routledge & Kegan Paul.

Leach, E.R., 1976. *Culture and Communication. The logic by which symbols are connected*. Cambridge : Cambridge University Press.

Lee, D.D., 1976. *Population Report. Ethnic Structures in Hawaii*. Honolulu : Research and Statistics Office of the Hawaiian Department of Health.

Lind, A.W., 1967. *Hawaii's People*. Third Edition. Honolulu : University of Hawaii Press.

Lopez, T.R., Jr., 1973. 'Cultural Pluralism : Political Hoax? Educational Need?' *The Journal of Teacher Education (Winter)*, pp. 277−281.

Lower, A., 1958. *Canadians in the Making*. Toronto : Longmans, Green.

Lupul, M.R., 1973. 'Multiculturalism within a bilingual framework : An essay in definition'. Paper presented at the Conference of the Western Association of Sociology and Anthropology, Banff, Alberta, December, 1973.

Lupul, M.R., 1978. 'Multiculturalism and Educational Policies in Canada'. *Multiculturalism*, 1(4), pp. 13−16.

Lynch, P. 1972. 'Australia's Immigration Policy'. Pp. 1−12 in H. Roberts (ed.) *Australia's Immigration Policy*. Perth : University of Western Australia Press.

Mackie, J.A.C., 1977. 'Asian Migration and Australian Racial Attitudes'. *Ethnic Studies*, 1(2), pp. 1−13.

MacKellar, M.J.R., 1976. *Towards a Population Policy for Australia*. Address to the Stable Population (Z.P.G.,S.A.) Forum, Adelaide, August 9, 1976. Canberra : Department of Immigration and Ethnic Affairs.

MacKellar, M.J.R., 1978. Speech by The Hon. M.J.R. MacKellar, M.P. Minister for Immigration and Ethnic Affairs on *Immigration Policies and Australia's Population*, Ministerial Statement. ('Parliamentary Debates', 7 June, 1978.) Canberra : Australian Government Publishing Service.

McLeod, K.A., 1975. 'A Short History of the Immigrant Student as "New Canadian" '. Pp. 19–31 in A. Wolfgang (ed.) *Education of Immigrant Students. Issues and Answers.* Toronto : O.I.S.E.

McLeod, K.A., 1978. Ministry of Education Course for Teachers : 'Multiculturalism in Education'. University of Toronto, Faculty of Education. Mimeographed.

McNaught, K., 1970. *The History of Canada.* London : Heinemann.

Malinowski, B., 1944. *A Scientific Theory of Culture.* Chapel Hill : University of North Carolina Press.

Mallea, J.R., 1977. 'Multiculturalism within a Bilingual Framework : A note on the Québécois Response'. *Multiculturalism*, 1(2), pp. 3–5.

Mallea, J.R., 1978. 'Ethnicity and Canadian Education'. Pp. 269–280 in M.L. Kovacs (ed.) *Ethnic Canadians : Culture and Education.* Regina.

Mallea, J.R. and Young, J., n.d. Teacher Education for a Multicultural Society. Toronto : O.I.S.E. Mimeographed (1978).

Mallea, J.R. and Shea, E.C. (eds.) 1979. *Multiculturalism and Education. A Select Bibliography.* Toronto : O.I.S.E.

Mannheim, K., 1968. *Ideology and utopia. An introduction to the sociology of knowledge.* New York : Harcourt, Brace & World.

Mara, Ratu Sir Kamisese, 1977. *Collected Speeches.* Suva.

Maraj, J.A., 1976. 'Education and an Integrated Society'. Key address presented to 46th Annual Conference of the Fiji Teachers' Union, May, 1976. *Fiji Teachers' Journal*, 3, pp. 9–16.

Martin, J.I., 1965. *Refugee Settlers. A Study of Displaced Persons in Australia.* Canberra : Australian National University Press.

Martin, J.I., 1971. 'Migration and Social Pluralism'. Ch. 3 in A.I.P.S. *How Many Australians? Immigration and Growth.* Sydney : Angus & Robertson.

Martin, J.I., 1972. *Migrants : Equality and Ideology.* Meredith Memorial Lectures, 1972. Bundoora : La Trobe University.

Martin, J.I., 1974. 'The Changing Nature of Australian Society: Pluralism Today'. In Australian Department of Education, *The Multicultural Society.* Proceedings of the National Seminar for Teacher Educators, Macquarie University, 28–31 August, 1974. Canberra: Australian Department of Education in co-operation with the Australian Department of Labor and Immigration.

Martin, J.I., 1976a. 'The Education of Migrant Children in Australia'. Pp. 1–65 in C.A. Price and J.I. Martin (eds.) *Australian Immigration A bibliography and digest.* Number 3, 1975, Part 2. Canberra : The Australian National University, Department of Demography, Institute of Advanced Studies.

Martin, J.I., 1976b. 'Education in a Multicultural Society'. Paper presented to Conference on Education in a Multicultural Society, New South Wales Teachers' Federation, Sydney, 26–27 November. Mimeographed.

Martin, J.I., 1978. *The Migrant Presence.* Sydney : George Allen & Unwin.

Masemann, V.L., 1978–9. 'Multicultural Programs in Toronto Schools'. *Interchange*, 9(1), pp. 29–45.

Maxwell, W., 1978. 'Foreword' in *Degree Handbook 1978 Revised.* The University of the South Pacific, School of Education. Mimeographed.

Mercer, J., 1978/79. 'Test "Validity", "Bias", and "Fairness" : An Analysis from the Perspective of the Sociology of Knowledge'. *Interchange*, 9(1), pp. 1–16.

Merrington, J., 1977. 'Theory and Practice in Gramsci's Marxism'. Pp. 140–75 in New Left Review (ed.) *Western Marxism A Critical Reader*. London : NLB.

Merry, D., Zangalis, C. and Zangalis, G., 1978. 'Migrant Education Action in Victoria'. *Ethnic Studies*, 2(1), pp. 59–69.

Merton, R.K., 1957. *Social Theory and Social Structure*. Glencoe, Ill. : The Free Press.

Minister of State Multiculturalism, 1978. *Multiculturalism and the Government of Canada*. Ottawa : Minister of Supply and Services, Canada.

Ministry of Education Ontario, 1977. *Multiculturalism in Action*. A support document for *The Formative Years*. Toronto : Ministry of Education.

Ministry of Education, Youth and Sport (FIJI), 1974. *Report for the year 1973*. Parliamentary Paper No. 27 of 1974. Suva : Government Printing Department. See also 1975 *Report for the year 1974*; 1977 *Report for the year 1975*.

Ministry of Education, Youth and Sport (FIJI), 1978. *Report for the year 1976*. Parliamentary Paper No. 27 of 1978. Suva : Government Printing Department.

Moag, R.F., 1977. 'What kind of Second Language Teaching and Why?'. *Fiji Teachers' Journal*, 4, pp. 15–19.

Moag, R.F., 1978. 'Vernacular Education in Fiji'. *The South Pacific Journal of Teacher Education*, 6(2), pp. 134–139.

Musgrave, P.W., 1970. 'Towards a Sociology of the Curriculum, *Paedagogica Europaea*, VI, 1970/71, pp. 37–49.

Musgrave, P.W., 1973. *Knowledge, Curriculum and Change*. Melbourne : Melbourne University Press.

Myrdal, G., 1944. *The American Dilemma : The Negro Problem and Modern Democracy*. New York : Harper & Bros.

Myrdal, G., 1974. 'The Case Against Romantic Ethnicity'. *The Center Magazine*, July – August.

Nagtalon-Miller, H., 1977. 'Pluralism and Bilingual/Multicultural Education in Hawaii'. *Educational Perspectives. Journal of the College of Education/ University of Hawaii*, 16(4), December, pp. 14–17.

Nasinu Teachers' College, 1978. *Handbook 1978*. Suva : Nasinu Teachers' College.

National Association for Multi-racial Education (N.A.M.E.), n.d. *The National Association for Multi-racial Education* (History & Activities).

National Council for Accreditation of Teacher Education, 1977. *Standards for Accreditation of Teacher Education*. Washington, D.C. : N.C.A.T.E.

National Education Association, 1975. *Roots of America*. Washington, D.C. : National Education Association.

National Education Association, 1977. *Ethnic Heritage Studies Program. Assessment of the first year*. Washington, D.C. : National Education Association.

National Education Association Task Force on Human Rights, 1968. 'Certain American Truths'. *Report of the Task Force on Human Rights*. Washington, D.C. : National Education Association.

National Population Enquiry, 1975. *Population Projections for the States and Territories of Australia, Research Report No. 1.* (The Borrie Report). Canberra : Australian Government Publishing Service.

National Seminar for Teacher Educators, 1974. *The Multi-Cultural Society.* Seminar, Macquarie University, 28–31 August, 1974. Canberra : Australian Department of Education in co-operation with the Australian Department of Labor and Immigration.

NCSS Task Force, 1976. *Curriculum Guidelines for Multiethnic Education Position Statement.* Washington, D.C. : National Council for the Social Studies.

Newman, W.M., 1973. *American Pluralism : A Study of Minority Groups and Social Theory.* New York : Harper & Row.

Newsam, P., 1978. *The Richer Heritage. ILEA Contact Supplement.* London : ILEA.

Nicoll, P., 1976. *A Conceptual Basis for Research in Migrant Education.* Canberra : Commonwealth Department of Education.

Nissel, M. and Lewis, C. (eds.), 1974. *Social Trends No. 5, 1974.* London : H.M.S.O.

Nordyke, E.C., 1977. *The Peopling of Hawaii.* Honolulu : The East-West Center and University Press of Hawaii.

Norton, R., 1977. *Race and Politics in Fiji.* St. Lucia : University of Queensland Press.

Novak, M., 1971. *The Rise of the Unmeltable Ethnics : Politics and Culture in the Seventies.* New York : Macmillan.

Novak, M., 1976. 'Presentation'. Pp. 181–200 in The Canadian Consultative Council on Multiculturalism, *Multiculturalism as State Policy. Conference Report.* Second Canadian Conference on Multiculturalism, Government Conference Centre, Ottawa, February 13–15, 1976. Ottawa : Minister of Supply and Services Canada.

Nunes, S.S., 1977. 'Institutional and Political Factors in Curriculum Development'. *Educational Perspectives. Journal of the College of Education/ University of Hawaii,* 16(2), May, pp. 9–13.

O'Bryan, K.G., Reitz, J.G. and Kuplowska, O.M., 1976. *Non-official languages. A Study in Canadian Multiculturalism.* Ottawa : Printing and Publishing Supply and Services Canada.

Ontario Ministry of Culture and Recreation, 1976. 'Black Students in Urban Canada'. *T.E.S.L. Talk (Special Issue),* 7(1), January.

Ontario Secondary School Teachers' Federation, 1976. *At What Cost : A Study of the Role of the Secondary School in Ontario.* Toronto : O.S.S.T.F.

Organization for Economic Co-operation and Development (OECD), 1975. *Educational Policy in Canada : External Examiners' Report.* Toronto : Canadian Association for Adult Education and the Students' Administrative Council, University of Toronto.

Pacheco, A., 1977. 'Cultural Pluralism : A Philosophical Analysis'. *Journal of Teacher Education,* XXVIII(3), May – June, pp. 16–20.

Palmer, H., 1976. 'Reluctant Hosts : Anglo-Canadian Views of Multiculturalism in the Twentieth Century'. Pp. 81–118 in The Canadian Consultative Council on Multiculturalism, *Multiculturalism as State Policy. Conference Report.* Second Canadian Conference on Multiculturalism, Government Conference Centre, Ottawa, February 13–15, 1976. Ottawa : Minister of Supply and Services Canada.

260 *The Pluralist Dilemma in Education*

Petersen, W., 1969. 'The classification of subnations in Hawaii : an essay on the sociology of knowledge'. *American Sociological Review*, 34, pp. 863–877.

Peterson, P.E., 1976. *School politics Chicago style*. Chicago : University of Chicago Press.

Phenix, P.H., 1964. *Realms of Meaning. A Philosophy of the Curriculum for General Education*. New York : McGraw-Hill.

Piaget, J., 1958. *The development of logical thinking from childhood to adolescence*. London : Routledge & Kegan Paul.

Porter, J., 1965. *The Vertical Mosaic : An Analysis of Social Class and Power in Canada*. Toronto : University of Toronto Press.

Porter, J., 1975. 'Ethnic Pluralism in Canadian Perspective'. Pp. 267–304 in N. Glazer & D.P. Moynihan (eds.) *Ethnicity : Theory and Experience*. Cambridge, Mass. : Harvard University Press.

Price, C.A. and Martin, J.I. (eds.), 1976. *Australian Immigration. A bibliography and digest*. Number 3, 1975, Part 2. Canberra : The Australian National University, Department of Demography, Institute of Advanced Studies.

Rado, M., 1978. 'What bilingual education can tell us'. *Ethnic Studies*, 2(1), pp. 48–58.

Ram, H., 1974. 'Teacher Education'. *Fiji Teachers' Journal*, Term III, pp. 21–31.

Ram, H., 1975. 'Looking ahead in education'. *Report of the 45th Annual Conference of the Fiji Teachers' Union, May 1975, Suva, Fiji*. Suva : Fiji Teachers' Union.

Reid, V., 1978. 'Multi-cultural education : its function'. *Education Journal*, 1(2), June – July, pp. 5–6.

Renaud, B., 1972. *Population Dynamics and Population Policy in Hawaii*. Honolulu : Economic Research Center, University of Hawaii.

Richmond, A.H., 1967. *Post-war immigrants in Canada*. Toronto : University of Toronto Press.

Richmond, A.H. and Lakshmana Rao, G., 1976. 'Recent Developments in Immigration to Canada and Australia'. *International Journal of Comparative Sociology*, XVII, 3–4, pp. 183–205.

Riffel, J.A., 1977. 'Situational problems in the process of policy research'. In CEA *Educational Research and Policy Formation*. CEA/CERA Research Conference. Calgary, Alberta, September 26–7. Toronto : The Canadian Educational Association.

Rivett, K., (ed. for the Immigration Reform Group), 1975. *Australia and the non-white migrant*. Melbourne : Melbourne University Press.

Robbins Committee, 1963. *Higher Education. Report of the Committee appointed by the Prime Minister under the Chairmanship of Lord Robbins*. London : H.M.S.O.

Rocher, G., 1973. *Le Québec en mutation*. Montreal : Hurtubise.

Rodger, G., 1972. 'Fiji education : some facts and figures'. *Occasional Paper of the School of Education, No. 2*. Suva : University of the South Pacific.

Rooth, J.S., 1968. 'The immigration programme', Pp. 57–72 in H. Throssell (ed.) *Ethnic Minorities in Australia. The Welfare of Aborigines and Migrants*. Sydney : Australian Council of Social Service.

Rose, E.J.B., 1969. *Colour and Citizenship*. London : Oxford University Press.

Royal Commission on Bilingualism and Biculturalism (RCBB), 1967. Report

Vol. 1 : *General Introduction : The Official Language*. Ottawa : Queen's Printer.

Royal Commission on Bilingualism and Biculturalism (RCBB), 1970. Report Vol. 4 : *The Cultural Contribution of the Other Ethnic Groups*. Ottawa: Queen's Printer.

Schatzman, L. and Strauss, A.L., 1973. *Field research. Strategies for a natural sociology*. Englewood Cliffs, N.J. : Prentice-Hall.

Schermerhorn, R.A., 1970. *Comparative Ethnic Relations. A Framework for Theory and Research*. New York: Random House.

Schmitt, R. and Kawaguchi, P., 1977. *Population Characteristics of Hawaii 1976*. Honolulu : Research and Statistics Office, Hawaii Department of Health.

Schneider, L. and Bonjean, C. (eds.), 1973. *The Idea of Culture in the Social Sciences*. Cambridge : Cambridge University Press.

Schools Commission, Australian, 1975. *Report for the Triennium 1976–78*. Canberra : Australian Government Printer.

Schools Commission, Australian, 1978. *Report for the Triennium 1979–1981*. Canberra: A.G.P.S.

Schools Commission, Australian. Committee on Multicultural Education, 1979. *Education for a Multicultural Society*. Report to the Schools Commission. Canberra: Schools Commission.

Singh, Gurmit, 1975. 'Looking ahead in Curriculum'. *Report of the 46th Annual Conference of the Fiji Teachers' Union, May 1975, Suva, Fiji*. Suva : Fiji Teachers' Union.

Singh, Gurmit, 1976. 'The Changing Primary Curriculum in Fiji'. *Fiji Teachers' Journal*, 3, pp. 32–40.

Singh, Gurmit, 1978. 'Curriculum Development and Related Issues'. *The South Pacific Journal of Teacher Education*, 6(2), pp. 118–124.

Sizemore, B.A., 1969. 'Separatism : A Reality Approach to Inclusion?'. Pp. 249–279 in R.L. Graan (ed.) *Racial Crisis in American Education*. Chicago : Follett Educational Corporation.

Smith, D.J., 1977. *Racial Disadvantage in Britain (The PEP Report)*. Harmondsworth : Penguin.

Smith, M.G., 1957. 'Ethnic and cultural pluralism in the British Caribbean'. In *Ethnic and cultural pluralism in intertropical countries*, Pp. 439–447. Brussels : INCIDI.

Smith, M.G., 1965. *The Plural Society in the British West Indies*. Berkeley : University of California Press.

Smolicz, J.J., 1971. 'Is the Australian school an assimilationist agency?'. *Education News*, 13(4), August, pp. 4–8.

Smolicz, J.J., 1972. 'Integration, Assimilation and the Education of Immigrant Children'. Pp. 42–60 in H. Roberts (ed.) *Australia's Immigration Policy*. Perth : University of Western Australia Press.

Smolicz, J.J., 1974a. 'Some Impressions of Polish Sociology'. *The Australian and New Zealand Journal of Sociology*, 10(1), pp. 17–23.

Smolicz, J.J., 1974b. 'The Concept of Tradition : A Humanistic Interpretation'. *The Australian and New Zealand Journal of Sociology*, 10(2), pp. 75–83.

Smolicz, J.J., 1975a. 'Humanistic Sociology and the Study of Ethnic Cultures'. Paper given to Section 27 : Sociology of the 46th ANZAAS

Congress, Canberra, January 1975.

Smolicz, J.J., 1975b. 'Migrant Cultures and Australian Education'. *Education News*, 15(1), pp. 16–21.

Smolicz, J.J., 1976a. 'Ethnic Cultures in Australian Society : A Question of Cultural Interaction'. Pp. 41–74 in S. Murray-Smith (ed.) *Melbourne Studies in Education 1976.* Melbourne : Melbourne University Press.

Smolicz, J.J. 1979. *Culture and Education in a Pluralist Society.* Canberra : Curriculum Development Centre.

Smolicz, J.J. and Secombe M.J., 1977. 'Cultural Interaction in a Pluralist Society'. *Ethnic Studies*, 1(1), pp. 1–16.

Smolicz, J.J. and Wiseman, R., 1971. 'European Migrants and their Children : Interaction, Assimilation, Education'. *Quarterly Review of Education*, 4(2/3). Melbourne : Australian Council for Educational Research.

Stamp, R., 1971. 'Canadian Education and the National Identity'. *Journal of Educational Thought*, 5.

State of Hawaii, 1977. *Data Book 1977. A Statistical Abstract.* Honolulu : DPED.

Statistics Canada, 1975. *Canada 1976 English Edition.* Ottawa : Statistics Canada Information Division.

Statistics Canada, 1977. *Canada Year Book 1976–77. Special Edition.* Ottawa : Minister of Supply and Services Canada.

Stent, M.D., Hazard, W.R. and Rivlin, H.N. (eds.), 1973. *Cultural Pluralism in Education : A Mandate for Change.* New York : Appleton-Century-Crofts.

Stockley, D., 1978. 'The Fraser Governments, Migrants and Education'. Paper presented at Australasian Political Studies Association Annual Conference, 30 August – 1 September. Adelaide : Mimeographed.

Storer, D. (ed.), 1975. *Ethnic Rights Power and Participation. Toward a Multi-Cultural Australia.* Melbourne : Clearing House on Migration Issues, Ecumenical Migration Centre, and Centre for Urban Research and Action.

Symons, T.H.B., 1975. *To Know Ourselves. The Report of the Commission on Canadian Studies.* Volumes I and II. Ottawa : Association of Universities and Colleges of Canada.

Taft, R., 1972. 'Ethnic Groups'. Ch. 4 in F.J. Hunt (ed.) *Socialization in Australia.* Sydney : Angus & Robertson.

Taft, R., 1975a. 'Aspirations of Secondary School Children of Immigrant Families in Victoria'. *Education News*, 15(1), pp. 38–41.

Taft, R., 1975b. 'The career aspirations of immigrant school children in Victoria'. *La Trobe Series in Sociology*, Paper No. 12. Bundoora : La Trobe University.

Taft, R., 1975c. 'Some recent facts about the educational achievements of working-class immigrants'. *Migration Action*, 2, pp. 14–16.

Taft, R., 1977a. 'The Study of Immigrant Adjustment : Science or just Common Sense?'. *Ethnic Studies*, 1(2), December, pp. 14–19.

Taft, R., 1977b. 'Coping with Unfamiliar Cultures'. In N. Warren (ed.) *Studies in Cross-Cultural Psychology*, Vol. 1. London : Academic Press.

Taft, R., 1978. 'Ethnic Groups'. Ch. 7 in F.J. Hunt (ed.) *Socialization in Australia.* Second Edition. Melbourne : Australia International Press.

Taft, R. and Cahill, D., 1978. *Initial Adjustment to Schooling of Immigrant Families.* Canberra : Australian Government Publishing Service.

Tatz, C., 1977. 'Teacher Education to counter prejudice and discrimination'. Pp. 41–53 in G. Coffey (ed.) *Teacher Education for International Under-*

standing. The proceedings of the Australian UNESCO Seminar, Adelaide, April 17–20, 1977, Canberra : Curriculum Development Centre.

Taylor, F., 1974. *Race, School and Community. A Survey of Research and Literature on Education in Multiracial Britain*. Slough : N.F.E.R. Publishing Co.

Theodorson, G.A. and Theodorson, A.G., 1970. *A Modern Dictionary of Sociology*. London : Methuen.

Thompson, L., 1969. *The Secret of Culture, Nine Community Studies*. New York : Random House.

Tindale, N.B., 1974. *Aboriginal Tribes of Australia*. Vols. 1 & 2. Canberra : Australian National University Press.

Tonkin, C., 1976. 'The Social Education Materials Project'. *Study of Society*. Special Supplement, September.

Townsend, H.E.R. and Brittan, E.M., 1972. *Organization in Multiracial Schools*. Slough : N.F.E.R.

Townsend, H.E.R. and Brittan, E.M., 1973. *Multiracial Education : Need and Innovation*. London : Evans Brothers.

Troper, H., 1977. 'Cultural Diversity and the History Curriculum of Canadian Public Schools'. A Paper presented to the American Historical Association Annual Meeting, Dallas, Texas, 1977. Mimeographed.

Trudeau, P., 1978. *A Time for Action*. Ottawa : Minister of Supply and Services Canada.

Tumin, M.M., 1977. 'Introduction'. Pp. xii–xx in M.M. Tumin and W. Plotch (eds.) *Pluralism in a Democratic Society*. New York: Praeger.

Tylor, E.B., 1871. *Primitive Culture*. London: John Murray.

U.S. Commission on Civil Rights, 1974. *Toward Quality Education for Mexican Americans*. Report VI : Mexican American Education Study. Washington, D.C. : The Commission.

U.S. Department of Commerce, Bureau of the Census, 1974. *Statistical Abstract of the United States 1974*. Washington, D.C. : Bureau of the Census.

U.S. Department of Commerce, Bureau of the Census, 1976. *Statistical Abstract of the United States 1976*. Washington, D.C. : Bureau of the Census.

U.S. Department of Commerce, Bureau of the Census, 1977. *Statistical Abstract of the United States 1977*. Washington, D.C. : Bureau of the Census.

Valpay, M., 1978. 'The fading dream of a bilingual nation'. *The Vancouver Sun*, Tuesday, September 19 p. A4.

Vaughan, M. and Archer, M.S., 1971. *Social conflict and educational change in England and France 1789–1849*. Cambridge : Cambridge University Press.

Wells, T.L., 1978. 'Education and Cultural Development'. *Multiculturalism*, 1(5), pp. 3–5.

Werner, W., Connors, B., Aoki, T. and Dahlie, J., 1977. *Whose Culture? Whose Heritage? Ethnicity within Canadian Social Studies Curricula*. Vancouver : Centre for the Study of Curriculum and Instruction, Faculty of Education, U.B.C.

White, J.P., 1973. *Towards a Compulsory Curriculum*. London : Routledge & Kegan Paul.

White, N.R., 1978. 'Ethnicity, culture and cultural pluralism'. *Ethnic and Racial Studies*, 1(2), April, pp. 139–153.

Whitehead, C., 1975. Education in Fiji. Unpublished Ph.D. Thesis. University of Otago.

Whitt, S. and Clark, R., 1978. *1976—1977 Summative Evaluation Report for the Pacific Northwest Indian Reading and Language Development Program.* Portland, Oregon : Northwest Regional Educational Laboratory.

Wilson, J., 1978. 'Come, Let Us Reason Together'. Pp. 167—188 in V. D'Oyley (ed.) *Black Presence in Multi-Ethnic Canada.* Vancouver : Centre for the Study of Curriculum and Instruction, Faculty of Education, U.B.C.; Toronto : O.I.S.E.

Wilson, T.P., 1971. 'Normative and Interpretive Paradigms in Sociology'. Ch.3 in J.D. Douglas (ed.) *Understanding Everyday Life.* London : Routledge & Kegan Paul.

Wiseman, R., 1974. 'Some issues involved in ethnic pluralism and education in Australia'. *The Forum of Education,* 33(2), September, pp. 146—163.

Wiseman, R., 1978. 'A study of social interaction and ethnic typifications between British-Australian and Italian-Australian high school students in Adelaide'. *Ethnic Studies,* 2(1), pp. 73—74.

Wolff, R.P., Moore, B., and Marcuse, H. (eds.), 1965. *A Critique of Pure Tolerance.* Boston : Beacon Press.

Wolfgang, A. (ed.), 1975. *Education of Immigrant Students. Issues and Answers.* Toronto : O.I.S.E.

Woodroffe, B., 1978. 'Growth through the Curriculum'. In P. Newsam, *The Richer Heritage ILEA Contact Supplement.* London : ILEA.

Worth, W.H., 1977. 'Perspectives on policy-formation : an administrator's view'. Pp. 15—21 in CEA *Educational Research and Policy Formation.* CEA/CERA Research Conference. Calgary, Alberta, September 26—7. Toronto : The Canadian Educational Association.

Wright, L., 1973. 'The Bilingual Education Movement at the Crossroads'. *Phi Delta Kappan,* 55, pp. 183—186.

Wyatt, J.D., 1978a. 'Native Involvement in Curriculum Development : the Native Teacher as Cultural Broker'. *Interchange,* 9(1), 1978—79, pp. 17—28.

Wyatt, J.D., 1978b. Course Outline : EDUC.441, 'Cultural Differences in Education'. Simon Fraser University, School of Education. Mimeographed.

Year Book Australia, No. 62, 1977 and 1978, 1979. Canberra : Australian Bureau of Statistics.

Young, M.F.D. (ed.), 1971. *Knowledge and Control : New Directions for the Sociology of Education.* London : Collier-Macmillan.

Young, R., 1977. 'Multicultural Education in New South Wales'. Paper presented to the Education Section of the ANZAAS Congress, August, 1977. Mimeographed.

Zubrzycki, J., 1977. 'The Formation of the Australian Ethnic Affairs Council'. Speech to the Inaugural Meeting by Chairman, Professor Jerzy Zubrzycki, MBE, FASSA, Canberra, 23 March, 1977. *Ethnic Studies,* 1(2), pp. 62—67.

Index

affirmative discrimination 127–8
Ali, A. 78, 79, 81, 82, 83, 86, 97, 99, 219–20
Americanization 112–13, 115
Asians
  in Australia 174–7
  in Britain 15, 16–17, 19
assimilation 65–6, 112, 117, 129–30, 153, 159–60, 171–4, 177, 180, 182, 212, 213, 224–5
Australian Ethnic Affairs Council 200, 201–5, 206, 235, 236–7
Australian Institute for Multicultural Affairs 188–9, 239

Baba, T. 89, 102
Banks, J. 137–9, 141, 155, 225
bilingualism 3
  in Australia 194, 203, 210
  in Canada 45–6, 55–6, 57, 58–9, 61, 63, 64, 66–70, 193, 229
  in Hawaii 157, 158–9, 164
  in U.S. 119–20, 128–9, 164
Birrell, T. 212, 226, 238
'Black Power' 10, 18, 63–4, 162
Blakeley, M. 25, 27, 36–7, 38, 39, 222
Burnet, J. 44, 48, 49, 51, 52–3, 65, 67, 70, 74–5, 193, 221, 222, 223

Callander, J. 28, 30
Canadian Consultative Council on Multiculturalism (CCCM) 56–7, 58–9, 66, 69, 71
Chattergy, V. 157, 164–5
Chicanos see Mexican Americans
Child Migrant Education Programme (Australia) 181
Civil Rights Acts (U.S.) 111, 119
Commission for Racial Equality (Britain) 33, 34–5
Committee on Multicultural Education (Australia) 191–3, 207–8, 226, 232–3, 236–8

Committee on the Teaching of Migrant Languages in School (Australia) 193–4
comprehensive schools (Britain) 23–4
counter-ideologies 11, 12, 13, 234–5
  in Australia 186, 203–16
  in Britain 26, 37–40
  in Canada 59, 61–76, 207
  in Fiji 97–103
  in Hawaii 153–4, 162–5
  in U.S. 129–40, 207
culture
  defined 2–3, 4
  and education 2
  transmission of 3, 4–6, 7
curriculum
  and culture transmission 4–6
  defined 4, 5
  in Hawaii 157–61
  and multiculturalism 69, 70–1, 72–3, 100, 235–6, 241
Curriculum Development Centre (Canberra) 193, 194–6, 222

Ecumenical Migration Centre (Australia) 214–15
Education for a Multiracial Society (Britain) 27, 28
Education Research and Development Committee (Australia) 196
Eggleston, J. 28, 29, 41
emigration
  from Fiji 84
Epstein, C. 122–3, 185
ethnic hegemony 226–8, 235–6, 241
  strategies for 228–38
Ethnic Heritage Studies Program (U.S.) 121–3, 137, 138, 185
European Economic Community 25

Falk, B. 211–12, 226, 244
Findlay, P.C. 75, 134
Foot, P. 21, 22

Forman, M. 158, 160, 161, 163, 164
French Canadians 45–7, 49–50, 66–70

Galbally Committee (Australia) 187, 188–9, 192, 194, 200, 201, 208, 209–11, 222, 226, 237, 239
Giles, R. 26–7
Glazer, N. 111, 112, 117, 136–7, 222, 237, 244
Good Neighbour Council (Australia) 200–1
Gould, J. 11
government policy
  in Australia 189–90
  in Britain 28–30
  in Canada 54–8, 74
  in Fiji 92–4, 95–6, 100
  in Hawaii 152–5
  in U.S. 118–19, 120–3
Gramsci, A. 227, 239
Grassby, A. 174, 183–6, 191
Greeley, A.M. 116, 117, 136, 205
Green Paper, 1977 (Britain) 8, 23, 30, 36

Hamnett, D. 162–3
Higham, J. 132, 243
Hilliard, A. 125–6, 127
Howard, A. 163–4

ideologies 10–13, 222–6
  in Australia 183–203
  in Britain 25–6
  in Canada 55–61
  defined 10–12
  in Fiji 92–6
  in Hawaii 151–61
  in U.S. 120–9
  see also pluralism, ideology of immigration
immigration
  Australia 48, 166–8, 170–83, 186–7
  Britain 15–16, 18–23
  Canada 44–5, 47–50
  controls on 26
  Fiji 84
  Hawaii 144–5, 147, 148
  U.S. 111–12, 117
Indians
  in Britain 16, 17, 19, 22
  in Fiji 77, 78, 79, 81, 82, 83, 85

James Report (Britain) 24

Kallen, H. 112–13, 115, 243
knowledge managers 8, 10, 13, 129, 220–2, 227, 234–5, 241, 243

knowledge/power 9, 10–11, 220–2, 228, 232–4, 241

language and culture 3
  see also bilingualism, multilingualism, Teaching English as a Second Language
Lashley, H. 33–4, 39
Lawton, D. 38–40, 222
Lind, A. 147, 148, 149–51

Manners, P. 37–8, 40
Mannheim, K. 11, 13
Mara, Ratu 92, 93–4
Martin, J. 1, 10, 12, 177, 178, 179–80, 181, 182, 198–9, 206, 211, 212–13, 216, 229–30
'melting pot' 50–1, 111–12, 116–17, 122, 130, 131, 132, 153
Mexican Americans 105, 106, 107, 111, 118, 119, 130–1, 219
Migrant Education Action (Australia) 216
migrant education, in Australia 177–83
migration, within U.S. 108–10
Moag, R. 89, 90, 99, 101–2
Mukherjee, T. 26, 38
multicultural concept viii, 35, 36, 41, 218, 228–32, 240
  in Australia 166, 167, 173, 174, 183–4, 185–6, 187–93, 194–200, 201, 203–4, 206–7, 208, 209–11, 212, 214–15, 230–3
  in Britain 32, 33–4, 36, 37–8, 166, 230
  in Canada 55–62, 64–6, 68–76, 166, 189, 192–3, 229
  in Fiji 97–8, 99–102, 228–9
  in Hawaii 155
  in U.S. 122–3, 123–7, 128–9, 130, 132–4, 166, 192
multiethnic concept viii, 1, 34, 41, 226
  in Britain 31–2, 36, 37–8, 40–1
  in Canada 71
  in Fiji 103
  in Hawaii 164–5
  in U.S. 121, 122–3, 124, 134–5, 136, 137–9
multilingualism 10, 26
  in Australia 169–70, 206
  in Fiji 81–2, 90
  in Hawaii 143
  in U.S. 124
  see also bilingualism
multiracial concept viii 35, 36, 41, 225
  in Australia 201, 206
  in Britain 26–9, 32, 33, 230

multiracial concept (continued)
in Fiji 88−9, 90, 92−6, 97, 100, 101−2
in Hawaii 151, 156, 164−5
Myrdal, G. 109−10, 132

National Association for Multiracial Education (NAME) Britain 26, 27, 35−7, 230
National Foundation for Education Research (NFER) Britain 26, 27, 28, 32−3
Negroes, American 111, 219
education 118
employment 107−8
migration 105−6
Newsam, P. 31, 40
Norton, R. 84−5, 86, 87
Novak, M. 122, 135

organization of education
in Canada 54−5
in Fiji 87−90, 96

Pacheco, A. 114, 115, 116, 132−4
Pakistanis/Bangladeshis
in Britain 16, 17, 19, 22
Paris, Dr 127, 128−9
PEP Report (Britain) 18, 21
pluralism
in Australia 135, 173, 204, 205, 213, 216
in Britain 28−9, 33−7
in Canada 59, 134
in Fiji 103
in Hawaii 163−4
ideology of 196, 218, 226−8, 236, 237−41, 244
in U.S. 112−17, 123−5, 132−4, 137−8
pluralist dilemma 207, 241−2, 244
defined 1, 13, 14
polyethnic concept 185, 186, 226, 242−4
Porter, J. 46−7, 49, 50, 65, 71, 74
pressure groups 9−10
Puerto Ricans 105, 106−7, 108, 111, 118, 119, 219

race and racism
in Australia 175−6
in Britain 31−4
in Canada 47, 63

race and racism (continued)
in Hawaii 157−8, 159
racial disturbances 20−1, 22
religion 17−18, 82
Robbins Committee (Britain) 23
'roots syndrome' 122, 153−4, 237
Royal Commission on Bilingualism and Biculturalism (Canada) 46−7, 52, 185

Schools Commission, The (Australia) 190−1, 192−3, 206−7, 222
Schools Council (Britain) 26, 27, 28
segregation 127−8
Smith, D.J. 17, 18, 19, 20, 21
Smolicz, J.J. 213

teacher education 4, 6−7, 23
in Australia 179, 181, 197−8, 199
in Britain 24−5, 33, 36, 38
in Canada 55, 63, 64
in Fiji 90−1, 95−6, 102−3
in Hawaii 160−1, 164−5
in U.S. 124, 126
teacher organizations
in Australia 196−8
in Britain 23, 27, 28
in Fiji 91−2, 98−9
Teaching English as a Second Language (TESL) 3, 23, 35, 156−7, 164, 178−9, 191, 203
see also bilingualism
Troper, H. 48, 50−1, 52, 53, 70

unemployment
in Britain 19−21
in Fiji 85
in Hawaii 154
unity in diversity 113, 152

West Indians
in Britain 16, 17, 18, 19, 22, 23
White Australia Policy 174−7
White, N. 211
Work Group on Multicultural Programs (Canada) 62−3

Zubrzycki, J. 169, 202−3, 203−5, 205−6, 231−2